The Heart of Judgment

Practical Wisdom, Neuroscience, and Narrative

In *The Heart of Judgment*, Leslie Paul Thiele explores the historical significance and present-day relevance of practical wisdom. Though primarily a work in moral and political philosophy, the book relies extensively on the latest research in cognitive neuroscience to confirm and extend its original insights. While giving credit to the roles played by reason and deliberation in the exercise of judgment, Thiele underscores the central importance of intuition, emotion, and worldly experience. In turn, he argues that narrative constitutes a form of ersatz experience, and as such is crucial to the development of the faculty of judgment.

Ever since the ancient Greeks first discussed the virtue of *phronesis*, practical wisdom has been an important topic for philosophers and political theorists. Thiele observes that it remains one of the qualities most demanded of public officials and that the welfare of democratic regimes rests on the cultivation of good judgment among citizens. *The Heart of Judgment* offers a new understanding of an ancient virtue while providing an innovative assessment of the salience of practical wisdom in contemporary society.

Leslie Paul Thiele is professor of political science at the University of Florida. He is the author of *Friedrich Nietzsche and the Politics of the Soul, Timely Meditations: Martin Heidegger and Postmodern Politics, Environmentalism for a New Millennium,* and *Thinking Politics.*

The Heart of Judgment

Practical Wisdom, Neuroscience, and Narrative

LESLIE PAUL THIELE

University of Florida

CAMBRIDGE UNIVERSITY PRESS
Cambridge, New York, Melbourne, Madrid, Cape Town, Singapore, São Paulo

Cambridge University Press
32 Avenue of the Americas, New York, NY 10013-2473, USA

www.cambridge.org
Information on this title: www.cambridge.org/9780521864442

First published 2006

Printed in the United States of America

A catalog record for this publication is available from the British Library.

Library of Congress Cataloging in Publication Data

Thiele, Leslie Paul.
The heart of judgment : practical wisdom, neuroscience, and narrative /
Leslie Paul Thiele.
p.   cm.
Includes bibliographical references and index.
ISBN 0-521-86444-5 (hardback)
1. Judgment.   2. Wisdom.   3. Experience.   4. Subconsciousness.   5. Affect
(Psychology)   6. Narration (Rhetoric)   7. Neurosciences.   I. Title.
BD435.T42   2006
121–dc22   2005033367

ISBN-13   978-0-521-86444-2 hardback
ISBN-10   0-521-86444-5 hardback

Contents

List of Figures

Preface

This book was conceived as a theoretical account of human judgment, the offspring of a traditional marriage of political philosophy and intellectual history. In time, however, it came to benefit from a broader parentage. In the end, it might be considered a child of miscegenation.

During the book's long gestation, I was often subject to doubts of the sort first voiced to me by an applicant for a faculty position in my department. This young political theorist had written a paper on judgment as a preamble to his doctoral thesis some years earlier. It seemed promising work. His dissertation, I now learned, was on a completely different topic. Why, I asked, had he changed course? He answered that he found the question of judgment inherently interesting and of great significance to moral and political thought. But after examining the available literature on the topic, he found himself with little to add, and, what was perhaps more disconcerting, with few enduring intellectual achievements to build upon. Practical judgment, he held, was simply too enigmatic a faculty to allow much in the way of cogent theorizing.

This widely shared experience helps explain the relative dearth of scholarship addressing practical judgment in the 2,500-year history of moral and political thought. If we continue the millennia-old search for the "Holy Grail of good judgment," recent scholars have concluded, we do so not because there are reasons to expect success, but because giving up hope is unconscionable. In any case, the nature of practical wisdom and the workings of the judging mind will likely remain a "permanent mystery."[1] After digesting much of what there was to read on the topic, I, too, sensed that the nut of judgment could not be cracked, and that those who tried were simply spinning their wheels. The subject appeared to have been taken about as far as it could go by conventional means, including anything I might add to the theoretical literature.

Two events changed my mind. First, I came across a number of philosophers who focused on the role of literature in the cultivation of moral virtues, including the virtue of practical wisdom. In turn, I began reading works in cognitive neuroscience, a field of study increasingly occupied with the nature of decision-making and human judgment. Initially there appeared to be no linkage between these two new avenues of study, the humanistic and the scientific. Then I discovered neuroscientists who were addressing the role of narrative in human consciousness. They did not forgo empirical analysis to extol the virtues of fiction. Rather, they offered sound scientific arguments for understanding the development of the brain in terms of narrative structures. In turn, they posited the faculty of judgment, among other cognitive abilities, as a product of narrative knowledge. The more I explored these diverse fields, the more it became apparent that the study of practical judgment had not reached a dead end in the history of thought. In an important sense, it was just beginning. What follows is a political philosopher's attempt to grapple with this renaissance.

With neuroimaging (brain scanning) increasingly employed to develop advertising techniques, influence decision-making among citizens during election campaigns, combat mental illness, and improve moral awareness, the nascent fields of neuroeconomics, neuropolitics, neuropsychology, and neuroethics are thriving.[2] There are dangers as well as opportunities here. The most rewarding aspect of delving into cognitive science for me has been the empirical vindication of some of the most insightful theoretical accounts of judgment, from Aristotle through contemporary pragmatism. But my use of science to vindicate philosophy is not meant to suggest that the latter has been surpassed by the former. Science has a privileged status in contemporary society, and that

---

[1] Peter J. Steinberger, *The Concept of Political Judgment* (Chicago: University of Chicago Press, 1993), pp. 295–96. Philip E. Tetlock, *Expert Political Judgment: How Good Is It? How Can We Know?* (Princeton: Princeton University Press, 2005), p. 66.

[2] Terry McCarthy, "Getting inside your head," *Time*, October 24, 2005, pp. 94, 97.

is often a good thing. Its ability to invest our lives with meaning, however, is quite limited. To the extent that it accomplishes this feat at all, science, like analytic efforts in philosophy, remains parasitic on narrative resources. The increasing use of narrative as a matrix for understanding neurological processes is, therefore, an intriguing development. It offers tantalizing glimpses of a more holistic approach to the human condition. And, refreshingly, it cuts squarely against earlier, mechanistic models of science. A growing number of the most advanced empirical studies – those that investigate the neurophysics of the brain – do not lead in the direction of biological determinism or crass reductionism. Rather, they affirm the importance of (self-)consciousness as a narrative process and confirm our creative ability to interact with and shape internal and external environments. To the extent that cognitive neuroscience further develops a relationship to humanistic understanding, it may ward off the hubris that doomed so many of its imperialistic forebears.

In the pages that follow, I provide readers from a wide variety of academic disciplines and lay perspectives with a historically informed, philosophically grounded, and scientifically defensible account of the judging mind. My effort has been to place contemporary neuroscientific research in the context of conceptual treatments of judgment found in works of moral and political philosophy, and vice versa. In turn, I provide a sustained investigation of the narrative foundations of judgment and, more generally, the narrative foundations of ethico-political life. My hope is that humanistically oriented readers will be stimulated by the opportunity to supplement introspection, historical investigation, and conceptual analysis with new sources of knowledge from the neurosciences. Scientifically oriented readers, in turn, might be equally pleased with the fruits of philosophical and historical reflection. Of course, neither the scientific nor the humanistic community may look favorably upon such a hybrid effort. The only apology available at this stage is the assertion that human judgment is itself a hybrid faculty. Blending rational, perceptual, and affective capacities, operating at the conscious level and below the threshold of awareness, taking heed of hard facts as well as narrative coherence, the human judge manages to forge meaningful patterns from a blooming, buzzing world. Making sense of human judgment demands an equally synthetic approach.

As to my motivation for writing this book, I defer to Solon and Sophocles. Solon was one of ancient Athens' greatest lawmakers. His political reforms set the stage for the rise of democracy. "The hardest thing of all,"

Solon avers, "is to recognize the invisible mean of judgment, which alone contains the limits of all things."[3] Sophocles was one of Athens' greatest playwrights. His *Antigone* depicts a mighty king brought low by his own misrule. In the midst of the carnage, a messenger arrives, offering insight to redeem the tragedy. "Of all the ills afflicting men," the messenger observes, "the worst is lack of judgment."[4] Exercising good judgment is the most difficult task for human beings, and the most needful. This ancient wisdom presents the contemporary world with an urgent challenge and provides the impetus for what follows.

[3] Fragment 16 in Diehls, quoted in Werner Jaeger, *Paideia: The Ideals of Greek Culture*, Vol. 1, 2nd ed. (New York: Oxford University Press, 1973), p. 148.

[4] Sophocles, *Antigone*, in *The Norton Book of Classical Literature*, ed. Bernard Knox (New York: W. W. Norton, 1993), p. 398.

The Heart of Judgment

Practical Wisdom, Neuroscience, and Narrative

Introduction

Perforce, a political theory is, among many other things, a sum of judgments, shaped by the theorist's notion of what matters, and embodying a series of discriminations about where one province begins and another leaves off... [A] theoretical judgment which, by definition, must discriminate can only be restrained from rendering inappropriate determinations if it is civilized by a meditative culture.

Sheldon Wolin[1]

Ever since Plato first discussed practical wisdom, or *phronesis*, and Aristotle, his student, raised it to ethical and political preeminence, the faculty of judgment has been an important topic for philosophers and political theorists. Good judgment is no less of a concern for lay people. Today, as in years past, citizens have demanded it of their public officials, as fates and fortunes depend on leaders making prudent assessments and wise decisions in diplomatic, economic, ecological, legal, moral, military, and political affairs. Indeed, citizens consistently deem good judgment one of the most important and essential traits for elected officials and heads of state.[2] Napoleon Bonaparte was half right to insist that

---

[1] Sheldon Wolin, "Political Theory as a Vocation," *American Political Science Review* 63 (1969):1076–77.

[2] Over three-quarters of all Americans believe sound judgment to be an "essential" trait for a president, ranking it as more important than high ethical standards, compassion, frankness, experience, willingness to compromise, and party loyalty. This appraisal holds across the ideological spectrum. Perhaps because of the difficulty of defining it, however, sound judgment is seldom directly addressed in political campaigns. See Stanley A. Renshon, "Appraising Good Judgment Before It Matters," in *Good Judgment in Foreign Policy: Theory and Application*, eds. Stanley A. Renshon and Deborah Welch Larson (New York: Rowman and Littlefield, 2003), pp. 61, 66–67.

"Nothing is more difficult, and therefore more precious, than to be able to decide."[3] The real difficulty, of course, is to decide well.

In representative systems of government, one might hope, citizens share in the virtue of practical judgment. For Aristotle, the distinguishing mark of a citizen of the *polis*, or city-state, was "his participation in judgement and authority."[4] The more participatory the democracy and the greater the liberties accorded to its citizens, presumably, the more will its health and welfare rest on the widespread exercise of good judgment. Democratic leadership entails persuading others to follow while preparing them to rule. The welfare of democratic societies, it follows, depends up the cultivation of judicious citizens. Freedom cannot be gained, or long maintained, in the absence of such a public. Indeed, it has recently been argued that judgment – more than any other human faculty – manifests our individual freedom, safeguards our civil liberties, and preserves us from tyranny.[5] With this in mind, some suggest, the cultivation of judgment should displace the formulation of theory as the foremost occupation of moral and political philosophers.[6]

Practical judgment is celebrated as a primary virtue and a preeminent concern by philosophers. It is, at the same time, the most banal of activities. Albert Camus observed that "To breath is to judge."[7] Camus exaggerates, but not by much. Everytime we act, speak, think, or merely perceive, we are exercising something akin to judgment. The phenomenologist Maurice Merleau-Ponty states that "Judgment is . . . *what sensation lacks to make perception possible.*"[8] His point is that our perceptions are not raw sensations. Perceptions are sensations that we have made sense of. We never actually see a house or a person, for instance, but only, at best, one side of a house or person. The visible facet, by way of an unconscious judgment, Merleau-Ponty states, "presents itself as a totality and a unity."[9] When we perceive, we are making judgments about the world, and thereby making sense of it.

---

[3] Robert Fitton, ed., *Leadership* (Boulder: Westview Press, 1997), p. 71.

[4] Aristotle, *The Politics*, trans. T. A. Sinclair (New York: Penguin Books, 1962), p. 102.

[5] Samuel Fleishacker, *A Third Concept of Liberty: Judgment and Freedom in Kant and Adam Smith* (Princeton: Princeton University Press, 1999). Dick Howard, *Political Judgments* (Lanham, MD: Rowman & Littlefield, 1996), p. 311.

[6] Ronald Beiner, *Philosophy in a Time of Lost Spirit: Essays on Contemporary Theory* (Toronto: University of Toronto Press, 1997). John Dewey, Hans-Georg Gadamer, and Hannah Arendt also hold this conviction, as subsequent chapters illustrate.

[7] Albert Camus, *The Rebel* (New York: Vintage Books, 1956), p. 8.

[8] Maurice Merleau-Ponty, *Phenomenology of Perception*, trans. Colin Smith (London: Routledge and Kegan Paul, 1962), p. 32.

[9] Merleau-Ponty, *Phenomenology of Perception*, p. 42.

Experimental psychology confirms the phenomenologist's assertion: our perceptions – visual, tactile, auditory, olfactory, and gustatory – entail implicit judgments that transform the data of raw sensation into sensible apprehensions. Neuroscientist V.S. Ramachandran maintains that "every act of perception . . . involves an act of judgment by the brain."[10] Oftentimes, this act of judgment takes significant liberties with raw sensation. People quickly viewing anomalous playing cards, for example, will identify a black four of hearts as a four of spades. They do so without awareness that they have transformed (novel) raw sensations into fabricated observations that conform better to the conceptual categories of previous experience.[11] To see is to judge – sometimes to the point of radically revising what we actually see. The same can be said, *a fortiori*, for thinking, speaking, and acting.

Judgment permeates our lives. The only alternative to its exercise would be an insensate, thoughtless, and inactive silence – the cessation of life itself. While this statement is most easily defended with regards to perceptual judgment, it also applies, in a social context, to moral and political judgment. Seyla Benhabib observes that "to withdraw from moral judgment is tantamount to ceasing to interact. . . . Moral judgment is what we 'always already' exercise in virtue of being immersed in a network of human relations."[12] We cannot escape ethico-political judgment without quitting a shared world.

Notwithstanding its indispensability, the faculty of judgment suffers some ill repute. Cicero, the ancient Roman orator and statesman, deemed prudence the greatest of the virtues. Today, in contrast, prudence or practical judgment connotes a certain stodginess that begs apology. To be prudent means that one spends more time preparing and preventing than repairing and repenting. As the Chinese proverb goes, "The more you sweat in peace, the less you bleed in war." That seems good advice – the sort elders are likely to impart. And that, perhaps, is the problem. There is, for lack of a better word, an *old-fashioned* character to prudence. The term, one scholar observes, "does not fit well with the boundless initiative and astonishing rates of change in modern life, much less the personal

---

[10] V. S. Ramachandran and Sandra Blakeslee, *Phantoms in the Brain* (New York: William Morrow and Company, 1998), p. 67.

[11] Thomas Kuhn, *The Structure of Scientific Revolutions*, 2nd ed. (Chicago: University of Chicago Press, 1970), pp. 62–63.

[12] Seyla Benhabib, "Judgment and the Moral Foundations of Politics in Hannah Arendt's Thought" (183–204), in *Judgment, Imagination, and Politics: Themes from Kant and Arendt*, ed. Ronald Beiner and Jennifer Nedelsky (New York: Rowman and Littlefield, 2001), p. 187.

freedom and self-expression of liberal individualism. It does not rhyme conceptually with either 'entrepreneur' or 'artist,' or with 'romance' or 'revolution.'"[13] Niether does prudence rhyme conceptually with righteousness or moral rectitude. It is a pragmatic virtue, often taken to be synonymous with expedience. Prudence is equated with self-protective reserve, an unwillingness to stick one's neck out. The prudent or politically expedient, in our times, stands opposed to the morally upright and ethically obligatory. Acting out of a sense of prudence today, in diametric opposition to the classical understanding voiced by Aristotle and Cicero, suggests a lack of moral courage.

To add to the problem, practical judgment does not rhyme conceptually with certainty or truth. As one commentator observes, "To label an issue a question of judgment is a cognitive put-down. The implication is that such issues are outcasts from knowledge, that worthwhile issues deserve something better than judgment."[14] In the same vein, practical judgment does not rhyme conceptually with impartiality or universality, as does law. There seems an arbitrary character to practical judgment that leaves it suspect. In the context of contemporary "value relativism," judgment is further depreciated, as the distinction between a well-considered judgment and a mere matter of taste evaporates. In sum, the faculty of judgment is often understood to be too old-fashioned, restrictive, self-serving, variable, uncertain, and subjective to merit the prerogatives, and bear the responsibilities, of guiding moral and political life.

For these reasons, practical judgment is often taken to constitute a faculty of last resort, something that is called upon when truth, ethical principle, or law, for whatever reason, forfeits its mandate and jurisdiction. The exercise of practical judgment becomes a kind of fall-back position that one endorses reluctantly when circumstances do not permit decisions to be made on the basis of firm knowledge, moral certainty, or valid rules.

To be sure, practical judgment is called for when firm knowledge, moral certainty, and valid rules – whether promulgated by an authoritative institution or derived from an internal process of cogitation – do not supply us with clear solutions to our problems. But that is not to say that the practical judge abandons herself to passing fancy. Rather, she employs a wide range of faculties and aptitudes, including common

---

[13] Robert Harriman, "Preface" to *Prudence: Classical Virtue, Postmodern Practice,* ed. Robert Harriman (University Park, PA: Pennsylvania State University Press, 2003), p. vii.
[14] F. H. Low-Beer, *Questions of Judgment* (Amherst, NY: Prometheus Books, 1995), p. 13.

sense, to navigate a complex world. She adeptly integrates these diverse capacities, coaxing them to operate fruitfully in tandem. To understand this integrative and admittedly mysterious skill, we need to investigate the human mind scientifically while exploring its experiential foundations and narrative resources.

Judgment, Rules, and Law

Practical judgment is an aptitude for assessing, evaluating, and choosing in the absence of certainties or principles that dictate or generate right answers. Judges cannot rely on algorithms. Their efforts always exceed adherence to rules and are not tightly tethered to law. Still, the practical judge reveres good rules and laws. The word *judge*, after all, derives from the Latin *judicem*, which refers to a speaker (*dicus*) of law (*jus*). The activity of judging, though not circumscribed by the boundaries posed by tenets and precepts, is complementary to rule-making and rule-following. The exercise of judgment relies on rules, principles, and laws for support, even as it transcends or transforms them. Hence Aristotle's man of practical wisdom, the *phronimos*, does not ignore rules and models, or dispense justice without criteria. He is observant of principles and, at the same time, open to their modification. He begins with *nomoi* – established law – and employs practical wisdom to determine how it should be applied in particular situations and when departures are warranted. Rules provide the guideposts for inquiry and critical reflection.

When established principle or law comes to serve as a final destination rather than a launching pad for inquiry and deliberation, practical judgment is precluded. Justice is thereby placed in jeopardy. The Roman dramatist Terence was invoking an Aristotelian conviction when he stated that "The extreme rigour of the law is oftentimes extreme injustice."[15] Two millennia later, Alexander Pope put the point most eloquently when he wrote:

> Mark what unvaried laws preserve each state,
> Laws wise as nature, and as fixed as fate.
> In vain thy reason finer webs shall draw,
> Entangle justice in her net of law,
> And right, too rigid, harden into wrong.[16]

[15] Terence, *Heautontimorumenos* (Oxford: Dodsley, Payne and Jackson, 1777), p. 50.
[16] Alexander Pope, *An Essay on Man*, Vol. 2 of *The Works of Alexander Pope* (London: John Murray, 1871), p. 415.

Justice is commonly assumed to thrive under the rule of law, which places individuals and their actions in uniform categories so that adjudication may occur in an unbiased fashion. Such legal impartiality is indispensable to a political society. But it cannot stand alone. Practical judgment supplements the rule of law in ways that makes socio-political life more practicable and humane. It digs underneath strict categorizations to uncover specificities and arbitrate in light of them. Only thus can equity be pursued. And equity, as Aristotle observed, is the highest form of justice.

In Sophocles's *Antigone*, Creon pushes the rule of law and reasons of state beyond their proper boundaries, rejecting counsel and exhibiting the worst of all human ills, poor judgment. As a result, a tragic conflict of values and duties turns catastrophic. Two limitations are suggested. First, positive law must be restricted in its application and enforcement. Its scope must be bounded by realms of human life that escape its reach. Second, the legitimate application and enforcement of positive law remains ever needful of adjustment. In both cases, determining what is truly just entails practical wisdom.

There are no rules to determine when, where, and how new rules should be invented and old rules bent or broken. Only practical judgment can ensure that the dead letter of the law does not suffocate its dynamic spirit. The scales held by the goddess of justice suggest that the balance she establishes is static. Her blindfold portrays justice as heedless of particularities. Yet justice must be readily adaptive and contextually sensitive. What is said here of legal codes applies equally to ethical rules. While the effort is always fraught with danger, as Edmund Burke observed, it is sometimes necessary for "morality [to] submit to the suspension of its own rules in favour of its own principles."[17]

One judges well by discerning in the midst of uncertainty how the concrete informs the abstract, how the contextual informs the comprehensive, how facts inform principle, and how the expedient informs the ideal. Because judgment always pertains to things particular, contingent, and concrete, it cannot be reduced to a wholly deductive enterprise. In this sense, practical judgment is similar to musical improvisation: training in theory is most helpful, but responsive flexibility is key. The difference in quality between a novice punching out the required notes and a master musician interpreting a score is patent. It is the difference between mechanically heeding the letter of the law and skillfully realizing its spirit.

---

[17] Edmund Burke, *Reflections on the Revolution in France* (Garden City: Doubleday and Co., 1961), p. 149.

Empirical studies demonstrate something we all know: people tend to exhibit self-serving biases when exercising judgment. That should give us pause whenever we contemplate bending or breaking rules. But the same brush can be used to tar principles and law. Certainly the history of moral and political philosophy no less than the history of legal institutions demonstrates that bias is no stranger to systems of thought and law. People exhibit partiality in the construction of "just" rules and the conceptualization of "fair" institutions no less than in their exercise of practical judgments.[18] The French novelist Anatole France once observed that "The law, in its majestic equality, forbids the rich as well as the poor to sleep under bridges, to beg in the streets, and to steal bread." People gravitate toward standards of justice that best serve their own interests. For all its impartiality, law is not above prejudice and preference. That is why it must remain subject to practical judgment, or risk losing its spirit.

Judgment and Rationality

If our assessments, evaluations, and choices were immune to self-serving biases, the faculty of judgment would not have its work cut out for it. Counteracting the prejudices that plague decision-making is intrinsic to its task. In turn, the practical judge must account for the prejudices of the people with whom she interacts. Notwithstanding great success in thwarting our own biases, we will not become good judges if we operate on the assumption that others are bias-free, are purged of common sources of error, or act out of straightforward, one-dimensional interests. That is to say, the good judge understands that the world is not populated by rational people, but by people who selectively employ rationality. In such a world, good judgment makes use of much more than reason.

Consider the story of the village idiot who preferred dimes to dollars.[19] Offered the choice by neighbor or passerby, the lad would always select the shiny coin to the paper money. It appeared a blatant bit of bad judgment on the youth's part. Clearly, he had lost his reason. As everyone likes to make fun, the lad's reputation grew. Soon he was visited by peasants and princes from far and wide, each offering him a dime and a dollar, and each leaving with the dollar bill in hand and a good laugh to boot. Day

---

[18] Jon Elster, *Alchemies of the Mind: Rationality and the Emotions* (Cambridge: Cambridge University Press, 1999), p. 346, 363.

[19] Gerd Gigerenzer relates this tale, and its lesson for decision science. Gerd Gigerenzer, *Adaptive Thinking: Rationality in the Real World* (Oxford: Oxford University Press, 2000), p. 265.

after day, the misguided youth suffered the ridicule of scores of acquaintances and strangers. And at the end of each day, the lad wandered home with a large sack of coins. He reputedly died a very rich man.

The moral of the story is that good judgment is grounded on the insight that others often misjudge. To judge well, one must comprehend the subtle interplay of motivations and calculations, aversions and desires, passions and prejudices, beliefs and misbeliefs that inform human thought and action. Practical judgment requires a thorough "knowledge of the human soul."[20] Such knowledge develops less from perusing books than from participating in worldly life. Good judgment is not so much gained in the classroom as in the school of hard knocks. Here, reason is but one of many players.

To exercise judgment, Peter Steinberger eloquently states, "is to invoke a kind of insight – a faculty of *nōus* or common sense, a certain *knowing how*, a 'je ne sçay quoy' [sic] – the mechanisms of which defy analysis.... [I]t is to be distinguished from the methodical, step-by-step manner of thinking that characterizes all forms of inferential reasoning."[21] As cognitive neuroscientists shed more light on the complex workings of the human brain, the enigma of judgment is beginning to unravel. These painstaking efforts, though inspiring, still shine only a dim beam into a very dark and convoluted process. But one thing has become clear: practical judgment is not simply rationality at work. Reason often proves of service to the practical judge, but it typically works in tandem with non-inferential faculties, and often comes into play subsequent to their exercise. Understanding the reasoning mind only gets one part way to understanding the judging mind.

President John F. Kennedy observed that "The essence of ultimate decision remains impenetrable to the observer – often, indeed, to the decider himself.... There will always be the dark and tangled stretches in the decision-making process – mysterious even to those who may be most intimately involved."[22] The mysterious aspect of judgment, its superseding of inferential reasoning, is tied to one of its most crucial features: the discernment of relevance. In moral and political life, nothing of importance issues from a single cause, generates a single effect, or has a single meaning. The task of practical judgment is to sift through the jumble of

---

[20] Ronald Beiner, *Political Judgment* (Chicago: University of Chicago Press, 1983), p. 165.

[21] Peter J. Steinberger, *The Concept of Political Judgment* (Chicago: University of Chicago Press, 1993), pp. 295–96.

[22] Quoted in Graham Allison, *The Essence of Decision* (Boston: Little, Brown and Company, 1971), i.

potential causes, effects, and meanings and settle upon those that are, for some particular purpose, the most apposite and weighty. When we judge, we are not simply manipulating predetermined variables to solve for 'x' or 'y'. Practical judgment is not algebraic calculation. Prior to any deductive or inductive reckoning, the judge is involved in selecting objects and relationships for attention and assessing their interactions. Identifying things of importance from a potentially endless pool of candidates, assessing their relative significance, and evaluating their relationships is well beyond the jurisdiction of reason.[23]

All this suggests that practical judgment is inherently a normative faculty. It imposes a sense of relevance and significance upon particular features of its world. Sheldon Wolin observes that the judge operates with a "notion of what matters" and discriminates "about where one province begins and another leaves off."[24] In selecting phenomena for attention, demarcating boundaries of significance, and assessing relative merits, the practical judge cannot rely upon determinative calculations. She must comparatively appraise within a field of shifting values.

There is much disagreement as to the form and substance of practical judgment. Yet there is something of a consensus concerning a key feature. Good judgment always demonstrates "a self-reflective ability to...shift one's style of reasoning in response to situational demands."[25] Good judgment is attentive to context and contingency. The practical judge cultivates responsiveness to a world in flux.

The Nature of Moral and Political Judgment

Many things fall into the realm of the contingent and contextual: human health, business relations, and military expeditions, not to mention the weather and seismic activity. The judgments that discern (and predict) medical problems, business opportunities, and military maneuvers bear important similarities to moral and political judgments. Such assessments and evaluations probe what might be called *deep complexity*. Deep complexity arises wherever relationships among diverse variables are so intricate and interdependent as to preclude the deductive calculation of reactions and outcomes. If a phenomenon is not inherently contingent and

[23] See Low-Beer, *Questions of Judgment*, p. 51.
[24] Sheldon Wolin, "Political Theory as a Vocation," *American Political Science Review* 63 (1969):1076–77.
[25] Philip E. Tetlock, "Is it a Bad Idea to Study Good Judgment," *Political Psychology* 13 (3): 429–434, 1992.

contextual, its assessment may require various human aptitudes. But practical judgment is not one of them. Bank tellers and accountants, in this sense, may make mistakes in their trades, but not poor judgments. To miscalculate – when there is an available algorithm or procedure for reaching the correct answer – is not to misjudge.

Most of the mental faculties involved in making decisions under conditions of deep complexity are the same regardless of whether one is engaged in a medical diagnosis, a business decision, the devising of a military strategy, or an ethico-political choice. Professionals and corporate executives employ many of the same skills as individuals negotiating moral and political relationships. It is not an accident that statesmanship is often preceded by a professional or business career. In the contemporary world, the judgment demanded in politics often finds its testing ground in the courtroom or executive suite.[26] The basic components of good judgment – such as broad socio-economic, psychological, and historical knowledge, aptitude in probabilistic reasoning and logic, openmindedness, thoroughness, perspicacity, empathy, imagination, common sense, and patience – prove beneficial regardless of whether one is embroiled in a moral conundrum, a political bargain, a professional dispute, a business decision, or a military confrontation.

Given this common foundation, some scholars take the next step, insisting that there are no important distinctions between ethico-political judgment and other sorts of decision-making. The mental faculties of the judge are identical, they argue, regardless of whether she is grappling with moral, political, medical, business, or military affairs. As one "field guide" in decision-making states, the same investigative methodology should apply whether we want to know "why and how Abraham Lincoln decided to free the slaves" or why and how "the Coca-Cola company . . . went wrong in replacing the old Coke with the New Coke."[27] Ending slavery or tweaking soft drink flavors – both are decisions made in the face of contingency. Both require good judgment to be successful in achieving their respective goals. Both are amenable, it is suggested, to standardized methods of analysis.

Notwithstanding the many commonalities shared by moral and political judges with decision-makers in other realms of life characterized by deep complexity, there is an important distinction. Moral and political

---

[26] See Low-Beer, *Questions of Judgment*, p. 112.

[27] John Carroll and Eric Johnson, *Decision Research: A Field Guide* (Newbury Park, CA: Sage Publications, 1990), p. 14.

judgments are never uncontestably right or wrong. They prove difficult to make not simply because they grapple with deep complexity – that is to say, with diverse, interactive variables – but because the very determination of ends and means – as well as the standards by which these ends and means might be evaluated – remain forever open to dispute. In moral and political affairs, the "canons of success" one might appropriately employ in assessing and evaluating judgments remain essentially contested.[28]

The individual engaged in a moral or political judgment, the radio-logist deciding when a detail on an x-ray merits further investigation, the business executive trying to capture greater market share through an advertising campaign, and the meteorologist deciding whether it will rain tomorrow are all grappling with deep complexity. For each of these decision-makers, multiple contingencies involved in the interaction of multiple variables disallow a purely calculative effort. Good judgment is required. However, the latter three judges, at least retrospectively, may secure an uncontested confirmation of the merit of their efforts. Surgery will determine whether the patient has, or does not have, a tumor. The end of the fiscal quarter will determine whether the company's market share rose or fell. And tomorrow will bring either rain or shine. For the ethico-political judge, in contrast, neither the ends selected nor the means chosen to achieve these ends, even after the fact, can be indisputably validated.

Many moral and political philosophers reject this assertion. Deontologically oriented theorists would insist with Kant that the moral realm is available to axiomatic certainty in the selection of ends, if not means. I defend a contrary position in later chapters. For now, I assert only that in moral and political affairs, contingency and essential contestability go hand in hand. Moral and political judges partake of many of the same skills and faculties as other decision-makers grappling with deep complexity. But moral and political judges face one contingency that medical practitioners, business people, and meteorologists do not face (qua medical practitioners, business people, and meteorologists): the indeterminacy of the criteria of success and failure. There exists a *multi-dimensionality* to moral and political life that undermines any effort to assess and evaluate it along a single axis.

To say that ethico-political life is multi-dimensional is not merely to assert that it is populated with multiple variables. The claim is that these variables and their means of evaluation are radically diverse.

---

[28] Fleishacker, *A Third Concept of Liberty*, p. 16.

Ethico-political life partakes of reason, but it is also nourished by embodied understandings and affective relations. Neither cognition, nor embodied understanding, nor affect taken alone will allow its comprehensive assessment, evaluation, and skillful navigation. There is no trump card to be found in this game. No one account, no single story can capture the full import of moral and political life or settle, once and for all, the rightness or wrongness of its components. A plurality of narratives compete for our allegiance. To judge well in the face of this inherent contextuality and essential contestability requires moral and political acumen and courage.

It has been argued that "The exercise of judgment offers one of the best sorts of evidence for virtue."[29] Cautiously interpreted, the statement may bear itself out. Those most adept at moral judgment, as assessed through a variety of moral reasoning tasks, also prove to be more "pro-social" in their behavior.[30] Virtue and the skills of judgment often go hand in hand. But correlation does not bespeak causation. The exercise of judgment does not necessarily foster laudable convictions or behavior. Indeed, it is possible that causality runs in the other direction: people who (naturally) are more pro-social will probably find greater opportunity to exercise moral judgment, and hence cultivate this faculty with practice. The exercise of judgment, therefore, does not offer evidence for values that most of us would consider morally and politically worthy (assuming most of us might actually agree on what these values were). As Machiavelli first argued, the skills of the practically wise man may be employed for sundry purposes, not all of which would fall within the ambit of the uprighteous.

I employ the terms *moral judgment* and *political judgment* interchangeably throughout this book. This equation requires justification, as moral judgment is often thought to stand in contrast to political judgment. The former generally refers to assessments, evaluations, and choices pertaining to personal or individual obligations, rights, or relationships. The latter refers to assessments, evaluations, and choices pertaining to collective obligations, rights, or relationships. It also refers to the tactics and strategies that best ensure the acquisition, exercise, and retention of the power needed to exercise our choices in the public realm. These

---

[29] Charles E. Larmore, *Patterns of Moral Complexity* (Cambridge: Cambridge University Press, 1987), p. 12.

[30] J. Philippe Rushton, "Social Learning Theory and the Development of Prosocial Behavior," in *The Development of Prosocial Behavior*, ed. Nancy Eisenberg (New York: Academic Press, 1982), p. 83. Rushton cites eight separate studies.

are worthwhile distinctions. But the *means* by which we think through and develop moral and political judgments are much the same, despite differences in their objects and objectives. In our daily lives, moreover, moral and political problems and solutions prove to be hopelessly entwined. To avoid sins of commission in the moral realm often forces us into sins of omission in the political realm, and vice versa.

Notwithstanding the various distinctions proffered by philosophers and theorists over the ages, therefore, I hold practical wisdom, prudence, practical judgment, moral judgment, and political judgment to be largely synonymous terms. This nomenclature is grounded in an argument, made toward the end of the book, that a rigid distinction between ethics and politics, between morality and prudence, between the right and the practicable is both unnecessary and, ultimately, untenable.

What Lies Ahead

Philosophy, Martin Heidegger stated, is correctly understood as "knowledge of the essence."[31] Might we, with this in mind, develop a philosophy of judgment? Can we gain theoretical access to the essence of this mysterious faculty? I doubt it. The human capacity for judgment is an evolutionary adaptation and a product of history. In this sense, practical judgment has no enduring, unified, and immutable set of characteristics. To be sure, the human animal, since the dawn of civilization, has been a genetically and culturally stable enough creature to allow the identification of its faculties with some confidence. But judgment is complicated, and, as philosopher Daniel Dennett observes, "Nothing complicated enough to be really interesting could have an essence."[32] Judgment may be described in great detail, but cannot be defined once and for all.

To say that judgment cannot be defined is not to say that theorists' characterizations are without merit. We can learn much from their insights no less than their shortcomings. With this in mind, Chapter 1 offers an intellectual history of judgment. It examines the development of the concept, focusing on philosophers and theorists whose works have advanced our understanding. And it reveals how judgment, though seldom in the

[31] Martin Heidegger, *The Fundamental Concepts of Metaphysics: World, Finitude, Solitude*, trans. William McNeill and Nicholas Walker (Bloomington: Indiana University Press, 1995), p. 154.

[32] Daniel C. Dennett, *Darwin's Dangerous Idea: Evolution and the Meanings of Life* (New York: Simon and Schuster, 1995), p. 201.

limelight of the intellectual arts, has consistently demonstrated its pivotal role in moral and political inquiry.[33]

The relationship of experience to judgment is the topic of Chapter 2. Ever since Aristotle, scholars have acknowledged that worldly experience is the chief, if not sole, foundation of practical judgment. Yet few thinkers have ventured to explain how and why experience gains this status, and none, I think it fair to say, have succeeded in doing so. The explanation requires an understanding of the neuroscience of experience. At issue is both the personal experience of the individual – that undergone over a single lifespan – as well as the embedded experience each individual inherits through her genetic constitution. Both sorts of experience inform judgment. Indeed, from a neurological point of view, personal and "ancestral" experience are structurally parallel and complementary phenomena.

Education usefully supplements experience in cultivating good judgment, but cannot supplant it. Instruction chiefly differs from experience in the way knowledge and skills are gained and employed. Formal education relies on explicit acts of information acquisition, retention, and retrieval. In contrast, the vast majority of what we absorb from worldly experience is not explicitly acquired, retained, or retrieved. Rather, it forms the basis of *implicit cognition*, a covert, unconscious acquisition and exercise of knowledge and skills. In Chapter 3, I explore the neuroscience of the implicit pathways that feature prominently in the exercise of judgment. While acknowledging the role played by reason and deliberation, this chapter underlines the importance of our more intuitive capacities, and argues that the role of the unconscious[34] should not be underestimated.[35]

---

[33] Sections of this chapter are adapted from Leslie Paul Thiele, "Judging Hannah Arendt: A Reply to Zerilli," *Political Theory* 33 (October 2005): 706–714. Copyright © Sage Publications 2005. Reprinted with kind permission.

[34] As the concern here is the "cognitive unconscious" rather than the "psychoanalytical unconscious," the term bears no Freudian overtones of repressed memories or urges. It is simply a shorthand for *unconscious mind*, understood as the panoply of mental capacities over which we have little or no conscious control and of which we have little or no awareness. Perhaps the term "preconscious" might be the better term, at least in some cases, as many of our unconsciously formed orientations eventually develop conscious features. See Lancelot Law Whyte, *The Unconscious before Freud* (New York: St. Martins, 1978); James Uleman, "Introduction: Becoming Aware of the New Unconscious," in *The New Unconscious*, ed. Ran Hassin, James Uleman, and John Bargh (Oxford: Oxford University Press, 2005), pp. 3–15; and Seymour Epstein, *Constructive Thinking: The Key to Emotional Intelligence* (Westport: Praeger, 1998), p. 81.

[35] Sections of this chapter are adapted from Leslie Paul Thiele, "Making Intuition Matter," in *Making Political Science Matter: The Flyvbjerg Debate and Beyond*, eds., Sanford F. Schram

In Chapter 4, I examine another way in which formal instruction differs from worldly experience. Instruction is a cognitive process. In contrast, most experience is emotion-laden. As cognitive neuroscientists have recently demonstrated, emotions are crucial to most forms of learning and prove necessary for the execution of rational behavior. In turn, emotions provide the relational linkages that define the ethico-political world while supplying the motivational levers for our assessments, evaluations, and choices. In the absence of affect, Chapter 4 demonstrates, moral and political judgment could not arise.

Experience remains the fountainhead of judgment as a result of its implicit and affective components. We gain direct experience from living our lives, confronting our world, and learning from our mistakes. But experience also has a mediated form. We gain such indirect experience from listening to, reading, and reflecting upon stories. Chapter 5 argues that stories, both historical and fictional, offer a kind of ersatz experience. This ersatz experience plays a prominent role in the development and exercise of good judgment. "Any fool can learn from his own mistakes," the old adage goes. "It takes a wise man to learn from the mistakes of others." Narrative allows us to learn from both the good and the bad judgments of others. As Alexander Solzhenitsyn observed in his Nobel lecture, the "condensed experience" one derives from literature, and we might add from other forms of narrative including history, is the only known "substitute" for worldly encounters.[36]

Narrative facilitates the cultivation of judgment because narrative, like direct experience, is conducive to implicit cognition and affect-based learning. The relationship between narrative and judgment is further established by empirical studies that identify the neurological basis for a narrative understanding of the self. Chapter 5 demonstrates that grappling with the enduring yet shifting role of narrative is crucial to understanding the nature of the self and the fate of judgment in contemporary society.[37]

The Conclusion reviews the multi-dimensional nature of judgment in light of these philosophical and scientific investigations. Here I underline

---

and Brian Caterino (New York: New York University Press), 2006. Copyright © New York University Press 2005. Reprinted with kind permission.

36 Alexander Isayevich Solzhenitsyn, *Nobel Lecture*, 1972.

37 An early version of this chapter benefited from the thoughtful comments of participants in the University of Florida, Political Theory Symposium, including Peggy Kohn, Dan Smith, Dan O'Neill, and Ryan Hurl. Sections of the chapter are adapted from Leslie Paul Thiele, "Ontology and Narrative," *The Hedgehog Review*, Vol. 7, No. 2: 77–85, Summer 2005. Copyright © The Hedgehog Review 2005. Reprinted with kind permission.

the central importance of practical judgment to our lives and ask whether it is up to the task of helping us navigate an epistemologically fractured, socially diverse, technologically expansive, and quickly changing world. This question rightfully provokes philosophers, scientists, politicians, civic leaders, and parents, who look to good judgment as a lantern in dark times.

What follows, then, is an effort to ground a historical overview of the concept of judgment in a phenomenological and scientific investigation of its experiential and narrative foundations. The book does not resolve the issue of whether the faculty of judgment is up to the task of meeting contemporary challenges. But the discussion is sufficiently informed to establish the importance of furthering inquiry.

1

An Intellectual History of Judgment

So vain and frivolous a thing is human prudence, and athwart all our plans, counsels, and precautions, Fortune still maintains her grasp on the results.
Michel de Montaigne[1]

A systematic theory of prudence would be a contradiction in terms.
Robert Harriman[2]

Judgment is an understudied phenomenon in the history of moral and political thought. Unlike the concepts of reason, liberty, power, or justice, judgment has seen no treatises devoted to its explication, with the exception of a small number of works written in recent years.[3] Only a few significant philosophers or theorists have shown an abiding concern with it. In this respect, a thorough history of the topic is made tractable, for there is relatively little ground to cover. Notwithstanding its feasibility, what follows is not a comprehensive account of the history of the concept. Rather, by way of a selective interpretation of key figures, this

[1] Montaigne, *The Complete Essays of Montaigne*, trans. Donald Frame (Stanford: Stanford University Press, 1965), p. 92 (I:24).
[2] Robert Harriman, "Theory without Modernity" (1–32) in *Prudence: Classical Virtue, Postmodern Practice*, ed. Robert Harriman (University Park, PA: Pennsylvania State University Press, 2003), p. 19.
[3] As Hannah Arendt observes, "Not till Kant's *Critique of Judgment* did this faculty become a major topic of a major thinker" (Hannah Arendt, "Postscriptum to *Thinking*," in *The Life of the Mind* [New York: Harcourt Brace Jovanovich, 1978], p. 215). Notably, Kant's third *Critique* dealt only with aesthetic judgment, and explicitly excluded moral and political judgment. See also Ronald Beiner, *Political Judgment* (Chicago: University of Chicago Press, 1983), pp. 4–5.

chapter charts the developmental milestones in the intellectual history of judgment. In turn, it suggests that judgment, while often rejected as an explicit focus of study, has proved itself to be a guiding thread of moral and political thought. Readers of later chapters will discover that the theoretical insights of thinkers who have grappled with the faculty of judgment over the last two and a half millennia – from Plato through the post-modernists – are frequently vindicated by contemporary empirical research.

Plato (c. 427–347 b.c.)

For Plato, the best part of the soul is rational or calculative. It is the part concerned with assessment and evaluation. But Plato is seldom focused on practical, worldly measurements. Rather, he is concerned with how things measure up to ideals, to the forms. For this reason, Plato did not write extensively on the virtue of *phronesis*, generally translated as *practical wisdom* or *prudence*. While Plato is the first major thinker explicitly to address the faculty, *phronesis* consistently plays second fiddle to the purely intellectual virtues in his work, particularly in the early dialogues.

Apart from a brief misadventure in Syracuse, where Plato served in the court of the tyrant Dionysius before wearing his welcome out and being sold into slavery, the philosopher spurned practical politics. His readers are given to assume, as Socrates suggests in the *Republic*, that it is good judgment to mind the eternal things of the soul rather than the passing affairs of the city. Socrates himself, of course, did not take this counsel to heart, and he paid for his political involvement, deemed by his detracters as a "corruption" of youth, with his life. The lesson that Plato learned from this painful experience, the trial and execution of his beloved mentor, is that security and sanctity were to be found in philosophical reflection unsullied by public involvement. Notwithstanding his accolade of Socrates as the "most prudent" (*allos phronimotatou*) of human beings at the conclusion of the *Phaedo*, Plato appears to have mixed feelings about the virtue of *phronesis*. He rued that his teacher was not sufficiently prudent to keep Athens from sinning against philosophy. Unwilling to degrade his mentor with the absence of a preeminent virtue, he lowered his estimation of the virtue in question.

Still, Plato was not oblivious to the need for practical wisdom. He was aware that judgment, in distinction to law modeled on the eternal forms, must have its due in a world of variability and change. In the *Cratylus*, Socrates observes that *phronesis* signifies an ability to perceive flux. And in Plato's later works, particularly *The Sophist, The Statesman,* and *The Laws,* the virtue of worldy understanding comes into its own. The Eleatic stranger in Plato's *Statesman,* for instance, gains Socrates' emphatic agreement with his observation that

> Law can never issue an injunction binding on all which really embodies what is best for each.... The differences of human personality, the variety of men's activities, and the inevitable unsettlement attending all human experience make it impossible for any art whatsoever to issue unqualified rules holding good on all questions at all times.... It is impossible, then, for something invariable and unqualified to deal satisfactorily with what is never uniform and constant.[4]

Given the uniqueness of individuals and the variability of circumstances, there is no substitute for practical wisdom.

To the extent that one values the human world, a place of shadows dancing on cave walls, one must value the faculty that allows its navigation. Plato acknowledged this much. And as we shall see in Chapter 5, Plato's dialogues themselves, like the shadows dancing on the cave walls, are uncertain figures that solicit, and cultivate, the hermeneutic judgment of attentive readers. It is fitting that Plato's relationship to *phronesis* is ambiguous. We must judge it carefully.

Aristotle (384–322 B.C.)

Aristotle is undisputably the preeminent ancient theorist of practical judgment and arguably the foremost authority on the subject to this day. His discussion of *phronesis,* primarily in the *Nicomachean Ethics,* remains unsurpassed for its insight and, one might say, its intrigue. Aristotelian *phronesis* might best be thought of as a "resourcefulness of mind and character."[5] It facilitates understanding of the ethico-political world and one's flourishing within it. *Phronesis* promotes the achievement of specific goods in specific contexts by providing a view of the good life as a whole and a sense of how the good life is best achieved in particular circumstances.

---

4 Plato, "The Statesman," (294b) in *Collected Dialogues* (Princeton: Princeton University Press, 1989), p. 1063.

5 Joseph Dunne, *Back to the Rough Ground: 'Phronesis' and 'Techne' in Modern Philosophy and in Aristotle* (Notre Dame: University of Notre Dame Press, 1993), p. 312. Likewise, Hannah Arendt describes "understanding," which she deems the better part of judgment, as a "resourcefulness of the human mind and heart." Hannah Arendt, "Understanding and Politics," in Hannah Arendt, *Essays in Understanding, 1930–1954,* ed. Jerome Kohn (New York: Harcourt Brace & Company, 1994), p. 310.

No one can truly be happy, Aristotle observes, without the opportunity to exercise a full range of virtues. *Phronesis* ensures that all the virtues find their respective roles in an individual's life and get exercised at the appropriate time and place. "For let a man have the one virtue of practical wisdom," we read in the *Ethics,* "all the moral virtues will be added unto him."[6] To exercise any virtue well requires *phronesis,* for only the view of the whole (a good life) allows one to know when, where, and how each part – that is, each particular virtue – ought to be called into action. One can only exercise courage most virtuously, for example, if one employs practical wisdom to determine which dangers ought to be faced, to what extent, and for what purpose. Putting oneself in harm's way for no good reason is the vice of foolhardiness, not the virtue of courage. In short, practical wisdom regulates the virtues by moderating or encouraging their exercise and limiting or expanding their respective domains. Every virtue is a mean between excess and deficiency. Practical wisdom determines where this mean is to be found and motivates its embrace.[7]

Along with the minor virtues, the four cardinal virtues of courage (*andreia*), moderation (*sophrosyne*), wisdom (*sophia*), and justice (*dikaiosyne*) are ordered within the soul by *phronesis*. They depend on practical wisdom for their worldly realization.[8] Contemplation or the exercise of theoretical wisdom (*sophia*) is the highest form of human life, Aristotle maintains, but it cannot create or maintain the conditions for its own exercise. The life of contemplation is "self-justifying," but is not, for that reason, "self-sustaining."[9] Only *phronesis* ensures the conditions for its own exercise, while also ensuring the conditions for the exercise of other virtues. In this respect, practical wisdom accomplishes "an integration of all the virtues sufficient for living well with regard to the full range of one's needs and obligations."[10]

---

[6] Aristotle, *The Ethics of Aristotle: The Nichomachean Ethics,* trans. J. A. K. Thomson (New York: Penguin Books, 1953), p. 191.

[7] Aristotle, *Ethics,* p. 66. See also J. O. Urmson, "Aristotle's Doctrine of the Mean," in *Essays on Aristotle's Ethics,* ed. Amelie Oksenberg Rorty (Berkeley: University of California Press, 1980), pp. 157–170.

[8] Aristotle, *Ethics,* p. 191. See also Alasdair MacIntyre, *Whose Justice? Which Rationality* (Notre Dame: University of Notre Dame Press, 1988) p. 123, 137; Zdravko Planinc, *Plato's Political Philosophy: Prudence in the Republic and the Laws* (Columbia: University of Missouri Press, 1991), pp. 11–12.

[9] Dunne, *Back to the Rough Ground,* p. 242.

[10] Harriman, "Theory without Modernity," p. 6.

Despite his celebration of *phronesis*, Aristotle finds it "strange" that anyone would want to assert its sovereignty. Practical wisdom restricts itself to human affairs, which are "matters susceptible of change." To assert the sovereignty of practical wisdom, one would have to elevate concern for the changing over concern for the transcendent. That would be to assume, falsely, "that man is what is best in the world."[11] Notwithstanding this inherent self-limitation, *phronesis* is in a class of its own. Only practical wisdom can determine its own limits while securing the social, economic, and political conditions that allow the cultivation and practice of other virtues. Practical wisdom makes the good life possible.

As an intellectual virtue, *phronesis* is likened to *episteme* (scientific reasoning), *techne* (technical or productive reasoning), and *noesis* (intellection). The practically wise man is intelligent; he exhibits the power of *nous*, the ability to recognize and identify universal principles (*arche*). In this respect, he shares traits with the (theoretically) wise man embodying *sophia*. But those who wield the power of *nous* are not always practically wise.[12] While it is not possible to be practically wise without demonstrating intelligence, it is possible to be brainy and, at the same time, quite ignorant of the ways of the world.

Aristotle's man of practical wisdon, the *phronimos*, employs his intelligence to discover what is good for the individual and community, what "conduces to the good (*eudaimonic*) life as a whole."[13] But the *phronimos* goes beyond recognizing the components of a good life; he is disposed to achieve them. That is to say, the exercise of *phronesis* is not solely a theoretical venture. Unlike the other intellectual virtues, practical wisdom has an explicitly moral character. *Phronesis* is not simply knowledge; it is the capacity for knowledge in action. Practical wisdom is "imperative," Aristotle states: "it gives orders."[14] The *phronimos* practices rather than simply understands the virtuous life, while securing rather than simply identifying its worldly requirements.

---

[11] Aristotle, *Ethics*, pp. 178–79.

[12] Aristotle, *Ethics*, p. 189.

[13] Aristotle, *Ethics*, p. 176. Aristotle's term *proairesis*, meaning deliberate choice, is often rendered as *judgment* by translators. Importantly, *proairesis* only concerns deliberation about means, when these means are multiple and the task at hand is choosing the best one. It does not concern the selection of ends. He who is practically wise, the *phronimos*, demonstrates the capacity for *proairesis*. But he also knows how to choose between competing ends, comparatively judging the merits of each. Aristotle, *Ethics*, p. 84.

[14] Aristotle, *Ethics*, p. 185 and see p. 216.

Practical wisdom employs more than sound reason to issue its imperatives. It also marshals "correct desire."[15] That is what makes *phronesis* inherently practical, a moral as opposed to a purely intellectual virtue. The ethical practicality of *phronesis* is a difficult concept for many contemporary thinkers to grasp. Immersed in a Cartesian understanding of the (disembodied) mind, most scholars posit a clear demarcation between knowledge (of right and wrong), and action that may or may not follow from such knowledge. Thus they depict the *phronimos* as someone who, having aquired moral knowledge, develops the disposition and discipline to apply it. In addition to and separate from his knowing the right thing to do, the *phronimos* (somehow) also manages to do it.[16] He puts his knowledge into practice.

This formulation is inadequate and misrepresentative. For Aristotle, moral knowledge does not preexist its enactment. We apprehend moral knowledge only in the context of virtuous behavior. Our actions, and the desires they embody, serve as the lens through which the ethical world becomes visible.[17] Effective knowledge of the virtuous arises only in its worldly incarnation. In effect, practice comes before preaching. The *phronimos* is a knower of the good only insofar as he is a doer of the good. Indeed, the *phronimos* intellectually integrates the effect of being transformed by his own practice. He acts to realize the good, and subsequently comes to know the good, and himself, through the prism of his actions.[18]

Aristotle's habit theory of virtue helps us understand this phenomenon. Plato's Socrates argued that no one does wrong knowingly;

---

[15] Aristotle, *Ethics*, p. 173. See also Arash Abizadeh, "The Passions of the Wise: *Phronesis*, Rhetoric, and Aristotle's Passionate Practical Deliberation," *The Review of Metaphysics* 56 (December 2002): 267–296.

[16] Peter Steinberger takes this position. Peter J. Steinberger, *The Concept of Political Judgment* (Chicago: University of Chicago Press, 1993). Scholars remain much divided as to the nature of Aristotelian *phronesis*. For a concise summary of some of the key debates, see the Afterword in Carlo Natali, *The Wisdom of Aristotle*, trans. Gerald Parks (Albany: State University of New York Press, 2001), pp. 183–89.

[17] See C. D. C. Reeve, *Practices of Reason: Aristotle's* Nicomachean Ethics (Oxford: Clarendon Press, 1992), pp. 48–52.

[18] See Dunne, *Back to the Rough Ground*, pp. 244, 263, 290. "What Aristotle has in mind in his discussion of *phronesis*," Ronald Beiner writes, "is the idea that real moral knowledge comes to life at the moment when the wise or virtuous person *concretizes* his or her abstract understanding of ethical requirements in particular situations; in that sense, there is no antecedent moral knowledge that awaits application." Ronald Beiner, *Philosophy in a Time of Lost Spirit: Essays on Contemporary Theory* (Toronto: University of Toronto Press, 1997), p. 180.

knowledge and virtue are one. Aristotle disagreed. He insisted that knowledge or cognitive insight may often prove insufficient in the realm of ethics. Reasoned arguments may supplement, but cannot supplant, the formation of virtuous character through habit. With this in mind, Aristotle insists that one should not try to reason with children, or with "the many." What they need is not rational argument but good habits. Here Aristotle is not simply saying, as some assume, that you cannot reason with unreasonable people. He is saying that knowing the good must be achieved by doing the good: "the moral virtues we do acquire by first exercising them."[19]

Practical judgment is a moral virtue. It cannot be improved through pedagogy or persuasion unless its foundation has already been laid through (habitual) practice. That is simply to say that our moral and political judgments arise in the context of our characters, and our characters, including their virtuous and vicious attributes, develop mostly out of our habits. When we judge, a panoply of habits figures prominently in the process. Quoting Evenus, Aristotle writes: "Habit . . . is practice long pursued, that at the last becomes the man himself."[20] The *phronimos* is a well-habituated man, a *spoudaios*, or person of sound character. Building this excellence of character and employing his intellectual virtues, he can deliberate and determine how best to pursue the *eudaimonic* life.

To be learned in affairs moral and political in the absence of excellence of character is not to be practically wise but simply to be well educated. It is to remain, notwithstanding any intellectual achievements, a moral and political invalid. Aristotle writes:

It is therefore fair to say that a man becomes just by the performance of just, and temperate by the performance of temperate, actions: nor is there the smallest likelihood of a man's becoming good by any other course of conduct. It is not, however, a popular line to take, most men preferring theory to practice under the impression that arguing about morals proves them to be philosophers, and that in this way they will turn out to be fine characters. Herein they resemble invalids, who listen carefully to all the doctor says but do not carry out a single one of his orders. The bodies of such people will never respond to treatment – nor will the souls of such 'philosophers.'[21]

The educated man may be able to instruct others in moral and political doctrine, but he will not inspire. Oftentimes, the educated prove most

[19] Aristotle, *Ethics*, p. 55.
[20] Aristotle, *Ethics*, p. 217.
[21] Aristotle, *Ethics*, p. 62.

in need of the moral learning they profess. We often teach best what we most need to learn.

Phronesis is oriented to *eupraxia,* or good action. Good action, while having ends beyond itself, also serves as its own end. Whereas the end of *techne* is outside itself, in the finished work produced by means of technical expertise, the end of *phronesis* is, in significant measure, internal. Aristotle argues that virtue is its own reward because it serves to ameliorate its practitioner, regardless of whether it achieves any external goals. Moral and political action, *praxis,* transforms the actor, increasing his (potential) for moral knowledge and setting in place or solidifying his (habitual) propensity for virtue.

The *phronimos* is habituated to virtuous action. But he is not, for that reason, inflexible. Habit orients but does not predetermine behavior. In large part, that is because one of the *phronimos's* most crucial habits is that of reflective deliberation. He is habituated to action informed by thought and, as importantly, to thought informed by action. Aristotle typically begins his disquisitions with a brief assessment of common opinion and traditional forms of behavior. Likewise, the *phronimos* begins his deliberations with an assessment of *nomoi,* established law. Subsequently, he employs practical judgment to determine how laws or principles should be applied in particular situations and when departures are warranted. In the absence of such principles, the activity of the *phronimos* would quickly degenerate into the calculations of the *deinos,* the clever or cunning person.[22]

Good rules help the practical judge begin his journey, but they never dictate his destination.[23] That is why, for Aristotle, the just, practically wise person rather than an abstract, unchanging rule is the true "standard and yardstick" of justice.[24] And that is why Aristotle deems equity (*epieikeia*), understood as the prudential correction of the law, "the highest form of justice."[25] Rules and principles have their place. However, their role is not to spare us from exercising judgment, but to support the effort.

The superiority of practical judgment to static rules or principles follows from the variability of the human condition. Aristotle, not unlike his mentor, but with greater consistency, maintained that "the *data* of human

---

[22] See Richard Bernstein, *Beyond Objectivism and Relativism: Science, Hermeneutics, and Praxis* (Philadelphia: University of Pennsylvania Press, 1985), p. 157.
[23] Aristotle, *Ethics,* p. 66. See also Martha Nussbaum, *Love's Knowledge: Essays on Philosophy and Literature* (New York: Oxford University Press, 1990), pp. 93, 99.
[24] Aristotle, *Ethics,* p. 89.
[25] Aristotle, *Ethics,* p. 228, and see also p. 166.

behavior simply will not be reduced to uniformity."[26] With this in mind, he argued that "Ethics admits of no exactitude. . . . Those who are following some line of conduct are forced in every collocation of circumstances to think out for themselves what is suited to these circumstances."[27] Aristotle celebrates scientific and theoretical knowledge (for example, in the *Metaphysics*) for its capacity to grasp universal principles. But he also acknowledges that contextual knowledge gained from practice generally produces better judgments than abstract scientific or theoretical inquiry. In the absence of practical insight, theoretical knowledge is often useless and potentially pernicious.[28]

To say that the data of human behavior are inherently plural is an epistemological assertion. It is also a normative claim. The good life is multi-dimensional. Its diverse components prove to be ends in themselves; they cannot be reduced to a single, overarching goal. Aristotle is denying the strict commensurability of the components of *eudaimonia*. There is no single metric that might be employed for their comparative evaluation. In a non-uniform world, practical judgments of particularities assume precedence over theoretical representations of the universal.[29]

Attunement to the pluralism of the moral realm develops less from theorietical acumen – which is predisposed to simplify for the purpose of conceptual clarity – than from familiarity with the interdependent, irreducible, and protean components of worldly life. For this reason, Aristotle insists, practical wisdom develops only from experience.[30] Those lacking in experience, even if intellectually brilliant, will want the strength of habit, the moral sensitivity, and the responsiveness to dynamic

[26] Aristotle, *Ethics*, p. 167.

[27] Aristotle, *Ethics*, p. 57, and see also 66. David Wiggins concludes his insightful essay on Aristotle's understanding of practical reason by observing that "those who feel they *must* seek more than all this provides want a scientific theory of rationality not so much from a passion for science, even where there can be no science, but because they hope and desire, by some conceptual alchemy, to turn such a theory into a regulative or normative discipline, or into a system of rules by which to spare themselves some of the agony of thinking and all the torment of feeling and understanding that is actually involved in reasoned deliberation." David Wiggins, "Deliberation and Practical Reason," in *Essays on Aristotle's Ethics*, ed. Amelie Oksenberg Rorty (Berkeley: University of California Press, 1980), p. 237.

[28] See Dunne, *Back to the Rough Ground*, pp. 252–53, 287; MacIntyre, *Whose Justice?* pp. 92, 123, 137; Richard S. Ruderman, "Aristotle and the Recovery of Political Judgment," *American Political Science Review* 91 (1997): 416.

[29] See Nussbaum, *Love's Knowledge*, pp. 38, 55, 79.

[30] Aristotle, *Ethics*, p. 182.

complexity that allow for an astute understanding and adept navigation of the world.

Marcus Tullius Cicero (106–43 B.C.)

Like Aristotle, Cicero held moral excellence to be a matter of practice, not theory. Its highest manifestation was to be found in political life, and its greatest exemplar was the prudent statesman.[31] Unlike Aristotle, Cicero saw no need to limit his accolades of practical wisdom because of its contingent and contextual subject matter. For this pragmatic Roman interested in "teaching philosophy to speak Latin," the valorization of prudence was complete. In one of his earliest works, *De Inventione*, a treatise on rhetoric written when he was still a youth, *prudentia* is elevated to the status of a cardinal virtue. It takes the place of theoretical wisdom (*sapientia*), joining justice, courage, and temperance.[32] By the time of the writing of his *Republic*, Cicero formally equated *prudentia* with *sapientia*.[33]

Accepting equity as the highest form of justice, Cicero observes in *De Officiis* that particular circumstances may change what otherwise would be considered just action into injustice. Our obligations, therefore, must change with circumstances. Only practical wisdom, which "safeguards human interests," can inform us when circumstances dictate the correction of law and the emendation of rules. In *De Oratore*, Cicero further develops the notion of prudence, highlighting its worldly function. Prudence is cultivated from *humanitas*, the combination of rhetoric and philosophy that Cicero held to be his singular achievement. Civic life, for the Roman, rightly claimed supremacy over the purely contemplative life. A well-ordered state is deemed the greatest blessing and practical wisdom the chief feature of the most blessed minds. Prudence is elevated to a supreme position.[34]

---

[31] Cicero, *The Republic and The Laws*, trans. Niall Rudd (Oxford: Oxford University Press, 1998), p. 4, 17.

[32] Cicero, *De Inventione* (Cambridge: Harvard University Press, 1949), p. 326.

[33] Robert Cape, Jr., "Cicero and the Development of Prudential Practice at Rome," (35–65) in *Prudence: Classical Virtue, Postmodern Practice*, ed. Robert Harriman (University Park, PA: Pennsylvania State University Press, 2003), pp. 40–41.

[34] Cicero, *The Republic and The Laws*, trans. Niall Rudd (Oxford: Oxford University Press, 1998), pp. 83, 119. See also Cape, "Cicero and the Development of Prudential Practice," p. 36. Robert Harriman, "Preface" to *Prudence: Classical Virtue, Postmodern Practice*, ed. Robert Harriman (University Park, PA: Pennsylvania State University Press, 2003), p. vii.

For Cicero, practical wisdom was a common sense that allowed fore-sight.[35] Formal learning contributed little to its sharpening. Like Aristotle, Cicero maintained that prudence was generated out of worldly experience. And, like Aristotle, he maintained that in practical matters, the walker was generally the better judge of the shoe than the cobbler. While Cicero lauded philosophy, his prudent man finds more use for general-purpose knowledge and keen powers of observation. Employing his worldly wits, he may "divine the course of public affairs, with all its twists and turns."[36] Subscribing to the skepticism of the New Academy, Cicero defended the use of probabilistic reasoning as a respectable and warranted tool of moral and political life. In turn, the man of practical wisdom speaks to a broad audience in ways that appeal both to aspirations and needs. The prudent man, Cicero held, employs worthy stories to reveal truths and direct action. He can plumb the souls of those around him, and he inspires by his skills no less than his character. "What we want," Cicero writes, "is an intelligent man, with a good brain sharpened still further by experience, who is able to form an incisive assessment of the thoughts and feelings and beliefs and hopes entertained by his fellow-countrymen."[37] The practical judge knows the good, keenly perceives the values, predilections, and limitations of his fellow citizens, and motivates them through rhetorical power to realize their virtues and to serve their country well. Very few, since Cicero, have placed a larger burden of responsibility, or larger hopes, on the cultivation of practical wisdom.

Niccolò Machiavielli (1469–1527)

Machiavelli took inspiration from the ancient Romans. Like other Renaissance figures, he was interested in rejuvenating the humanist tradition, including its focus on *prudentia* that Cicero was largely responsible for cultivating. In at least one respect, however, Machiavelli sided with his Christian forebears against the pagans. He was at one with Cicero in celebrating the power of the human mind. But, like Thomas Aquinas, Machiavelli sought to distance practical wisdom from ethical life.

---

35 Cicero, *The Republic and The Laws*, trans. Niall Rudd (Oxford: Oxford University Press, 1998), p. 85.
36 Cicero, *The Republic and The Laws*, trans. Niall Rudd (Oxford: Oxford University Press, 1998), p. 49.
37 Cicero, "On the Orator (I)," in *On the Good Life*, trans. Michael Grant (New York: Penguin, 1971), p. 316.

Aquinas did so in order to elevate morality above prudence. A truly moral man seeks to imitate Christ, not, as Aristotle had it, the *phronimos*. The yardstick of justice, though often bent to accommodate the ways of the world, is forged hard and unyielding in the heavens. Like Augustine before him, albeit with less vehemence, Aquinas warned against overweening pride in the human mind. Revelation, not human intellection, would blaze the path of righteousness.[38] Practical wisdom was meant to supplement, not usurp, the role of religious creed in determining and directing moral practices.

Machiavelli would have none of this. Indeed, he takes the opposite tack, distancing *prudentia* from moral life by raising the former above the latter. The worldly Florentine wanted to undermine the ability of ethical norms to restrict what might otherwise be achieved through practical intelligence. Though he is often portrayed as pitting himself against religious tradition, Machiavelli was not so much responding to Christian thinkers as he was building upon, and significantly modifying, the humanist tradition handed down from the Roman republicans.

Machiavelli undermines the Ciceronian tradition more than he fulfills it. He weds prudence to ruthless calculations of power, and this marriage ended a longstanding relationship between the morally good and the practically wise. To be successful in the world, Machiavelli insists, one has to adapt to the times. Obeisance to stagnant norms is a nuisance, and in the high-stakes game of state politics, often a deadly one. From a prince's perspective, ethical principle is a burden that can derail strategic efforts in a treacherous world.

Scholars of practical wisdom suggest that Machiavelli celebrates corrupt behavior and rejects the value of moral character.[39] Machiavelli clearly takes the discourse on prudence in a new direction. But he also highlights many of its traditional features. He upholds a concern for contingency and he values experience over formal pedagogy. These two themes prove to be related. Prudence is insight into the realm of contingent affairs. To be successful in this realm, one must experience the trials and errors of life and remain responsive to the whims of fortune. Here the limitations of theoretical knowledge are revealed, as is the indispensability of courage.

---

[38] Douglas J. Den Uyl, *The Virtue of Prudence* (New York: Peter Lang, 1991), p. 87.

[39] Eugene Garver, "After Virtù: Rhetoric, Prudence, and Moral Pluralism in Machiavelli," in *Prudence: Classical Virtue, Postmodern Practice*, ed. Robert Harriman (University Park, PA: Pennsylvania State University Press, 2003), pp. 67–97.

To avoid all risk in an uncertain and at times chaotic world is cowardly. It is also imprudent. The prudent man plays to win, but victory entails a willingness to gamble. Political and military success, in particular, depend in no small part on perilous ventures. Taking a risk is often the wisest course of action, even when the odds are stacked against one. Machiavelli embraced the Roman admonition that fortune favors the brave. Fortune is a woman, Machiavelli famously observed, and she requires a bold master. Victory is often gained by sheer daring.

In effect, Machiavelli argues that it is not prudent to be too prudent. In wrestling with fortune, the practically wisest course of action may on occasion entail throwing caution to the wind.[40] Prudence enjoins us to adapt. We should always heed this call. When circumstances confront us with the erratic whims of fortune, the most prudent course may also be an audacious one.

Still, putting oneself in peril unnecessarily displays faulty judgment. The point is to take well-calculated risks. Failure is always possible and, over the long run, inevitable. But it is not a mark of imprudence to fail in a great venture. It *is* a mark of imprudence not to have studied all opportunities for success, exploited them to their fullest, and anticipated, if not avoided, inherent dangers. Napoleon Bonaparte was issuing a Machiavellian decree when he observed that "To be defeated is pardonable; to be surprised – never!"[41]

Machiavellian prudence is knowledge of where, when, and how to take risks. This knowledge is developed, in large part, through trial and error. Machiavelli agrees with Aristotle that prudence is primarily gained from experience. Yet Machiavelli innovates even here. He maintains that experience need not be direct to achieve its end. Prudence may be developed by modeling oneself on great men of the past. The study of history is crucial – if not for the prince, then for his advisors.

Machiavelli observes that men generally walk on previously trodden trails. His advice to those who seek power is to follow leaders who have displayed wordly wisdom. Machiavelli's counsel is not primarily intended for men naturally disposed to distinction. He is writing for those who

[40] Hannah Pitkin interprets Machiavelli's counsel: "No one policy, even prudence itself, can successfully guide action in all situations. Prudence teaches its own insufficiency.... Thus, no simple rule will do; neither 'be prudent' nor 'be bold.' Rather, one can only say that to succeed, a man must adapt 'his way of proceeding to the nature of the times.'" Hannah Fenichel Pitken, *Fortune is a Woman: Gender and Politics in the Thought of Niccolo Machiavelli* (Berkeley: University of California Press, 1984), p. 151.

[41] Robert Fitton, ed., *Leadership* (Boulder: Westview Press, 1997), p. 47.

have to earn their stripes the hard way. For such aspirants, exemplars are crucial. We read in *The Prince* that "a prudent man should always follow the footsteps of the great and imitate those who have been supreme. His own talent (*virtù*) may not come up to theirs, but at least it will have a sniff of it."[42] It is not what you know, but whom you know (and imitate) that counts. By associating with great men, albeit through the medium of historical narrative, greatness may rub off. The focus is as much on style as substance, as much on appearance as reality. By imitating the exemplars of old, the new prince may gain the respect and allegiance he requires from his subjects – not because he deserves it, but because he appears to deserve it. It is who you *seem* to be that matters most. Actual greatness may not be necessary; its semblance will suffice. In both *The Prince* and the *Discourses on Livy*, achieving goals by circuitous means is the craft of statesmanship.

This counsel to engage in deception puts Machiavelli in stark disagreement with Aristotle and Cicero, not to mention Aquinas. Yet the point of smelling like a virtuous man is not simply to gain what is not deserved. Rather, the point is to become more like the great men of history. To be sure, one feigns mastery of capacities yet to be achieved. But this deception is meant to produce an overall increase in *virtù*. Indeed, the mechanism bears a notable resemblance to Aristotle's habit theory of virtue. Machiavelli, charitably interpreted, is simply saying that it is prudent to benefit from the semblance of virtue en route to its actual achievement.

The problem, of course, is that smelling virtuous is easier than becoming virtuous. Many a prince may forego the difficult task of matching reality to appearance, of coming to own what he displays. In the hard-and-fast world of power politics, there may be neither the time nor motivation to embody aspirations. In such cases, treachery may replace virtue as the defining feature of the statesman. Thus the cunning *deinos* usurps the role of the honorable *phronimos*. Machiavelli's achievement was to blur the line separating these characters.

Immanuel Kant (1724–1804)

Aristotle, Cicero, and Machiavelli all agree that practical wisdom is gained from experience. What experience yields, in large part, is an encounter with exemplary thought and action. One's direct experience, combined

---

[42] Niccolò Machiavelli, *The Prince*, trans. Robert Adams (New York: Norton, 1977), p. 16.

with the study of history, provides a rich source of examples – concrete illustrations of good judgments and misjudgments. From this fertile soil, practical wisdom grows.

Immanuel Kant rejects this counsel – at least so far as ethical life is concerned. "We cannot do morality a worse service," he insists, "than by seeking to derive it from examples."[43] For Kant, moral life is structured by universal, a priori rules, and these rules cannot be derived from concrete experiences. Moral instruction is the product of pure practical reason, unsullied by the conditional or the particular: "Morality cannot be abstracted from any empirical, and therefore merely contingent, knowledge."[44] According to Kant, our moral obligations arise directly from the activity of reasoning. Prudence has no role to play in determining these obligations, or even amending them given circumstantial constraints.[45] Prudence, Kant suggests, is a threat to legality. Hence he gave equity, as determined by the practical wise judge, no jurisdiction in courts of law.[46] There was little room for practical wisdom to maneuver given the firm constraints of Kant's axiomatic morality and the rigidity of legal principle.

By severing morality from the empirical world, Kant challenges the status and significance of practical wisdom. For this reason, and notwithstanding the damage done earlier by Machiavelli, Kant is often seen as the philosopher who dealt prudence its deadliest blow.[47]

---

43 Immanuel Kant, *Groundwork of the Metaphysics of Morals*, trans. H. J. Paton (New York: Harper and Row, 1964), p. 408. Kant writes that "Good example (exemplary conduct) should not serve as a model but only as a proof that it is really possible to act in accordance with duty." Immanuel Kant, *The Doctrine of Virtue*, trans. Mary Gregor (Philadelphia: University of Pennsylvania Press, 1964), p. 152.

44 Kant, *Groundwork of the Metaphysics of Morals*, p. 411.

45 See Beiner, *Political Judgment*, p. 66.

46 Immanuel Kant, *The Metaphysical Elements of Justice: Part I of the Metaphysics of Morals*, trans. John Ladd (Indianapolis: Bobbs-Merrill, 1965), p. 40.

47 Douglas Den Uyl writes: "The perspective Kant brings to prudence is simple enough: morality is one thing, prudence is another. Prudence is another name for self-interest; morality is disinterested. Prudence is tied to experience; morality is not. Prudence is caught up in the particular; morality represents the universal. Prudence is hypothetical; morality is categorical. . . . Kant self-consciously sought to oppose the virtue of prudence in all its manifestations." Den Uyl, *The Virtue of Prudence*, pp. 143, 157. Robert Harriman writes that "The greatest threat in the history of prudence came from the Enlightenment, and particularly with Kant's subordination of self-interest and social context alike to universal moral principles." Harriman, "Preface," p. ix. See also Peter J. Diamond, "The 'Englightement Project' Revisited," in *Prudence: Classical Virtue, Postmodern Practice*, ed. Robert Harriman (University Park, PA: Pennsylvania State University Press, 2003), p. 103.

Kant understood that one cannot rationally derive rules that dictate how rules are to be applied; the effort to do so pitches one into an infinite regress. Hence a certain *knack* is required. Although the principles of morality are derived from pure, practical reason, the ability to apply these rules in the concrete world remains a skill grounded in experience. This is where judgment comes in. Like most earlier theorists of practical wisdom, Kant held judgment to be a talent that could be practiced but not taught. While he rejected the Aristotelian claim that practical judgment plays a role in determining our moral ends and amending our ethical obligations in light of circumstances, he acknowledged that good judgment was indispensable to ascertaining how (predetermined) moral ends were to be pursued in the concrete particularities of daily life.[48] This instrumental service is of no small consequence.

Kant distinguishes two types of judgment: determinative and reflective. Determinative judgment operates when the universal (rule) is given, and the task at hand is to apply it to particular cases. This is what judges do in courts of law when they determine which, if any, law has been broken by a defendant's act. The subsumption of the particular under the universal is largely a deductive enterprise. Determinative judgment is a matter of application: how to apply a law to concrete particulars or how to assign particulars to their respective laws. Reflective judgment, in contrast, operates when the particular is available, and the task at hand is to forge the universal (rule). It is what judges do when they set precedents. Here the universal is initially absent. It is the object of discovery. Reflective judgment inductively derives the general from the particular.

In purely Kantian terms, what we commonly call moral judgment is not judgment at all. Rather, it is the product of pure, practical reasoning. Subjective feelings are not involved in its exercise. While we may feel positively about the goodness of an action, its moral worth arises not from these feelings but from the rational concept of the law that determines the will.[49] Kant insists, in his *Critique of Practical Reason,* that the moral law must determine the will directly and not gain influence by means of

---

[48] In his *Groundwork of the Metaphysics of Morals,* Kant distinguished between perfect and imperfect duties. Perfect duties oblige us to perform specific actions, such as keeping promises or paying debts. Imperfect duties oblige us to act in general ways, benevolently or courageously, for instance. Imperfect duties harbor a much larger role for judgment, and their instantiation is much aided by examples.

[49] See Patricia M. Mathews, "Kant's Sublime: A Form of Pure Aesthetic Reflective Judgment," *The Journal of Aesthetics and Art Criticism,* Vol. 54 (1996), p. 165.

a (subjective) feeling of any kind. Indeed, allowing moral actions to be motivated by feelings sets one on the slippery slope to evil.[50]

In aesthetic matters, in contrast, feelings matter. The sense of the pleasing and displeasing is a crucial component. Kant addresses this phenomenon in his *Critique of Judgment*. Whereas morality follows directly from the application of ethical principles under the strict constraints of rationality, aesthetic judgment is a matter of taste. Grounded in pleasure or displeasure rather than truth or falsehood, aesthetic judgment cannot be wholly objective. At the same time, it is not wholly subjective, as it is based on external experiences that are widely shared, or common to all.[51] Aesthetic judgment is a form of reflective judgment nourished by intersubjectivity. With this in mind, Kant underlines the public nature of aesthetic judgment. It requires an "enlarged mentality" to develop, while examples serve as its indispensable "go-cart" (*Gängleband*).

Kant understands aesthetic judgment to be more closely related to the faculty of taste than the faculty of reason. It is therefore without bearing in the realm of ethics. Subsequent theorists, focused on the intersubjectivity and public nature of this reflective capacity, appropriated its features to illuminate the nature of moral and political judgment.

Friedrich Nietzsche (1844–1900)

The death of God and the abandonment of metaphysics leaves humankind the task of ordering its aspirations without recourse to transcendental norms. In such a world, Nietzsche insists, judgment is a preeminent virtue. With the disappearance of eternal, universal standards, principles, and rules, the capacity for drawing boundaries and determining rank proves indispensable.[52] If passive nihilism is not to destroy life, earthly judges must be capable of setting goals, allotting praise and blame,

---

[50] Kant leaves some room for moral feelings to play a role as an impetus to action subsequent to the determination of the will by the law. But feelings do not and cannot foster moral judgment. The partial exception is the obscure *feeling* of respect for the law. See Immanuel Kant, *Religion Within the Limits of Reason Alone*, trans. Theodore Greene and Hoyt Hudson (New York: Harper and Row, 1960), pp. 23, 31. See also Richard McCarty, "Motivation and Moral Choice in Kant's Theory of Rational Agency," *Kant-Studien* 85 (1994): 15–31; Jeanine Grenberg, "Feeling, Desire and Interest In Kant's Theory of Action, *Kant-Studien* 92 (2001): 153–179.

[51] See Kennan Ferguson, *The Politics of Judgment: Aesthetics, Identity, and Political Theory* (Lanham, MD: Lexington Books, 1999), p. 5.

[52] Friedrich Nietzsche, *The Gay Science*, trans. Walter Kaufmann (New York: Vintage, 1974), p. 143.

and determining values. Not the nihilistic abdication of judgment – the relativist's claim that anything goes – but a this-worldly means of assessment and evaluation is demanded. Nietzsche did not write extensively on the nature of judgment, but it provides the linchpin to his thought.

Nietzsche wanted to affirm life. But the love of life is always accompanied by the danger of infatuation. Infatuation is a form of self-deception, a kind of mendaciousness.[53] It idealizes rather than strives to promote the birth of ideals. The true lover of life, consequently, is also its unflinching judge. He adds a grain of contempt to every kilo of love as an inoculation against infatuation and its delusions.[54]

Judgment entails the capacity to administer justice and therefore to condemn that which receives more than its due. At the same time, the judge must demonstrate that criticism is only a means to a fuller affirmation, that destruction is the prerequisite for creation – in short, that the desire for change that arises from the judge who finds life wanting is part of a great celebration of the state of becoming. One must be a naysayer, a judge, a struggler, and a destroyer if one is to become something different – namely, a yea-sayer.

The Nietzschean judge is severe. But it would be wrong to characterize him as rigid or self-serving. For one, the exercise of judgment never ceases, lest it calcify into conviction.[55] Beliefs, Nietzsche held, are the prisons one builds to escape the burden of judging anew each and every moment of the day. The same may be said of the biases that stem from a shallow egoism. To see things as they are, and judge accordingly, entails seeing them "out of a hundred eyes, out of *many* persons."[56] To see through multiple eyes, feel with multiple hearts, and touch with multiple hands is basic to the judge's task. Nietzsche's perspectivism is a call for judgment unanchored to transcendent norms and free of restrictive biases.[57] As the Nietzschean judge is no less critical of himself than his world, he lives in a constant state of self-overcoming. Accordingly, he celebrates battles more than victories.

---

[53] Nietzsche, *Ecce Homo*, trans. Walter Kaufmann (New York: Vintage, 1967), p. 258. See also Friedrich Nietzsche, *The Will to Power*, trans. Walter Kaufmann and R. J. Hollingdale (New York: Vintage, 1968), p. 506.

[54] Nietzsche, *Gesammelte Werke, Musarionausgabe*, vol. 20 (Munich: Musarion Verlag, 1880–82), p. 132.

[55] Nietzsche, *The Anti-Christ*, trans. R. J. Hollingdale (New York: Penguin, 1968), pp. 114, 166, 172.

[56] Nietzsche, *Gesammelte Werke*, p. 138.

[57] Nietzsche, *The Gay Science*, trans. Walter Kaufmann (New York: Vintage, 1974), p. 215.

Nietzsche claims that his "overall insight" was "the ambiguous character of our modern world – the very same symptoms could point to decline or to strength."[58] One man's meat is another man's poison. What is beneficial and what is dangerous to health depends on who is at the table. The strong will be able to transform into an elixir that which remains a toxin for others.[59] In such a world, a keen sense of discrimination is crucial. Echoing the Sophoclean dictum that good judgment is the greatest gift, Nietzsche insists that "the best thing we gain from life" is the "art of nuance."[60]

Fully developed, this art combats "the worst of all tastes, the taste for the unconditional."[61] As there exist no ultimate truths or values, the judge must ask in each circumstance why particular truths and values have been adopted, what purpose they serve, and what sort of person would require them. Nietzsche prided himself on his ability to infer the rank order of individuals from the beliefs that they found necessary. He did so by employing the "most difficult and captious form of backward inference . . . from the work to the maker, from the deed to the doer, from the ideal to those who need it, from every way of thinking and valuing to the commanding need behind it."[62] To this end, "psychological antennae" are required. The Nietzschean judge discerns the health of souls, diagnoses their disorders, and provides therapeutic prescriptions.

Nowhere is the Nietzschean judge in greater need of his skills than in the evaluation of nihilism. Does a hatred of life or an excess of joy predominantly characterize the nihilist? The value of nihilism rests on the answer to this question. Nihilism *tout court*, Nietzsche declared, is ambiguous. Active nihilism is a sign of "increased power of the spirit"; passive nihilism marks a "decline and recession of the power of the spirit." Nihilism may be a "divine way of thinking," or an invitation to spiritual anarchy.[63] Again, it depends on why and how one is a nihilist.

There are, at base, two possibilities. One may deny God, a heavenly afterlife, and transcendental norms out of a reverence for the self, a love

---

[58] Nietzsche, *The Will to Power*, p. 69. Friedrich Nietzsche, *Human, All Too Human: A Book for Free Spirits*, trans. R. J. Hollingdale (Cambridge: Cambridge University Press, 1986), p. 27.

[59] Nietzsche, *The Gay Science*, p. 92.

[60] Nietzsche, *Beyond Good and Evil*, p. 44.

[61] Nietzsche, *Beyond Good and Evil*, p. 44.

[62] Nietzsche, *The Gay Science*, p. 329.

[63] Nietzsche, *The Will to Power*, p. 17, see also p. 15.

of worldly life, the desire to be creative, and the courage to judge. Or one may reject ideals out of a need to escape the threat of being weighed and found wanting. The former nihilist approaches the overman. The latter nihilist is the last man. The last man murdered God, Nietzsche insists, because he could no longer bear the burden of judging and being judged.[64] It is in light of this charge that we should interpret Nietzsche's love for a particular Greek deity who represented the fullest affirmation of life. "Dionysus is a judge!" Nietzsche declared, and then asked: "Have I been understood?"[65]

John Dewey (1859–1952)

Like Nietzsche, John Dewey valorizes judgment because it fosters psychological and cultural development without recourse to transcendent norms. Unlike Nietzsche, Dewey places his hope in democracy, understood as the crucible within which the virtue of practical judgment might achieve its most potent form.

Dewey defines judgment as "a sense of respective or proportionate values." The judge determines which concerns merit attention, ascertains their significance, and grades them according to their respective claims.[66] This process of ascertaining, weighing, and ranking "must be more than merely intellectual."[67] Cognitive, perceptual, and emotional faculties are all called to action. To judge is not simply to render a disinterested assessment. Rather, judgment is the product of the individual's empathetic investment in the social world.

Dewey identifies judgment as the human faculty that brings thought into action. Like Aristotle, he insists that "The difference between mere knowledge, or information, and judgment is that the former is simply held, not used; judgment is ideas directed with reference to the accomplishment of ends."[68] Judgment makes thought useful. But it is not to be equated with a concern for "narrow and coarse utilities."[69] Judgment

---

[64] Nietzsche, *Thus Spoke Zarathustra: A Book for Everyone and No One*, trans. R. J. Hollingdale (New York: Penguin, 1969) p. 276.

[65] Nietzsche, *The Will to Power*, p. 541. See also Leslie Paul Thiele, "Love and Judgment: Nietzsche's Dilemma," *Nietzsche-Studien*, 20 (1991):88–108.

[66] John Dewey, *The Political Writings*, ed. Debra Morris and Ian Shapiro (Indianapolis: Hackett, 1993), p. 106.

[67] Dewey, *The Political Writings*, p. 106.

[68] Dewey, *The Political Writings*, p. 106.

[69] Dewey, *The Political Writings*, p. 6.

secures nothing less than human freedom. For Dewey, there is no greater ideal.

The freedom to act is generated and safeguarded by freedom of thought. However, freedom of thought develops only through its practical exercise. It is not automatically realized in the absence of restrictions to thought, or even in the actual process of thinking. Rather, freedom of thought arises in the opportunity to bring thinking to bear upon life. It is realized by way of discerning judgments that allow thought to secure worldly effects. Dewey writes:

> It has been assumed, in accord with the whole theory of Liberalism, that all that is necessary to secure freedom of thought and expression, is removal of external impediments: take away artificial obstructions and thought will operate.... Thinking, however, is the most difficult occupation in which man engages.... It requires favorable conditions, just as the art of painting requires paint, brushes and canvas. The most important problem in freedom of thinking is whether social conditions obstruct the development of judgment and insight or effectively promote it.[70]

Social conditions promote the development of judgment, and thereby safeguard freedom of thought, when they place individuals – both children and adults – in situations that demand the exercise of judgment. Only the transformation of thought into action via judgment fosters the stimulation of further thought. Dewey argues that judgment secures freedom of thought, and subsequently all other freedoms, by stimulating thinking to change its world.

Dewey is perhaps best known for his writings on education. It is seldom observed, however, that his pedagogical theory pivots around the cultivation of judgment. He writes: "The child cannot get power of judgment excepting as he is continually exercised in forming and testing judgment. He must have an opportunity to select for himself, and then to attempt to put his own selections into execution that he may submit them to the only final test, that of action."[71] Education does not end with childhood, nor does growth. Life itself is an extended pedagogical experience. Learning and growing are indefinite activities. Indeed, growth is the only moral absolute for Dewey.

Freedom and growth stand inextricably entwined. Dewey writes that "We are free not because of what we statically are, but inasfar as we

---

[70] Dewey, *The Political Writings*, p. 140.
[71] Dewey, *The Political Writings*, p. 108

are becoming different from what we have been."[72] Only intelligence
directed toward growth is deemed truly free. It alone ensures "a quick-
ened and enlarged spirit."[73] The social conditions that best facilitate
freedom and growth, for adults no less than for children, are found in
a democratic society. The health of democratic society, in turn, rests on
the widespread cultivation of judgment.

Democracy is a lived experiment. Self-government and self-realization
develop together through efforts to solve social problems. Thus Dewey
advocates not a "plann*ed* society... [but a] *continuously* plann*ing* society."[74] To this end, the propagation of knowledge must ensure "a
public opinion intelligent enough to meet present social problems."[75]
But more so than knowledge, scientific or otherwise, what safeguards
the democratic experiment is the unencumbered experience of putting
intelligence into action. Democracy stands or falls with the use of
"intelligence to liberate and liberalize action... for the sake of possibilities not yet given."[76] Bringing intelligence to bear in the unending work
of freedom is achieved only by way of assessing our social conditions –
perceptually, cognitively, emotionally, and normatively – grading them
according to their respective claims, evaluating their dangers and merits,
and, subsequently, engaging ourselves in their transformation.[77] Absent

---

[72] Dewey, *The Political Writings*, p. 136.
[73] Dewey, *The Political Writings*, pp. 7–8.
[74] Dewey, *The Political Writings*, p. 171.
[75] Dewey, *The Political Writings*, p. 57.
[76] Dewey, *The Political Writings*, pp. 7–8.
[77] Though he ignores Dewey's writings, Samuel Fleishacker argues that judgment constitutes the fullest exercise of individual freedom. Fleishacker holds that judgment is best
understood as a third concept of liberty, richer than the negative liberty of freedom from
constraint as well as the positive liberty of self-mastery and collective empowerment. Since
judgment is an individual's most important means of exercising and preserving liberty,
Fleishacker argues, the state should maximize opportunities for individual judgment.
Fleishacker and Dewey agree that the malaise of contemporary society is largely the
result of a lack of "phronetic activities" in people's lives. Indeed, Fleishacker stipulates
that "the solution to the alienation, the anomie, so many people experience can be neither cheap nor theatrical.... Instead, it requires the real costs in efficiency of... giving
low-level workers and officials more responsibility than, at least in the beginning, one has
any reason to think they can competently handle; and giving power to unreliable people
rather than reliable machines. If we refuse to do these things in our political, social, and
economic arenas, then we may indeed build technology that gives us smoother, healthier,
and more bodily pleasurable lives, but the people living those lives will more and more
resemble dumb animals rather than human beings." Samuel Fleishacker, *A Third Concept
of Liberty: Judgment and Freedom in Kant and Adam Smith* (Princeton: Princeton University
Press, 1999), p. 114. In the end, Fleishacker opts for a trickle-down theory of judgment,
wherein its regular exercise in commercial activity spills over into political life. Dewey

the judgment required for this endeavor – continuously and universally engaged by citizens – there is no hope that democracy will deliver on its promise of freedom.

Martin Heidegger (1889–1976)

Martin Heidegger explicitly addressed the question of practical wisdom in his Marburg lecture course on *Plato's Sophist.* The lecture, delivered in 1924–25, also explored Aristotle's discussion of *phronesis* in the *Nicomachean Ethics.*[78] Although Heidegger reengaged the topic periodically in his later works, notably in *A Question Concerning Technology,* the attention devoted to *phronesis* in his thought was limited in scope. Nonetheless, Heidegger provides a stunning vision of the workings of practical wisdom, though access is limited to those willing to excavate his dense texts. We should not be surprised that two of his students, Hans-Georg Gadamer and Hannah Arendt (discussed later), went on to become key scholars in the twentieth-century reappraisal of judgment.

For Heidegger, *Being-in-the-world* is not simply a brute fact for human beings; it bespeaks their intrinsic envelopment in defining relationships. Most fundamentally, these relationships are navigated by way of an unreflective know-how consisting of quasi-habitual skills. By subjecting these skills and the relationships they navigate to an intentional gaze, to reflection, the individual develops practical wisdom as a deliberative capacity. Thus the exercise of judgment typically occurs during the "breakdown" of habitual, everyday coping when our unreflective but skillful efforts are brought into the light of consciousness for questioning.

The narrow, concentrated light illuminating objects of our intentional scrutiny – what Heidegger calls the "present-at-hand" – causes their surroundings to fall into shadows and be temporarily obscured. Things come into focus for abstract consideration, in other words, only with their contexts already established and, generally, taken for granted. To be revealed as present-at-hand, something must arise for scrutiny and evaluation *out* of a context that forms an unreflective background to thought and action. The obscurity of the surroundings serves to define the object of attention, just as shadows demarcate an object that is illuminated. Judgment, as an

---

held the obverse to be true and normatively required. Fleishacker's disregard of Dewey and focus on Kant and Adam Smith accords with this distinction.

78 Martin Heidegger, *Plato's Sophist,* trans. Richard Rojcewicz and Andre Schuwer (Bloomington: Indiana University Press, 1997).

intentional exercise in analysis and evaluation, is grounded upon a host of non-deliberative, skillful interactions with the "ready-to-hand" world.

In this respect, judgment resembles the formal act of (textual) interpretation, which proceeds intentionally on the foundation of (unreflective) linguistic competence. Interpretation is the act of bringing into focus that which otherwise would remain obscurely embedded in its background text. Heidegger insists that interpretation is not a matter of imposing meaning on a passive, objective world lying before us. Human beings do not first stand opposite their world, as a subject to a present-at-hand object, and then become further involved in it through the individual's use of intrusive interpretative techniques. Rather, human beings always already exist in a ready-to-hand world, a contextual world of embedded involvement. They cope with this world, navigating its multiple relationships, more or less skillfully, and in large part habitually and unconsciously, in their day-to-day lives. Heidegger's word for this embedded involvement is "pre-ontological." Interpretation is the act of giving meaning to this pre-ontological, skillful navigation of the world.[79]

Heidegger affirms that "Our skills *have us* rather than our having them."[80] He means to suggest that we are not primordial subjects bearing essential natures who subsequently appropriate skills to achieve particular goals. Rather, our worldly skills are definitive of who and what we are. Only subsequent to and based upon our skillful involvement in the ready-to-hand world can we engage in the interpretive distillations that carry us beyond pre-ontological understanding. Just as interpretation consists in subjecting to scrutiny a world that is already negotiated by way of unreflective linguistic skills, so *phronesis* consists in subjecting to examination a world that is already negotiated by way of unreflective, practical skills. For this reason, Heidegger deemed *phronesis* a hermeneutic virtue.

Aristotle declared *sophia* to be the highest form of life because of its concern with the eternal and unchanging. In his early writings, Heidegger pushes *phronesis* onto this pedestal.[81] Aristotle understood *phronesis* to meld practice with principle, allowing one to act prudently in specific situations because the parts were seen in the context of the (good life as a)

---

[79] Martin Heidegger, *Being and Time* (New York: Harper and Row, 1962), pp. 190–91.

[80] See Hubert L. Dreyfus, *Being-in-the-World: A Commentary on Heidegger's* Being and Time, *Division I* (Cambridge, MA: MIT Press, 1991), pp. 107, 117, 202.

[81] Michael Gillespie writes: "Heidegger recognizes that for Aristotle, *sophia* is higher than *phronesis*, but he himself is convinced of the reverse and strives to make the strongest case possible on an Aristotelian foundation for the superiority of *phronesis*." Michael Gillespie, "Martin Heidegger's Aristotelian National Socialism," *Political Theory* 28 (April 2000):147.

whole. For Heidegger, the 'whole' in question is less an ethical projection than an ontological, world historical vision. When inauthentic, we confront particulars (specific entities or relationships) without appreciation of the whole (of Being – the mysterious Being of beings, in its full historicity). Heideggerian *phronesis* relates the parts to *this* whole. The *phronetic* individual displays an authentic relationship to Being in the face of everyday coping. He ably interprets the actions of others, placing them within the most revealing, ontologically informed, context.[82] He remains capable of worldly competance, without losing sight of his historic embeddedness, his *Geworfenheit*, or thrownness.

The later Heidegger largely abandons interest in *phronesis* as a form of knowledge that has its locus in *praxis*, focusing instead on *techne* as a form of knowledge that has its locus in *poeisis*. Heidegger makes the switch after his political escapade with the Nazis in 1933. Heidegger was retreating into the hope that thinking and art, rather than politics and *praxis*, might provide a better means of forging a new relationship to Being. Heidegger comes to reject politics, and lose interest in *phronesis*, its key virtue, after his own scandalous involvement with fascism.[83] With politics dismissed as a unique and substantial mode of human being, the post-war Heidegger slots the remaining possibilities into the antipodal categories of philosophic-poetic thought and technological mastery.

Some interpreters take a diametrically opposed view, maintaining that "Heidegger seeks to solve the problem of technology by establishing the rule of *phronesis*."[84] Christopher Rickey, for example, depicts Heidegger as involved in a politico-religious crusade to rid the world of inauthenticity through *phronetic* activity. Like any number of commentators, Rickey misunderstands authenticity, depicting it as "the criterion for distinguishing what is superior or better in human existence."[85] For Heidegger, however, inauthenticity and authenticity are ontological, not ethical, categories. Thus he explicitly rejects the terminology of 'superior' or 'better.' Authentic speech and action are not improvements upon everyday talk and activity. They are, at once, less forgetful of Being and, for that very

[82] See Martin Heidegger, "Phenomenological Interpretations with Respect to Aristotle: Indications of the Hermeneutic Situation," *Mind and World* 25 (1992): 381. See also Gillespie, "Martin Heidegger's Aristotelian National Socialism," p. 150.

[83] See Richard Bernstein, *The New Constellation: The Ethical-Political Horizons of Modernity/ Postmodernity* (Cambridge: MIT Press, 1991), pp. 121, 122.

[84] Gillespie, "Martin Heidegger's Aristotelian National Socialism," p. 151.

[85] Christopher Rickey, *Revolutionary Saints: Heidegger, National Socialism and Antinomian Politics* (University Park, PA: Pennsylvania State University Press, 2002), p. 42.

reason, less adequate to our everyday transactions. Inauthenticity, in turn, bears no pejorative connotation. As a distinct, essential, and inevitable mode of human being, inauthenticity is neither deplorable nor regrettable. "The inauthenticity of Dasein," Heidegger writes, "does not signify any 'less' Being or any 'lower' degree of Being."[86] It follows that inauthentic existence should not be disparaged. "On the contrary," Heidegger writes, "this everyday having of self within our factical, existent, passionate merging into things can surely be genuine, whereas all extravagant grubbing about in one's soul can be in the highest degree counterfeit or even pathologically eccentric."[87] An authentic existence can only be gained on the foundation of our quasi-habitual, skillful, inauthentic involvement with the world. Likewise, practical judgment can only be exercised on the foundation of a plethora of largely unconscious strategies of skillful coping.

Rickey asserts the central importance of *phronesis* to Heidegger's magnum opus, *Being and Time*, and to his philosophy as a whole. Textual evidence does not support this claim.[88] The significance of *phronesis* to Heidegger's thought is patent, but its centrality is doubtful. While the early Heidegger celebrated this practical virtue, the later Heidegger increasingly leaves it out of the picture. In turn, and as importantly, Heidegger distanced *phronesis* from moral life, for better or for worse. His chief and lasting contribution to our understanding of practical judgment, with this in mind, is his insistence that its exercise only ever occurs upon the foundation of a skillful, unreflective navigation of relationships. The deliberative and analytic features of judgment are always preceded by and remain parasitic upon a practical and embodied worldliness.

Hans-Georg Gadamer (1900–2002)

While attending Heidegger's lectures on Aristotle in Freiburg, Hans-Georg Gadamer was introduced to *phronesis* as a hermeneutic virtue.[89]

---

[86] Heidegger, *Being and Time*, p. 68.

[87] Heidegger, *The Basic Problems of Phenomenology* (Bloomington: Indiana University Press, 1982), p. 160.

[88] See Rickey, *Revolutionary Saints*, pp. 40, 61, 116, 160. See also Leslie Paul Thiele, "A (Political) Philosopher by Any Other Name: The Roots of Heidegger's Thought," *Political Theory*, 32 (August 2004):570–579. As the reader of the two most popular translations of *Being and Time* may easily determine, *phronesis* does not appear in the very extensive English and Greek indexes.

[89] Hans-Georg Gadamer, *Heidegger's Ways*, trans. John Stanley (Albany: State University of New York Press, 1994), p. 141. See also Hans-Georg Gadamer, *Philosophical Hermeneutics*, trans./ed. David Linge (Berkeley: University of California Press, 1976), pp. 196, 201.

Like his mentor, Gadamer postulated practical judgment as a specific type of interpretation, one that engages the concrete world as if it were a text. The practical judge is first and foremost a worldly hermeneut.

With Heidegger, Gadamer insists that explicit interpretation is possible only on the basis of an array of implicit understandings. Whenever we attempt to know something, we are always projecting our "fore-conceptions" upon it.[90] The goal for the interpreter is not to eliminate these fore-conceptions. Indeed, prejudices constitute "the initial directedness of our whole ability to experience.... They are simply conditions whereby we experience something – whereby what we encounter says something to us."[91] Prejudices, for Gadamer, are not distortions that mar the purity of understanding. Rather, they constitute the initial conditions under which understanding becomes possible. Gadamer formulates a "positive concept of prejudice," understood as the "initial directedness of our whole ability to experience."[92] The point is not to retain one's prejudices. Fore-conceptions simply provide a starting point. "The important thing," Gadamer writes, "is to be aware of one's own bias, so that the text may present itself in all its newness and thus be able to assert its own truth against one's own fore-meanings."[93] Good interpretation constantly seeks to replace initial preconceptions with more suitable ones as the reading of a text progresses.

Good judges, like good hermeneuts, are porous. They are capable of absorbing and integrating other points of view. Gadamer calls this inter-subjective understanding a "fusion of horizons."[94] It bespeaks the development, from initially divergent positions, of a sufficient level of understanding such that conversation becomes meaningful. As a hermeneutic virtue, practical judgment prompts the extension of the self in an effort to fuse horizons with those one interprets and evaluates. This interpretive "adventure" leaves one vulnerable but also poised for growth.[95]

Unlike technicians engaged in rule-governed activity, the judge understands that moral and political decisions demand more than the application of axiomatic knowledge. In forging judgments, he is attentive, but not tethered, to rules. Gadamer is fundamentally Aristotelian in this regard. Only good judgment, not set procedures, can determine in any given

---

90 Gadamer, *Truth and Method* (New York: Crossroad, 1975), p. 358.
91 Gadamer, *Philosophical Hermeneutics*, p. 9.
92 Gadamer, *Philosophical Hermeneutics*, p. 9.
93 Gadamer, *Truth and Method*, p. 238.
94 Gadamer, *Truth and Method*, p. 273.
95 Gadamer, *Reason in the Age of Science*, trans. Frederick Lawrence (Cambridge: MIT Press, 1981), pp. 109–110

circumstance the appropriateness of specific action (or specific laws). The practical judge does not simply apply rules; he "co-determines" them.[96] Only thus can equity be achieved.

The co-determination of rules is not a purely calculative or analytic effort. It activates reflective rather than determinative judgment. Good taste is an "indispensable element" of the judge's craft. This good taste or "undemonstrable tact" allows one to distinguish right from wrong and effective from ineffective. While reason has its role to play in practical judgment, it is a supra-rational, intuitive knack that allows the judge, in ambiguous and uncertain circumstances, to "hit the target."[97]

As a kind of taste or tact, good judgment does not generate provable or falsifiable truth claims. But it is not for that reason merely subjective, in the sense of relating to purely personal preferences. Gadamer is concerned with the faculty of taste insofar as it can be cultivated. People are not born connoisseurs. They develop a knack for appreciating fineness by way of experience. Good taste, like good judgment, can be developed. And the judgments that ensue from this sort of knack, while not strictly verifiable or falsifiable, are available (as Kant also observed[98]) to informed debate.

Good taste, for Gadamer, is not the whole of judgment. It supplements rational and deliberative activities. What Gadamer says of tact or taste, in this regard, bears a striking similarity to what Aristotle says of correct desire. It is a necessary but not sufficient condition of good judgment, an indispensable supplement that ensures embodied knowledge. For Gadamer, "taste is not the ground, but the supreme perfection of the moral judgment. The man who finds that what is bad goes against his taste has the greatest assurance in the acceptance of the good and the rejection of the bad – as great as the assurance of the most vital of our senses which chooses or rejects food."[99] Acceptance or rejection is not simply a cognitive matter. Rather, it constitutes a lived understanding informed by our deepest desires. Moral knowledge, for Gadamer as for Aristotle, is only truly discovered by grappling with situations that demand our practical involvement.

Gadamer is mainly known for his interpretations of ancient texts. For the most part, he shared Heidegger's distrust of modern technology and its scientific foundations. He is, in this respect, a far cry from Dewey, who, for the most part, uncritically celebrated the power of science. Yet, on

---

[96] Gadamer, *Truth and Method*, pp. 16, 37, 283–84.
[97] Gadamer, *Truth and Method*, p. 38.
[98] Immanuel Kant, *Critique of Judgment* in *The Philosophy of Kant*, ed. Carl J. Friedrich (New York: Modern Library, 1949), pp. 302–307.
[99] Gadamer, *Truth and Method*, p. 38.

the question of judgment, Gadamer and Dewey share many of the same concerns. Like Dewey, Gadamer held that practical judgments display our "real freedom" as we "participate in the performance of life itself."[100] Like Dewey, Gadamer worried that the "autonomy" of judgment and opportunities for its exercise were threatened in an increasingly bureaucratized society. "The more rationally the organizational forms of life are shaped," Gadamer lamented, "the less is rational judgement exercised and trained among individuals."[101] Like Dewey, Gadamer held the practical judgments of average citizens in high esteem. And, like Dewey (though with a different assessment of the role played by science), Gadamer held the task of contemporary philosophy to be the promotion of the democratic skills of judgment. Gadamer writes:

> I think, then, that the chief task of philosophy is to . . . defend practical and political reason against the domination of technology based on science. That is the point of philosophical hermeneutic. It corrects the peculiar falsehood of modern consciousness: the idolatry of scientific method and of the anonymous authority of the sciences and it vindicates again the noblest task of the citizen – decision-making according to one's own responsibility – instead of conceding the task to the expert. In this respect, hermeneutic philosophy is the heir of the older tradition of practical philosophy.[102]

In claiming this lineage for hermeneutic philosophy, Gadamer weds Heideggerian phenomenology with a proto-Deweyian pragmatism. Whereas Dewey believed decision-making could be greatly enhanced by modern science, Gadamer worried that scientific expertise might usurp the role of practical judgment altogether. Dewey believed that citizen-judges were mature enough to wield science as a powerful tool in the struggle for freedom. Harking back to Heidegger, Gadamer feared that citizen-judges were themselves becoming tools in the hands of a scientific elite. In an age of increasing technocratic power, Gadamer suggests, the embodied skills and desires that inform practical wisdom might simply wither away.

Hannah Arendt (1906–75)

Hannah Arendt concurred with Gadamer that good judgment was related to good taste. Like Gadamer, she understood judgment to be fundamentally grounded in a shared world. Given their common mentorship by

---

[100] Gadamer, *The Enigma of Health*, trans. Jason Gaiger and Nicholas Walker (Stanford: Stanford University Press, 1996), pp. 53–54. See also Gadamer, *Philosophical Hermeneutics*, p. 40.

[101] Gadamer, *The Enigma of Health*, p. 17.

[102] Gadamer, "Hermeneutics and Social Science," *Cultural Hermeneutics* 2 (1975): 316.

Heidegger, that is hardly surprising. Yet Arendt approached the topic of human judgment not through Heidegger's appropriation of *phronesis,* as did Gadamer, but by way of Kant's critique of aesthetic judgment. In doing so, she raised the faculty to a position of importance that it arguably had not held since Aristotle. Indeed, the concept of judgment was of such consequence to Arendt that she planned to devote an entire book to its analysis: the final section of *The Life of the Mind,* which remained unfinished at the time of her death.

Arendt's writings on judgment are controversial. Many find them "paradoxical," in large part because she attempts to blend Aristotelian *phronesis* with Kantian aesthetic judgment, effectively politicizing the latter.[103] In this respect, Arendt utilizes Kant for "un-Kantian, anti-Kantian" purposes.[104] While Kant clearly provides a springboard for her thought, and the focus of much of her writing on the subject, Arendt unmistakably diverges from Kant in order to reappropriate classical concerns. Like Aristotle, Arendt conceives judgment as the faculty that allows one to tell right from wrong. Kant insists that this task belongs not to reflective judgment, or even to determinative judgment, but to pure, practical reason, the topic of his second *Critique.* In turn, Arendt considers judgment "the most political of man's mental abilities."[105] Like Aristotle, she deems judgment to be the preeminent virtue of the *zoon politikon,* the political animal.

Recalling Kant's observation that the faculty of aesthetic judgment presupposes the presence of others, Arendt states that "when one judges, one judges as a member of a community."[106] But for Arendt, unlike Kant, the judgments that emerge from this membership structure moral and political no less than aesthetic life. We employ judgment to tell right from wrong as we navigate a public realm of intersubjective meanings.[107]

---

[103] Seyla Benhabib, *The Reluctant Modernism of Hannah Arendt* (Thousand Oaks, CA: Sage, 1996), p. 175. See also Seyla Benhabib, "Judgment and the Moral Foundations of Politics in Hannah Arendt's Thought" (183–204), in *Judgment, Imagination, and Politics: Themes from Kant and Arendt,* ed. Ronald Beiner and Jennifer Nedelsky (New York: Rowman and Littlefield, 2001), p. 185.

[104] George Kateb, "The Judgment of Arendt," in *Judgment, Imagination, and Politics: Themes from Kant and Arendt,* ed. Ronald Beiner and Jennifer Nedelsky (New York: Rowman and Littlefield, 2001), pp. 121–122.

[105] Hannah Arendt, "Thinking and Moral Considerations: A Lecture," *Social Research* 38 (1971), p. 446.

[106] Arendt, *Lectures on Kant's Political Philosophy,* ed. with an interpretive essay by Ronald Beiner (Chicago: University of Chicago Press, 1982), p. 72. Hannah Arendt, *Between Past and Future: Eight Exercises in Political Thought* (New York: Penguin Books, 1954), p. 221.

[107] Arendt, *Between Past and Future,* p. 221. See also Benhabib, *The Reluctant Modernism of Hannah Arendt,* pp. 188–89.

To make this un-Kantian claim, Arendt invokes Kant's notion of the "enlarged mentality" that grounds aesthetic judgment. This enlarged mentality allows one to think from the place of others.

Citing Kant, Arendt states that reflective judgment is a way of training "one's imagination to go visiting."[108] Herein we gain appreciation of the world of others, not so much the actual thoughts and feelings of others but their possible thoughts and feelings, given their respective standpoints. Our imagined encounter with multiple points of view liberates us from the unitary perspective of the individual. In this manner, Arendt affirms, one becomes capable of "representative thinking."[109] As such, judgment is a "political rather than a merely theoretical activity."[110]

Arendt surmises that the ability to think representatively originated with "Homeric impartiality," first demonstrated in the ancient bard's depiction of the Trojan war from the standpoints of both protagonists, Achilles and Hector.[111] Representative thinking is not empathy. The difference, for Arendt, is that empathy requires one to experience another's emotional state, whereas representative thinking requires only an understanding of how one would feel and think were one in another's place. This imaginative insight may develop without losing the (emotional) distance required to render an impartial judgment. Representative thinking may exist amidst the starkest disagreement. It demands not concord or sympathy but a rich, nuanced understanding of how others, given their respective points of view, came to form particular judgments.

The faculty of judgment is nourished by the "truthfulness" of seeing things from multiple perspectives. Providing this impartial assessment of unique events, Arendt states, is the "political function of the story-teller – historian or novelist."[112] The Arendtian judge, first and foremost, is engaged with worldly tales. Not the compulsion of reason but narrative understanding and persuasion is his *modus operandi*.

The narratives that foster representational thinking and judgment are not mere chronologies of events. They are storehouses of examples. What Kant said of aesthetic judgment, Arendt maintained for moral and political judgment: examples constitute its irreplaceable go-carts. Furnished either by history or fiction, examples allow one imaginately to "go visiting," to see and feel the contours of other standpoints without being

---

[108] Arendt, *Lectures on Kant's Political Philosophy*, p. 43.
[109] Arendt, *Between Past and Future*, p. 220.
[110] Arendt, *Between Past and Future*, p. 219.
[111] Arendt, *Between Past and Future*, p. 51.
[112] Arendt, *Between Past and Future*, p. 262.

compelled through logic or reason to accept or reject them.[113] Examples are the narrative accountings that allow persuasion in the midst of common experiences and disparate opinions. It is validation through examples, Arendt holds, that provides the most cogent solution to the problem of how particulars can be judged without subsuming them under rules. Our judgments prove to be good or bad, in large part, depending upon which examples, which narratives, inform them.[114]

Citing Thomas Jefferson, Arendt observes that Shakespeare goes much further than "dry volumes of ethics" to instill a sense of what duties are required of us. The only way for "an ethical principle to be verified as well as validated," she insists, is "when it manages to become manifest in the guise of an example."[115] The examples that populate history and fiction – stories of men and women in dark times who judge well (or badly) and act courageously (or cowardly) – provide banisters to guide our ethico-political lives. They serve the judge as illustrations of commendable (or, in the case of bad examples, deplorable) speech and action. "In the last analysis," Arendt observes, "our decisions about right and wrong will depend upon our choice of company, with whom we wish to spend our lives. And this company is chosen through thinking in examples, in examples of persons dead or alive, and in examples of incidents, past or present."[116] Selecting the right examples is the better part of judgment. The "cultivated" person, Arendt insists, chooses well in this regard.[117]

Political judgments, like the aesthetic judgments and matters of taste addressed by Kant, are open to discussion and debate but cannot be decided by rational processes. The judge solicits agreement but cannot compel it (with logic, reason, or any other cognitive tool). When judging, Arendt states, we actively seek to "woo the assent of others." Indeed, judgments are made in anticipation of the need for accord. Unlike the self-enclosed process of reasoning, the activity of judging is grounded in "an anticipated communication with others with whom I know I must finally come to some agreement."[118] To this end, judgments invoke common sense, shared experience, and resonant examples.[119] In this regard,

---

[113] Arendt, *Lectures on Kant's Political Philosophy*, p. 43.

[114] Arendt, *Lectures on Kant's Political Philosophy*, pp. 76–77, 84.

[115] Arendt, *Between Past and Future*, pp. 248–49.

[116] Quoted in Ronald Beiner, "Interpretive Essay," in Arendt, *Lectures on Kant's Political Philosophy*, p. 113.

[117] Arendt, *Between Past and Future*, p. 226.

[118] Arendt, *Between Past and Future*, p. 220.

[119] In a very Arendtian fashion, Wayne Booth writes: "Judgment requires a community: no judge can operate outside a legal system; no just weighing can take place on scales

judgment – while not bound by the strictures of logic, rules, and truth claims – is not reducible to subjective preferences. It always appeals to commonly held, if not universal, dispositions and understandings. Unlike truths, judgments grounded in examples cannot ensure assent. They do not demonstrate objective validity. But the judge can legitimate her assessments, evaluations, and choices by rendering an account of their development, referencing commonly shared experiences and worthy examples along the way. Reason may (and should) play a role in this account, but it remains in service to narrative meaning.

Like Dewey and Gadamer, Arendt holds that judgment arises out of, generates, and preserves freedom of thought. She characterizes thinking as the "soundless dialogue" of the "two-in-one" that constitutes consciousness, a kind of split identity that forms by way of silent conversations. *Con-sciousness*, as its Latin roots indicate, is a knowing-with. It mimics by way of an internal duality the plurality of the public realm. Conscience – the knowing of right from wrong – is a "by-product" of the knowing-with of consciousness. It arises, Arendt suggests, not from universally shared reason (as Kant argues), but from the common sense and knowing-with of those who live and grow in communities.[120] Freedom of thought is not exercised by the isolated thinker who remains unfettered in his ideas or utterances. Rather, it is demonstrated by the individual engaged in representative thinking who imaginatively shares the world with others.[121]

As a faculty of its own, judgment depends upon thought but is not reducible to it. Judgment allows the constant back-and-forth of thought

---

not calibrated with other scales. . . . All judgment is pointless unless it can be shared with other judges who rely in turn on their past experiences. . . . But we need a term that suggests even more strongly than the legal metaphor the reliance (rational but by no means logical in any usual sense of the word) on the past experiences of many judges who do not have even a roughly codified set of precedents to guide them. The term must imply a communal enterprise rather than a private, 'personal' calculation logically coercive on all who hear it. Since I find no term that meets these demands, I must for once reluctantly resort to neologism: *coduction*, from *co* ("together") and *ducere* ("to lead, draw out, bring, bring out"). . . . Coduction can never be "demonstrative," apodeictic: it will not persuade those who lack the experience required to perform a similar coduction. And it can never be performed with confidence by one person alone. The validity of our coductions must always be corrected in conversations about the coductions of others whom we trust." Wayne C. Booth, *The Company We Keep: An Ethics of Fiction* (Berkeley: University of California Press, 1988), pp. 72–73.

120 See Ronald Beiner and Jennifer Nedelsky, "Introduction" in *Judgment, Imagination, and Politics: Themes from Kant and Arendt*, ed. Ronald Beiner and Jennifer Nedelsky (New York: Rowman and Littlefield, 2001), p. xi.

121 In the same vein, Arendt maintains that freedom of action is exercised only by those who enter the public realm.

to find its bearings in the concrete world, helping it escape from an otherwise endless dialogue. Judgment, Arendt writes, is the "mysterious endowment of the mind by which the general, always a mental construction, and the particular, always given to sense experience, are brought together."[122] It helps the "thinking ego," which otherwise would not stray from generalities, enter the phenomenal world of particularities. The mind needs the "gift" of judgment to make this passage.[123]

Aware of Tocqueville's lament that the past no longer illuminates the future, Arendt suggests that today we are often forced to think without banisters.[124] But judgment is more than thinking. Judgment liberates us from the *aporias* of thought and the spirals of solitary speculation such that we might embrace or reject specific features of a shared world. It channels the metaphoric streams of consciousness into concrete geographies of interest. Thinking may survive without banisters, but judgment cannot. It relies on the guidance of examples, narrative accounts of the phenomenal world. As such, judgment constitutes a moral faculty. Arendt explains:

> If thinking – the two-in-one of the soundless dialogue – actualizes the difference within our identity as given in consciousness and thereby results in conscience as its by-product, then judging, the by-product of the liberating effect of thinking, realizes thinking, makes it manifest in the world of appearances, where I am never alone and always too busy to be able to think. The manifestation of the wind of thought is not knowledge; it is the ability to tell right from wrong, beautiful from ugly. And this, at the rare moments when the stakes are on the table, may indeed prevent catastrophes, at least for the self.[125]

While thinking is goalless, judgment is firmly tethered to the world. And while Arendt celebrates thinking in its own right, she nonetheless indicates that the life of the mind culminates – both in a temporal and normative sense – in the worldliness, and ethico-political impact, of judgment.[126]

Though worldly and practical, judgment is not inherently partisan. While attentive to the political game and its stakes, the judge is neither a

---

[122] Hannah Arendt, *The Life of the Mind – Thinking* (New York: Harcourt Brace Jovanovich 1978), p. 69.

[123] Arendt, *The Life of the Mind*, p. 215.

[124] Arendt, "On Hannah Arendt," in Melvyn A. Hill, *Hannah Arendt: The Recovery of the Public World* (New York: St. Martin's Press, 1979), p. 336.

[125] Arendt, *The Life of the Mind*, p. 193; and see 123.

[126] See Robert Dostal, "Judging Human Action: Arendt's Appropriation of Kant," in *Judgment, Imagination, and Politics: Themes from Kant and Arendt*, ed. Ronald Beiner and Jennifer Nedelsky (New York: Rowman and Littlefield, 2001), p. 159.

player nor a fan. Impartiality is in order: "Withdrawal from direct involvement to a standpoint outside the game is a condition *sine qua non* of all
judgment."[127] Like the magistrate in a court of law, the individual exercising practical judgment takes a step back from the fray. This is a conscious effort, a struggle even, and not an easy retreat. Judgment, Arendt
argues, "presupposes a definitely 'unnatural' and deliberate withdrawal
from involvement and the partiality of immediate interests as they are
given by my position in the world and the part I play in it."[128] While
a process of assessment and evaluation may conclude with the judge's
choosing sides in a partisan struggle, the exercise of judgment itself is
characterized by representative thinking that bespeaks a plurality of viewpoints. While representative thinking that makes good use of examples
"does not tell one how *to act*... how to apply the wisdom, found by virtue
of occupying a 'general standpoint,' to the particulars of political life," it
does orient one's moral compass.[129] And it may well tell one what *not* to
do, especially when the stakes are on the table.

An enlarged mentality allows for impartiality. But the function of judgment is not simply the provision of fair and balanced assessments. It also
anchors the ebb and flow of life and, as such, stabilizes and preserves the
world. Building on Kant's understanding of aesthetics, Arendt depicts the
judge as a disinterested spectator who gains retrospective clarity. Seen this
way, judgment is ontologically redeeming. It lends durability to a world
of fleeting appearances. Judgment redeems an ultimately tragic, transitory world of phenomena by way of narrative accounts that distinguish
right from wrong, worthy from unworthy, meaningful from meaningless.[130] Indeed, it is our capacity for judgment that begets "our human
dignity."[131]

In mass societies, where the realm of political thought and action has
been substantially shrunk as a result of the scale of markets, bureaucracies,
and technological development, Arendtian judgment salvages citizenship
and the public realm.[132] To be sure, Arendt's early placement of judgment
within the *vita activa* gives way, by the time she wrote the *Life of the Mind*,
to its depiction as a component of the *vita contemplativa*. At the same
time, judgment remained firmly tethered in both her early and later

---

[127] Arendt, *Lectures on Kant's Political Philosophy*, p. 55.
[128] Arendt, *The Life of the Mind*, p. 76.
[129] Arendt, *Lectures on Kant's Political Philosophy*, p. 44.
[130] Arendt, *Between Past and Future*, p. 262.
[131] Arendt, *The Life of the Mind*, p. 216.
[132] See Ronald Beiner, "Interpretive Essay," p. 153.

works to the expression of freedom. Its public nature coupled with its independence from the coerciveness of truth keeps judgment squarely within the field of politics.

For Arendt, the judge is less an advocate than a voice of reserve. He does not push forward with all deliberate speed. Rather, the exercise of practical wisdom keeps him from making egregious missteps, from slipping into morally or politically dark waters. This is no small feat. A sole dissenter often proves to be the catalyst that transforms a mob into a political body where dispute is once again possible and fruitful. In a world of accelerating technological change and socio-political disruption on a global scale, the role of courageous resistance should not be undervalued.

Arendtian judgment is enigmatic. It is, at once, an act of freedom and a stabilizing force, a firm arbiter of right and wrong and a purveyor of multiple perspectives. Judgment spans these chasms by linking the ephemeral world of thought with the concrete world of action. Only a paradoxical faculty, Arendt suggests, could redeem the human condition.

Judgment in Post-Modernity

Post-modernists constitute a broad constellation of thinkers exhibiting many fundamental disagreements. Few accept the moniker. To the extent that post-modernists are identifiable as a group, their status arises primarily by their serving as the target of traditionalist and modernist criticism. In rallying against the grand specter of normalization, post-modernists often suggest their neutrality with regard to the relative worth of specific cultures and cultural achievements. Thus they abdicate moral responsibility, critics charge, and undermine political judgment. When post-modernists do target institutions or behavior for censure, critics hold, they advance only a tactical choice rather than a principled claim. The moral force of judgment is consequently depleted. In turn, post-modernists are denounced for replacing ethics with aesthetics. They advocate the creation of the self as a work of art. This effort undermines ethico-political responsibilities and the sound judgment needed to fulfill them.[133] In a post-modern world, there is no telling right from wrong.

---

[133] See, for example, Beiner, *Philosophy in a Time of Lost Spirit*, and Leslie Paul Thiele, "Common Sense, Judgment and the Limits of Political Theory," *Political Theory*, 28(2000): 565–588. See also James P. McDaniel and John Sloop, "Hope's Finitude," in *Judgment*

Many of these concerns and criticisms hit the mark, or do not miss by much. While post-modernists reject axiomatic moral theory, however, many explicitly valorize ethico-political judgment. They embrace practical judgment because it fills the void left by the collapse of metaphysical foundations. While post-modern judgment still aims at justice, its inherent fallibility is explicitly acknowledged. In turn, it is exercised not as distilled rationality, but rather as a historically developed mix of affective loyalties and expedient calculations. A sustained case for this assertion will be presented in Chapter 5, where the work of Martin Heidegger, Michel Foucault, and Richard Rorty will be addressed. For now, I summarize how and why key figures placed in the post-modern camp commend practical judgment.

Jean-François Lyotard has written perhaps the best-known account of post-modernity.[134] In a number of his works, he celebrates the faculty of judgment and pursues its relationship to justice. Lyotard writes that "Justice ... does not consist merely in the observance of the rules ... it consists in working at the limits of what the rules permit, in order to invent new moves, perhaps new rules and therefore new games."[135] He goes on to say that "a judge worthy of the name has no true model to guide his judgments ... the true nature of the judge is to pronounce judgments, and therefore prescriptions, just so, without criteria. This is, after all, what Aristotle calls prudence. It consists in dispensing justice without models."[136] Lyotard mischaracterizes Arisotle. But in doing so, he highlights the significance of judgment for his own thought. Practical judgment is both the foundation and summit of moral and political life for Lyotard. In the absence of metaphysical certainties and firm foundations, practical judgment takes on an unprecedented mandate in the contemporary world.

Notwithstanding his valorization of judgment, Lyotard argues that even the most judicious decision necessarily falls short of the mark. Every judgment commits some injustice, failing to give each person his due. To acknowledge this lapse is to appreciate what Lyotard calls the "differend." The differend is that feature of ethico-political life that resists

Calls: Rhetoric, Politics, and Indeterminacy, ed. John Sloop and James McDaniel (Boulder: Westview Press, 1998), p. 3.

[134] Jean-François Lyotard, *The Postmodern Condition* (Minneapolis: University of Minnesota Press, 1984).

[135] Lyotard, *Just Gaming*, trans. Wlad Godzich (Minneapolis: University of Minnesota Press, 1985), p. 100.

[136] Lyotard, *Just Gaming*, pp. 25–26.

closure. Disputes defy truly just resolutions because every resolution in the
name of justice creates injustice, doing some ill to the undeserving.[137] By
dint of its unforeseeable pathways through the intricate interdependencies of social life, all action bears within it the seeds of discrimination and
wrongdoing. The burden of navigating the moral transgressions of political life in a plural world must be borne, however, for justice could never be
pursued if the commission of moderate injustice were wholly proscribed.
In this vein, Lyotard recommends "a politics that would respect both
the desire for justice and the desire for the unknown."[138] Such a politics
would guard against "the encroachment of the discourse of justice by the
discourse of truth."[139] To establish and preserve such a political realm,
one must ensure that the role of practical judgment is not usurped by
ethico-political 'truths' and the duties they dictate.

Jacques Derrida develops a number of Lyotard's themes, speaking also
to the relation of justice and judgment. Best known as a deconstructionist,
Derrida is famous for skewering sacred cows with impenetrable prose.
Everything becomes grist for his deconstructive mill. Nothing is out of
bounds.

Still, there is one exception. Derrida writes that "Justice in itself, if
such a thing exists, outside or beyond law, is not deconstructible."[140] As
if bringing Aristotle's theory of equity up to date, Derrida argues that
"Justice is what gives us the impulse, the drive, or the movement to
improve the law, that is, to deconstruct the law. Without a call for justice we would not have any interest in deconstructing the law. That is
why I said that the condition of possibility of deconstruction is a call
for justice."[141] Following the thought of Emmanuel Levinas, Derrida
insists that the idea of justice is infinite: "infinite because it is irreducible,
irreducible because owed to the other, owed to the other, before any contract, because it has come, the other's coming as the singularity that is

---

[137] Lyotard, *The Differend: Phrases in Dispute*, trans. Georges Van Den Abbeele (Minneapolis:
University of Minnesota Press, 1988).

[138] Lyotard, *The Postmodern Condition*, p. 67.

[139] Lyotard, *Just Gaming*, p. 98.

[140] Jacques Derrida, "Force of Law: The 'Mystical Foundation of Authority'," trans. Mary
Quaintance, in *Deconstruction and the Possibility of Justice*, ed. Drucilla Cornell, Michel
Rosenfeld, and David Gray Carlson (New York: Routledge, 1992), p. 14.

[141] Jacques Derrida, "The Villanova Roundtable: A Conversation with Jacques Derrida," in
Deconstruction in a Nutshell, ed. John D. Caputo (New York: Fordham University Press,
1997), p. 16. See also Richard Rorty, *Philosophy and Social Hope* (New York: Penguin,
1999), p. 212.

always other."[142] As the other is beyond calculation, it demands a justice that is infinite. This creates an insuperable obligation for the practical judge.

Derrida writes: "A judge, if he wants to be just, cannot content himself with applying the law. He has to reinvent the law each time. . . . Justice, if it has to do with the other, with the infinite distance of the other, is always unequal to the other, always incalculable. You cannot calculate justice."[143] The Derridean judge pursues an impossible task. He is, in this respect, always a failure and always guilty.[144] But Derrida does not give up on judgment. Like Lyotard, he asserts its need, indeed its indispensability and primacy in the ethico-political realm. However, he wants the judge to remain humbly aware of his Sisyphean task.

Justice must go beyond calculation, Derrida insists, but "This does not mean that we should not calculate. We have to calculate as rigorously as possible. But there is a point or limit beyond which calculation must fail, and we must recognize that."[145] The law is never more than a guide always in need of surpassing. Justice is as fundamental, as undeconstructible, as it is unattainable – cognitively or concretely. Justice, while never wholly realized, Derrida insists, must be vigorously pursued. The foremost means to its pursuit is practical judgment.

Judgments are always, ultimately, ungrounded. While one may and should employ rules and principles as guideposts, one judges in the end from a position of radical uncertainty. Derrida employs the term "aporetic experience" to describe the moment when a judgment is made. It is the moment of the incalculable and the calculable passing through each other. Just as judgment defines the blending of the particular and the universal, so it merges the unknown and the known. Referencing Kierkegaard, Derrida goes so far as to suggest that the act of judging is a display of madness. In his pursuit of an incalculable justice, in wrestling with "the ghost of the undecidable" by means of the most thorough calculations, the judge courts folly.[146]

---

142 Derrida, "Force of Law," p. 25.
143 Derrida, "The Villanova Roundtable," p. 17.
144 The "scrupulous conscience," according to Levinas, understands that "the more I am just, the more I am guilty. " Emmanuel Levinas, *Basic Philosophical Writings*, ed. Adrian T. Peperzak, Simon Critchley, and Robert Bernasconi (Bloomington: Indiana University Press, 1996), p. 21.
145 Derrida, "The Villanova Roundtable," p. 19.
146 Derrida, "Force of Law," p. 24.

Rules fail the judge, yet decisions must be made. An inventive leap is required. Derrida explains his complex position:

> To be just, the decision of a judge, for example, must not only follow a rule of law or a general law but must also assume it, approve it, confirm its value, by a reinstituting act of interpretation, as if ultimately nothing previously existed of the law, as if the judge himself invented the law in every case. No exercise of justice as law can be just unless there is a 'fresh judgment.' ... This 'fresh judgment' can very well – *must* very well – conform to a preexisting law, but the reinstituting, reinventive and freely decisive interpretation, the responsible interpretation of the judge requires that his 'justice' not just consist in conformity, in the conservative and reproductive activity of judgment. In short, for a decision to be just and responsible, it must, in its proper moment if there is one, be both regulated and without regulation: it must conserve the law and also destroy it or suspend it enough to have to reinvent it in each case, rejustify it, at least reinvent it in the reaffirmation and the new and free confirmation of its principle. Each case is other, each decision is different and requires an absolutely unique interpretation, which no existing, coded rule can or ought to guarantee absolutely.[147]

Correcting for the mischaracterization of Aristotle by Lyotard, Derrida acknowledges the presence of models, principles, and laws for the judge. But rules provide only a starting place, never a destination. Thus the journey of judgment demands courage and ingenuity. The judge must strenuously reach for that which, inevitably, escapes his grasp.[148]

Unlike Derrida and Lyotard, Richard Rorty does not wax enthusiastic about the infinity of the other. His goal is to celebrate Enlightment liberalism while shedding its rationalistic core as a remnant of metaphysical thought.[149] Having spurned epistemological rationalism in his early work, Rorty later follows suit in the realm of ethics and politics. He straightforwardly asks us to "give up on the idea that there are unconditional, transcultural moral obligations, obligations rooted in an unchanging, ahistorical human nature."[150] As a substitution for the philosophical pursuit of the "antecedently real," Rorty follows Dewey in suggesting that we embrace the priority of practical judgments.[151]

While Rorty is morally committed to diminishing human suffering, constraining cruelty, and increasing equality such that, at a minimum,

---

[147] Derrida, "Force of Law," p. 23.
[148] Derrida, "Force of Law," pp. 16, 23.
[149] Richard Rorty, "Justice as a Larger Loyalty," in *Justice and Democracy: Cross-Cultural Perspectives*, eds. Ron Bontekoe and Marietta Stepaniants (Honolulu: University of Hawai'i Press, 1997), p. 20.
[150] Rorty, *Philosophy and Social Hope*, p. xvi.
[151] Rorty, *Philosophy and Social Hope*, p. 29.

children begin life with as equal a chance of happiness as possible, he admits that these ethical ends bear no transcendental status. No argument for them can rightly claim to have Reason or God on its side.[152] Rather, they reflect particular loyalties. Indeed, the demands of justice are simply the demands of an expanded sense of loyalty.[153] Rather than grounding justice in principles begat from transcendental reason, Rorty links it to the growing sense of inclusion that is generated when we admit more people into our conversation. Rationality, from this perspective, indicates the willingness and ability to engage others in meaningful discussion. As the conversation expands, so do our loyalties, and as our loyalties expand, so do the obligations to diminish suffering, constrain cruelty, and increase equality among participants. That is the general work of justice. Practical judgment gives us the details.

As loyalties grow beyond the family to the clan, from clan to tribe, from tribe to village, from village to city-state, from city-state to nation-state, and, in contemporary times, from nation-state to global community, the desire to create a more egalitarian, less cruel, and less painful social life increasingly becomes a moral imperative. That is simply a matter of cultural development. But how does the pragmatist demonstrate that the expansion of loyalties is a good thing? Rorty's answer is straightforward. An expanded sense of loyalty better serves human needs in this day and age. It produces a world of happier, more prosperous people – and that is argument enough. Or, in any case, there is no appeal available to a higher standard.

Once we understand that our ethico-political commitments and judgments ultimately derive from an expanded sense of loyalty, Rorty argues, "the opposition between rational argument and fellow-feeling thus begins to dissolve."[154] The better argument is simply that which produces more uncoerced agreement. In the absence of a natural, unconditional, transcultural rationality, uncoerced agreement is as close to truth as we get. The pursuit of something more, of a natural order of reasons, Rorty chides, is simply the "secularized version" of an earlier appeal to God's will.[155]

Rorty asks that we "abandon the traditional philosophical project of finding something stable which will serve as a criterion for judging the

---

[152] Rorty, "Justice as a Larger Loyalty," p. 19.
[153] Rorty, "Justice as a Larger Loyalty," pp. 18–19.
[154] Rorty, "Justice as a Larger Loyalty," pp. 18–19.
[155] Rorty, "Justice as a Larger Loyalty," p. 19.

transitory products of our transitory needs and interests. This means, for example, that we cannot employ the Kantian distinction between morality and prudence."[156] In the ethico-political realm, all we can do is make increasingly persuasive arguments to expand loyalties. In mustering our resources to this end, we realize that "no sharp break divides the unjust from the imprudent, the evil from the inexpedient."[157] All ethico-political assessments, evaluations, and choices, optimally, would be products of practical judgment exercised by free and equal individuals who have been socialized to value the expansion of loyalties.

 Of course, the devil is in the details. There is, for example, the problem of determining when coercion steps in to muddy the waters, and when the ostensibly free and equal individuals making practical judgments are actually victims of ignorance, misinformation, propaganda, emotional intimidation, or other forms of manipulation. Rorty largely neglects to address these concerns.

In a book devoted to the topic of judgment in the post-modern age, Alessandro Ferrara follows the lead of Lyotard, Derrida, and Rorty, addressing current developments in political philosophy after the "linguistic turn."[158] Ferrara characterizes the contemporary scene as centered around a "radically reflexive form of self-grounding" that calls for "situated judgment."[159]

Ferrara asks *the* post-modern question – namely, "What notion of justice can ensure the integration of a society of free and equal citizens who subscribe to different conceptions of the good by means of helping these citizens to solve their controversies of interest and value without appealing to any standpoint, criterion or principle external to the parties involved in the contention?"[160] Though tempted by the Aristotelian notion of *phronesis* and the Kantian understanding of reflective judgment, Ferrara eventually foreswears these options. While both Aristotle and Kant contributed to the notion of "validity severed from the postulation of general principles," their understandings of *phronesis* and reflective judgment were ultimately grounded in assumptions about human nature and transcendental essences that cannot be squared with the linguistic turn of post-modernity.[161]

[156] Rorty, *Philosophy and Social Hope*, p. xvi.
[157] Rorty, *Philosophy and Social Hope*, p. xxix.
[158] Alessandro Ferrara, *Justice and Judgment* (London: Sage, 1999), p. x.
[159] Ferrara, *Justice and Judgment*, p. 12.
[160] Ferrara, *Justice and Judgment*, p. x.
[161] Ferrara, *Justice and Judgment*, pp. 179, 180.

In contemporary times, we are confronted with the need for practical judgment that cannot rely on transcendental reason or any other metaphysical foundation. In the face of this problem, Ferrara, like Rorty, wants to continue the historical expansion of our loyalties to include "equal respect owed to all the parties involved," with the parties in question referring to "a superordinate collectivity which ideally, in the case of the *moral* point of view, can be coextensive with humanity in its entirety."[162] If we ask why our practical judgments should be directed toward this superordinate collectivity, Ferrara, like Rorty, can only tell a story about the historical development of our species, and how we might want the next chapter to unfold. Ferrara accepts the historical constitution of our identities and denies any transcendental aspects to our nature.[163] Like Rorty, he insists that the cultural developments that made us, broadly speaking, into liberals (and subsequently into post-modern liberals) must be acknowledged. But they should not be reified into unconditional truths. Things could change.

Lyotard, Derrida, Rorty, and Ferrara valorize practical judgment while underlining its limitations. All deem it the most needful, indeed indispensable, faculty for humankind. They accept Nietzsche's assessment of the vital role of judgment after the death of God, but do so having vouchsafed the basic equality and inherent freedom of all persons. In effect, they have internalized a belief that Nietzsche identified as a "folly" – namely, the conviction that every human being, "simply because he is human," bears a redeeming greatness of spirit.[164] Nietzsche, too, held this belief – but only periodically and, as he ironically noted, against his better judgment.

Contemporary Decision Theory

This chapter has summarized the historical efforts of key individuals who address the nature of practical judgment and grapple with its ethico-political significance. But I would be remiss in sketching these conceptual developments were no mention made of recent efforts to craft a science of decision-making. During the 1950s and 1960s, the field of psychology underwent a "cognitive revolution." Freudian and behaviorist orientations gave way to theories of information processing. In turn,

---

[162] Ferrara, *Justice and Judgment*, pp. 188, 201.
[163] Ferrara, *Justice and Judgment*, p. 218.
[164] Nietzsche, *The Gay Science*, pp. 76–77.

philosophers of mind became increasingly analytical in orientation. A cognitively based approach to the study of mental faculties, and, more specifically, to the study of rationality and decision-making processes emerged. The field of decision science was born. No understanding of human judgment could be considered well informed without taking into account the valuable insights provided by this diverse discipline.

While born of psychology's cognitive revolution, decision science, also known as decision theory, was informed by a vast interdisciplinary literature, including micro-economics, game theory, social choice theory, utility theory, voting studies, social statistics, and subjective probability theory. It quickly developed into something of a growth industry. Decision science became the focus of attention for psychologists, philosophers, political scientists, sociologists, business and administration analysts, organization theorists, and computer scientists. By the mid-1980s, the Society for Judgment and Decision Making had been founded.[165] A parallel society was formed in Europe shortly thereafter. Numerous journals were devoted to the field.[166]

The *locus classicus* of the discipline might be traced back to an article published in 1954 by Ward Edwards.[167] Edwards equated good decision-making with rational decision-making. In turn, he equated rationality with probabilistic reasoning. Edwards's work focused on the internal coherence of judgments as determined by their mathematical and logical consistency. Tools and methodologies often inform theoretical perspectives. In the 1950s and 1960s, psychologists and philosophers deemed the computer – a tool increasingly in use and gaining widespread attention – a fitting model for the human mind.[168] Early scholars in the field of decision science, like Edwards, imagined the human brain as a complex machine. Decision-making at its best, from this perspective, was a matter of carrying out rational calculations, logical operations, and statistical computations. Good judgment was an efficient form of "information

---

[165] See the Society for Judgment and Decision Making website at http://www.sjdm.org

[166] For helpful reviews of the history of decision science, see Peter Fishburn, "The Making of Decision Theory," in *Decision Science and Technology*, ed. James Shanteau, Barbara Mellers, and David Schum (Boston: Kluwer Academic Publishers, 1999), pp. 369–388; Ray W. Cooksey, *Judgment Analysis: Theory, Methods, and Applications* (San Diego: Academic Press, 1996).

[167] Ward Edwards, "The Theory of Decision Making," *Psychological Bulletin*, 41:380–417.

[168] See Gerd Gigerenzer, *Adaptive Thinking: Rationality in the Real World* (Oxford: Oxford University Press, 2000), pp. 26–43.

processing."[169] The conclusion often reached by experts in the field was that human beings were notoriously bad judges.

To this day, many scholars of decision-making adopt the information-processing model, invoking complex, rationalized schemes for the crafting of choices. One of the more popular efforts, grounded in multi-attribute utility theory (MAUT), is meant to generate an exhaustive reasoning process that forces "all relevant considerations out into the open, and suppresses irrelevant considerations."[170] It achieves this feat by clearly identifying for the decision-maker the attributes of every goal or alternative in question, quantifying the utility associated with these by weighing or prioritizing each of their dimensions, and comparatively evaluating all weighted scores before rendering a final choice.[171]

Critics of the "mind-as-machine" approach argue that the effort to ground judgment in analytic reason harbors a *reductio ad absurdum*. Good judgment can only proceed on the basis of sound knowledge of alternative options and their relative worth. The decision to seek (particular kinds of) information or examine (particular) alternatives before making a judgment, however, must be based on a set of reasons. These reasons should be well chosen, which is to say that their selection should be based on yet another set of reasons. But the soundness of these reasons rests on the merit of the reasons employed in their selection. An infinite regress threatens. In turn, one must justify the judgment that there is enough time available for the pursuit of (still more) information, or justify the judgment that enough information has already been collected. Any reasons given to validate *these* judgments will necessarily be based on other judgments, which will require their own information-backed reasons. Ultimately, an authoritative judgment is called for that says the buck (and rational analysis) stops here.

Pondering the (skeptic's) effort exhaustively to justify action through reason, David Hume observed that "no durable good can ever result from it while it remains in its full force and vigor.... all action would immediately cease, and men remain in a total lethargy till the necessities of

---

[169] Milton Lodge and Kathleen M. McGraw, eds., *Political Judgment: Structure and Process* (Ann Arbor: The University of Michigan Press, 1995).

[170] John Mullen and Byron Roth, *Decision–Making: Its Logic and Practice* (Savage, MD: Rowman and Littlefield, 1991), p. 67.

[171] See Leigh Thompson, *The Mind and Heart of the Negotiator*. 2nd ed. (Upper Saddle River, New Jersey: Prentice Hall, 2001), p. 295.

nature, unsatisfied, put an end to their miserable existence."[172] The practical inability of sustaining the pursuit of sufficient reason is a *prima facie* argument for its *ir*rationality. Herbert Simon's notion of "bounded rationality," developed in the 1950s, was a response to this problem. Simon, a political scientist known for his work in economics, cognitive psychology, computer science, and philosophy, argued that fully rational decision-making requires more information and computational ability than people have at their disposal. Bounded rationality characterizes the effort to assess and navigate a complex world in the face of ambiguity, contraints in time, and limited information.[173]

Bounded rationalizers do not attempt to optimize their choices based on exhaustive analysis. Rather, they "satisfice. " Simon explains: "We cannot within practicable computational limits generate all the admissible alternatives and compare their respective merits. Nor can we recognize the best alternative, even if we are fortunate enough to generate it early, until we have seen all of them. We satisfice by looking for alternatives in such a way that we can generally find an acceptable one after only moderate search."[174] The satisficer is willing to employ rules of thumb in an effort to satisfy, rather than optimize, his needs and wants.

In the field of philosophy, critics of *act* utilitarianism arrived at a similar conclusion. To be exhaustively engaged in a felicific calculus aimed at maximizing pleasure (or the greatest good of the greatest number) would deprive one of the time and resources needed to experience or propagate the pleasures (or goods) one seeks to maximize. For this reason, act utilitarianism has no practitioners who actually manage their lives in accordance with its demands. It is a self-defeating doctrine. What is the alternative? Philosophers proposed something called *rule* utilitarianism. Rule utilitarians are satisficers who rely on rules of thumb to produce acceptable results with only a moderate investment of resources.

---

[172] David Hume, *An Inquiry Concerning Human Understanding* (Indianapolis: Bobbs-Merrill, 1955), p. 168.

[173] See Herbert Simon, "Alternative visions of rationality," in *Judgment and decision making: An interdisciplinary reader*, ed. H. R. Arkes and K. R. Hammond (Cambridge: Cambridge University Press, 1986), pp. 97–113. For a more recent application of bounded rationality as it applies to decision-making, see Gerd Gigerenzer, Peter M. Todd, and the ABC Research Group, *Simple Heuristics That Make Us Smart* (New York: Oxford University Press, 1999).

[174] Herbert Simon, *The Sciences of the Artificial*, 2nd ed. (Cambridge: M.I.T. Press, 1981, p. 139. Cited in Amitai Etzioni, *The Moral Dimension* (New York: The Free Press, 1988), p. 116.

Blending philosophical and psychological insights, Jon Elster has explored the limits of rational decision-making. He criticizes the effort to reduce judgment to the process of (deductive and inductive) calculation as "an addiction to reason." Like any other addiction, hyper-rationality undermines optimal performance. Elster observes that "Some people do indeed have a craving to make all decisions on the basis of 'just' or sufficient reasons. That, however, makes them irrational rather than rational. A rational person would know that under certain conditions it is better to follow a simple mechanical decision rule than to use more elaborate procedures with higher opportunity costs."[175] The higher opportunity costs that Elster refers to reflect the common exigencies of life – namely, the general scarcity of time, useful information, and calculative power.

It would be misleading to employ the term *decision rule* to capture the panoply of means employed to escape the infinite regress of exhaustive reasoning. A significant portion of the means people commonly employ remain unarticulated, and many operate below the level of conscious awareness. Collectively, they have become known as *heuristics* and *biases*.[176] Heuristics are mental shortcuts that reduce the complex task of assessing probabilities, predicting values, and weighing alternatives to simpler operations. Many heuristics effectively piggyback on innate mental processes.[177] Most are useful and sensible means of estimating values and have withstood the test of time because they pay off for their users. Biases are the products of inappropriately applied heuristics that yield systematic errors. One might say that heuristics and biases allow, respectively, quick and dirty judgments. Heuristics facilitate speedy decisions. But the cost of such efficiency, not infrequently, is systematic error. Whether a particular heuristic proves to be beneficial or pernicious in a specific situation demands empirical study. Much psychologically oriented decision science provides this valuable service.

Just as the computer became a model for the human mind among early decision scientists, so the tool of probability theory, with the rise of statistics as a social science methodology, provided a model for human

[175] Jon Elster, *Alchemies of the Mind: Rationality and the Emotions* (Cambridge: Cambridge University Press, 1999), pp. 290–91.

[176] See Daniel Kahneman, Paul Slovic, and Amos Tversky, eds. *Judgment under uncertainty: Heuristics and biases* (Cambridge: Cambridge University Press, 1982).

[177] See Thomas Gilovich and Dale Griffin, "Introduction – Heuristics and Biases: Then and Now," in *Heuristics and Biases: The Psychology of Intuitive Judgment*, Thomas Gilovich, Dale Griffin, and Daniel Kahneman, eds. (Cambridge: Cambridge University Press, 2002), p. 3.

reasoning in subsequent decades. Many decision scientists today model the human judge on the optimal performance of a statistically astute rationalizer. In doing so, they target those heuristics that inhibit the understanding or application of the laws of probability. Consider five such heuristics:

The *anchoring heuristic* fosters the linkage of estimates to previously provided, and quite possibly arbitrary, values. Initial values anchor the values (estimates) that follow, with subsequent adjustments generally failing to make up the difference. Barterers are very familiar with this effect: buyers will start low and sellers high in the hope that their counterparts will not adjust sufficiently from the initial value provided. Whether purchasing goods or estimating distances, weights, ages, populations, or costs, people will incrementally adjust their estimates from any anchor value, even though the anchor value may not closely approximate the actual value of the variable.

When the *availability heuristic* is in play, people inflate their estimations of the probability of an event occurring because of the ease with which the event can be brought to mind. The most easily remembered or imagined events (or solutions), of course, may not be the most probable (or best) ones. For instance, most people falsely believe that there are more words that start with 'r' than there are words with 'r' as the third letter. They make this false judgment simply because words that start with 'r' are more easily brought to mind. The availability heuristic is widespread, if not universal.

When we base our predictions about an event on the degree to which it represents a preconceived notion of reality rather than on the statistical likelihood of its occurrence, we are subject to the *representativeness heuristic*. Given a detailed description of a person said to have been picked randomly from a group of eighty elementary school teachers and twenty lawyers, for example, people tend to identify that person as a teacher or lawyer according to how well the description of the person fits their stereotyped images of these two professions. In doing so, they will wholly ignore the base rate of the population (80/20) and the statistical probabilities that derive therefrom given a random selection.

Most people tend to view chance as a "self-correcting process." Coin tosses producing a series of 'heads,' for instance, will falsely raise expectations that a series of 'tails' are due.[178] This bias is known as the *gambler's*

---

[178] Amos Tversky and Daniel Kahneman, "Judgment of and by representativeness," in *Judgment under Uncertainty: Heuristics and Biases*, Daniel Kahneman, Paul Slovic, and Amos Tversky, eds. (Cambridge: Cambridge University Press, 1982), p. 7.

fallacy. Of course, the chance of a heads turning up on a fair coin toss after a long run of tails remains 50/50. Past chance events have no effect on, and will not secure compensation in, future chance events. Chance events do not correct for 'runs' to restore equilibrium (as if coins had memories); they merely dilute deviations over time.

Notwithstanding the gambler's fallacy, it is true that extreme events (for example, a very long run of heads) are more likely than not to be followed by less extreme events (for example, alternations between, or shorter runs of, heads and tails). This relationship is not causal, however. It is merely statistical – a matter of probability given the relative rarity of extreme events. Most people do not predict this *regression toward the mean*. They adopt the bias that extreme events are more likely to be followed by similarly extreme events. For instance, people may buy stocks after an extended rise in the market, only to be surprised when stocks drop the following week. In turn, they may make false causal attributions. If a child improves on a subsequent exam after being scolded for doing unusually poorly on an earlier test, a parent might falsely attribute the improvement to the reprimand. In point of fact, it may simply indicate a regression toward the mean.

Contemporary decision scientists study a wide range of heuristics and biases, including those unrelated to people's ignorance or misapplication of the laws of probability. Such heuristics and biases are often known as *effects*. For the most part, they are attributable to basic human psychology. The literature addressing these effects demonstrates their pervasiveness in the general population. They are powerful contributors to misjudgment. Some of the more common effects include the following:

- The *contrast effect* describes a widespread tendency to (mis)interpret current experiences in light of and in contrast to (recent) past experience. While often exercised in cognitive assessments, the contrast effect also appears in purely perceptual assessments. Thus, a weight appears to be lighter if a heavier weight is lifted first, just as tepid water feels warmer to the touch if one's hand were just immersed in cold water.[179]

- The *sunk costs effect* fosters ongoing non-beneficial investments in a failing effort. That is to say, people are reluctant to acknowledge and absorb a loss, and thus prove willing to pay more or risk more for things they have already incurred costs for or devoted resources to, regardless of the likelihood of future payoffs.

[179] Scott Plous, *The Psychology of Judgment and Decision Making* (Philadelphia: Temple University Press, 1993), p. 38.

- The *out-group homogeneity effect* leads individuals to perceive themselves as less uniform in their internal constitution than other people. In turn, they perceive members of other groups as more uniform in characteristics than members of their own group.[180] The out-group homogeneity effect contributes to stereotyping and racial/ethnic biases.
- The related *actor/observer effect* prompts individuals to understand their own behavior in terms of situational requirements while viewing the behavior of others in terms of personal dispositions. That is to say, people tend to interpret their own actions as responsive to context while interpreting others' actions as a product of the characters of the actors involved.[181] Because we see others as more uniform in character (as a result of the out-group homogeneity effect), it is easier to posit their actions as stemming directly from their dispositions.[182]
- The *self-confirmation effect* leads people to seek and accept information that is consistent with their decisions while ignoring disconfirming evidence. As La Rochefoucauld observed, "There are few sensible people, we find, except those who share our opinions."[183]
- In the related *rationalization effect*, individuals search only for those reasons that support their pre-judgments. Here, reason becomes a rubber stamp.[184] The rationalization effect often prompts people, *post facto*, to bring their beliefs in line with their behavior. For instance, voters will voice lower assessments of the merits of candidates and their chances of winning an election prior to casting ballots for them. After voting, estimations of the merits of selected candidates and their probabilities of success rise.[185] The rationalization effect may reflect an effort to reduce cognitive dissonance, as people attempt to bring their beliefs in line with their behavior in order to lesson the (self)perception of inconsistency.[186]
- The *conformity effect* prompts individuals to amend their judgments to accord with majority decisions and group pressure. Much of this effect

---

[180] Plous, *The Psychology of Judgment*, p. 206.

[181] Plous, *The Psychology of Judgment*, p. 181.

[182] "Circumstances reveal us to others and still more to ourselves," La Rochefoucauld observed. He failed to mention that the differential is grounded in a common and quite misleading bias. La Rochefoucauld, *Maxims*, trans. Leonard Tanock (London: Penguin Books, 1959), p. 82; #345.

[183] La Rochefoucauld, *Maxims*, p. 82; #347.

[184] Jonathan Haidt, "The Emotional Dog and Its Rational Tail: A Social Intuitionist Approach to Moral Judgment," *Psychological Review* 108 (October 2001), 814–834.

[185] Plous, *The Psychology of Judgment*, p. 29.

[186] Plous, *The Psychology of Judgment*, p. 30.

is alleviated if the potentially dissenting decision-maker encounters at least one person who agrees with him.[187]

- Finally, the *overconfidence effect* leads individuals to inflate estimations their own merits and powers, including their capacity for sound judgment.

An education in the laws of probability and the psychology of common effects, one might expect, would correct for the aforementioned sources of misjudgment. To some extent this is true. Yet many common biases and effects are robust. Awareness of their existence does not automatically make them disappear. A bucket of tepid water will always feel warmer than it actually is to a hand that was just immersed in ice water. Cognitive prejudices are often as stable, and as unavailable to reform, as such perceptual illusions. Hence people well trained in the field of decision theory continue to make faulty judgments based on common biases and effects.[188] To make matters worse, the well-trained often have a much higher assessment of their own decision-making abilities. Expert prediction, it turns out, is "often wrong, but rarely in doubt."[189]

At the same time, learning about common biases and effects can mitigate some of their more pernicious influences. Ethnic stereotyping, for instance, increases when a subject's attention is decreased as a result of time pressure or distractions. Unable to deliberate rationally, the subject gives greater sway to prejudice.[190] In this case, reducing the effect of stereotyping may be as straightforward as allowing people more time for reflection.

None of this suggests that heuristics and common psychological tendencies are by nature wrong or perverse and should be eliminated whenever possible. Many play an indispensable role as useful rules of thumb, allowing us efficiently to navigate a complex world. Others serve

---

[187] Plous, *The Psychology of Judgment*, p. 202. John Mullen and Byron Roth, *Decision–Making: Its Logic and Practice* (Savage, MD: Rowman and Littlefield, 1991), p. 24. See also Irving Janis, *Victims of Groupthink* (Boston: Houghton Mifflin, 1972).

[188] Amos Tversky and Daniel Kahneman, "Judgment under Uncertainty," p. 18. Amos Tversky and Daniel Kahneman, "Extensional versus Intuitive Reasoning: The Conjunction Fallacy in Probability Judgment," in *Judgment under Uncertainty: Heuristics and Biases*, p. 44. See also Philip Tetlock, "Theory-Driven Reasoning about Plausible Pasts and Probable Futures in World Politics," in *Judgment under Uncertainty: Heuristics and Biases*, pp. 751–53.

[189] Dale Griffin and Amos Tversky, "The Weighing of Evidence and the Determinants of Confidence, in *Judgment under Uncertainty: Heuristics and Biases*, p. 230.

[190] Anthony Greenwald and Mahzarin Banaji, "Implicit Social Cognition: Attitudes, Self-Esteem, and Stereotypes," *Psychological Review* 102 (1995): 18.

beneficial exogenous purposes. The *overconfidence effect* often produces inaccurate judgments. But it may also help people maintain equanimity in the face of a demanding environment that would otherwise prove debilitating. Being 'right' much of the time is of little benefit if one is too depressed to get out of bed in the morning. A reasonably inflated self-image may promote psychological well-being and greater achievement.[191] In Chapter 3, we grapple more extensively with the ineradicability of biases as well as their potential benefits.

Early decision scientists devised sophisticated decision-making instruments grounded in expected utility principles to generate optimal judgments while accounting for compensatory trade-offs. Yet many experts now conclude that complex decision-tree analyses and computer-based aids do not produce particularly good results. Middle-range efforts that compensate for common biases and effects without requiring intricate calculations are often more successful. Studies designed to improve judgment without unduly complicating it offer the following advice to decision-makers:

- survey a wide range of objectives
- assess all relevant values
- canvass alternative courses of action while evaluating the positive and negative effects, costs, and risks of each
- search for and assimilate new information, including data that counters current biases and effects
- avoid rapid closure to the decision-making process
- make extensive provisions for the implementation of decisions
- produce contingency plans to address the ramifications of initial decisions

These are valuable recommendations and, if implemented, would improve most decision-making. They might appear little more than common sense. Yet, as Voltaire observed, common sense is not so common.

Modeling the human decision-maker on the digital computer and the statistically astute rationalizer has provided scholars with important insights, and considerable misdirection, in the study of judgment.[192] No doubt a basic education in social statistics and probability theory

---

[191] Plous, *The Psychology of Judgment*, p. 253.
[192] We should expect similar aid and excess in current efforts to ground human judgment in the nascent field of quantum computation. See Jeffrey Gray, *Consciousness* (Oxford: Oxford University Press, 2004), p. 245.

aids the development of judgment. In turn, an education in common psychological effects is indispensable to sound decision-making. The best judges are generally those who know when, where, how, and why people (including themselves) are predisposed to misjudgment.

Echoing Hegel, Aldous Huxley wryly observed that the most important lesson that history has to teach is that people do not learn much from history.[193] The same might be said regarding the lessons of decision theory. The science of decision-making demonstrates that formal learning does not immunize the scientist against the biases and effects he studies. We become better judges for acknowledging this humbling lesson.

[193] Quoted in Fitton, *Leadership*, p. 119.

2

The Indispensability of Experience

Experience is never limited, and it is never complete; it is an immense sensibility, a kind of huge spider-web of the finest silken threads suspended in the chamber of consciousness, and catching every air-borne particle in its tissue.... The power to guess the unseen from the seen, to trace the implication of things, to judge the whole piece by the pattern, the condtiion of feeling life in general so completely that you are well on your way to knowing any particular corner of it – this cluster of gifts may almost be said to constitute experience.

Henry James[1]

It is more important to study men than books.

La Rochefoucauld[2]

Following a Kantian line of thought, Anne Colby and Lawrence Kohlberg observe that "Moral judgments ... direct, command, or oblige us to take some action. Moral prescriptions are not merely commands to *perform* particular actions, however. They are imperatives deriving from some rule or principle of action that the speaker takes as binding on his own actions."[3] Moral judgments, Colby and Kohlberg are saying, are products of the application of abstract laws to particular cases. This Kantian position has enjoyed widespread endorsement.

---

[1] Henry James, "The Art of Fiction" in *Partial Portraits* (Ann Arbor: University of Michigan Press, 1970), pp. 388–89.

[2] La Rochefoucauld, *Maxims*, trans. Leonard Tanock (London: Penguin Books, 1959), p. 109; #550.

[3] Anne Colby and Lawrence Kohlberg, *The Measurement of Moral Judgment, Volume 1: Theoretical Foundations and Research Validation* (Cambridge: Cambridge University Press, 1987), p. 10.

Undoubtedly, some moral judgments do arise through a process that involves reflecting on and reasoning about general principles. But this is more the exception than the rule. For the most part, moral judgment is not a process of deriving imperatives for action from abstract propositions. Rather, it arises through the internalization of social values and the immediate perception of their violations. This process takes place without much in the way of recourse to theory.[4]

Judgments become available to us, in the sense that we gain awareness of their (conceptual) import, only with their articulation.[5] Prior to this event, proto-judgments formed experientially already inform our attitudes, beliefs, and actions in important ways. Consider the common event of 'discovering' one's judgment at the moment of its articulation. Novelist E. M. Forster captured this phenomenon well when he asked: "How do I know what I think, until I see what I say?" Before a judgment is put into words, we have no settled position. At least, we are aware of none. Only at the moment of voicing a judgment do we, along with our listeners, discover that an assessment, evaluation, and critical choice have been made. With its articulation, a judgment is professed and comes to claim our commitment. Subsequently, we may attempt to defend this judgment, and often do so by mustering rational arguments that rely on general principles.

The articulation of a judgment typically signals its conscious birth. Preceding this event was an extensive period of gestation. Most of the key features of the judgment were formed during the time spent *in utero*. While practical judgments may often invoke rules and principles, we should not put the cart before the horse. The rules and principles invoked are, as often as not, *post facto* rationalizations of intuited values. The cognitive neuroscience behind this phenomenon will be addressed in Chapter 3. Its general validity can be ascertained by examining the normative judgments exercised by non-linguistic species.

Most primates, and all great apes, display the deliberate enforcement of social standards. Troupes of great apes establish clear social norms and exact punishment on those who shirk or disregard them. The norms appear to arise, in part, as a means of mitigating the hierarchical

---

4 See Peter Levine, *Living Without Philosophy: On Narrative, Rhetoric, and Morality* (Albany: State University of New York Press, 1998), p. 50.

5 Scott Plous observes that "People discover their own attitudes, emotions, and other internal states partly by watching themselves behave in various situations." Scott Plous, *The Psychology of Judgment and Decision Making* (Philadelphia: Temple University Press, 1993), p. 25.

dominance of individuals. Such dominance develops naturally, but may lead to the arbitrary exercise of power. Violations are strongly and consistently responded to, either by isolation of the shirker or by reciprocation of the (mis)deed. Like human beings, primates (in general and great apes in particular), react much more strongly to losses arising from a violation of a norm of reciprocity than to losses arising from accidents or simple competition. Like us, our closest genetic neighbors employ norms to counter raw power and to grease the wheels of social interaction.[6] They navigate social relations in accordance with these standards and devote considerable energy to, and incur significant risks in, their enforcement. For this to occur, an elementary, pre-verbal form of moral judgment is required.

I do not wish to belabor the linkage between our ethico-political judgments and the more rudimentary forms of normative judgment exercised by other animals. My point is simply that the discernment of norms (of reciprocity) and the punishment of their violation among primates are achieved without the use of abstract reasoning and sophisticated language. There is no rational argument, no formulation of axioms, rules, or laws, and no "deriving" of imperatives for action from these principles. Normative judgments are not generated as the application of a general rule to a particular case. Rather, they follow from what can only be described as the "thick interpretation" of social life.[7]

Thick interpretation is particularistic; it determines the violation of social morality in its actual violation, as a departure from accepted norms of conduct. These norms are internalized not as abstract principles, but as habitualized patterns of behavior. Higher primates project past behavior into future expectation, and react negatively when expectations are thwarted.[8] The argument here is not that human moral

---

[6] Denise Dellarosa Cummins, "Social Norms and Other Minds: The Evolutionary Roots of Higher Cognition," in in Denise Dellarosa Cummins and Conlin Allen, *The Evolution of Mind* (New York: Oxford University Press, 1998), pp. 39–45.

[7] Thick interpretation builds upon the notion of "thick description," Gilbert Ryle's term, later popularized by Clifford Geertz. See Clifford Geertz, *The Interpretation of Cultures* (New York, Basic Books, 1973), p. 6 and *passim*. The concept of thick description is addressed later in this chapter.

[8] The capacity of various animals to plan for the future prompted Aristotle to ascribe *phronesis* to other species. St. Thomas Aquinas followed suit. Animals, he states, partake of "natural prudence." Thomas Hobbes shared this opinion. See Aristotle, *The Ethics of Aristotle* (New York: Penguin Books, 1953), p. 179. See also Hans-Georg Gadamer, *The Enigma of Health*, trans. Jason Gaiger and Nicholas Walker (Stanford: Stanford University Press, 1996), p. 47.

judgment is equivalent to the normative assessments and evaluations exhibited by other primates. The point is simply that moral judgment can and does occur in the absence of abstract theorization and principled argument.

At the same time, the articulation of a judgment plays an important role in its constitution. Speech is a selective process. Not all that is thought, felt, or intuited finds a voice; and what gets selected for articulation or relegated to silence can significantly alter the judgments we develop.[9] In turn, the (public) context of speech affects not only its stylistic expression but also its substance. Last, but far from least, the use of language inevitably introduces conscious thinking. Oftentimes, this takes the form of reasoning and abstract conceptualization, mental operations that can significantly amend or recast internalized values. Once articulated, principles may take on lives of their own, circling back to influence basic assessments and evaluations. In this respect, judgments are developed and transformed by way of the "reflective equilibrium" established between the socially cultivated sensibilities inhabiting our guts and the theoretically formalized principles that emerge from our mouths. Speech is where the unconscious and the conscious meet, grapple with each other, and produce the "considered judgments" that we find ourselves willing and able to defend.[10] Only by finding their voice do judgments rise above the primitive and impoverished.

Ancestral Experience

Words allow judgment its refinement, but they can only do their work upon a foundation laid by worldly experience. For this reason, experience – not the powers of logic or abstract conceptualization – is considered the *sine qua non* of good judgment. Strikingly, few scholars have investigated this relationship. Fewer still have explored the impact of genetically embedded experience on judgment. This form of experience finds its origins not in our worldly encounters as individuals – as crucial as these are to the development of practical judgment. Rather, our genetically embedded experience is a product of the worldly encounters

---

9 William E. Connolly, *Neuropolitics: Thinking, Culture, Speed* (Minneapolis: University of Minnesota Press, 2002), pp. 71–72. Jerome Bruner, "The Narrative Creation of Self," in *The Handbook of Narrative and Psychotherapy: Practice, Theory, and Research*, Lynne Angus and John McLeod, eds. (Thousand Oaks, CA: Sage Publications, 2004), pp. 3–14.

10 I borrow these terms from John Rawls, *A Theory of Justice* (Cambridge: Harvard University Press, 1971), pp. 48–51.

of hundreds of generations of our forebears. Its effect is known by way of the ease with which we exercise various aptitudes and skills.

Scholars informed by evolutionary psychology have opened up this field of inquiry.[11] The works of Steven Pinker, Gerd Gigerenzer, and Kenneth Hammond, for example, offer sustained reflection on the effect our heritage has had on practical judgment.[12] They see the human mind as the product of evolutionary history. Rather than posing the practical judge as an unsophisticated and often faulty computer grinding out probabilities and calculating the ramifications of consistent rule-following, they view her as a relatively successful biological adaptation.

In many respects, the point seems obvious. Clearly there was practical judgment among early humans before there was much in the way of abstract thought. The judgment exercised by primitive hominids occurred in the absence of sophisticated reasoning. Indeed, given what we know of primates, we can be assured that there was normative judgment before *homo sapiens* themselves evolved. From an evolutionary perspective, reasoning our way to the articulation of rules is a very recent development. Practical judgment preceded it by countless millennia.

An even more recent development is the exercise of judgment in accordance with notions of logic and probability. While the basic mental capacities for practical judgment have been evolving for at least 100,000 years, and perhaps, in more rudimentary fashion, for millions of years before that, the notion of logic has only been around for a few thousand years, and the notion of statistical reasoning only since the mid-seventeeth century.[13] We should not be surprised, therefore, if contemporary humans, while quite adept at exercising practical judgment in daily life, prove to be relatively unskilled in applying the laws of logic and probability.

---

[11] To embrace evolutionary psychology, one need not be committed to the belief that all morphological and behavioral features of a species exist because they (originally) improve(d) fitness. Various mental and behavioral capacities may constitute "exaptations" rather than adaptations. That is to say, they may have accompanied the development of other features that increased fitness without themselves increasing fitness at the time of their origin. Alternatively, they may have evolved under natural selection but only subsequently found their current uses. Stephen Jay Gould suspects that "many important functions of the human brain are co-opted consequences of building such a large computer for a limited set of adaptive uses." Stephen Jay Gould, *Bully for Brontosaurus: Reflections in Natural History* (New York: W.W. Norton, 1991), p. 144.

[12] See Leslie Paul Thiele, "Common Sense, Judgment and the Limits of Political Theory," *Political Theory*, 28(2000): 565–588.

[13] See Ian Hacking, *The Emergence of Probability* (Cambridge: Cambridge University Press, 1975). See also Hacking, *The Taming of Chance* (Cambridge: Cambridge University Press, 1990), p. 6.

In the year following Ward Edwards' seminal article on decision theory, Kenneth Hammond published an essay with a markedly different approach. Hammond's article, extending the work of his mentor, Egon Brunswik, did not focus on the *coherence* of judgments – that is to say, their internal logic and rational consistency. Rather, it focused on the *correspondence* of assessments and evaluations to actual facts. His concern was the empirical accuracy of judgments. Hammond was reacting to an emerging trend in decision science: the notion that people are poor judges because they are poor logicians and statisticians.[14] These studies almost exclusively investigated deficiencies in inferential or probabilistic reasoning. Hammond argued that we should not be surprised at, or unduly worried about, the uninspiring results.

Individuals who have not been trained in logic and statistics will generally exhibit poor inferential and probalistic reasoning. They will, for instance, consistently skew their judgment as a result of the availability or representativeness heuristics while ignoring regression toward the mean. Fortunately, there is a viable means of bettering the coherence of their efforts. When subjects gain formal training in logic and statistics, their inferential and probabilistic judgments improve. But formal education is not necessary for people to demonstrate relatively good correspondence judgment. That is because people have been equipped by hundreds of thousands of years of evolution to assess what Hammond calls the *multiple fallible indicators* provided by the natural environment.

Multiple fallible indicators are environmental "cues," each of which on its own has limited reliabilty. When taken together and well integrated, however, these indicators supply the foundations for sound judgment. We might assess the likelihood of rain, for example, by the smell of the air, the darkness of clouds, the feel of the wind, our physical reaction to dropping barometric pressure, and the behavior of birds. Likewise, we might assess the character of a new acquaintance by the gestures she employs, her facial expressions and body language, the tone of her voice, and the content of her speech. Most of the indicators employed by practical judges are directly provided by the environment. Some may be human artifacts. A weathervane is a constructed indicator of the direction and force of the wind. The Dow Jones index is a constructed indicator of the strength of the stock market in general. Whatever the mix of natural and constructed

---

[14] See L. J. Cohen, "Can Human Irrationality Be Experimentally Demonstrated?" *The Behavioral and Brain Sciences* 4 (1981): 317–331. Lola L. Lopes, "The Rhetoric of Irrationality," *Theory and Psychology* 1 (1991): 65–82.

indicators, the accuracy of correspondence judgments depends on their selective use and interpretation.

While our capacity to assess the coherence of judgments is largely the product of education and, more specifically, the product of studying logic and statistics, our capacity to assess environmental indicators is innate. Hammond explains that

> [C]orrespondence competence is a product of evolution. We should therefore expect such competence among all *Homo sapiens* in circumstances affording multiple fallible indicators and not expect it when these are absent.... Whereas correspondence competence is phylogenetic (it benefits from perhaps millions of years of evolution), coherence competence is ontogenetic (it benefits only from each person's opportunity and ability to acquire the appropriate concepts from education and training). We cannot expect coherence competence when these are lacking. Therefore, we achieve vastly different levels of coherence competence, depending on our education.[15]

Our evolutionary background (hundreds of thousands of years living as members of hunter-gatherer tribes) did not give us innate knowledge of the laws of probability or syllogistic reasoning. It did provide us with innate or easily developed capacities of perceptual judgment. It also gave us innate or easily developed capacities of normative judgment, skills that proved increasingly important with the growth and sophistication of collective life among early hominids. This genetically embedded experience is crucial to the exercise of practical judgment.

It might be thought misleading to characterize genetic inheritance as a form of embedded experience. After all, natural selection is a product of adaptation that (mostly) occurs as a result of chance genetic mutations. It does not arise from experiential learning in the usual sense of the term. Still, genetic development might reasonably be viewed as a product of species-wide experience. The evolution of a form of life is a kind of genetic sorting mechanism. Only those individuals fortunate enough to have been born with genetic compositions relatively well-adapted to their environments have a good chance to pass on their genes to offspring. While an individual's genes are not affected by lived experience, they do represent the evolutionary experience of forebears who were fit enough to procreate and raise young. This ancestral experience – the aptitudes and skills of forebears that facilitated their survival and procreation – gets passed on to progeny in the form of adaptive traits. In contrast, the

---

[15] Kenneth R. Hammond, *Human Judgment and Social Policy: Irreducible Uncertainty, Inevitable Error, Unavoidable Injustice* (New York: Oxford University Press, 1996), p. 351.

genetically encoded experience representing maladaptive traits is not reproduced. This experience is lost to us as a species, and, quite likely, we are better off for it.

Ancestral Experience and the Brain

The evolutionary experience of the species and the personal experience of the individual find common ground in the synaptic constitution of the human brain. The brain's neurological structure – its genetically inherited foundation – reflects the species' evolutionary experience. The ongoing development of the brain's synaptic pathways over the life of the individual, as interactions with the environment stimulate the creation of particular neural connections while allowing the atrophy of others, reflects the effect of personal experience. To better understand the effects and interaction of these two sorts of neurologically captured experience, we must first survey the morphology and operation of the brain.

The human brain represents approximately 2% of an individual's body weight but consumes 20% of its available energy. This energy is utilized to keep 100 billion elongated cells, known as neurons, firing. Connections between these brain cells – gaps one-millionth of a centimeter wide known as synapses – link the multiple dendrites or spines of one neuron to the arm or axon of another neuron, and vice versa. Electrical charges moving at about 200 miles per hour travel from neuron to neuron across these synaptic gaps, facilitated by a molecular bath known as a neurotransmitter, released by the nerve ending. The average human brain cell has about a 1,000 synapses, though some neurons in the cerebellum boast 100,000 synaptic links. The electrochemical activity of pulses dispersing across 100 trillion synapses constitutes the bio-physics of (unconscious and conscious) thought, emotion, and sensory processing.

The human brain encodes what happens to it, and within it, on its synaptic networks. These extensive neural relays chart the history of the individual, from its pre-natal experiences to its various encounters with the world, including the internal reactions and mental (re)processings that these environmental encounters generate. Collectively, the neural relays are known as "brain maps." The brain's synaptic structure, in effect, can be read like "a map of lived experience."[16] Brain maps constitute a neural inventory of the individual's life.

---

[16] Jeffrey M. Schwartz and Sharon Begley, *The Mind and the Brain: Neuroplasticity and the Power of Mental Force* (New York: HarperCollins, 2002), p. 200.

Like the muscles in our bodies, brain maps gain strength with use. As particular synaptic relays fire and refire, they become increasingly dominant. That is to say, the more a particular neural network is used, the more it is likely to be relied upon in the future. Neurons that fire together, wire together. Neural networks are like the paths rainwater takes down a gentle slope. At first, the paths are multiple and develop in an apparently random fashion as water drawn by gravity skirts obstacles and areas of resistance on its downward journey. Increasingly, fresh rainwater finds its way into previously blazed trails. Some of these pathways deepen and widen with use. Others dry up as their potential load becomes diverted into neighboring conduits. Eventually, a few key rivulets are formed, sufficient in number and distribution to carry most of the rainwater to its destination.

Similarly, the brain's development occurs by way of the growth of synaptic pathways, some of which, as a result of repeated use, are increasingly likely to prevail in the future. As Joseph LeDoux observes, "synapses in the brain, like animals in their environments, compete to stay alive. Synapses that are used compete successfully and survive, while those that are not used perish."[17] A "neural Darwinism" effectively operates in the brain. During critical periods of life, such as early childhood, the wiring together of particular synapses is crucial to the development of various aptitudes and skills (eye alignment, for example). If they do not wire together during this crucial period as a result of the proper stimulation from the environment, it is very difficult, if not impossible, for it to happen later. The synaptic pathways required for the development and exercise of specific capacities may be lost forever.[18]

Genetic and environmental factors interact in the initiation, reinforcement, and rewiring of synaptic circuitry. The average neuron of a newborn baby has about 2,500 active synapses. During the next three years of its life, a peak of about 15,000 synapses will develop per neuron. Then a process of "pruning" takes place, marking a steady decline in synaptic connections. Synapses that fire relatively infrequently wither and die – a case, as one neuroscientist observed, of "survival of the busiest."[19] This loss of neuronal connections does not indicate a decline of intelligence or skill. Rather, as superfluous synaptic connections wither, active brain

---

[17] Joseph LeDoux, *The Synaptic Self: How Our Brains Become Who We Are* (New York: Penguin Books, 2002), p. 73. And see Gerald Edelman, *Neural Darwinism* (New York: Basic Books, 1987).

[18] LeDoux, *The Synaptic Self,* p. 94.

[19] Schwartz, *The Mind and the Brain,* p. 117.

maps allow increasingly effective adaptation to specific environments. For example, the newborn's brain is equally primed to learn any language. But it attunes itself in early life to the phonemic repertoire of its caregivers. The initial capacity to easily recognize a myriad of non-native phonemes slowly dissolves as the synaptic relays that allow such recognition wither and die. This process facilitates the quick recognition and learning of a native tongue. But it comes at the cost of increased difficulty of aquiring a new language in later life. Like the selective process involved in language acquisition, the neural pruning involved in attaining other aptitudes and skills represents the construction of effective (brain) maps out of a clutter of surplus connections.

A large number of neural relays are built into the structure of the brain. These circuits do not need to be stimulated by the environment to gain effect and become dominant: they already claim a certain neurological hegemony. The healthy newborn does not try out a number of different neural pathways over a period of hours, days, weeks, or months before figuring out which brain circuits allow it to breathe air. Rather, the neural pathways that dictate the expansion of lungs are part of the baby's neurological hardware. This is the realm of instinct. The development of non-innate skills supplements these innate relays. When non-innate skills become habitual, in the sense of becoming largely perfected, we speak of their gaining the status of *second nature*. The skills of walking and talking fit into this category. Here, synaptic pathways developed after birth become increasingly dominant as they build upon and interact with the relatively sparse brain maps provided by first nature, allowing the individual a much larger repertoire of proficient behavior.

Explaining the relationship between innate and subsequently acquired neural pathways, LeDoux aptly observes that "Learning involves the nurturing of nature."[20] He goes on to state that "Nature and nurture both contribute to who we are, but . . . they actually speak the same language. They both ultimately achieve their mental and behavioral effects by shaping the synaptic organization of the brain. . . . Nature and nurture function similarly: they are simply two different ways of making deposits in the brain's synaptic ledgers."[21] From a species point of view, the trial and error experiment of matching evolving genes to a constantly changing environment constitutes an embedding of experience in the genes of ancestors and, consequently, the embedding of experience in the innate

---

[20] LeDoux, *The Synaptic Self*, p. 9
[21] LeDoux, *The Synaptic Self*, pp. 3, 5.

brain maps of progeny. This embedded experience features prominently
in structuring human behavior. But the embedding of ancestral experience through inheritance is only half the story. There are approximately 35,000 human genes, about half of which appear to be actively
involved in the brain. Yet the brain boasts trillions of synaptic connections.
Lived experience – an individual's personal interactions with its environment – determines how the vast majority of these neural pathways will
develop.

Neuropsychiatrist Jeffrey Schwartz and Sharon Begley write:

If each gene carried an instruction for a particular [synaptic] connection, we'd
run out of instructions long before our brain reached the sophistication of, oh,
a banana slug's. Call it the genetic shortfall: too many synapses, too few genes.
Our DNA is simply too paltry to spell out the wiring diagram for the human
brain.... The basic principle is this: genetic signals play a large role in the initial
structuring of the brain. The ulimate shape of the brain [in the sense of its working
synaptic relays], however, is the outcome of an ongoing active process that occurs
where lived experience meets both the inner and the outer environment.[22]

The trial and error experiments of life that constitute the personal experience of the individual build upon the trial and error experiments that
constitute the evolutionary experience of the species. LeDoux explains:
'We commonly think of experiences as leaving their mark on the brain
through the record of memory, and . . . memory is a product of synapses.
It is less common, but no less appropriate, to think of genes as also influ-
encing us in the form of memory. In this case, though, the synaptic memory comes about as a result of ancestral rather than personal history."[23]
Whether experience is ancestral or personal, it has the effect of producing brain maps. These brain maps provide the neural wherewithal
for decision-making. This is simply to say that (ancestral and personal)
experience (re)maps brains to equip them for practical judgment.

Making Good Use of Ancestral Experience

Like Hammond, Gigerenzer looks to evolutionary psychology to inform
our understanding of practical judgment. Rather than invoking analytical rules for decision-making, he argues, we should be employing Darwinian principles to better understand the psycho-social foundation of

---

[22] Schwartz, *The Mind and the Brain*, pp. 112, 117.
[23] LeDoux, *The Synaptic Self*, p. 66.

competent judgment in an uncertain world.[24] Gigerenzer, like Hammond, rues the take-home message of much of the literature in decision science – that peope are "bad reasoners" because they neglect the laws of probability.[25] And, like Hammond, he notes that these statistical laws are latecomers to the historical scene. The mathematics of probability only emerged in the mid-seventeeth century, and it took another century before the concept of probability took precedence over cruder notions of expectation. In turn, the widespread use of probability percentages to represent levels of uncertainty only became prevalent in the nineteenth and twentieth centuries.[26] Until very recently, the representation of uncertainty was achieved through other means. When decision scientists depreciate human judgment because of its weak and faulty powers of probabilistic reasoning, Gigerenzer argues, it is not human judgment per se that is deficient, but the tools scholars employ to measure it.

Throughout history, natural frequencies grounded in natural samples have been used to measure levels of certainty and uncertainty. A natural frequency corresponds to the way people encountered data, and evaluated multiple fallible indicators, before the invention of probability theory. It is a raw numerical observation, the final tally of a natural sample that has not been normalized with respect to base rates.[27] Say six out of ten snakes that the forest dweller encounters one day have the look of the brightly banded and deadly coral snake, while the other four are non-poisonous black racers. From past experience, the forest dweller knows that of every three brightly banded snakes in the forest, only one turns out to be a poisonous coral snake. The other two are king snakes, harmless (and delicious) mimics. Now the forest dweller wants to tell his son how many of the snakes seen today in a particular neck of the woods are likely to be poisonous. The answer, he easily calculates, is two. Rather than computing base rates, hit rates and false positives in terms of percentages, the data are maintained in their actual numbers or ratios.[28] The calculation is relatively straightforward.

---

[24] Gerd Gigerenzer, *Adaptive Thinking: Rationality in the Real World* (Oxford: Oxford University Press, 2000), p. 225. Unfortunately, Gigerenzer mistakenly saddles Aristotle with the Enlightment's elevation of formal principles over social-psychological observation.

[25] Gigerenzer, "Ecological Intelligence: An Adaptation for Frequencies," in Denise Dellarosa Cummins and Conlin Allen, *The Evolution of Mind* (New York: Oxford University Press, 1998), pp. 11–12.

[26] Gigerenzer, "Ecological Intelligence," pp. 11–12.

[27] Gigerenzer, *Adaptive Thinking*, p. 63.

[28] Gigerenzer, *Adaptive Thinking*, p. 63.

Now consider a physician who has 114 patients, 12 of whom have a new disease. Of these 12, 8 show a symptom. In turn, 16 of the 102 remaining patients without the disease also display the symptom. The physician sees a new patient who has the symptom. On the basis of her clientele alone (assuming no other data are available), what should she say the chances are that the new patient has the disease? If the physician attempted to transform her observations into probabilities and percentages, calculate base rates, hit rates, and false positives, rather complicated rules of Bayesian inference would need to be applied. But by keeping to natural frequencies, the answer is again relatively straightforward. The likelihood that the new patient has the disease is calculated by taking all those patients with the disease and symptom (8) and dividing that number by all those who exhibit the symptom (8 + 16). The physician should say that the symptomatic patient has a 1 in 3 chance of having the disease.

Physicians and other professionals are often confronted with such problems. Those who employ probabilities, percentages, and Bayesian inference make mistaken estimates that are often an order of magnitude larger or smaller than those who employ natural samples and natural frequencies.[29] Indeed, both lay people and professionals make fewer mistakes (and much fewer big mistakes), estimating uncertainties when they are presented as natural frequencies. Gigerenzer explains:

The lesson of these results is not to blame physicians' or students' minds when they stumble over probabilities. Rather, the lesson is to represent information in textbooks, in curricula, and in physician-patient interactions in natural frequencies that correspond to the way information was encountered in the environment in which human minds evolved. . . . The thesis is that mental algorithms were designed for natural frequencies, the recurrent format of information until very recently. . . . Mental computations are simpler when information is encountered in the same form as in the environment in which our ancestors evolved, rather than in the modern form of probabilities and percentages.[30]

Early decision science was based on the assumption that human rationality and probability theory were two sides of the same coin. Gigerenzer tells a different story, where the parvenu of probabilistic reasoning does not neatly map onto a mind adapted to the assessment of natural frequencies.

What Gigerenzer demonstrates regarding predispositions for the calculation of natural frequencies also applies to other facets of practical

---

[29] Gigerenzer, *Adaptive Thinking*, pp. 60–65.
[30] Gigerenzer, "Ecological Intelligence," pp. 17, 26. See also Gigerenzer, *Adaptive Thinking*, p. 76.

judgment. Much decision science is founded on the premise that more information is better, and that common heuristics, by shortcutting extensive efforts at information gathering and rational processing, thwart good judgment. In an impressive array of studies, Gigerenzer provides compelling evidence for the virtues of the "fast and frugal heuristics" that human beings have naturally developed over the millennia. These tried and true rules of thumb often prove more effective than the more sophisticated, deliberative, and rational models of decision-making developed in recent decades.[31]

For instance, Gigerenzer observes that Germans predict the relative sizes of U.S. cities more accurately than Americans do. They do so not because they know *more* about the United States of America than its own citizens, but because they know *less*. The Germans correctly identify San Diego as bigger than San Antonio, for example, simply because they have heard of San Diego, but have not heard of San Antonio. Americans, acquainted with both cities, stop to assess their relative knowledge and deliberate. That process often produces less accurate judgments.[32]

Frequently, the first (and perhaps only) good reason a person has to choose among alternatives is that only one of them is recognized. The predisposition to embrace the recognized and reject the unknown is a fast, frugal, and often helpful rule of thumb. This predisposition is an evolutionary adaptation evident in many species. Rats have been shown to prefer food that they have eaten before or smelled on another rat's breath to completely foreign food. They choose the known over the unknown instinctively, reducing the likelihood of ingesting something poisonous. Likewise, the common heuristic of choosing the recognized over the unrecognized often proves to be an effective aid to human decision-making, though it may also contribute to prejudice.

Many heuristics that are problematic from the point of view of probabilistic reasoning prove to be useful rules of thumb in daily life. Such is the case with the gambler's fallacy. Underlining the evolutionary nature of our capacities for judgment, Steven Pinker writes:

An astute observer *should* commit the gambler's fallacy and try to predict the next occurrence of an event from its history so far, a kind of statistics called time-series analysis. There is only one exception: devices that are *designed* to deliver events independently of their history. What kind of device would do that? We call them

---

[31] Gerd Gigerenzer, Peter M. Todd, and the ABC Research Group, *Simple Heuristics That Make Us Smart* (New York: Oxford University Press, 1999), p. 29.
[32] Gigerenzer, *Adaptive Thinking*, pp. 174, 234.

gambling machines. . . . So in any world but a casino, the gambler's fallacy is rarely a fallacy. Indeed, calling our intuitive predictions fallacious because they fail on gambling devices is backwards. A gambling device is, by definition, a machine designed to defeat our intuitive predictions. It is like calling our hands badly designed because they make it hard to get out of handcuffs.[33]

From a statistical point of view, it makes no sense to expect a run of heads to increase the chance of a tail's occurring on any particular toss. Those who succumb to the gambler's fallacy, in effect, are overcompensating for the assumed fairness of the coin, as if the coin had a memory and a desire to return to a 50/50 distribution of heads and tails as quickly as possible. In the natural world, however, one seldom encounters the equivalent of a fair coin toss. That is because there are few events in the world that have a 50/50 chance of (re)occurring regardless of their history. Tossed coins and gambling devices fit this profile, but not much else. Asked which side of a mammoth vertebrae will land upward, and knowing that his next meal depends on a correct prediction, the Pleistocene dweller would do well by choosing the side that has landed up in most of the previous tosses. Mammoth vertebrae, unlike coins, are not completely symmetrical and weight-balanced. So the history of their landings is not a function of pure chance; rather, it provides a fallible indicator of future behavior. Basing predictions on past behavior is a good rule of thumb. Though it may get you in trouble in casinos, it serves well enough in the jungle.

The human mind displays its most reliable assessments, evaluations, and predictions when it can call into play its evolutionary experience. This applies both to perceptual skills as well as cognitive aptitudes. Children incapable of judging how abstract geometric shapes will move across a computer screen, for example, quickly learn to predict the pattern of movement when the geometric shapes are changed into sketches of animals that they are asked to catch.[34] The lesson, again, is that the nature and limits of human judgment are best assessed by conducting tests that mimic naturally encountered circumstances. As a rule, the more an act of judgment demands abstract conceptualization, the less will it be able to rely upon ancestral (and, for all but the highly educated, personal) experience.

---

[33] Steven Pinker, *How the Mind Works* (New York: W. W. Norton, 1997), p. 346.

[34] S. Ceci and U. Bronfenbrenner, "Don't forget to take the cupcakes out of the oven: Strategic time-monitoring, prospective memory and context," *Child Development* 56 (1985): 175–90.

The conclusion reached by decision theorists informed by evolutionary psychology is that human beings are innately predisposed to learn some lessons better than others, and hence to judge best when they employ skills that were selected for in the natural environment. This relationship applies not only to humans, but to all creatures that learn and judge. Consider how rodents make practical associations. Melvin Konner observes that

it is very easy to teach a rat an association between a taste and artificially induced nausea, so that it will avoid the taste thereafter; and it is easy to teach it to associate a light or sound with an electric shock, with similar results in avoidance behavior. But it is very difficult indeed to make the rat learn the converse associations.... Now while these findings may have startled learning psychologists ... they came as no surprise to biologists. They are obviously adaptive in the most meaningful sense. The ancestors of rats, in the wild, must surely have gotten into situations where tastes or smells led to nausea, and where lights and sounds led to external physical pain. But natural selection very likely had no opportunity to favor rats who could associate lights and sounds with nausea.... It produced, instead, genetically based tendencies to learn some lessons better than others.[35]

Genetic constitution does not determine every aspect of the rat's behavioral repertoire. Rather, it determines the limits within which the rodent may behaviorally adapt to its environment. The rat's genetically embedded experience determines the boundaries within which it may efficiently learn from personal experience. Human beings are capable of adaptive learning orders of magnitude greater than rats. But the fact remains that we are programmed by our neural structure to learn some lessons more easily than others.[36] Inherited brain maps determine what sort of experiences will have the upper hand in restructuring our neural networks. Skills of judgment develop best when they build upon lessons that we are "biologically primed" to learn.[37]

Personal Experience and the Brain

Notwithstanding their important investigations of innate capacities, Hammond, Gigerenzer, and Pinker do not squarely face an important

---

35 Melvin Konner, The Tangled Wing: Biological Constraints on the Human Spirit (New York: Holt, Rinehart and Winston, 1982), pp. 27–28.

36 See Steven Pinker, *The Blank Slate* (New York: Viking, 2002), pp. 40–41.

37 See Steven R. Quartz and Terrence J. Sejnowski, *Liars, Lovers, and Heroes: What the New Brain Science Reveals about How We Became Who We Are* (New York: William Morrow, 2002), p. 183.

issue. For the most part, these scholars focus on the inherited components of human judgment. Yet we are not born with the ability to exercise practical judgment any more than we are born with, say, the ability to speak. We come into the world not with language competence, but with the capacity to develop speech given a sufficiently supportive environment. We only become competent speakers (and social interacters) by being exposed to speech (and social interaction) as young children. Likewise, our innate *capacities* for perceptual and social judgment require extensive exercise to become functional *abilities*.

The rats in Konner's experiment did not innately associate new sights and sounds with electric shocks or new foods with nausea. Rather, they learned to make these primitive judgments by experiencing the nasty effects of certain events. Similarly, we are born not as practical judges, but with a capacity to develop the skills of practical judgment given an environment that fosters learning. Typically, this education is of the trial and error sort. Most of the abilities that figure prominently in practical judgment are not innate. They are developed by way of worldly experience.

Nature lays down the original tracks of the mind. But most of the brain is left unmapped. Environmental learning takes advantage of this open space. It exploits the plasticity of the brain, its availability for (re)mapping. For many decades now, neuroplasticity has been documented in young children. Experiential learning physically alters children's brains, both increasing the number of new neural circuits in use and reprogramming existing circuits. That is the stuff of typical childhood development. In cases of brain trauma or surgery in children, the effects of neuroplasticity are even more evident. Indeed, young brains (at least before the age of four or five) are so plastic that they may undergo a truly radical restructuring. In medical cases where the entire left hemisphere of a child's brain had to be removed, the remaining right hemisphere thoroughly restructured itself so as to take over standard left-brain functions.[38]

One might say that children's brains are genetically structured to remain receptive to continual rewiring. Ancestral experience makes them neurological sponges of personal experience. The phenomena of developing new circuits to grapple with novel experience, however, extends later in life than was once assumed. Recent studies document growth of brain cells in adolescents, directly before and after puberty, followed by the further pruning of synaptic links.[39] And specific areas of the brain,

[38] Schwartz, *The Mind and the Brain*, p. 99.
[39] Schwartz, *The Mind and the Brain*, pp. 127–29.

such as the pre-frontal cortex, where assessment of risk, impulse control, and many other operations of practical judgment occur, are not fully developed until people reach their mid-twenties or later. This late maturity is primarily a function of the tardy myelination of axons. Only when sheathed with an insulating, fatty layer of myelin, do the cortical neurons become fully functional.[40]

Beginning in the 1990s, advanced brain-imaging techniques also documented elements of "cortical remapping" in older adults. Mature individuals extensively practicing a certain skill, for instance, exhibited an expansion of the brain space devoted to that type of activity. One study demonstrated that the posterior of the hippocampus of London taxi drivers grew in direct proportion to the number of years the drivers sat behind the wheel navigating London's streets and exercising geographic memory.[41] The hippocampus, a curved ridge located on the floor of each lateral ventricle, is directly involved in memory. Alternatively, certain areas of the adult brain can become reprogrammed to grapple with new demands. The visual cortex of blind people who learn to read Braille may be reassigned to process information from touch.[42] Likewise, deaf people may employ part of their auditory cortex to process sign language.[43] Plasticity is not only a matter of the expansion, contraction, or reassignment of brain regions devoted to the exercise of certain skills, however. It is also exhibited by the increase in strength of synaptic connections within given brain regions. Whether laying down new neural tracks or co-opting and strengthening existing circuits, our interactions with the environment alter the wiring of our brains.[44]

Neuroscientists Michael Merzenich and R. Christopher deCharms were pioneers in the exploration of the ability of mature neurons to forge

[40] Elkhonon Goldberg, *The Wisdom Paradox: How Your Mind Can Grow Stronger As Your Brain Grows Older* (New York: Gotham Books, 2005), pp. 40–42.

[41] E. A. Maguire et al., "Navigation-related structural change in the hippocampi of taxi drivers, "*Proceedings of the National Academy of Sciences of the United States of America,* 97 (2000): 4398–4403. Cited in Schwartz, *The Mind and the Brain,* p. 250. The region may slowly shrink back to its original size once the activity responsible for its expansion ceases. See also Goldberg, *The Wisdom Paradox,* pp. 254–55.

[42] N. Sadato, A. Pascula-Leone, J. Grafman, V. Ibanez, M. P. Deiber, G. Dold, and M. Hallett, "Activation of the primary visual cortex by Braille reading in blind subjects," *Nature* (1996) 380: 526–28.

[43] Pinker, *The Blank Slate,* p. 84.

[44] LeDoux, *The Synaptic Self,* p. 79. Schwartz, *The Mind and the Brain,* p. 131. V. S. Ramachandran and Sandra Blakeslee, *Phantoms in the Brain* (New York: William Morrow and Company, 1998). M. M. Merzenich and R. C. deCharms, "Neural Representations, Experience, and Change," in *The Mind-Brain Continuum: Sensory Processes,* ed. Rodolfo Llinas and Patricia Churchland (Cambridge: MIT Press, 1996), pp. 61–81.

new connections, effecting a rewiring of the circuits of the adult brain. They argue that "moment by moment we choose and sculpt how our ever-changing minds will work, we choose who we will be the next moment in a very real sense, and these choices are left embossed in physical form on our material selves."[45] Well beyond childhood, personal experience continues to leave its mark on the neural circuitry of the brain. To be sure, the malleability of the brain is limited. It demonstrates innate regional specialization (especially in sub-cortical areas) that remains defiant to reorganization. However, plasticity is significantly evident in the cerebral cortex – that is, the area of the brain that mediates practical judgment.[46] In this respect, the cortex proves to be a dynamic entity that is "remodeled continually by experience."[47] As a result of the brain's plasticity – the development of new neural relays and the ongoing pruning and co-optation of old relays – the mature individual learns to cope with an ever-changing environment.

Adult neuroplasticity is not solely a function of the brain's reprogramming itself in response to environmental stimuli. A significant role is played by conscious, mental effort. Brain maps are modified throughout the life of the individual as a product of the interaction of changing (patterns of) input from the senses and variable mental output from the mind. Schwartz and Begley write: "Now there is no question that the brain remodels itself throughout life, and that it retains the capacity to change itself as the result not only of passively experienced factors such as enriched environments, but also of changes in the ways we behave . . . and the ways we think. . . . If the brain is like a map of lived experience, then the mind can, with directed effort, function as its own internally directed mapmaker."[48] A crucial component of the experience that serves to sculpt

---

[45] Merzenich, "Neural Representations, Experience, and Change," p. 77.

[46] For a reserved estimation of neural plasticity, see Pinker, *The Blank Slate*, pp. 83–102.

[47] Schwartz, *The Mind and the Brain*, p. 166.

[48] Schwartz, *The Mind and the Brain*, pp. 253–54, 200. There is increasing evidence that the capacity of mental effort to affect the physical functioning of neural circuits is best explained by the laws of quantum physics. Specifically, it is hypothesized to be a product of the collapse of the "wave function" in accordance with the "Quantum Zeno Effect." This quantum event triggers the synaptic flow of calcium ions through the nanometer-wide channel in the nerve terminal and the subsequent release of neurotransmitters. See Schwartz, *The Mind and the Brain*. See also Jeffrey Gray, *Consciousness* (Oxford: Oxford University Press, 2004). Roger Penrose argues that consciousness itself develops as a product of such "non-computational" quantum physical processes in the brain. This occurs at the neuronal level, though Penrose believes that the non-computable physics occurring here is actually "a mere *shadow* of the deeper level of cytoskeletal action [the cytoskeletan being the protein framework of a cell, including a neuron, and the

the brain, then, is that which occurs within the mind itself, as it grapples with and integrates the meaning of its worldly encounters.

Our interactions with the world, as well as our mind's interactions with itself, reshape our brains. This neural sculpting alters the habits of our thoughts and changes the ways we grapple with existence.[49] Just as we become competent speakers by being exposed to a supportive linguistic environment, so we become competent judges by exposure to an environment that challenges us to assess, evaluate, and choose while providing opportunities for correction. Aristotle and John Dewey had it pretty much right. Through experiential learning we cultivate the skills of perception and assessment that yield accurate correspondence judgments as well as the social aptitudes that facilitate ethico-political judgment. Formal instruction is not much involved in the process. An education of a different sort is required. It occurs, for the most part, in the school of hard knocks.

The Worth of Worldly Experience

Proverbs are notorious for gainsaying each other. A book of maxims reveals an abundance of ambiguous, paradoxical, and in the aggregate, contradictory truisms. Pondering a crucial decision about furthering a relationship with a new acquaintance, one might turn to such a tome. One reads that "Haste makes waste." The wisdom of these words is patent. Accordingly, the decision is made not to jump to conclusions regarding the acquaintance's apparent virtues (or vices). In accord with the counsel offered, one decides to look a while longer before leaping. The matter seems settled. But turning the page, one notes that "He who hesitates is lost." Any number of examples of costly delays come to mind. Perhaps the opportunity for friendship will be squandered if the day is not seized.

Unable to decide whether to forge ahead or defer, one leafs ahead. The adage "Birds of a feather stick together" appears. An abundance of shared traits suggest that the friendship will be sustainable. Moving ahead again seems to be a good idea. But having made this decision, one's

microtubules that compose it] – and it is at this deeper level where we must seek the physical basis of *mind*." As a result of their quantum investigations, Penrose observes, physicists today "tend to take a less classically mechanistic view of the world than do the biologists." Roger Penrose, *Shadows of the Mind* (Oxford: Oxford University Press, 1994), pp. 50, 216, 217, 376.

49 John T. Cacioppo and Gary Berntson, "Social Neuroscience," in *Foundations in social neuroscience.* ed. John T. Cacioppo et al. (Cambridge, Mass.: MIT Press, 2002), p. 8.

eyes fall upon the maxim "Opposites attract." Perhaps too many similar characteristics will produce a dull, unleavened relationship. Familiarity grounded in similarity may breed contempt. Perhaps variety really is the spice of life. Foiled again, one begins to wonder whether personal gains or losses should be the focus of one's attention. A less egoistic, more expansive concern for the new acquaintance may be in order. Countless proverbs buttress this call to altruism. But then, turning back to the book, one reads that "Self-interest blinds some, but enlightens others."[50] At a loss, one turns the page, revealing the adage that "Two heads are better than one." Perhaps seeking the advice of a confederate would be in order. The initiative is stymied by the following entry, which announces that "Too many cooks spoil the broth." Nonplussed, one senses that reading further will not lead to enlightment. Indeed, one might go blind before securing clear, uncontradicted counsel.

In such cases, any number of equally tried-and-true and mutually incompatible nuggets of folk wisdom fit the bill. How to choose among them? A good judge presumably has to know, lest she inappropriately and ineffectually appeal to the wrong principle. Unfortunately, there are no principles that spell out which principles to choose, or how and when to apply them. Perhaps decision science might come to the rescue. An exhaustive list of common effects and biases, however, proves to be an insufficient resource unless one can determine, for any particular case, which effects and biases are most likely to be in play. Moreover, any rules of thumb that we might wish to apply have their own antipodes – counterweight heuristics that would have us going in opposite directions.

To make matters more complicated, contradictory heuristics, effects, and biases often operate simultaneously. Jon Elster has artfully brought this point home.[51] People making choices about desired objects or courses of action will exhibit a wide variety of competing psychological effects. Certain individuals in particular contexts will disdain that which they cannot possess or achieve, while others will hanker for it all the more. That is to say, a sour grapes effect and a forbidden fruit effect may be in play simultaneously. Or consider the rule of thumb, often employed by democratic theorists, that participation in one realm of public life leads to involvement in another.[52] People who become invested in a political

---

[50] La Rochefoucauld, *Maxims*, p. 42; #40.

[51] Jon Elster, *Alchemies of the Mind: Rationality and the Emotions* (Cambridge: Cambridge University Press, 1999).

[52] See Carole Pateman, *Participation and Democratic Theory* (Cambridge: Cambridge University Press, 1970).

activity often find themselves active in related areas. This is known as the *spillover* effect. But a *crowding out* effect is also evident. Here, participation in one realm uses up the time and resources that might otherwise have been available for other forms of involvement. The problem with political participation, one might say with a nod to Oscar Wilde, is that it consumes too many evenings, leaving one reluctant to take on any other obligations. At the same time, if participation is denied in one realm, it might increase demand for it in another. This is known as the *compensation* effect.[53] The compensation effect is the obverse of the spillover effect, and militates against the crowding out effect. All three effects may be at work at once in any given population or person. The problem is to determine what vector is formed by the intersection of the effects in play at any given time and place for any particular individual.

There is no psychological rule or body of knowledge that facilitates the determination of which effect will prevail, or how it will interact with other effects, in any given circumstance. Of course, one can study aggregate trends. But these will be of limited value in determining particular cases. As Elster observes, various effects may cancel each other out in large populations. The study of aggregate trends may consequently lead to false conclusions. If, for instance, the sour grapes effect occurs in subpopulation 'A' whereas the forbidden fruit effect occurs in subpopulation 'B,' statisticians observing aggregate trends in the population as a whole might assume there is no clear tendency.[54] In fact, there are two clear tendencies.[55]

What are we to make of a multitude of principles, proverbs, heuristics, and effects that potentially contradict each other? Notwithstanding his own penchant for rationally derived rules, Kant acknowledges that the determination of the applicability of a rule – that is to say, knowing when an object or event falls within its scope – must rest on a different kind of ability than that involved in the stipulation of a rule and the determination of its internal (logical) consistency. The determination of the applicability of a rule, upon threat of an infinite regress, cannot be a rule-governed procedure. Rather, it is, as Kant said, a kind of knack. Among other things, practical judgment is the knack that allows one to determine, in any particular context, which rules to apply. It is in particular demand when

---

53 Elster, *Alchemies of the Mind*, pp. 24–25.
54 Empirical studies indicate that the forbidden fruit effect is slightly more prevalent in the aggregate. Elster, *Alchemies of the Mind*, p. 22.
55 Elster, *Alchemies of the Mind*, p. 45.

the principles at our disposal are contradictory and mutually exclusive. "There are trivial truths and great truths," the physicist Niels Bohr stated. "The opposite of a trivial truth is plainly false. The opposite of a great truth is also true." Practical judgment is required whenever one is embroiled in matters that exceed the parameters of trivial truths, as is the case in most, if not all, moral and political affairs. Practical judgment helps us determine whether a great truth, or its equally true opposite, is more fitting given the circumstances at hand.

Practical judgment does not shy away from factual information (trivial truths), scientific research, or the study of maxims, principles, laws, and rules of thumb. If there is one thing that scholars of judgment have agreed on over the ages, however, it is that formal instruction proves insufficient. There is no substitute for experience. Bent Flyvbjerg underlines this fact in his plea for "*phronetic* social sciences." Expertise, Flyvbjerg argues, cannot be achieved without extensive worldly experience. Novices in a field typically demonstrate book knowledge, and gauge their success by the extent to which their practice stays true to the letter of the law. As novices gain experience, however, contextual assessments begin to play a larger role. For those who reach the status of experts, practical judgment proves to be all important. Following rules and abiding by logic allows competency. But the proficiency of an expert is only achieved through skills and understanding acquired over years of physical, mental, and emotional experience. If one is limited to a strictly analytical rationality and remains caught in rule-following procedures, progress towards virtuosity will be stymied.

Flyvbjerg illustrates this assertion by way of an empirical study that recorded whether CPR instructors, CPR practitioners, and novices could distinguish between professionals and trained novices practicing CPR skills. While experts could identify experts-in-action very well, and novices could pick out expert practitioners reasonably well, CPR instructors did very poorly in their selections. Flyvbjerg explains that instructors, whose job it was to teach novices to follow rules, assumed that professionals remained rigorous rule-followers. Because professionals did not strictly follow rules but responded based on knowledge and skills acquired over years of work in the field, instructors failed to identify them as experts.

The moral of the story is that if you insist on a monopoly for analytical rationality and context-independent knowledge, you will never gain expertise. This truth, Flyvbjerg insists, applies as much to the training of social scientists as to the training of paramedics. To become an expert social scientist, one must move beyond the antiseptic massaging of data and get one's hands dirty grappling with the real world.[56]

There is no set procedure for getting one's hands dirty in a productive manner. Some social scientists, aware that operational rules are unavailable, call it "mucking around." Guy Claxton describes how learning occurs while mucking around: "One needs to be able to soak up experience of complex domains – such as human relationships – through one's pores, and to extract the subtle, contingent patterns that are latent within it."[57] This soaking up of worldly experience takes time. There is no quick route to the integration of its lessons. Sophocles famously stated, with more than a hint of pessimism, that wisdom comes only to the aged.[58] Aristotle provided the reason, observing that "knowledge must be worked into the living texture of the mind, and this takes time."[59] The remark is prescient of the contemporary research in neuroscience. New practices and skills, including those of observation, assessment, and evaluation, slowly reconstruct brain maps. Practical wisdom is the product of a lifetime of such reconstructive learning.

Becoming an expert is time-consuming. Herbert Simon cites empirical research confirming that expert status is seldom achieved without an apprenticeship of ten or more years. "Almost no person in these disciplines [of chess, music composition, painting and mathematics] has produced world-class performances without having first put in at least ten years of intensive learning and practice....A *sine qua non* for outstanding work is diligent attention to the field over a decade or more."[60] Simon notes that even so-called child prodigies reach their peak performance after many years of learning and practice. Mozart, for instance, did not write world-class music until he was seventeen years old, thirteen years after he first started composing at the age of four.

---

[56] The business world operates similarly, according to Malcolm Gladwell. Gladwell observes that "the best instincts belong to those with experience. And the ability to make a successful snap judgment is largely a function of years of training and knowledge and experience – all kinds of things that allow people to educate their unconscious." Quoted in Teresa K. Weaver, "In a blink," *Gainesville Sun*, March 6, 2005, p. 5D. See also Malcolm Gladwell, *Blink: The Power of Thinking without Thinking* (New York: Little, Brown: 2005).

[57] Guy Claxton, *Hare Brain Tortoise Mind: Why Intelligence Increases When You Think Less* (Hopewell, NJ: The Ecco Press, 1997), p. 192.

[58] Sophocles, *Antigone* (1348–52) in *Sophocles I* (Chicago: University of Chicago Press, 1954), p. 204.

[59] Aristotle, *Ethics*, p. 200.

[60] Herbert A. Simon, "Alternative visions of rationality," in *Judgment and decision making*, ed. H. R. Arkes and K. R. Hammond (Cambridge: Cambridge University Press, 1986).

While expertise develops only after extended practice, certain fields of study are known to favor youth. Great strides in mathematics, for instance, are typically made by relatively young scholars. The aged mathematician still doing original work is a rarity. In contrast, practical judgment is generally the purview of more mature individuals. Aristotle maintains that politics, unlike mathematics, is not an appropriate field for the young because its end is not knowing but doing. The art of doing requires experience, absent in youth. Importantly, Aristotle insists that the immaturity that makes the young unfit for politics is not strictly correlated to age. Maturity is gauged by the development of character, not the mere accumulation of years. In order for knowledge to be worked into the living texture of the mind, time must be spent in the trenches. But involvement in real-world politics is not a sufficient condition. Aristotle argues that experience has to be well-absorbed and well-integrated to become a viable source of practical wisdom.[61] Old fools, after all, exist in abundance. While practical wisdom is seldom, if ever, a trait of the very young it may also elude the aged. Wisdom does not simply accumulate over the years.[62] It has to be earned.

Michael Oakeshott observes that a busy person can be party to a very "crowded" life. While her days will be replete with "happenings," however, they may evidence a dearth of truly memorable "experiences." Though continually occupied and engaged, she may remain inexperienced. Her time will evidence "a ceaseless flow of seductive trivialities which invoke neither reflection nor choice but instant participation."[63] Such a life, given over to distracted involvement, does not allow for the integration of experience. Practical wisdom will not mark its path.

Neuroscientists confirm this relationship. Merzenich and deCharms observe that experience needs to be *coupled with attention* to produce "physical change in the structure and future functioning of the nervous system."[64] Experience is indispensable. But it is the intentionality with

---

[61] Aristotle, *Ethics*, p. 28. Jean-Jacques Rousseau concurred, writing that "The man who has lived the most is not he who has counted the most years but he who has most felt life." Jean-Jacques Rousseau, *Emile*, trans. Allan Bloom (New York: Basic Books, 1979), p. 42.

[62] See Ursula Staudinger, "Older and wiser? Integrating results on the relationship between age and wisdom-related performance," *International Journal of Behavioral Development*, 23 (1999): 641–664. See also Gisela Labouvie-Vief, "Wisdom as integrated thought: historical and developmental perspectives," in *Wisdom: Its nature, Origins, and Development* (Cambridge: Cambridge University Press, 1990), p. 79.

[63] Michael Oakeshott, *The Voice of Liberal Learning* (Indianapolis: Liberty Fund, 2001), p. 33.

[64] Merzenich, "Neural Representations, Experience, and Change," p. 77. Italics added.

which experience is integrated, not its mere extension over time, that matters most. To yield practical wisdom, experience must be soaked up with one's pores and worked into the living texture of the mind. Instant participation will not do the trick. In other words, experience enhances the skills of judgment only by way of the exercise of judgment. To bear fruit, experience must be subject to reflection and choice. As Dewey maintained, experience participated in but not reflected upon, assessed, and evaluated is wasted. Such under-utilized worldly encounters fail to create or strengthen the synaptic networks that enable the skills of practical judgment to develop.

Common Sense

Practical judgment is akin to and partakes of common sense – the most basic, and perhaps most important, product of our lived experience.[65] Common sense defies straightforward definition. None who have tried to corral it conceptually have met with much success.[66] Arendt's definition is as good as any: "Common sense is only that part of our mind and that portion of inherited wisdom which all men have in common in any given civilization."[67] Common sense is a widespread if not universal perceptual and cognitive ability that facilitates our quotidian navigation of the world.

Common sense is not a single sense. We have many common senses, such as the ability to gauge distances or weights, assess visual perspective, recognize faces, and attribute goals and intentions to actors. We also have the common sense that allows us to posit correlation as causation. Hence, when two objects (billiard balls, for example) meet in time and space and subsequently change their respective behavior (direction), we understand the meeting (collision) as the cause of the changed behavior. We all have a common, but not infallible, sense that tells us which correlations bespeak causation (the interactions of balls on billiard tables) and which do not (the arrival of the morning newspaper and the reveille of songbirds).

---

[65] Peter J. Steinberger, *The Concept of Political Judgment* (Chicago: University of Chicago Press, 1993), pp. 295–96.

[66] Thomas Reid of the Scottish realist school and, more recently, G. E. Moore are the two philosophers who have most extensively grappled with the notion.

[67] Hannah Arendt, "Understanding and Politics," in Hannah Arendt, *Essays in Understanding, 1930–1954*, ed. Jerome Kohn (New York: Harcourt Brace & Company, 1994), pp. 316–17.

It is common sense to assume that the cue ball's movement is the cause of the red billiard ball's movement after the former strikes the latter. It is common sense to assume that a room will begin warming up the moment the sun's rays enter its windows in the morning. After repeatedly watching an unmanned railroad crossing gate close, its lights begin to flash, and its bells ring minutes before the arrival of a train, it is common sense to assume that the approaching train somehow signals the crossing apparatus to begin its performance. Understanding cause and effect is a common sense, at least when the relationship in question is relatively straightforward.

Of course, there are many cause and effect relationships that far exceed the purview of common sense. No one would suggest that a person lacks common sense were she unable to describe the connection between increased carbon dioxide emissions in the United States and altered patterns of global precipitation. Many causal relationships escape the grasp of the most brilliant scientists, and certainly fall well beyond common sense understanding. That is because we do not directly confront these associations in our daily lives. Hence we have limited opportunities to apprehend them. There is no hard-and-fast rule that allows us to distinguish common sense from its lack. Neither is there a hard-and-fast rule that separates common sense from genius, the superior ability to discern or discover qualities or patterns that escape the perceptive and cognitive capacities of most other people. Nonetheless, when we say that someone lacks common sense, or has good common sense, we generally know what we mean.

Common sense is not innate. It develops over time, as a product of experience. For most, it requires relatively limited experience. Children begin to gauge distances, posit causation, and recognize faces after a few months of life. Figuring out that people act in relation to goals and intentions, that the sun warms up rooms, or that trains interact with unmanned crossings takes a little longer. Regardless of how elementary the issue, some experience is required. Common sense is not simply instinct doing its work. A lack of common sense reflects an inability to learn that which most of us learn with little if any conscious effort. To have common sense is to have learned the lessons that human beings are predisposed to learn. It is, in this respect, something we share with others, the product of common experiences gained through a common form of life. That is why Arendt insists that "common sense . . . [is] the political sense par excellence."[68]

***

[68] Arendt, "Understanding and Politics," p. 318.

David Hume observed that reason, understood as the intellectual capacity for logic and rational deliberation, is insufficient to the task of cultivating common sense. Common sense learning is experiential rather than conceptual or analytical. Speaking to the common sense understanding of correlation and causation, Hume writes:

> Were a man such as Adam created in the full vigor of understanding, without experience, he would never be able to infer motion in the second [billiard] ball from the motion and impulse of the first. It is not anything that reason sees in the cause which makes us *infer* the effect.... The mind can always *conceive* any effect to follow from any cause.... It follows, then, that all reasonings concerning cause and effect are founded on experience, and that all reasonings from experience are founded on the supposition that the course of nature will continue uniformly in the same. We conclude that like causes, in like circumstances, will produce like effects.... It is not, therefore, reason which is the guide of life, but custom. That alone determines the mind in all instances to suppose the future conformable to the past. However easy this step may seem, reason would never, to all eternity, be able to make it.[69]

Our common senses are those we have acquired through experiential learning, what Hume calls "custom." Reason may supplement our common sense. But only experience, in the sense of worldly practice, can map the brain in a way that fosters the development of the most fundamental perceptive and inferential abilities.

Hume maintains that the common sense ability to determine cause and effect is "the foundation of moral reasoning."[70] Common sense is indeed the most basic component of practical judgment, its *sine qua non*. One cannot be a good judge and lack common sense. To be at the lower end of the scale of its development is to be, colloquially speaking, dull or stupid. And if one is found wanting in this capacity, notwithstanding the experiences that normally would have fostered its development, there is little recourse. "Deficiency in judgment," Kant wrote, "is just what is ordinarily called stupidity, and for such a failing there is no remedy."[71] Becoming learned through study, Kant went on to say, does not compensate for the shortcoming. To be stupid, to lack common sense, is to be without the foundation upon which practical judgment is built. It means that one does not easily learn from experience. To lack common sense

---

[69] David Hume, "An Abstract of A Treatise of Human Understanding," in David Hume, *An Inquiry Concerning Human Understanding* (Indianapolis: Bobbs-Merrill, 1955), pp. 186–89.

[70] Hume, *An Inquiry Concerning Human Understanding*, p. 172.

[71] Immanuel Kant, *Critique of Pure Reason*, trans. N. Kemp Smith (London: MacMillan, 1985), p. 178.

is to be deficient in the knowledge and skills most human beings are neurologically predisposed to acquire. In such cases, no amount of formal
instruction will make it good. Arendt referred to the "Ariadne thread
of common sense."[72] When, for whatever reason, this thread is severed,
there is little hope that we will successfully learn to navigate our worldly
maze.

Practical wisdom is heightened common sense that spans not only the
perceptual and cognitive domains but the social field as well. Practical wisdom entails knowledge of human psychology. One might easily imagine
a loner – perhaps a hermit from an early age – exhibiting fine common
sense in her mundane perceptions and inferences. Divorced from human
affairs, however, she is unlikely to boast much in the way of practical wisdom. Having little experience of the breadth, depth, and multi-faceted
nature of ethico-political life, the hermit cannot become an astute judge
of its participants. Though experiencing cause and effect in the natural
world, she would lack its parallel understanding in the social world.

Isaiah Berlin well captures the nature of practical judgment and its
relation to common sense. He defines judgment as the "art of diagnosis
and prognosis" and, like Aristotle, understands it as a distinct faculty that
stands in contrast to theoretical knowledge.[73] Judgment bespeaks a capacity for "imaginative insight" that allows one to distinguish the "unique
flavours" of each situation – and to act or give advice accordingly. It is
an achievement of the "profounder students of human beings." Falling
along a spectrum that runs from "common sense" to "genius," practical
wisdom, Berlin maintains, is exhibited not so much by the "learned" as
by "ordinary persons endowed with understanding of life."[74] The student of (social) life whose understanding is particularly acute rises to the
status of a "political genius." This practically wise person, Berlin writes,
possesses "the gifts of ordinary men, but these in an almost supernatu-
ral degree."[75] In short, the practical judge builds upon a foundation of
common sense, acquiring diagnostic and prognostic psychological skills
through extensive experience in human affairs.

---

[72] Arendt, "Understanding and Politics," p. 311.
[73] Isaiah Berlin, *Concepts and Categories*, ed. Henry Hardy (New York: Viking Press, 1979),
   p. 116.
[74] Berlin, *The Sense of Reality: Studies in Ideas and their History*, ed. Henry Hardy (London:
   Chatto and Windus, 1996), p. 25. See also Ryan Patrick Hanley, "Political Science and
   Political Understanding: Isaiah Berlin on the Nature of Political Inquiry," *American Political Science Review* 98: (May 2004): 327–339.
[75] Berlin, *The Power of Ideas*, ed. Henry Hardy (Princeton: Princeton University Press, 2000),
   p. 187.

Berlin was an admirer of the eighteenth-century Neapolitan scholar, Giambattista Vico. Celebrating the wisdom of the ancients, particularly the Roman republicans, Vico insisted that prudence and rhetoric were of the greatest importance to life. What grounds prudence, Vico argues, is not abstract reason or scientific knowledge, but training in the "*sensus communis.*" A common faculty that combines the five senses, the *sensus communis* allows judgments to be made about its world.[76] Berlin, like Vico, insists that practical wisdom, like common sense, is available to all – given the right experiences and opportunities. Rhetoric supplies the images that abet its cultivation. (We will address this relationship further in Chapter 5.)

The experiences and opportunities required for the cultivation of practical wisdom is a shared, interactive life. "To try to be wise all on one's own," La Rochefoucauld counseled, "is sheer folly."[77] Rendering sound judgment entails putting oneself in the place of others, seeing things, as Arendt suggested, from their points of view. Developing this "enlarged mentality" is not simply an exercise in speculative rationality. Unless one has experience interacting with others, the effort to explore other points of view will generally result not in an expanded mentality but in the transference of one's own opinions, fears, and concerns. For example, most people say that they would rather die than face life in a wheelchair. The vast majority of physically disabled people, however, are quite happy (relative to the able-bodied population), and the suicide rate among them is low. Clearly, when trying to imagine life with paralysis, able-bodied people project their own fears, and consequently misrepresent the lives and orientations of those they seek to understand.[78] To escape this distortion, the "otherness" of others must not simply be imagined, but concretely confronted through dialogue and direct engagement.[79] Extensive experience interacting with physically disabled people would likely reduce projection and alter judgments accordingly. Isolated (cognitive or affective) speculation is insufficient. Worldly experience entailing direct engagement is indispensable.

Though grounded in common sense, practical wisdom has an elite flavor to it. Indeed, it is often described as an aristocratic virtue.

---

[76] See Hans-Georg Gadamer, *Truth and Method* (New York: Crossroad, 1985), p. 21.

[77] La Rochefoucauld, *Maxims*, p. 67; #231.

[78] Iris Marion Young, "Asymmetrical Reciprocity: On Moral Respect, Wonder, and Enlarged Thought" in *Judgment, Imagination, and Politics: Themes from Kant and Arendt*, ed. Ronald Beiner and Jennifer Nedelsky (New York: Rowman and Littlefield, 2001), p. 209.

[79] See Seyla Benhabib, *Situating the Self: Gender, Community and Postmodernism in Contemporary Ethics* (New York: Routledge, 1992), p. 168.

Aristotle insisted that *phronesis* is an achievement of the few, not the many, a virtue displayed by rulers rather than the masses. John Dryden echoed Aristotle's conviction, writing: "If by the people you understand the multitude, the *hoi polloi*, tis no matter what they think; they are sometimes in the right, sometimes in the wrong: their judgement is a mere lottery."[80] Even staunch democrats who advocate the proliferation of practical wisdom by way of direct, political engagement acknowledge that good judgment retains an aristocratic countenance. It arises from the capacity to make fine discriminations. These discriminations may be undermined in a democratic culture that fosters equality by occluding difference. Sheldon Wolin writes of Alexis de Tocqueville:

His aristocratic eye would make for attentiveness to the value of discriminations, subtleties, nuances, gradations, idiosyncrasies, in a word, to all manner of particularities. The aristocratic mode of perception would be a rich source of insight, supplying endless contrasts and colors in an increasingly monochromatic world. It would also be a basis for resistance, insisting that democracy submit to being understood by its Other, by principles that were not only predemocratic but antidemocratic. Aristocratic perception, when it was able to transcend nostalgia, encouraged a theoretical sensitivity to the special claims of differences, less as a matter of right or of empirical observation, than because of the potential resistance embodied in cultural differences now jeopardized by a world inclining toward sameness."[81]

For Wolin, the practical judge is aristocratic in the sense that she is habituated to the perception of difference. To the extent that democracy operates as a force of homogenization, rather than, say, a celebration of diversity and its fecundity, democratic life bears the potential to undermine the cultivation of good judgment.

Encomia of practical judgment easily translate into celebrations of elite leadership. Posited as an aristocratic virtue, prudence is often understood as a conservative force. It is portrayed as "a means to moralize power,"[82] as defensive of the status quo. Certainly prudence has often been so employed. Aristotle deemed practical wisdom an aristocratic virtue. It was available only to the few, and would forever elude the many. For Cicero, prudence was decidedly a conservative force, identified with restraint

---

[80] John Dryden, in his *Essay on the Dramatic Poetry of the Last Age*, in *The Oxford Dictionary of Quotations*, 3rd ed. (Oxford: Oxford University Press, 1979), p. 198.

[81] Sheldon S. Wolin, *Tocqueville Between Two Worlds: The Making of a Political and Theoretical Life* (Princeton: Princeton University Press, 2001), p. 158.

[82] Stephen Browne, "Edmund Burke's *Letter to the Sheriffs of Bristol* and the Texture of Prudence," (127–144) in *Prudence: Classical Virtue, Postmodern Practice*, ed. Robert Harriman (University Park, PA: Pennsylvania State University Press, 2003), p. 141.

rather than reform. When discerning the "direction things are taking," he writes, the role of the prudent man is to "hold them back or else be ready to meet them."[83] Though himself a New Man without a blue-blooded pedigree, Cicero consistently sided with the aristocratic and conservative *optimates* against the *populares* during his political career.[84] Edmund Burke argued vociferously that prudence entailed the maintenance of customary practices, and the hierarchies they enabled.[85] Likewise, Heidegger's attraction to Hitler and the Nazis has been directly linked to his embrace of *phronesis*.[86]

While a highly developed form of practical judgment is indeed an achievement of the few, as Berlin observes, its most basic form is available to the many. As an enhanced form of common sense coupled with rudimentary social-psychological insight, practical wisdom remains fully in the public domain. And anything that might replace practical judgment as a tool for navigating moral and political life is equally if not more prone to elitism. Certainly the exercise of pure reason, as defined by Kant for example, is largely unavailable to the masses. Comprehending its dictates is difficult enough for bookish philosophers. In turn, science is equally restricted to trained practitioners, those well versed in its methodology, conceptual foundations, and empirical manifestations. By their very nature, both the philosophic discourse of reason and the scholarly pursuit of science produce an elite group of experts and specialists. The effort to integrate the philosophic/humanistic and natural scientific specialties into a social science does not alleviate the problem. Those who decry the aristocratic nature of practical wisdom and suggest that rigorous social science should take its place often end up justifying the prerogatives and defending the rule of a professional elite.[87]

Notwithstanding his own aristocratic leanings, Aristotle maintained that the best judge of the merit of a political regime is not the ruler,

---

[83] Cicero, *The Republic and The Laws*, trans. Niall Rudd, Oxford: Oxford University Press, 1998, p. 49.

[84] Anthony Everitt, *Cicero: The Life and Times of Rome's Greatest Politician* (New York: Random House, 2003).

[85] See Daniel I. O'Neill, *The Burke-Wollstonecraft Debate: Savagery, Civilization, and Democracy* (University Park, PA: Penn State University Press, forthcoming 2007). Stephen Browne, "Edmund Burke's *Letter to the Sheriffs*," pp. 127–144.

[86] See Christopher Rickey, *Revolutionary Saints: Heidegger, National Socialism and Antinomian Politics* (University Park, PA: Pennsylvania State University Press, 2002) and Michael Gillespie, "Martin Heidegger's Aristotelian National Socialism," *Political Theory* 28:2 (April 2000): 140–166.

[87] Berlin, *The Sense of Reality*, p. 43.

but the citizen, just as the best judge of the fit of a pair of shoes is not the cobbler, but the person who sports the footwear. But how could Aristotle affirm the relative scarcity of practically wise people while, at the same time, lauding the widespread ability of average citizens to match if not exceed the skills of specialists in the assessment of worldly affairs? The answer is that the caliber of a judgment in any particular domain is directly proportional to the relevance of the judge's experience. The cobbler's expertise in fabrication is no match for the more direct experience of wearing shoes if the issue is not craftsmanship per se but the question of comfort and durability. The shoe-wearer lacks the precise technical knowledge demonstrated by the skilled craftsperson. But the shoe-wearer's ability to select the right shoes for her feet is not, for that reason, impeded. Indeed, precise, technical knowledge may actually cloud the holistic perception that informs good judgment.

John Coates updates this Aristotelian insight in *The Claims of Common Sense*. Coates argues that greater power derives from the relative vagueness of common sense assessments and evaluation than arises from the precise determinations of the technical expert. Technical precision and conceptual sophistication often result in terminology and ideas too cumbersome or precise to facilitate general understanding. Coates observes John Maynard Keynes's argument that the mathematization of economics may cause us to lose sight of "the complexities and interdependencies of the real world in a maze of pretentious and unhelpful symbols."[88] Likewise, the technical rigor of the specialist may cause us to lose sight of the complex interdependencies of human affairs that the person of practical wisdom always keeps well within view.

Citing G. E. Moore, Coates argues that our capacity for good judgment far exceeds our capacity to explain its components. Most of us would be very hard pressed to explain precisely how we make the distinction between correlation and causation, just as we could not explain how we assess distances, weights, and perspective, or recognize familiar faces. Yet this lack of conceptual knowledge in no way impedes our judgments. As Moore observed in his defense of common sense, "We are all, I think, in this strange position that we do *know* many things ... and yet we do not know how we *know* them."[89] The shoe-wearer's direct experience provides indubitable evidence of the fit of the shoes. She knows

---

[88] From John Maynard Keynes, "Theory of Prices." Quoted in John Coates. *The Claims of Common Sense: Moore, Wittgenstein, Keynes and the Social Sciences* (Cambridge: Cambridge University Press, 1996), p. 96.

[89] Quoted in Coates. *The Claims of Common Sense*, p. 47.

whether a particular pair are right for her feet or not, though she may be unable to describe the structural features of the shoes that account for this judgment. The cobbler, in contrast, knows the material components and compositional requirements of a good pair of shoes. But this technical knowledge, while crucial to the fabrication of footwear, does not get one very far in determining their fit on an actual pair of feet. Indeed, swayed by the power of his own expertise, the cobbler may take on the perspective of Procrustes.

It would come as no surprise to Berlin, or Coates, to learn that so-called political experts (such as academic political scientists, policy analysts in think tanks, and intelligence analysts in governmental service) are only slightly more accurate at predicting the occurrence of political phenomena than one would expect from wholesale guesswork.[90] Moreover, the technical pursuit of precision can produce gross misjudgments in practical affairs. Common sense will seldom lead one so far astray. As Aristotle observed: "It is a mark of the educated man and a proof of his culture that in every subject he looks for only so much precision as its nature permits."[91] Moral and political life is like water or fine sand. It is easy enough to weigh and assess in a loosely cupped hand. The more one tightens one's grip, however, the more it slips through the fingers. Likewise, technically precise terminology and sophisticated conceptual analysis, oftentimes, capture the substance of moral and political life less adequately than common sense judgment.

Albert North Whitehead wrote that "Science is rooted in . . . the whole apparatus of common sense thought. That is the *datum* from which it starts, and to which it must recur. . . . You may polish up common sense, you may contradict it in detail, you may surprise it. But ultimately your whole task is to satisfy it."[92] Pace Whitehead, the instrumental and mathematical extensions of our scientific discoveries often surprise and contradict common sense beyond any effort to satisfy it. Einstein's theory of relativity, which maintains that time slows down and mass increases as one approaches the speed of light, flies in the face of common sense. Humans have no lived experience of mass varying with velocity, or of time

---

[90] Philip Tetlock, "Theory-Driven Reasoning about Plausible Pasts and Probable Futures in World Politics," in *Heuristics and Biases: the Psychology of Intuitive Judgment,* ed. Thomas Gilovich, Dale Griffin, and Daniel Kahneman (Cambridge: Cambridge University Press, 2002), pp. 751–53. Philip E. Tetlock, *Expert Political Judgment: How Good Is It? How Can We Know?* (Princeton: Princeton University Press, 2005).

[91] Aristotle, *Ethics,* p. 28.

[92] Kenneth R. Hammond, *Human Judgment and Social Policy: Irreducible Uncertainty, Inevitable Error, Unavoidable Injustice* (New York: Oxford University Press, 1996), p. 53.

moving in any direction but forward at a relatively uniform speed. In turn, our common sense is restricted to three-dimensional space. Yet physicists work with many more dimensions in their efforts to understand the fundamental forces of the universe. Likewise, statistical knowledge and the laws of probability do not always satisfy common sense. On occasion, they seem downright counter-intuitive or paradoxical.

Such surprises and dissatisfactions should not prompt us to abandon common sense. After all, one of its key virtues is an appreciation of its own limitations. In any case, we rely on common sense to determine when, and to what extent, a more rigorous assessment employing analytical reason or science is warranted in any given situation. Absent common sense, we would neither gain the most basic understanding of cause and effect that is the foundation of science and reason nor be able to determine when the precise tools of scientific inquiry or rational analysis are appropriate for the job at hand. While science can teach us a great deal about the nature of practical judgment, and reason can aid us in its extension and consistent application, neither can substitute for a firm foundation of common sense.

Learning Good Judgment

That good judgment is the child of experience rather than formal education was recognized by Cicero, who observed "how little difference there is between the learned and the ignorant in judging."[93] Arendt cites Cicero's remark with approval, and seconds Kant's dictum that there is no remedy to be found in pedagogy for a dearth of good judgment.[94] Practical wisdom, like its common sense foundation, is a product of experiential knowledge. It arises neither from book learning nor ratiocination nor solitary introspection. Rather, it develops in the midst of life, as an outcome of reflective participation. Rousseau captured this notion when he insisted that a "true education consists less in precept than in practice."[95] Of course, grappling with precepts can be very beneficial, no less than familiarity with various forms of specialized knowledge. In such cases, however, it is the 'how' of learning much more than its 'what' that affects

[93] Quoted in Hannah Arendt, *Lectures on Kant's Political Philosophy*, ed. Ronald Beiner (Chicago: University of Chicago Press, 1982), p. 64. See also Hannah Arendt, *The Life of the Mind – Thinking* (New York: Harcourt Brace Jovanovich 1978), p. 215.
[94] Arendt, *The Life of the Mind*, p. 69.
[95] Rousseau, *Emile*, p. 42.

judgment. Precepts and principles prove to be most valuable to the practical judge not when they are read in a book, but when they are revealed in life. The proper educator, Rousseau insists, "ought to give no precepts at all: he ought to make them be discovered."[96]

Building on Rousseau, Benjamin Barber makes the strongest case for judgment as a product of direct experience, and in particular, direct, political experience. Barber argues that political judgment arises only in the

whirl of public activity.... Political judgment is defined by activity in common rather than by thinking alone. It is what politics produces and not what produces politics.... Private men, even when they are prudent private judges, will not be able to figure out what the public good is, for it depends on – indeed, it only exists through – the interaction of that public assembled and voting.... Political judgment is the multitude deliberating, the multitude in action.... [It depends] on continuous political engagement and experience.[97]

Barber overstates the case. He insists that reason in general and philosophy in particular must remain silent in the whirl of public activity that generates political judgment.[98] Yet practical wisdom entails the fertile combination of reflection and worldly experience.

Too be sure, regular involvement in the rough-and-tumble of life is the surest means to developing practical wisdom. A "hands-on" education is indispensable. But without the supplement of reflection, constant political activity would not foster practical wisdom. Rather, it would produce what Michael Oakeshott called the "crowded life," replete with a ceaseless flow of happenings. Such a life seduces "instant participation" but is lacking in both the memorable experiences and the meaningful choices that solicit and cultivate good judgment. Ignoring the reflective, deliberative side of practical judgment is as mistaken as neglect of its experiential foundation.

Some take the opposite tack of Barber, insisting that practical judgment can only be well exercised in the relative calm of solitude. That is, perhaps, the conviction behind Federalist 55, which states: "Had every

---

96 Jean-Jacques Rousseau, *Emile*, p. 52.
97 Benjamin Barber, *The Conquest of Politics: Liberal Philosophy in Democratic Times* (Princeton: Princeton University Press, 1988), pp. 199, 204, 210. See also Benjamin Barber, "Foundationalism and Democracy," in *Democracy and Difference: Contesting the Boundaries of the Political*, ed. Seyla Benhabib (Princeton: Princeton University Press, 1996), p. 354.
98 Barber, *The Conquest of Politics*, pp. 199–200. Barber also reifies political judgment, insisting that it stands isolated and wholly distinct from moral, legal, or aesthetic judgment, which he suggests are products of solitary individuals.

Athenian citizen been a Socrates, every Athenian assembly would still have been a mob." A "whirl" of public activity without pause for reflection will often produce a dearth of judgment, as is exhibited by mobs whipped into a frenzy by demagogues. After her investigation of totalitarian regimes, Arendt suggested that the opportunity for politics itself vanishes when the individual becomes dissolved in the collective and the opportunity for reflection evaporates in the heat of constant activity. We might conclude that good judgment is typically displayed in pauses from activity, assuming these pauses have been fertilized with the compost of well-digested experience. Good judgment develops in the wake of the habit of reflecting upon experience. It cannot be learned in the absence of experience or in the absence of sustained effort to absorb and integrate its lessons.

Public engagement is never a sufficient condition, only a necessary one for the development of practical wisdom. There is no contradiction in Aristotle's assertion that experience is the key to practical wisdom and his insistence that education remains the most essential task of a government intent on cultivating responsible citizens.[99] To be a good judge, one must be trained to reflect upon experience. Education can offer such training. While worldly experience rather than formal education is the *sine qua non* of judgment, there is a good deal to be gained from formal education. Oakeshott has written most eloquently on the acquisition of practical wisdom that occurs in such settings.

Teaching, Oakeshott maintains, entails a "twofold activity." First, there is the communication and transmission of information. Oakeshott labels this "instructing." In turn, there is the learning of judgment. Judgment is not the product of instruction. Rather, it is "imparted." Instructing and imparting are not wholly separate events. The imparting of judgment is a by-product of instruction, the side-effect of the manner in which information is transmitted and acquired. Judgment is impossible to teach in "a separate lesson," apart from substantive instruction that addresses the actual data of the moral and political world. Judgment, Oakeshott insists, can only be "imparted obliquely in the course of instruction."[100] The aptitude for judgment is gained by way of the student's active interpretation of the teacher's own performances of thinking and judging. The task for the student, with this in mind, is "to detect the individual intelligence

---

[99] See Martha Nussbaum, *Love's Knowledge: Essays on Philosophy and Literature* (New York: Oxford University Press, 1990), p. 102.
[100] Oakeshott, *The Voice of Liberal Learning*, p. 58.

which is at work in every utterance, even in those which convey impersonal information. . . . We may listen to what a man has to say, but unless
we overhear in it a mind at work and can detect the idiom of thought,
we have understood nothing. . . . Learning, then, is acquiring the ability
to feel and to think, and the pupil will never acquire these abilities unless
he has learned to listen for them and to recognize them in the conduct
and utterances of others."[101] Judgment, in other words, is experientially
absorbed rather than pedagogically transmitted.[102]

The experience of learning is more than the acquisition of information. It is the gaining of insight into the unscripted lessons that teachers
offer by way of their embodied pedagogy. That is why one can learn judgment by reading men and women but not by reading books. Oakeshott
writes that judgment "is implanted unobtrusively in the manner in which
information is conveyed, in a tone of voice, in the gesture which accompanies instruction, in asides and oblique utterances, and by example."[103]
The transmission of raw information does not teach one how to think,
and certainly not how to judge. Information, like the capacity for reason
described by Hume, proves to be quite useless in the absence of experientially generated understanding. Pedagogically speaking, we learn to
judge by discerning the assessments, evaluations, and choices others make
about the information they convey.

The Benefits of Bad Experience

Certain capacities and skills are products of tranquility. It is hard to imagine developing much mathematical intelligence, for instance, in the midst
of great hubbub and constant diversion. Practical wisdom is different.
Though entailing reflection, it arises only from involvement in the complex and taxing environment of social life. Often it is generated from the
adversity this involvement begets. The wisdom that Sophocles claimed for
the aged was theirs not as a product of years passively accumulated. It was
the result of existential blows actively borne.[104] Sophocles' contemporary,
albeit elder, dramatist, Aeschylus, put the point succinctly in his *Agamem-
non*: "Wisdom comes only through suffering." Pain helps us learn not to

---

[101] Oakeshott, *The Voice of Liberal Learning*, p. 59.
[102] Oakeshott, *The Voice of Liberal Learning*, pp. 53–54.
[103] Oakeshott, *The Voice of Liberal Learning*, p. 60.
[104] Sophocles, *Antigone* (1348–52) in *Sophocles I* (Chicago: University of Chicago Press, 1954), p. 204.

make the same mistake twice. It is one of the most effective inducements
to take the education of experience seriously.

Goethe observed that "A talent is formed in stillness, a character in the
world's torrent."[105] Character develops amidst the skirmishes of life. Practical wisdom, as Aristotle insists, reflects strength of character; it bespeaks
one's capacity to meet adversity squarely and rise above it.[106] The practical judge learns her craft in the wake of frays and mishaps. She develops
character by personally paying for the costly lessons of experience. The
word *experience* derives from the Latin *perire,* to make a trial of. Experience
refers to that which is learned from personal trials. The events that chiefly
edify the practical judge are her trials and tribulations.

Worldly life teaches us that the unforeseen is to be expected. That
is why we run practice drills to test programs and systems. In theory,
everything should come off without a hitch, according to plan. In practice,
the world proves to be more complex than any philosophy. Knowing that
some things will go wrong, notwithstanding good planning, is one of the
most valuable lessons experience has to offer. For the practical judge, this
insight is painfully obvious.

Those who avoid risk, Machiavelli knew, were not rich in experience
and could not, therefore, become good judges. Risk-avoidance curtails
the opportunity for valuable experience. Risk-avoiders, having ventured
little, prove all too successful at avoiding failure. And failure is of great
educational value. "Learning begins not in ignorance," Oakeshott writes,
"but in error."[107] Bad experiences generally outperform good experiences as educators. Or, perhaps better said, whether bad or good,
experience teaches best when we fail to anticipate its lesson. "Every experience worthy of the name runs counter to our expectation," Gadamer
observes.[108]

The best way to improve a person's judgment is to provide her with
opportunities to make mistakes and be surprised. Studies in contemporary decision science generally focus on one-time "discrete" decisions
made by individuals. There are no feedback loops. Yet the development
of judgment is a continuous, adaptive phenomenon. Studies that focus on
discrete incidents fail to account for the fact that good judgment arises, in
large part, from having to cope with and reflect upon the effects of prior

[105] Quoted in Robert A. Fitton, *Leadership.* (Boulder: Westview Press, 1997), p. 5.
[106] "He among us who best knows how to bear the goods and the ills of this life," Rousseau
offered, "is to my taste the best raised." Rousseau, *Emile,* p. 42.
[107] Oakeshott, *The Voice of Liberal Learning,* p. 57.
[108] Gadamer, *Truth and Method,* p. 319.

(bad) judgments.[109] "No people are more often wrong than those who cannot bear to be," La Rochefoucauld wrote.[110] Likewise, the worst judge is generally unwilling to admit her mistakes, and hence fails to learn from them.

Good judges are, by definition, those who make more good judgments than bad ones. The Israeli diplomat and writer Abba Eban once said that "People and nations behave wisely – once they have exhausted all other alternatives." By these standards, we are all, potentially, good judges – that is, if we live long enough. But experience can be a very unforgiving teacher. It provides us the opportunity to better navigate our world by demonstrating our mistakes and allowing for their correction. However, egregious misjudgments will often severely curtail opportunities for new journeys and the improvement of judgment such journeys offer. The young captain who sinks his first ship seldom makes admiral. Practical wisdom, Sophocles says, is the prize of a full life. But it comes to Creon only after his misjudgments leave him ruling over a stack of corpses. Sophocles did not count Creon a *phronimos*. The King of Thebes learned from his misjudgments, but much too late in the game to matter much. The greater part of wisdom is being wise in time. Good judgment is the achievement of quick learners.

People may not learn from experience for any number of reasons. Perhaps they implement choices in ways that preclude the reception of reliable feedback, thus foregoing the opportunity to learn from mistakes. Or, from pigheadedness or some other intellectual or moral vice, they may not learn from their mistakes regardless of available feedback. Alternatively, they may not have a sufficient foundation in knowledge, skill, or common sense to make effective use of experience. In such cases, they fail to discern what their experience is really an experience of. In *Pudd'nhead Wilson*, Mark Twain observes that a cat is smart enough to learn from the experience of sitting on a hot stove never to do so again. But, Twain notes, the once-burned cat will never sit down on a cold stove either. We expect more of humans. Our understanding of cause and effect needs to be sufficiently fine-grained that we gain from experience the right lessons – neither less nor more than warranted. Empirical studies validate these claims. Experience is often squandered or misused. Some lessons never get learned. And to make matters worse, extensive

---

[109] Robin Hogarth, "Beyond discrete biases: Functional and dysfunctiional aspects of judgmental heuristics," in *Judgment and decision making*, pp. 680–704.
[110] La Rochefoucauld, *Maxims*, p. 86; #386.

experience, though ill-absorbed, often makes us overconfident in our ability to judge.[111]

How might experience be made most fruitful? Gadamer writes that "The experienced person proves to be ... someone who is radically undogmatic; who, because of the many experiences he has had and the knowledge he has drawn from them is particularly well equipped to have new experiences and to learn from them."[112] If experience is the fountainhead of good judgment, it is so only on condition that students remain open to its teaching.[113] A politician may boast twenty years of experience. But if learning stopped after the first anniversary of gaining office, she really has but one year of experience – twenty times over. Experience can be a lifelong teacher, but only to the right sort of student. Only some aging dogs will learn new tricks.

Many are disposed to believe – perhaps academics more so than others – that we can (and should) *think* our way into new ways of doing. But the far more common phenomenon is that we *do* our way into new ways of thinking. Marx was right: life produces consciousness more so than consciousness produces life. While Aristotle may have objected to the relationship, it is fair to say that Marx stands upon the Peripatetic's shoulders in this regard. Aristotle insisted that one becomes just, or charitable, or practically wise, by acting justly, or charitably, or wisely over an extended period. In turn, we come to think just, charitable, or wise thoughts in the wake of such practice.

Aristotle was harking back to the mimeticism of an oral culture, where one learned less by way of rational analysis and abstract thinking than by the imitation of forebears and past masters.[114] Embodied, experiential learning was held to be of utmost importance. The development of alphabetic literacy stimulated conceptual sophistication and heightened opportunities for analytical rationality. But this technological development did not undo millions of years of genetic coding. The manner in which human brains get mapped has not changed much over the last 10,000 years, alphabetic knowledge notwithstanding. Literacy gives us a skewed sense of how humans learn best.

[111] See Berndt Brehmer, "In a word: Not from experience," in *Judgment and decision making*, pp. 705–719.

[112] Gadamer, *Truth and Method*, p. 319.

[113] Empirical evidence for openness to experience as a predictor of wisdom is discussed in Mihaly Csikszentmihalyi and Jeanne Nakamura, "The Role of Emotions in the Development of Wisdom," in *A Handbook of Wisdom: Psychological Perspectives*, ed. Robert Sternberg and Jennifer Jordan (Cambridge: Cambridge University Press, 2005), p. 232.

[114] See David Abram, *The Spell of the Sensuous: Perception and Language in a More-Than-Human World* (New York: Pantheon Books, 1996), p. 109.

Gilbert Ryle observes that any event can be described thinly (the man's eyelid closed rapidly), or thickly (the man winked conspiratorily). In the latter case, the thickness of description supplies an event with a particular meaning. Thick description does not simply add more details. It supplies morally salient facts (about intentions or purposes) and as such allows us to place particular actions within broader contexts that bear ethical charges.[115] Building on Ryle's distinction, Michael Walzer has objected to the notion of morality as "a (thin) set of universal principles adapted (thickly) to these or those historical circumstances." He argues that moral ways of being do not begin with a "common idea or principle or set of ideas and principles, which [people of different cultures] then work up in many different ways." Rather, "morality is thick from the beginning, culturally integrated, fully resonant, and it reveals itself thinly only on special occasions, when moral language is turned to specific purposes."[116] What Walzer says of morality can be said, perforce, of practical wisdom. It arises not from precepts but from the thickness of concrete experience. Moral discourse may indeed produce precepts. But these "thin" principles are not foundational.[117] They are the effect rather the cause of practical judgment, the upshot of embodied wisdom, not its source.

Merleau-Ponty said that matter was "pregnant" with its form. He meant to suggest that we perceive and know the world only within the field of concrete events that generate perception and knowledge.[118] Likewise, good judgment is pregnant with its experiential form, the horizon of concrete events that stimulate its development. If rules and principles, maxims and dictums prove to be essentially ambiguous or contradictory, it is because practical wisdom arises from contextually specific experiences. This thick experience, not its subsequent distillation into a thin set of rationalized precepts, must be retrieved in order to judge well, and anew, in any particular circumstance.

The exercise of practical judgment is context-specific and restricted in scope, unlike a theory or principle that is valid across space and time. A crucial feature of practical judgment, then, is its self-conscious finitude. Gadamer has addressed the ramifications of this self-limitation.

---

[115] See Peter Levine, *Living without Philosophy: On Narrative, Rhetoric, and Morality* (Albany: State University of New York Press, 1998), pp. 31–32.

[116] Michael Walzer, *Thick and Thin: Moral Argument at Home and Abroad* (Notre Dame: University of Notre Dame Press, 1994), p. 4.

[117] Walzer, *Thick and Thin*, p. 18.

[118] Maurice Merleau-Ponty, "The Primacy of Perception and its Philosophical Consequences," in *The Essential Writings of Merleau-Ponty*, ed. Alden Fisher (New York: Harcourt, Brace and World, Inc., 1969), p. 47.

Experience, he observes, inevitably contradicts expectation. It is psychological if not physically painful. This disagreeable feature of experience is not grounds for pessimism or cynicism. It simply underlines the temporally and spatially bound nature of the human condition. Grasping this reality firmly, Gadamer suggests, constitutes wisdom. Aeschylus captured the "metaphysical significance" of the "inner historicality of experience" with his notion of "learning through suffering" (*pathei mathos*). Aeschylus, Gadamer writes,

... does not mean only that we become wise through suffering and that a more correct understanding of things must first be acquired through the disappointment of being deceived and then undeceived. Understood in this way, the formula is probably as old as human experience itself. But Aeschylus means more than this. He refers to the reason why this is so. What a man has to learn through suffering is not this or that particular thing, but the knowledge of the limitations of humanity, of the absoluteness of the barrier that separates him from the divine. It is ultimately a religious insight – that kind of insight which gave birth to Greek tragedy. Thus experience is experience of human finitude. The truly experienced man is one who is aware of this, who knows that he is master neither of time nor the future. The experienced man knows the limitedness of all prediction and the uncertainty of all plans.... Real experience is that in which man becomes aware of his finiteness. In it are discovered the limits of the power and the self-knowledge of his planning reason.[119]

Whereas "planning reason" is often thought to be the whole of judgment, Gadamer insists that it is not even the better half. Experience worthy of its name generates an understanding that reason is but one tool in the workshop of wisdom – a tool generally overrated and frequently mishandled.

Practical wisdom is embodied learning mindful of its own limits. But it is not, for that reason, prone to resignation or fatalism. The practical judge is very much aware of the indispensability of action. The tragic and heroic nature of life, as the ancient Greeks knew, arises from the need to act notwithstanding severe limitations in knowledge. It is, therefore, insufficient to say that the experienced and practically wise person is she who recognizes human finitude. Practical wisdom is not yet evident in the enervated Hamlet who finds his resolution "sicklied o'er by the pale cast of thought." Practically wise people are not mopers. They get things done. To seek more than a "relative" validity for one's convictions, Isaiah Berlin writes, is perhaps a "deep and incurable metaphysical need." But to allow this necessarily unfulfilled need to thwart all practice, he insists, is

[119] Gadamer, *Truth and Method*, pp. 319–20.

"a symptom of an equally deep, and more dangerous, moral and political immaturity."[120] Practical wisdom, if it means anything, signifies moral and political maturity.

Nietzsche acknowledged the appropriateness of the skeptic's statement "I have no idea how I am *acting!* I have no idea how I *ought to act!*" Yet, he insists, we cannot stop there. "You are right," Nietzsche responds, "but be sure of this: *you will be acted upon!* at every moment!"[121] Even those who refuse to "do" anything – and there is always a glut of reasons to be found for inaction – are nonetheless always being "done." Experience teaches us that much.

Nietzsche was an ardent skeptic who valorized doubt.[122] At the same time, he knew that life demands action and that action demands the end of rumination. To be healthy, strong, and fruitful, one must know when and how to place bounds on the power of the unknown. Nietzsche writes:

Cheerfulness, the good conscience, the joyful deed, confidence in the future – all of them depend, in the case of the individual as of a nation, on the existence of a line dividing the bright and discernible from the unilluminable and dark; on one's being just as able to forget at the right time as to remember at the right time; on the possession of a powerful instinct for sensing when it is necessary to feel historically and when unhistorically. This, precisely, is the proposition the reader is invited to meditate upon: *the unhistorical and the historical are necessary in equal measure for the health of an individual, of a people and of a culture.*[123]

Gadamer speaks of the wisdom that arises from a sense of "inner historicality." To ensure that this wisdom does not become an excuse for inaction requires a good measure of "the unhistorical." What Nietzsche says here about time-consciousness applies equally to other aspects of finitude. The practically wise person is aware of profound epistemological limitations, and equally in touch with the need to choose and act in spite of them. Were judgment to leave its practitioner enervated in the face of uncertainty, it would have no role to play in the world. It would not be, in any meaningful sense, practical.

Judgment is one thing, action another. Yet the opportunity to improve judgment inheres in learning from actions taken on the basis of prior

[120] Isaiah Berlin, *Four Essays on Liberty* (Oxford: Oxford University Press, 1969), p. 172.

[121] Friedrich Nietzsche *Daybreak: Thoughts on the Prejudices of Morality*, trans. R. J. Hollingdale (Cambridge: Cambridge University Press, 1982), pp. 76–77.

[122] Nietzsche, *The Anti-Christ*, trans. R. J. Hollingdale (New York: Penguin, 1968), pp. 166, 172.

[123] Nietzsche, "On the Uses and Disadvantages of History for Life," in *Untimely Meditations*, trans. R. J. Hollingdale (Cambridge: Cambridge University Press, 1983), p. 63.

assessments and evaluations. The fact that our misdirected actions often bring hardships does not mitigate the value of embodied knowledge. Rather, it suggests that the only wholly bad experiences are those that teach no lessons.

Bootstrapping and the Brain

The good judge is an attentive student of life. Her brain provides the best evidence. The neural circuitry of the brain, and particularly the circuitry of the cerebral cortex, chart an individual's interactions with the world. These brain maps are constantly being revised in light of (integrated) experience. The remappings, in turn, significantly affect the manner in which the individual undergoes future experiences. It is a circular process, but not a vicious one. Schwartz and Begley write:

> The experiences of our lives leave footprints in the sands of our brain like Friday's on Robinson Crusoe's island: physically real but impermanent, subject to vanishing with the next tide or to being overwritten by the next walk along the shore. Our habits, skills, and knowledge are expressions of something physical [in the brain's wiring] . . . And because that physical foundation can change, so, too, we can acquire new habits, new skills, new knowledge. . . . [T]he experiences we undergo, the choices we make, and the acts we undertake inscribe a diary on the living matter of our cortex. . . . It is the brain's astonishing power to learn and unlearn, to adapt and change, to carry with it the inscriptions of our experiences, that allows us to throw off the shackles of biological materialism, for it is the life we lead that creates the brain we have. Our new understanding of the power of mind to shape brain can advance not only our knowledge, but also our wisdom.[124]

Habits and skills, including those that figure prominently in practical judgment, are the behavioral expressions of neural remappings. They represent what cognitive scientist Francisco Varela calls "the bootstrapping effect." We lift ourselves up by way of judgments and actions that restructure neural circuits. These restructurings, in turn, regulate our future judgments and actions. Understanding and exploiting the vast possibilities and significant limitations to this bootstrapping effort, in ourselves and others, is the better part of practical wisdom.

Most everything that has been said regarding brain science in this chapter was foreshadowed by Aristotle's habit theory of virtue. One learns to be courageous, to embody the virtue of courage, Aristotle insists, by performing courageous acts. Likewise other virtues (and vices). "Our

---

[124] Schwartz, *The Mind and the Brain*, pp. 164, 373.

actions," he writes, "determine our dispositions."[125] The hand teaches the heart. These nuggets of wisdom have long been endorsed by experimental psychologists, and now have the backing of neuroscientists charting the changes in brain circuitry that accompany new practices.

The remapping of the brain in the wake of experience, though most prominent in youth, continues throughout life. These altered circuits channel thought and behavior. It is important to remember, however, that much of our neural atlas was sketched with the permanent ink of ancestral experience. Our genetic inheritance has congealed in the form of inherited brain circuits or strong propensities for their formation. It is this embedded experience, by and large shared species-wide, that largely determines what lessons we are predisposed to learn. Predispositions and dispositions are, respectively, products of ancestral and personal experience. The former almost always and the latter quite frequently operate below the threshold of awareness. In exploring this dark territory, we discover that the faculty of judgment often functions best when we exploit knowledge and skills that lie beyond our conscious reach.

[125] Aristotle, *Ethics*, pp. 55, 57.

3

The Power of the Unconscious

It is a profoundly erroneous truism, repeated by all copybooks and by eminent people when they are making speeches, that we should cultivate the habit of thinking of what we are doing. The precise opposite is the case. Civilization advances by extending the number of important operations which we can perform without thinking about them. Operations of thought are like cavalry charges in battle – they are strictly limited in number, they require fresh horses, and must only be made at decisive moments.

Alfred North Whitehead[1]

Attempts to give singular priority to the highest and conceptually most sophisticated brain nodules in thinking and judgment may encourage those invested in these theories to underestimate the importance of body image, unconscious motor memory, and thought-imbued affect.... Thinking and judgment are already well under way before they enter the picture as conscious processes.

William Connolly[2]

It seems obvious that the more deliberate, well analyzed, and thoroughly examined practical judgments are, the better. Most scholars of decision-making operate on the assumption that the systematic application of reason will result in more "favorable consequences."[3] Who, after all, would

---

[1] A. N. Whitehead, *Introduction to Mathematics* (London: Williams and Norgate, 1911), p. 61.
[2] William E. Connolly, *Neuropolitics: Thinking, Culture, Speed* (Minneapolis: University of Minnesota Press, 2002), pp. 10, 28.
[3] John Mullen and Byron Roth, *Decision-Making: Its Logic and Practice* (Savage, MD: Rowman and Littlefield, 1991), p. 6.

suggest that judgments would be better made in a rash, thoughtless, or reactive manner? The development of good judgment, one presumes, is a matter of learning how carefully to weigh evidence, rationally reflect upon principles and probabilities, and meticulously assess context and contingencies to arrive at a well-considered account of the current situation and a suitable course of action.

Yet this tidy portrait of the human judge is misleading. Notwithstanding much in the way of rumination and cogitation that goes into the effort, practical wisdom is intrinsically grounded in unconscious capacities and is, for that reason, more than a stone's throw away from a wholly deliberate, systematic, and analytical affair. This is not simply an unavoidable feature of moral and political judgment. In many, if not most, circumstances, it is a good thing. Any effort to expunge the role of what are commonly called our intuitive capacities is bound to be counterproductive, eliciting poorer not better judgments.

Perhaps the best way to set forth this thesis, before directing the reader's attention to suggestive evidence from the field of cognitive neuroscience, is by way of analogy. Some suggest that decision-making in the realm of morality and politics is akin to solving an algebraic equation. There is at least one unknown, usually the question of what is to be done. And there are, hopefully, enough known values that the unknown variable might be discovered inferentially. To arrive at the correct value for our unknown, 'x,' the decision-maker systematically examines the options available, assesses costs and benefits of various courses of action, and examines the applicability and weight of particular principles and obligations. Often the answer will be context-specific and cannot be precise. Given the ambiguities intrinsic to the moral and political world, it might be possible only to say that in circumstances approximating 'y,' one should do something like 'x.' The decision-maker arrives at such a judgment (the estimated value of 'x'), based on extensive analysis that sets forth the best solution available given the uncertainties at hand.

In fact, practical judgment is far removed from the deliberative, cognitive exercise in analytical assessment just described. Indeed, it more closely resembles the activity of typing out the words on this page. When we type, particularly if we touch-type, our concentration is not upon the work of our hands. Words, phrases, and whole sentences appear without conscious effort. It is as if our fingers were skilled laborers who listen attentively to what is going on inside our heads and then translate this conversation into script before our eyes. They are independent artisans, requiring little if any instruction or oversight. Free from having to supervise these digital workers, the mind is available for the higher-level activity of thinking, deliberating, and wordsmithing. We remain largely if not wholly unconscious of the process of typing, at least as long as it proceeds unproblematically. An error may bring the unconscious effort to a halt, and require a deliberate correction. But, quickly enough, we are back to the unreflective activity of letting our fingers effortlessly put our thoughts into black and white.

The moment typing becomes deliberate – as soon as we actually think about what we are doing – it suffers both in quality and quantity, increasing in errors and decreasing in words typed per minute. Typists' fingers select appropriate keys in 200–300 milliseconds or less. A conscious effort to select a key takes about twice as long, 500 milliseconds or more. The skilled typist (who types 120 words a minute) will go through all five of the movements required to type the word "quick" in the same time it would take him to carry out one conscious motion. Only the very poor typist, the novice, actually thinks about what he is doing. Typing is at its best when it is unanalyzed, unexamined, and largely unconscious in its execution. Can the same be said of judgment?

Philosopher Hubert Dreyfus and his brother Stuart believe so. They argue that only novices, those who demonstrate a minimal competence, act rationally and consciously in the execution of a skill, art, or trade. People who become "proficient" develop and utilize unconscious, intuitive capacities. And those who reach the status of the expert act "arationally," operating from intuition alone. These developmental stages also apply to the practical judge.

Building on the work of Martin Heidegger, Dreyfus and Dreyfus observe that much of our worldly life is given over to skillful, spontaneous coping. Most of our speech and action demonstrates an unconscious, intuitive "know-how" rather than a conscious, deliberative "knowing-that." In ethics, no less than in other realms of life, know-how supersedes knowing-that in significance. The Dreyfuses write: "We should try to impress on ourselves what a huge amount of our lives – working, getting around, talking, eating, driving, and responding to the needs of others – manifest know-how, and what a small part is spent in the deliberate, effortful, subject/object mode of activity which requires knowing-that."[4]

---

4 Hubert Dreyfus and Stuart Dreyfus, "What is morality: A phenomenological account of the development of ethical expertise," in *Universalism vs. Communitarianism: Contemporary Debates in Ethics,* ed. David Rasmussen (Cambridge: MIT Press, 1990), p. 244. See also

Having been corrupted by "intellectualism," most ethicists, including the otherwise insightful Aristotle, deny this reality and portray moral life chiefly as a display of knowing-that.[5] The Dreyfus brothers argue that the onus is on intellectualists to demonstrate that "the development of ethical expertise should follow a different course than the development of expertise in other domains."[6]

I want to support the approach taken by the Dreyfuses. But I get off the bus before it reaches their destination. The prevalence of know-how over knowing-that in our worldly life is patent. And their description of know-how applies well enough to most skills, trades, and arts, such as typing, athletics, and chess (the latter being one of their favorite top-ics and past-times). But in these skills, trades, and arts, the rules of the game are well-established, the goals are clear, the relevant actors are pre-determined, and variables remain relatively few. Moral and political life is different: the rules of the game are *not* well-established, goals are *not* clear, relevant actors are *not* pre-determined, and contingencies are *not* insignificant in number or import. For these reasons, I would argue, there are no "experts" to be found in practical morality, at least not in the same sense that there are acknowledged experts in the fields of chess or typing. The most we can aspire to in our moral and political life is *proficiency* of judgment, and this proficiency is gained, in part, by reflective, delibera-tive thought.

In many ways, this accords with our common understanding of practi-cal judgment. We would be stretching its meaning too far to suggest that it could be exercised in the complete absence of conscious effort. Not every action is the product of judgment. We might scream when suddenly frightened, for example, rather than silently flinching. Such an automatic response cannot be said to be grounded in judgment. To respond to the world on the basis of a largely involuntary physical reaction, or even on the basis of an unconscious bias, is not to judge. Judgment always entails some reflection and deliberation. But the role of the unconscious is much more at play in our moral and political judgments than is generally assumed.

Hubert Dreyfus and Stuart Dreyfus, "What is Moral Maturity: Towards a Phenomenology of Ethical Expertise," in *Revisioning Philosophy*, ed. James Ogilvy (Albany: State University of New York Press, 1992), pp. 111–131; and Hubert L. Dreyfus and Stuart E. Dreyfus (with Tom Athanasiou) *Mind over Machine: The Power of Human Intuition and Expertise in the Era of the Computer* (New York: The Free Press, 1988), p. 36.

5 Dreyfus, "What is Morality," p. 246.
6 Dreyfus, "What is Morality," p. 256.

Most contemporary scholarship on judgment concerns itself with how we might counteract biases that intrude on rational decision-making.[7] By means of rigorous training in (social) statistics and probability theory, this effort is designed to improve our judgment by strengthening our reason. There is much to be gained from this endeavor, for intuitive biases are many and their influence in decision-making is often pernicious. An education in reason is all for the good. The problem is that this education is generally portrayed as a means of *replacing* intuition with conscious, rational thought. Any such effort will prove counterproductive. The alternative, however, is not simply to give freer range to intuitions. The task is to educate them.

Most, if not all, cognitive skills, including judgment, dynamically mesh automatic, unconscious processes with reflective, conscious ones. The interaction constitutes the phenomenon of the human mind at work. If we are to become more proficient moral and political judges, we must acknowledge and cultivate rather than deny or deprecate the role of the unconscious in this interplay. The idea of explicitly cultivating a part of ourselves that we do not cognitively control, or even well comprehend, may seem strange, and perhaps dangerous. But it is a common feature of our efforts to achieve excellence in many other human endeavors. Research in cognitive neuroscience suggests that it is equally applicable to moral and political judgment.

Perceptual Skills and Implicit Memory

Unless we are capable of accurately perceiving our world, good judgments cannot arise. No doubt we can make a deliberate effort to cultivate fine perception, trying to be more attentive to the intricate features of human character and the complex interdependencies of opportunities, obligations, and constraints that structure the moral and political world. But most of our perceptions are not intentionally sought or gained. They arrive unannounced. We can deliberately choose to close our eyes and cover our ears. But once these conduits to the world are opened, what they take in and what they fail to take in is not much under conscious control.

Neuroscientists claim that our eyes absorb and pass on to the brain over 10 million signals each second. The other four senses also contribute

---

[7] See, for example, D. Kahneman, P. Slovic and A. Tversky, eds. *Judgment under Uncertainty: Heuristics and Biases* (Cambridge: Cambridge University Press, 1982; and Scott Plous, *The Psychology of Judgment and Decision Making* (Philadelphia: Temple University Press, 1993).

extensively. Our conscious mind, in contrast, can only process about 40 pieces of information each second. That is a small share of what is made available to us. Indeed, it is estimated that our sense organs collect between 200,000 and 1 million bits of information for every bit of information that enters our awareness.[8] Conscious perception represents only the smallest fraction of what we absorb from our worldly encounters. It is the tip of an iceberg.

Perceptions are next to useless unless they can be stored and retrieved. Memory, like perception, is a crucial skill without which judgment could not develop or be well-exercised. And memory, like perception, is not fully, or even primarily, within our conscious control.[9] We remember much more than we can ever recall.

Consider experiments that inform a field of cognitive psychology known as "implicit learning" or "implicit cognition."[10] Faced with a computer screen divided into four quadrants, participants of one study were asked to press one of four buttons corresponding to the quadrant upon which a target character, hidden among other characters, appeared in an apparently random fashion. The target character's actual distribution among the quadrants, unbeknownst to participants, was determined by a very complex algorithm. Participants became increasingly adept – that is to say, faster and more consistent – at pressing the correct buttons as the study proceeded. Yet they remained wholly unaware of the algorithm

---

[8] Timothy Wilson, *Strangers to Ourselves: Discovering the Adaptive Unconscious* (Cambridge: Belknap Press, 2002), p. 24. Manfred Zimmerman, "The Nervous System in the Context of Information Theory," in *Human Physiology*, ed. R. F. Schmidt and G. Thews. 2nd ed. (Berlin: Springler-Verlag, 1989), pp. 166–73. Ap Dijksterhuis, Henk Aarts, and Pamela Smith, "The Power of the Subliminal: On Subliminal Persuasion and other Potential Applications, in *The New Unconscious*, ed. Ran Hassin, James Uleman, and John Bargh (Oxford: Oxford University Press, 2005), p. 82.

[9] Jeffrey P. Toth, "Nonconscious Forms of Human Memory," (pp. 245–261) in *The Oxford Handbook of Memory*, ed. Endel Tulving and Fergus Craik (Oxford: Oxford University Press, 2000), p. 252. See also K. Koh and D. E. Meyer, "Function learning: Induction of continuous stimulus-response relations, *Journal of Experimental Psychology: Learning, Memory, and Cognition*, 17 (1991):811–836; P. Lewicki, M. Czyzewska and H. Hoffman, "Unconscious acquisition of complex procedural knowledge," *Journal of Experimental Psychology: Learning, Memory, and Cognition*, 13 (1987): 523–530.

[10] The term "implicit learning" was coined by Arthur Reber (Arthur Reber, "Implicit learning of artificial grammars," *Journal of Verbal Learning and Verbal Behavior* 6 (1967): 317–327. For a general review of the field, see Arthur Reber, *Implicit Learning and Tacit Knowledge: An Essay on the Cognitive Unconscious* (New York: Oxford University Press, 1993); Michael Stadler and Peter Frensch, eds. *Handbook of Implicit Learning* (Thousand Oaks: Sage Publications, 1998); and Geoffrey Underwood, ed. *Implicit Cognition* (Oxford: Oxford University Press, 1996).

that determined where the target character would appear. When the algorithm was changed (without notice), the participants' performance deteriorated.

What was happening? Without knowing it, the participants were acting in anticipation of the pattern of the target character's appearance. They had unconsciously perceived, stored, and retrieved for use – that is to say, learned – the complex algorithm that was determining the placement sequence on the computer screen. Yet they had no awareness of this knowledge. Participants, all college students, were even offered a cash reward ($100) to identify any systematic feature of the sequencing. Despite hours of efforts, none could identify a pattern.[11]

Studies exposing subjects to an apparently random series of letters that are actually generated by a complex algorithm demonstrate similar results. In short order, subjects prove able to discriminate between "legal" and "non-legal" strings of letters. Yet they remain unable to identify the criteria for their judgments. Reaction times to decisions decrease as the exercise proceeds, until the underlying algorithm is changed without notice. At that point, for no apparent reason from the subjects' point of view, their ability to make quick, accurate judgments deteriorates significantly.

Implicit cognition is demonstrated when traces of past experience affect behavior, yet the influential earlier experience remains largely unavailable to self-report or introspection.[12] In other words, proficiency grounded in unintentionally acquired knowledge develops without (or well in advance of) the ability to articulate or even detect useful patterns of information. There is ample evidence that distinct neural structures (particular areas of the brain) are devoted to or feature prominently in implicit cognition.[13] For example, conscious, short-term memory, also known as "explicit" or "declarative" memory, while stored in related cortical regions is wholly mediated by the hippocampus. If the hippocampus is damaged, a perfectly intelligent person may not remember what happened a day, hour, or few minutes earlier. Implicit memory, also known as "procedural" memory, is mediated by other brain regions, including the amygdala (an almond-shaped mass located in the medial temporal lobes, in front of the hippocampus).[14] Implicit

[11] Pawel Lewicki, Thomas Hill, and Maria Czyzewska, "Nonconscious acquisition of information," *American Psychologist* 47 (1992): 796–801. Wilson, *Strangers to Ourselves*, p. 26.
[12] Anthony Greenwald and Mahzarin Banaji, "Implicit Social Cognition: Attitudes, Self-Esteem, and Stereotypes," *Psychological Review* 102 (1995): 4–5.
[13] Daniel B. Willingham and Laura Preuss, "The Death of Implicit Memory," Psyche, 2 (15), October 1995; http://psyche.cs.monash.edu.au/v2/psyche-2-15-willingham.html
[14] Joseph LeDoux, *The Emotional Brain* (New York: Simon and Schuster, 1996), p. 202.

cognition is not a unified learning process; it often has perceptual, motor, affective, and cognitive components, each of which implicates various regions of the brain. Much of the research on implicit cognition is devoted to assessing how perceptions and memories unavailable to the conscious mind are formed, stored, and employed by these other brain regions.

The study of implicit cognition originated with an experiment conducted by the Swiss psychologist Edouard Claparede. In the early 1900s, Claparede worked with a forty-seven-year-old woman who had been in an asylum for five years suffering from Korsakoff's syndrome. The patient, as a result of her brain malady, had no capacity to access recent memories. Every morning, the woman would have to be reintroduced to her caretakers and co-patients, as she bore no recollection that the same event had taken place each of the previous mornings.

One day, Claparede concealed a pin in his palm when he shook hands with the amnesiac woman. She reacted as one might expect, by wincing and retracting her hand. Shortly thereafter, the woman completely forgot about the episode, as she forgot about all recent events. Yet when Claparede introduced himself again, the woman withheld her hand.[15] The patient did not recognize Claparede and could not recall the pinprick. The damaged hippocampus that would normally allow such short-term, declarative memory remained non-functional. The undamaged part of her brain that was involved in the formation of procedural (implicit) memory, however, worked well. Like the subjects who unconsciously learned the complex rules dictating the sequencing of target characters on a computer screen, the amnesiac woman was able to learn without consciousness, acting on the basis of memories she could not recollect.

The preponderance of information that comes our way every minute of our waking hours is processed through implicit cognition. Our conscious minds do not get much involved. But it is not simply the quantity of information that makes implicit cognition important. In many circumstances, it also has the edge over conscious learning in terms of quality. Our capacity for implicit learning is often more robust and resilient in the face of a complex, challenging world.[16] This is most

---

[15] Edouard Claparede, "Recognition and 'me-ness,'" in D. Rapaport, ed., *Organization and Pathology of Thought* (New York: Columbia University Press, 1951), pp. 58–75. See also Ian Glynn, *An Anatomy of Thought: The Origin and Machinery of the Mind* (Oxford: Oxford University Press, 1999), p. 318.

[16] See Reber, *Implicit Learning and Tacit.* Guy Claxton, *Hare Brain Tortoise Mind: Why Intelligence Increases When You Think Less* (Hopewell, NJ: The Ecco Press, 1997).

easily demonstrated when demands on our attention simultaneously
arise from multiple sectors. Subjects perform quite poorly, for instance,
when attempting to recall a list of words if, while reading the list, they
are asked to take on a secondary task, such as monitoring a sequence
of digits. Declarative (conscious) memory is noticeably impaired. In
contrast, implicit memories are not significantly weakened by multiple
demands on a subject's attention. Likewise, resorting to conscious rationality in taxing situations often produces a decline in skillful performance. People under stress who rely on implicit learning tend to perform
better.[17]

The conscious mind is like a serial processor that addresses tasks
sequentially. It is inhibited from taking on more than one job at a time.
The unconscious mind works more like a parallel-distributed processor.
It addresses numerous complex tasks simultaneously by funneling multiple independent sources of information through multiple information-
processing units.[18] To the extent that we engage in "multi-tasking," the
unconscious mind has to take over. As much of our lives are characterized by multiple demands on our attention and multiple sources of
information, it is unsurprising that implicit cognition plays a very large
role in our ability to function effectively. Marcus, Neuman and MacK-
uen write: "Learning is principally at the service of doing. And doing is
guided by procedural memory, not by declarative memory. While declarative memory makes what we know available to consciousness, thus aiding
introspection, it has very limited abilities as far as the actual execution
of behavior is concerned. So limited that it cannot directly control much
of what we do."[19] Conscious and implicit forms of learning are qualitatively discrete abilities making use of distinct neural networks that allow
the past to influence the present in different ways. Implicit cognition
plays a significant role in our lives and, oftentimes, produces qualitatively
superior results.

---

[17] R. S. W. Masters, "Knowledge, knerves and know-how: The role of explicit vs. implicit
knowledge in the breakdown of a complex skill under pressure." *British Journal
of Psychology* 83(1992): 343–58. Toth, "Nonconscious Forms of Human Memory,"
pp. 248–49.

[18] John Bargh, "The Automaticity of Everyday Life," in *The Automaticity of Everyday Life:
Advances in Social Cognition*, ed. Robert Wyer, Jr., Vol. X (Mahwah, NJ: Lawrence Erlbaum
Associates, 1997), p. 53. See also David E. Rumelhart, James L. McClelland and the
PDP Research Group, *Parallel Distrubuted Processing: Explorations in the Microstructure of
Cognition*, Volume 1 (Cambridge: MIT Press, 1986).

[19] George E. Marcus, W. Russell Neuman, and Michael MacKuen, *Affective Intelligence and
Political Judgment* (Chicago: University of Chicago Press, 2000), p. 30.

Evolutionary theory suggests as much. Early hominids were intuitive judges, with conscious, inferential reasoning, and, even more so, logic and probabilistic reasoning showing up much later in the development of the species. Unconscious processing has been the rule rather than the exception throughout the history of humankind. Arthur Reber writes:

Consciousness and phenomenological awareness are recent arrivals on the phylogenetic scene. Hence, consciousness and conscious control over action must have been 'built upon,' as it were, deeper and more primitive processes and structures that functioned independently of awareness. On these grounds it is assumed that the processes studied under the rubric *implicit learning*, operating independently of consciousness, are more primitive and basic than those that are dependent, in some measure, on consciousness and conscious control.[20]

Conscious processes that figure in the exercise of judgment are generally grounded in unconscious processes. Today, as in millennia past, the preponderance of forces at work in the act of judging operate below the threshold of awareness.

The Modularity of the Brain

Humans possess all sorts of skills that they are not consciously aware of or, in any case, do not and cannot consciously control. Consider a simple example. Pick up a pen and a piece of paper and quickly sign your name. Now turn the paper over and sign your name again, but this time do so with the other hand. Most people who conduct this experiment fail to achieve comparable results, the more so for those with idiosyncratic signatures that are not limited to orthogonal lettering. It becomes apparent, particularly for the latter group, that the problem is not simply a matter of one hand's being insufficiently dexterous. With the pen in the wrong hand, we find ourselves at a loss as to the sort of shapes to make, let alone how to scribe them fluidly. It is as if the dominant hand, not our conscious mind, held the information about how to sign our names. Like many other skills, such as riding a bicycle, playing a musical instrument, typing, or engaging in various athletic events, signing our names is not easily accessible to conscious control.

---

[20] Reber, *Implicit Learning and Tacit Knowledge*, p. 7. As Joseph LeDoux observes, it is a misleading "linguistic quirk, or a revealing cultural assumption" that the older, foundational *un*conscious processes are defined as negations of the more recent, superstructural, conscious processes. Joseph LeDoux, *The Synaptic Self: How Our Brains Become Who We Are* (New York: Penguin Books, 2002), p. 11.

The explanation for this phenomenon lies in the way the brain divides its workload. The hind brain, or cerebellum, controls fine motor movement and complex movement patterns. The pianist who completes a fast and intricate passage without a thought to the fingering, like the touch typist or the person signing his name, has stored the necessary instructions in his cerebellum.[21] The pre-frontal cortex, where most conscious thought occurs, remains largely uninvolved. Likewise, when grandmasters and good amateurs play chess, brain scans indicate that the amateurs are primarily using the medial temporal lobes of their brains whereas the grandmasters employ their frontal and parietal cortices.[22] One would expect analogous results for novices and experts engaged in other strategic or skill-based games. At a certain level of performance, when people operate most proficiently, distinct brain regions take over the show. These brain regions generally operate without conscious, cognitive control.

Such findings have led neuroscientists and psychologists to posit the brain as *modular* in structure and function. Rather than viewing the human mind as a general-purpose computer, modularists believe it operates more like a Swiss Army knife. Distinct neural networks, which may or may not occupy a single, discrete area of the brain, demonstrate distinct uses and capacities. Modules are specialized brain systems whose operations remain unavailable to conscious control. These modules carry out specific, independent tasks while remaining "cognitively impenetrable."[23] Over the evolutionary history of the species, thousands of these specialized circuits have developed in the human brain.

In the early nineteenth century, Franz Joseph Gall speculatively divided the brain into separate centers with domain-specific capabilities. And ever since the cognitive revolution in psychology began in 1959, with Noam Chomsky's severely critical review of B. F. Skinner's *Verbal Behavior*, scientific evidence for modularity has been mounting.[24] Many, if not most, of our mental capacities appear to be modular to some degree, though early proponents of modularity clearly overestimated

---

[21] Glynn, *An Anatomy of Thought*, p. 167.

[22] *The Gainesville Sun*, August 9, 2001, p. 6A.

[23] James E. Hoffman, "The Psychology of Perception," in *Mind and Brain: Dialogues in cognitive neuroscience*, ed. Joseph Ledoux and William Hirst (Cambridge: Cambridge University Press, 1986), p. 8. See also *Evolution and the human mind: Modularity, language and meta-cognition*, ed. Peter Carruthers and Andrew Chamberlain (Cambridge: Cambridge University Press, 2000).

[24] Noam Chomsky, "Review of *Verbal Behavior*," in *Language* 35 (1959): 26–58.

its scope while underestimating the brain's flexibility. Cognitive neuroscience has proven modularity at a basic level, though the precise extent to which it operates, the level of interactivity between modules, and the level of emergent rather than innate modulation remains unknown.[25]

Modularity is most evident in the (evolutionary) older regions of the brain, such as the thalamus. But even in the neocortex, which demonstrates more fluidity, parallel processing, and interconnection, a form of modularity is evident. The right hemisphere, for instance, primarily takes on the charge of grappling with novelty while the left hemisphere is concerned with more routine tasks and exercising well-developed mental skills.[26] The frontal lobes, in turn, are mostly involved in practical ("adaptive") judgments, those entailing a choice among alternatives whose relative merits are ambiguous. They do not participate much in purely calculative ("veridical") judgments, such as those produced by means of syllogistic logic or computation. Importantly, there is no specific, isolated part of the brain *solely* devoted to practical judgment. The faculty engages various brain regions, and each region so engaged is also implicated in other mental processes.[27]

Modularity is well demonstrated in the act of smiling. When asked to smile on command for a camera, or trying to smile in front of a mirror, many of us produce awkward grimaces. Yet beautiful smiles appear on our faces without effort when encountering a good friend. These two kinds of smiles differ so markedly because distinct brain regions handle them. The consciously orchestrated smile is produced by the motor cortex. The spontaneous smile is executed by the basal ganglia, clusters of cells found between the brain's higher cortex and the thalamus. A person who has had a stroke in the right motor cortex (which controls movement on the left side of the body) is only able to produce a half smile (on the right side of the face) with conscious effort. But this same stroke victim can exhibit a full spontaneous smile on both sides of his face. Likewise, voluntary

---

[25] Many modularists assume that modules are products of natural selection, but two of the most famous modularists, Noam Chomsky and Jerry Fodor, avoid all evolutionary theorizing. For a critique of modularism, see Elkhonon Goldberg, *The Wisdom Paradox: How Your Mind Can Grow Stronger As Your Brain Grows Older* (New York: Gotham Books, 2005), pp. 142–48.

[26] Elkhonon Goldberg, *The Executive Brain: Frontal Lobes and the Civilized Mind* (New York: Oxford University Press, 2001), pp. 79–80.

[27] Joshua Greene and Jonathan Haidt, "How (and where) does moral judgment work?" *Trends in Cognitive Sciences* 6 (2002): 522.

arm movements are impossible for such a stroke victim on both sides of his body. Try as he might, the person suffering from a stroke in his right hemisphere will not be able to lift his left arm.[28] But an involuntary yawn will raise both arms. The reason, again, is that the voluntary and involuntary movements are controlled by different brain regions, only one of which was damaged by the stroke.[29]

Such findings prompt the following questions. Is there a significant sense in which practical judgment, like smiling, is best accomplished by non-explicit, involuntary, unconscious means that are grounded in distinct brain regions? Is our practical judgment impoverished if it cuts itself off from the many forms of perceiving, remembering, assessing, evaluating, and learning that remain cognitively impenetrable? Would a person exercising practical judgment solely through conscious effort be in the position of the pianist who refused to employ his cerebellum, and consequently produced choppy, ear-bending executions rather than mellifluous music?

Consider an experiment that pits (semi)conscious visual assessments against largely unconscious motor assessments. Two disks, physically identical in diameter, are surrounded by different size objects, as in Figure 3.1. The disk surrounded by smaller objects appears larger than the disk surrounded by larger objects. Most of us have seen this sort of optical illusion before. Now comes the interesting part.

Standing an arm's length away from the illusion, known as the Titchener circles, reach out and attempt to "grab" the two central disks, each in turn, with your thumb and index finger. If you perform as most people do, your hand will have guessed the sizes quite accurately. Indeed, frame-by-frame photography of hands attempting to pick up identical objects (dominoes, in one experiment) that appear to be different sizes because they are surrounded by larger or smaller objects confirm that fingers are positioned exactly the same distance

---

[28] With extensive therapy, stroke victims and other brain-damaged patients can rewire their neural circuits, allowing hitherto impossible physical movement. An examination of such brain plasticity is found in Jeffrey M. Schwartz and Sharon Begley, *The Mind and the Brain: Neuroplasticity and the Power of Mental Force* (New York: HarperCollins, 2002).

[29] V. S. Ramachandran and Sandra Blakeslee, *Phantoms in the Brain* (New York: William Morrow and Company, 1998), p. 14. The spontaneous smile is, in part, elicited by emotional experience that produces an involuntary contraction of the outer strands of the eye muscle. This so-called *Duchene smile* cannot be willed into existence absent the requisite emotions. See Y. Susan Choi, Heather Gray, and Nalini Ambady, "The Glimpsed World: Unintended Communication and Unintended Perception," in *The New Unconscious*, ed. Ran Hassin, James Uleman, and John Bargh (Oxford: Oxford University Press, 2005), pp. 309–333.

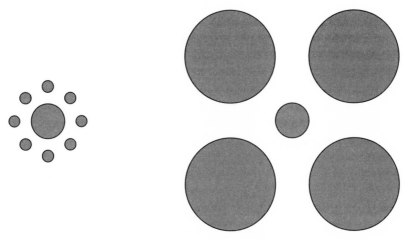

FIGURE 3.1. The Titchener circles.

apart.[30] The part of the brain that controls abstract visual assessment gets fooled by the illusion. The parietal lobes that control eye-hand coordination are not duped. In this instance, the less conscious judgment that goes into the physical movements determining the separation between fingers outperforms conscious visual assessment.

Of course, one is not consciously willing one's eyes to do anything. But our visual assessment of the sizes of the central disks demands a level of conscious attention and evaluation. We look at the disks, perhaps squint, and say something like, "The disk amongst the smaller objects seems the larger one. Yes, I'm quite sure now. It's definitely larger." When we reach for the disks, in contrast, we remain thoughtless. The mind is not consciously involved. If practical judgment is in any way analogous to the "guesswork" involved in determining the size of these disks, we would be better off lowering the volume of the conscious mind and relying more on its unconscious capacities.

Most musicians, athletes, typists, jugglers, and bicycle riders already know this. They perform best when their minds are turned off or, better said, when their attention is directed to something other than the conscious execution of particular (fine-motor and gross-motor) skills. These phenomena, as well as others more closely related to practical judgment, are best addressed under the rubric of tacit knowledge.

[30] See Ramachandran, *Phantoms in the Brain*, pp. 82–83. Jeffrey Gray, *Consciousness* (Oxford: Oxford University Press, 2004), p. 19. See also A. Milner and M. Goodale, *The visual brain in action* (Oxford: Oxford University Press, 1995).

Tacit Knowledge and Intuition

The notion of tacit knowledge was given a wide audience beginning in the late 1960s by Michael Polanyi. Polanyi described in phenomenological (rather than neuroscientific) terms how it is that we can have "subsidiary" knowledge of things without this knowledge ever rising to the level of consciousness. He posited as the paradigm case for tacit knowledge the way we "know" our own bodies.[31] The sense of balance exhibited in walking, running, or jumping demonstrates that we know how to do many things with our bodies without being able to explain how we do them. We subsidiarily know how to ride a bicycle, for instance, yet we remain largely if not wholly unable to identify the precise movements that allow this complex activity of balance and propulsion to take place.

The mental equivalent of knowing our bodies is common sense. As La Rochefoucauld observes, "Simple grace is to the body what common sense is to the mind."[32] Our common senses are the most basic, widespread, and widely acknowledged generators of tacit knowledge. We have many common senses, such as the ability to recognize a colleague's face, even in a crowd of thousands, or the ability to infer causation. For the most part, we cannot describe how we achieve these feats. Tacit knowledge, whether in the form of common sense or more specialized cases, is a type of "know-how." It is exemplified in fine and gross motor skills (for example, playing a piano or riding a bicycle), in skills involving one or more of the five senses (for example, that exhibited by wine tasters or music conductors, or the more general ability to discern and discriminate between particular smells, tastes, colors, shapes, sounds, and touch), in skills that employ various senses in combination (for example, the ability to predict weather patterns through sight, sound, smell, and bodily reactions to changes in barometric pressure), and in more cognitive but no less unconsciously-directed skills (for example, language use).

Some forms of tacit knowledge appear innate. Certain people, for instance, are "born" with perfect pitch. Most of our tacit knowledge, however, is acquired. That is a good thing, given the relative paucity of instinctive knowledge that human beings might claim. We do not arrive in the world with knowledge of how to walk, ride a bike, or speak a language. Rather, we are born with the potential, if we are typical, of

---

[31] Michael Polanyi, *Knowing and Being*, ed. Majorie Greene (Chicago: University of Chicago Press, 1969), p. 183.

[32] La Rochefoucauld, *Maxims*, trans. Leonard Tanock (London: Penguin Books, 1959), p. 45; #67.

developing the muscular coordination, sense of balance, and linguistic skills that make walking, riding a bike, and speaking possible. We are not "hard-wired" to do these things in the same sense that we are hard-wired to breathe. But we are hard-wired to learn to do these things given a sufficiently supportive environment. Our brains, while relatively plastic, are (genetically) predisposed to learn some lessons better than others.[33]

We can and generally do learn these lessons without ever consciously gaining an explicit understanding of them. We may learn to speak, walk, or ride a bike without acquiring explicit knowledge of grammar, physics, or physiology. Explicit learning in these arenas, if it ever occurs, happens long after we have acquired the respective tacit skills. When my four-year-old son remarked after sampling both his and my treats that "The chocolate ice-cream is the goodest," he was neither imitating something he had heard nor consciously applying memorized rules of grammar. Rather, he was (mis)applying tacitly learned knowledge. Explicit knowledge of grammar, in this case, will come mostly from school. It will serve to supplement an extensive base of tacit linguistic knowledge and skill.

When appropriating tacit knowledge, we are engaged in what Polanyi called "learning without awareness."[34] The phenomenon of learning without awareness was demonstrated in an experiment conducted by Jean Piaget. The Swiss psychologist had children practice hitting a target with a ball tethered to a rope. Whirling the ball in a circle, the children tried to let go of the rope at the right time such that the ball would strike the target. With practice, the children quickly learned to release the rope at the moment it became parallel to the target. When asked to explain to another child how best to hit the target, however, many children, including all the younger ones, incorrectly said that one should let go of the rope when it was pointing at the target – that is, when the rope was perpendicular rather than parallel to it. These children had all learned the skill of hitting the target without awareness.

Consider another example. Poultry egg producers once waited up to six weeks before the appearance of adult feathers allowed them to separate cockerels (males) from pullets (hens). At an earlier age, the chicks

---

[33] Reber helpfully clarifies this distinction by contrasting "process nativism" with "content nativism." The latter term refers, for example, to the Chomskian belief that the deep structure of a universal grammar is genetically encoded in the mind. The former refers to an innate predisposition to acquire certain sorts of knowledge and skills. Reber, *Implicit Learning and Tacit Knowledge*. See also LeDoux, *The Synaptic Self*, p. 85.

[34] Polanyi, *Knowing and Being*, pp. 141–42.

have no discernible physiological differences. That posed a problem, as it meant hatcheries had to feed and house twice the number of chicks for six weeks before being able to eliminate the non-egg-producing cockerels. In the 1930s, Australian hatcheries learned of Japanese 'chicken sexers' who could determine at a mere glance the sex of day-old chicks. Australian workers were subsequently trained by the Japanese, and after months of practice and supervision, the apprentices could almost match the skill of their mentors, sexing up to 800 chicks an hour with a 99% accuracy rate. Neither the Japanese experts nor the skilled apprentices could explain how they accomplished the task. The process, to this day, remains "too subtle" for words.[35] Similar cases regarding the learning of complex skills with little or no awareness of their mechanisms are well-documented. These capacities, though learned, remain unavailable to introspection.[36]

The cultural expression of tacit knowledge, occasionally referred to as local knowledge, has been explored by social scientists. In *Seeing Like a State,* James Scott examines the benefits of local forms of practical knowledge as alternatives to universal rationalism. Scott employs the Greek term for cunning, *metis,* to denote the practical knowledge displayed by local people as they employ contextually sensitive skills and rules of thumb. He contrasts *metis* to *techne* (which he problematically conflates with *episteme*). *Techne* is defined as universal, scientific judgment that allows quantitative precision and/or "logical deduction from self-evident first principles."[37] Scott celebrates local, culturally specific forms of tacit knowledge as an alternative to what he considers the potentially destructive technical systematizations of "high modernism."

Likewise, Stephen Toulmin illustrates the merits of tacit knowledge with a story of Balinese rice farmers. The farmers were forbidden in the late 1960s and early 1970s to plant native species and were required instead to double and triple crop high-yield varieties of rice developed in the Green Revolution. Productivity increased for a number of years

[35] David G. Myers, *Intuition: Its Powers and Perils* (New Haven: Yale University Press, 2002), p. 55. R. D. Martin, *The Specialist Chick Sexer: A History, A World View, Future Prospects* (Melbourne: Bernal Publishing, 1994).

[36] Pawel Lewicki, Maria Czyzewska, and Thomas Hill, "Nonconscious information processing and personality," in *How Implicit is Implicit Learning,* ed. Dianne Berry (New York: Oxford University Press, 1997), p. 52. Myers, *Intuition,* p. 44. Richard Horsey, *The art of chicken sexing,* 2002, http://www.phon.ucl.ac.uk/home/richardh/chicken.htm

[37] James C. Scott, *Seeing Like a State: How Certain Schemes to Improve the Human Condition Have Failed* (New Haven: Yale University Press, 1998), p. 319.

following the introduction of the high-yield rice. But then infestation by funguses and pests afflicted the crops, and the farmers were forced for the first time in their lives to purchase and use expensive pesticides. Eventually, the rice farmers begged to be allowed to return to the traditional sequencing of crops and irrigation employing native species. Since this sequencing took place under the direction of the "water temples," it was perceived to be a reversion to religion over science.[38] The farmers could not give (scientific) explanations for their customary agricultural practices. But there was much practical wisdom, understood as culturally specific forms of tacit knowledge, embedded in their traditional, sustainable methods of farming.

Ethico-political life, perhaps as much if not more so than farming and other livelihoods, is highly dependent on tacit knowledge. Borrowing directly from Polanyi, Sheldon Wolin observes that "tacit political knowledge" or political wisdom "is mindful of logic, but more so of the incoherence and contradictoriness of experience. And for the same reason, it is distrustful of rigor. Political life does not yield its significance to terse hypotheses, but is elusive, and hence meaningful statements about it often have to be allusive and intimative. Context becomes supremely important, for actions and events occur in no other setting."[39] In contrast to methodologically rigorous, highly directed inquiry, tacit political knowledge derives from "an indwelling or rumination in which the mind draws on the complex framework of sensibilities built up unpremeditatedly."[40] Wolin maintains the merits – and indispensability – of tacit knowledge for those who adopt political theory as a "vocation."

In like fashion, Isaiah Berlin writes that astute political judges are acutely aware of "the infinite variety of the social and political elements in which they live. Their antennae are extremely sensitive and record half-consciously a vast variety of experience; but instead of being overwhelmed by so much, their genius consists precisely in the fact that they are able to integrate it – not by any conscious process, but in some semi-instinctive fashion – into a single coherent picture."[41] Berlin understands practical judgment as an "empirical knack," effectively a tacit skill that allows for

---

[38] See Stephen Toulmin, *Return to Reason* (Cambridge: Harvard University Press, 2001), pp. 60–61.

[39] Sheldon Wolin, "Political Theory as a Vocation," *American Political Science Review* 63 (1969): 1070.

[40] Wolin, "Political Theory as a Vocation," p. 1071.

[41] Isaiah Berlin, *The Power of Ideas*, ed. Henry Hardy (Princeton: Princeton University Press, 2000), p. 188.

the synthesis of the multiple, variegated clues (fallible indicators) swirling around us.[42] The integration of these "fleeting, broken, infinitely various wisps and fragments that make up life" occurs largely in the absence of conscious analysis.[43] Given its enigmatic method of operation, Berlin identifies judgment as a "mysterious capacity."[44]

The grounding of practical judgment in tacit knowledge has also been affirmed by theorists on the other side of the political spectrum, such as Edmund Burke and Michael Oakeshott. Like Scott, Toulmin, Wolin, and Berlin, but with a notably conservative orientation, Burke and Oakeshott worry about the danger posed by the undermining of tacit capacities in modern times. Oakeshott specifically laments the effort to rationalize politics in modernity. And like his fellow political theorists, he decries the discounting of implicit forms of learning. "By 'judgment'," Oakeshott writes, "I mean the tacit or implicit component of knowledge, the ingredient which is not merely unspecified in propositions but is unspecifiable in propositions. It is the component of knowledge which does not appear in the form of rules and which, therefore, cannot be resolved into information or itemized in the manner characteristic of information."[45] Like Polanyi, Oakeshott differentiates between the 'knowing-how' of tacit knowledge and the 'knowing-what' of explicit knowledge (information). He submits that most, if not all, 'knowing-how' has within it certain elements of 'knowing-what.' But he argues that knowing how is foundational. In turn, he insists that tacit knowledge is exhibited not only in physical skills, but in "all abilities whatever, and, more particularly, in those abilities which are almost exclusively concerned with mental operations."[46] Empirical research supports Oakeshott's claim.[47]

When tacit knowledge is involved in mental efforts, such as decision-making, these efforts are often said to be *intuitive* in nature. Intuition

---

[42] Berlin, *Concepts and Categories*, ed. Henry Hardy (New York: Viking Press, 1979), p. 116.

[43] Berlin, *The Sense of Reality: Studies in Ideas and their History*, ed. Henry Hardy (London: Chatto and Windus, 1996), pp. 47–48.

[44] Berlin, *Concepts and Categories*, p. 116.

[45] Michael Oakeshott, *The Voice of Liberal Learning* (Indianapolis: Liberty Fund, 2001), p. 49.

[46] Oakeshott, *The Voice of Liberal Learning*, p. 51.

[47] Researchers have concluded that tacit knowledge facilitates the acquisition and application of more deliberative, explicit knowledge. Students who demonstrate high levels of tacit knowledge, for instance, achieve better academic grades than students who are low in tacit knowledge but equal or higher in explicit knowledge. See Anit Somech and Ronit Bogler, "Tacit Knowledge in Academia: Its Effects on Student Learning and Achievement," *The Journal of Psychology*, 133: 605.

is occasionally portrayed as a quasi-mystical capacity, as "perception beyond the physical sense."[48] It is not clear what this could mean. In any case, there is no need to leave the physical world. Intuition is not grounded in mystical awareness, but in perception and cognitive processing beyond directed effort. Intuition may simply be defined as a form of awareness that occurs without the involvement of conscious reasoning or attention. As such, it reflects our access to and use of tacit knowledge.

Intuition tends to be automatic (experienced passively), rapid, effortless, holistic (pattern oriented), and associational. It is idiographic, grasping reality in concrete images and metaphors, is self-evidently valid, and is prone to stereotyping. Intuition is immediately compelling and resistant to change; its alteration generally requires repetitive or intense experience. In contrast, rational thought is intentional, relatively slow, structured, analytical, and deductive or inductive. It grasps reality in abstract symbols, words, or numbers, requires logical justification and evidence, and is generally responsive to new evidence and arguments.[49] Both intuitive awareness and rational thought have their respective strengths and weaknesses. They often work separately, but can also fruitfully be utilized in tandem.

Intuition frequently has a conscious component. In experiments, subjects acquiring implicit knowledge generally become aware that they have learned something. They may demonstrate this awareness by noting that they feel more confident when making decisions. Although subjects feel that they have learned something, they cannot say exactly what it is that they have learned.[50] In this sense, tacit knowledge gains an explicit component without ever becoming fully conscious. To the extent conscious thought arises, it builds upon rather than replaces implicitly acquired knowledge and skill. When a grandmaster plays chess, for instance, he is operating in an analogous fashion to the expert pianist performing a concerto, or the tennis pro playing a match. In each case, intuition, understood as the utilization of tacit knowledge and skill, is at the forefront, leaving a much diminished but by no means absent role for deliberative reason. When conscious thought does come into play for the chess

---

[48] Sandra Weintraub, *The Hidden Intelligence: Innovation through Intuition* (Boston: Butterworth Heinemann, 1998), p. 4.

[49] See Seymour Epstein, Rosemary Pacini, Veronika Denes-Raj, and Harriet Heier, "Individual Differences in Intuitive-Experiential and Analytical-Rational Thinking Styles," *Journal of Personality and Social Psychology* 71 (1996): 390–405.

[50] Reber, *Implicit Learning and Tacit Knowledge*, p. 136.

expert, it is not manifested as a wholly separate, purely analytical activity. Rather, it involves critical reflection upon existing intuitions.[51]

Moral judgment operates much like other kinds of judgment, with the lion's share of its work accomplished by intuitive processes.[52] For most people most of the time, moral judgment is a product of intuitions that have been shaped through active participation in socio-cultural environments, and occasionally refined by propositional discussions. When conscious deliberation takes place, it typically occurs not as the imperial pronouncement of reason, but as the use of reason to break a deadlock between conflicting intuitions.[53] In the political realm, we witness a similar interplay between reason and intuition. Even at the highest levels of decision-making, intuition continues to play a leading role. As James Schlesinger, one time director of strategic studies for RAND and subsequently Secretary of Defense, observed: "Analysis is not a scientific procedure for reaching decisions which avoid intuitive elements, but rather a mechanism for sharpening the intuitions of the decision-maker."[54]

The last decade of social psychological research has seen a plethora of studies detailing the "automaticity" of everyday life. Much of what we perceive, remember, learn, say, and do is a product of implicit efforts that operate automatically, which is to say, without awareness or conscious control. Practical judgment is not a wholly automatic activity. It is composed of a well-integrated mix of intuitive and deliberative elements. When an individual makes an assessment, evaluation, or choice on a wholly intuitive or automatic basis, I would argue, this act should not be defined as a judgment at all. Lacking any conscious component, it is simply the expression of a *bias*.

A bias is a belief, orientation, or predilection that is not (currently) subjected to conscious review or critical engagement. The term as employed here, following Gadamer, bears no derogatory connotation. Biases are intrinsic components of judgment in that, minimally, they allow its exercise to get underway. Biases can become judgments, if we subject them to reflection. And judgments can become biases, when they stimulate forms of thought or behavior that are no longer subject to scrutiny. We often

[51] Dreyfus, *Mind over Machine*, p. 32.

[52] Jonathan Haidt, "The Emotional Dog and Its Rational Tail: A Social Intuitionist Approach to Moral Judgment," *Psychological Review*. 108 (2001): 814–834.

[53] Haidt, "The Emotional Dog and Its Rational Tail." Joshua Greene et al., "An fMRI Investigation of Emotional Engagement in Moral Judgment," *Science* 293(2001): 2105–8. Greene and Haidt, "How (and where) does moral judgment work? pp. 517–523.

[54] James R. Schlesinger, "Uses and Abuses of Analysis, "*Survival* 10 (October 1968): 35.

learn to do things through a series of conscious decisions and efforts, only to find that reflective activity ceases once the behavior is mastered. The acquisition of most habits fits this description. The acquisition of certain habits, in turn, requires the replacement of one bias with another, often with a period of deliberative activity marking the transition. Consider how a tennis player who takes up squash has to make a conscious effort to unlearn the bias of swinging the racquet from his shoulder (itself a skill consciously learned years ago, but now fully automatic) and appropriate a new bias of swinging the racquet from his wrist. We may think of decision rules, tacit knowledge, and intuitions as types of biases that figure prominently in judgments. However, as Derrida observes, the judge never simply acts on the basis of biases, not even on the basis of those legal biases known as laws. Rather, he reflectively reinvents (or reevaluates) the law or bias whenever he judges.

While it is often the case that we think and act wholly on the basis of biases, it is arguably never the case that we think or act wholly *without* their benefit. Michael Polanyi writes: "While tacit knowledge can be possessed by itself, explicit knowledge must rely on being tacitly understood and applied. Hence all knowledge is *either tacit* or *rooted in tacit knowledge*. A *wholly* explicit knowledge is unthinkable."[55] It follows, for Polanyi, that "any attempt to gain complete control of thought by explicit rules is self-contradictory, systematically misleading and culturally destructive."[56] Likewise, Hans-Georg Gadamer deems the effort wholly to eliminate one's biases "manifestly absurd."[57] Trying to think and reason in the absence of biases – Gadamer labels them "fore-conceptions" – is like trying to run on ice. Without the friction of biases, movement is impossible. There is no way to get the processes of reasoning and reflection started but by way of unexamined prejudices. To assume otherwise constitutes a "fallacious idealism" that ignores our "true dependencies" while giving reflective reason a "false power."[58] Oakeshott agrees. He writes:

I think 'knowing *how*' is an ingredient of all genuine knowledge, and not a separate kind of knowing specified by an ignorance of rules. Facts, rules, all that may come to us as information, itemized and explicit, never themselves endow us with an ability to do, or to make, or to understand and explain anything. Information has to be used, and it does not itself indicate how, on any occasion, it should be

55 Polanyi, *Knowing and Being*, p. 144.
56 Polanyi, *Knowing and Being*, p. 156.
57 Hans-Georg Gadamer, *Truth and Method* (New York: Crossroad, 1975), p. 358.
58 Gadamer, *Philosophical Hermeneutics*, trans./ed. David Linge (Berkeley: University of California Press, 1976), p. 33.

used. What is required in addition to information is knowledge which enables us to interpret it, to decide upon its relevance, to recognize what rule to apply and to discover what action permitted by the rule should, in the circumstances, be performed.[59]

The "knowledge" that allows one to make good use of information and apply rules intelligently, Oakeshott insists, is obliquely learned and tacitly employed. In the same vein, Hannah Arendt insists that "a preliminary, inarticulate understanding" is the basis for all knowledge.[60] This wordless understanding, which Arendt describes as "original intuition" or "prejudices," precedes and guides the pursuit of all explicit knowledge.[61]

You have to take some things for granted, in other words, before critical reflection can begin. Typically, a great deal is taken for granted, such as the stable meaning of words and common sense perceptions and understandings. The nature and composition of what is taken for granted, the tacit knowledge involved in our judgments, remains blocked from awareness. Even our most deliberative, meticulous efforts at reasoning rely on the inaccessible foundations of the unconscious mind.

The indispensable contribution of tacit knowledge to conscious thought is suggested by the difficulties facing technicians struggling to produce artificial intelligence (AI). A good judge must grapple with the implications of what he knows. But he does not entertain everything he knows, or grapple with all possible implications. At play is an implicit sense of relevance, what Wolin calls a "notion of what matters."[62] AI researchers have yet to impart this tacit sense to a machine. Efforts to get computers with vast computational power to exhibit even rudimentary "sub-symbolic" thinking – that is, common sense – have failed. Even staunch advocates of AI who have invested considerable time and resources in the effort to build machines that mimic human thought acknowledge that such sub-symbolic systems do most of the work of our minds.[63]

One might acknowledge the impossibility of the operation of reason in the complete absence of tacit knowledge and still seek to limit the role

[59] Oakeshott, *The Voice of Liberal Learning*, p. 50.

[60] Hannah Arendt, "Understanding and Politics," in Hannah Arendt, *Essays in Understanding, 1930–1954*, ed. Jerome Kohn (New York: Harcourt Brace & Company, 1994), p. 310.

[61] Arendt, "Understanding and Politics," pp. 311, 325.

[62] Wolin, "Political Theory as a Vocation," pp. 1076–77.

[63] Dreyfus, *Mind over Machine*, pp. xi, xii. Newly developed "neural network computers" may eventually prove to be up to the task. Such computers, modeled on the human brain, do not so much follow programmed rules as search and solve for patterns.

of non-deliberative, intuitive knowledge to a minimum while expanding rational analysis. Our implicit knowledge and skills may constitute a necessary starting point for critical reflection, but might it not be best to restrict their operation so as to maximize the role of reason?

The answer is no. When the conscious mind crowds out the unconscious mind, a tremendous resource is wasted. Cognitive psychologists have demonstrated that the performance of subjects working on a given problem may be significantly undermined if they are asked to "think aloud" through the problem solving. Thinking aloud effectively restricts subjects to conscious mental processes, eliminating the often more fecund capacities of the unconscious mind – namely, implicit memories and intuitive apprehension.[64] Likewise, many forms of tacit knowledge, such as that which operates in face recognition, become impaired if people are required to describe verbally the world they observe.[65] Words and the conscious thoughts behind them get in the way of acute perception. In turn, people often demonstrate improved recall of the perceptual cues or other memory traces that guide judgment when they relax their efforts to retrieve them. A willful, conscious attempt to focus the mind actually interferes with access to the memories and knowledge that abet the making of judgments.[66] Conscious efforts to solve difficult problems may also constrict the width of attention and consequently hinder the observation or recall of environmental signals. In contrast, "low arousal" states of mind, where conscious processes do not overpower unconscious ones, are often more conducive to the discovery of "insightful" solutions.[67] With this in mind, we can understand why the vast majority of Nobel laureates (seventy-two out of eighty-three in science and medicine, for example), indicate that intuition plays a significant role in their success.[68]

Consider a study in which implicit knowledge provided a good foundation for decision-making while the too-extensive search for and use of reasons impeded good judgment. Participants were asked to give their preferences for strawberry jams (based on tasting them) and college courses

[64] Dean Keith Simonton, *Origins of Genius: Darwinian Perspectives on Creativity* (New York: Oxford University Press, 1999), pp. 47–49.

[65] J. Schooler, and T. Engstler-Schooler, "Verbal Overshadowing of Visual Memories: Some Things Are Better Left Unsaid," *Cognitive Psychology* 22 (1990): 36–71.

[66] Greenwald and Banaji, "Implicit Social Cognition," p. 17. See also Henry Ellis and R. Hunt, *Fundamentals of Cognitive Psychology*, 5th ed. (Madison: Brown and Benchmark, 1993), pp. 93–94.

[67] Simonton, *Origins of Genius*, pp. 44–45.

[68] F. Marton, P. Fensham, and S. Chaiklin, "A Nobel's Eye View of Scientific Intuition." *International Journal of Science Education* 16 (1994): 457–73.

(based on the review of syllabi). Left to their own devices, control subjects produced preferences that corresponded very well to the rankings of trained sensory experts and faculty members, respectively. Subjects who were asked to think about why they liked or disliked the jams and why they would choose or not choose a particular course performed quite poorly.

How and why did this occur? The more deliberative decision-makers brought to mind, as requested, attributes and reasons to ground their judgments. But these did not correspond well to the attributes and reasons deemed important by experts. When the subjects proceeded to base their decisions on these faulty attributes and reasons, they produced suboptimal choices. The quality of judgments was worsened by the search for a rational justification.[69] Lord Mansfield may have had this in mind when he thus counseled a newly appointed colonial governor who had no experience in law but soon would have to serve as a magistrate: "Nothing is more easy; only hear both sides patiently – then consider what you think justice requires, and decide accordingly. But never give your reasons; for your judgement will probably be right, but your reasons will certainly be wrong."[70] Benjamin Disraeli offered similar counsel to those who would follow his footsteps, admonishing them to "never explain."[71]

Mansfield's and Disraeli's advice smacks of imperial power and elite prerogative. It is an inappropriate model for pubic judgments in a democratic society. But the search for reasons often does lead us astray. Seeking and employing reasons in decision-making does not guarantee that one will find and choose the right reasons. Intuitive efforts – based on unconscious sorting mechanisms – often prove to be more effective, yielding better results, and more efficient, requiring fewer metabolic resources.[72] This is particularly true if the task at hand is oriented less to the determination of facts or figures and more to the determination of attitudes and values.[73] In such cases, the effort to make judgments primarily or

---

[69] T. D. Wilson and J.W. Schooler, "Thinking too much: Introspection can reduce the quality of preferences and decisions," *Journal of Personality and Social Psychology*, 60 (1991): 2, 181–192. Choi, "The Glimpsed World," p. 326. See also Myers, *Intuition*, p. 44.

[70] John Campbell, *Lives of the Chief Justices of England*, vol. 4. ed. James Cockcroft (Northport: E. Thompson, 1894–99), p. 388.

[71] Quoted in Robert A. Fitton, *Leadership*. (Boulder: Westview Press, 1997), p. 5.

[72] See Leanne S. Woolhouse and Rowan Bayne, "Personality and the use of intuition: Individual differences in strategy and performance on an implicit learning task," *European Journal of Personality*, 14: (2000):157–169. Goldberg, *The Wisdom Paradox*, p. 138.

[73] J. McMackin and P. Slovic, "When does explicit justification impair decision-making?" *Journal of Applied Cognitive Psychology*, 14 (2000): 527–541.

wholly deliberative will frequently produce poorer results than (partial) reliance on unconscious, intuitive capacities. Indeed, in certain circumstances, biases can ameliorate judgment even when they stand in marked contrast to avowed explicit beliefs that have deliberative justifications.[74] In such cases, an accurate intuition may beneficially overcome a mistakenly held (conscious) conviction. Whereas the former is labeled a bias, it is the latter that deleteriously skews judgment.

The point is not that practical judgment should wholly rely upon the unconscious powers of the mind. Anything deserving of the name of judgment, to repeat, has a significant portion of its activity directed by reflective effort. Deliberation can be a prominent and beneficial component of judgment, and certain kinds of decision-making are almost always improved when consistent reasoning is involved.[75] But the question remains: how large a role, respectively, should conscious and unconscious capacities play. Our brains, over eons of evolution, have figured out which of its modules to employ to achieve the best results when attempting many physical feats. As often as not, the less conscious the activity the better. We have a lot further to go before we can speak authoritatively about the best balance between our unconscious and reflective capacities in moral and political judgments.[76]

Intuition has been identified as a "new cottage industry."[77] It is valorized in popular culture and, more recently, in business affairs, with magazines, web sites, pay-per-call "hot lines," and best-selling books devoted to it.[78] While abilities do vary, in general people tend to overrate their intuitive powers.[79] Individuals making "seat of the pants" decisions based on their "gut feelings" – including reputed experts in their

---

[74] Lewicki, "Nonconscious acquisition of information," pp. 796–801. See also Claxton, *Hare Brain Tortoise Mind.*

[75] Pizarro, David and Paul Bloom, "The intelligence of the moral intuitions: A reply to Haidt." *Psychological Review,* 110(2001): 193–196; Matthew D. Lieberman, "Intuition: A Social Cognitive Neuroscience Approach." *Psychological Bulletin,* 126 (2000): 109–137.

[76] Preliminary research suggests that "people can unconsciously monitor and correct for bias in judgments, just as they might consciously." Jack Glaser and John Kihlstrom, "Compensatory Automaticity: Unconscious Volition Is Not an Oxymoron," in *The New Unconscious,* ed. Ran Hassin, James Uleman and John Bargh (Oxford: Oxford University Press, 2005), p. 189.

[77] Myers, *Intuition,* p. 3.

[78] For a recent example of the prestige gained by intuitive decision-making in business affairs, see Malcolm Gladwell's best-seller, *Blink: The Power of Thinking without Thinking* (New York: Little, Brown: 2005).

[79] Woolhouse and Bayne, "Personality and the use of intuition," pp. 157–169. Myers, *Intuition,* p. 44. Myers Briggs Type Indicator scores categorize 25 percent of the U.S. population as "intuitive." Sandra Weintraub, *The Hidden Intelligence: Innovation through Intuition* (Boston: Butterworth Heinemann, 1998), p. 43.

own fields of expertise – often perform quite poorly.[80] Certainly intuition that does not issue from worldly experience is often untrustworthy.[81] One must approach the unconscious cautiously. Jonathan Baron writes:

> Intuitions can be useful when we correctly perceive them as *part* of the story rather than as the whole story. They become dangerous when we think in a way that protects whichever idea grips us first. . . . The important point is that we must be willing to think of decision making as a kind of balancing, with each argument put onto the scales and weighed. . . . All of these intuitions are reasonable rules of thumb. . . . The intuitions cause trouble because we conduct our thinking as if they were more than this. . . . *The intuitions become absolutes.*[82]

There are no hard and fast rules that might allow us to determine when and where a more intuitive or more rational approach to a problem will yield better results. We do know that the potential for harm from intuition is increased when it is employed without heed to context. Reflection and rational analysis are as indispensable to good judgment as the tacit knowledge and skills that precede and inform deliberative efforts. The better part of intuition may well be discerning when, where, and how the power of reason should be dutifully engaged.

Biases are often pernicious, and the contributions to judgment of the "intelligent unconscious," though significant, are easy to overstate.[83] Let there be no mistake: intuition is very fallible. Nonetheless, one cannot understand or develop good judgment without reference to or reliance upon the prominent, often positive, and generally indispensable role it plays. Neither reason nor intuition, neither explicit nor implicit

[80] Jon Elster, *Alchemies of the Mind: Rationality and the Emotions* (Cambridge: Cambridge University Press, 1999), p. 295; R. Dawes, D. Faust and P. Meehl, "Clinical versus actuarial judgment," *Science* 243 (1989), 1688–74; Robin Hogarth, *Educating Intuition* (Chicago: University of Chicago Press, 2001), pp. 144–45; C. F. Camerer and E. J. Johnson, "The process-performance paradox in expert judgment: How can the experts know so much and predict so badly?" in *Toward a General Theory of Expertise: Prospects and Limits,* ed. K. A. Ericsson and J. Smith (Cambridge: Cambridge University Press, 1991); and Irving L. Janis, *Crucial Decisions: Leadership in Policymaking and Crisis Management* (London: The Free Press, 1989).

[81] Asked about President George W. Bush's penchant for making big decisions on gut feelings, Malcolm Gladwell observed that intuitions, what he problematically calls "instincts," are generally only as good as the relevant worldly experience of the person making the decisions. To rely on intuition in the absence of integrated experience is folly. Teresa K. Weaver, "In a blink," *Gainesville Sun,* March 6, 2005, p. 5D.

[82] Jonathan Baron, *Judgment Misguided: Intuition and Error in Public Decision Making* (New York: Oxford University Press, 1998), pp. 2, 7, 8, 9.

[83] Claxton, *Hare Brain Tortoise Mind,* 1997.

cognition, neither deliberation nor habit can carry the show on its own. Judgment, as Baron argues, is a balancing act. But Baron's statement may be misleading. It is not only "arguments" that need to be weighed, and the "scales" employed to ascertain the right balance do not belong solely to reason. On pain of falling into an infinite regress, rational justification, too, must acknowledge its limits. Reason is a co-participant, not the final arbiter of good judgment.

Post Hoc Reasoning

In his magisterial study, Peter Steinberger elegantly summarizes the nature of practical judgment. He writes:

> Judgment involves a kind of noninferential faculty of insight or intuition, roughly equivalent to Aristotelian *nous*. Like sense perception, this faculty may be recognized and acknowledged as reliable despite our inability to understand fully how it operates. It can be nurtured and improved through an appropriate education curriculum, though this curriculum will largely be a matter of habituation and experience rather than discourse. The faculty is common – it is a faculty of common sense – but it is not plebiscitary; as such, it is widely shared in any community, but it is not always cultivated and employed in an appropriate manner. For either innate or experiential reasons, the faculty of insight is more acute and reliable in some individuals than in others. But in all cases, it is embedded in and invariably operates in light of the often implicit conceptual and theoretical materials that compose the intellectual foundations of a culture.

Steinberger does not rely on cognitive neuroscience to guide his efforts. Still, he gleans most of the right lessons from the historical and theoretical literature, and provides as concise and accurate a description of practical judgment as can be found anywhere. But then he takes a step too far. He insists that

> The exercise of this faculty absolutely presupposes a capacity to reconstruct those foundations rationally, to describe the implicit element of *knowing that* which is required if there is to be a genuine *knowing how*, to "recollect" (*anamimnesko*) the tacit, socially and historically generated propositions about particulars and universals that one would have employed if the process of judgment had been inferential.[84]

This is an untenable position. All judgments are not analytically reducible to reasoned arguments, even after the fact. The intuitive elements of

---

[84] Peter J. Steinberger, *The Concept of Political Judgment* (Chicago: University of Chicago Press, 1993), pp. 247–48.

judgment cannot always (or even often) be weighed on the scales of reason.

Steinberger is sensitive to the non-inferential, tacit, unconscious means by which practical judgment is acquired and exercised. With Polanyi, he believes that "Disembodied thought is inimical to, and leads to the destruction of, judgment properly understood."[85] But Steinberger un-waveringly maintains that judgment is always retrospectively *reducible* to rational foundations. Judgment can always be "reconstructed" by placing "preunderstandings ... on the table" and making its components fully "explicit and manifest."[86] Steinberger argues for

> ... the absolute necessity of *post festum* explanations. We expect our judges to be able to justify their decisions in rational terms. This expectation is both appro-priate and, I think, conceptually necessary. Imagine a judge who simply cannot account in any way for his or her decision. Such a judge has not rendered a judgment at all. Something else has occurred. The judge's "decision" is more like a nervous tic, a biochemical reaction, a mechanical response to an exter-nal stimulus; it is the behavior of an animal or a machine, not an intelligent performance. . . . Political judgment, like any species of intelligent performance, presupposes a capacity to adduce after the fact some kind of propositional calcu-lus involving, as any such calculus must, both the opportunity and the obligation to engage in a process of rational evaluation and critique.[87]

Notwithstanding his nuanced account, Steinberger fudges the issue here. Since judgment always involves an element of conscious deliberation, *some* explanation will always be possible. So it is true that a judge who cannot account "in any way" for his decision did not render a judgment at all but has, at best, given voice to a bias. Yet Steinberger argues that a rational *post festum* accounting can and should be exhaustive. This assertion is quite mistaken.

We cannot kick away the ladder of the unconscious, even once we have ascended to the roof of a deliberative judgment. The embodied dispositions and intuitions that serve as the foundation of judgment are not simply proxies for reason. It has been said that "if you *have* reasons, you must be able to *give* reasons."[88] That is true enough, and every good judgment has its reasons. But a judgment does not have and cannot give *all* the reasons that brought it into being.

[85] Steinberger, *The Concept of Political Judgment*, p. 235.

[86] Steinberger, *The Concept of Political Judgment*, pp. 240–41.

[87] Steinberger, *The Concept of Political Judgment*, pp. 237–39.

[88] Brian Barry, *Political Argument* (New York: Humanities Press, 1965), p. 2.

By way of analogy, one might portray Steinberger's position as follows. A basketball player has little if any conceptual understanding of how he gets clear of the defense and shoots a basket. Rather, he lets his skills carry the day. But a sideline team of physiologists and physicists could, in theory, give a full explanation of the bio-mechanical forces involved in the player's successful drive to the hoop. Steinberger acknowledges that the good judge renders judgments much as the basketball player shoots baskets. Implicit cognition and tacit skills are at the fore. Embodied knowledge is crucial. But like the team of scientists, Steinberger maintains, the good judge can fully explain his actions in rational terms, when interviewed after the game.

How exhaustive is this post-game analysis? Will the judge be able fully to account for his judgment in rational terms? Or will he, like the basketball player, be forced to state – after some discussion, no doubt – that decisions were made and actions taken instinctively, and leave it at that.

Perhaps the analogy itself is misleading. After all, the basketball player on the court seems to be engaged in something much closer to expressing biases than making judgments. Consider, then, a different scenario: a parent stands confronted by a child who persistently questions the legitimacy of a recent decision. As any parent knows, at some point the provision of justificatory reasons must end. The termination to the rationalizing process is, among other things, a matter of practicality. The child's incessant "But why?" – voiced after each new reason is provided – will generally outlast a parent's patience. Eventually an appeal to an authority is heard, perhaps voiced in that handy conversation stopper, "Because I said so!"

Other authorities may of course be invoked, such as the law, social mores, moral principle, or religious scripture. Alternatively, one might simply appeal to a habit or decision rule that has been developed over time. One might adopt the heuristic: once fatigued to the point of irritation in the search for sufficient reasons, choose the most appealing alternative produced thus far. In any case, something other than reason must be called upon to end the interrogation.

Russell Hardin writes that "One of the first lessons of any serious attention to the problem of rationality . . . is that a complete account of everything involved in one's significant decisions is not possible."[89] This is not to say that finding and articulating reasons for judgments is not a useful exercise. Certainly, as Steinberger suggests, we require an extensive chain

---

[89] Russell Hardin, *Morality with the Limits of Reason* (Chicago: University of Chicago Press, 1988), p. 1.

of reasoning from judges on the bench rendering legal verdicts. And we expect *some* effort at rational explanation, however limited, from political leaders and, for that matter, from colleagues, friends, and family members rendering judgments. Nonetheless, rationality ultimately proves insufficient, as each reason proffered can always be subject to further questioning. Unable to deliver reasons for all her reasons, the judge attempting to render an exhaustive account of a judgment is eventually reduced to silence, an admission of ignorance, or an appeal to intuition, habit, a decision rule, or some form of authority. In the end, the buck has to stop in a court other than that of reason.

This fact has been recognized by the most distinguished jurists. In Jacobellis v. Ohio, Justice Potter Stewart concurred with the majority in reversing the obscenity conviction of a movie theater manager in Cleveland Heights for showing the 1959 Louis Malle film, *Les Amants*. Stewart insisted that the First Amendment protected all but "hard-core pornography." He wrote: "I shall not today attempt further to define the kinds of material I understand to be embraced within that short-hand description, and perhaps I could never succeed in intelligibly doing so. But I know it when I see it, and the motion picture involved in this case is not that."[90] The decision rendered by the Supreme Court justices demonstrated sound judgment. Yet Stewart explicitly recognized that at its very core the verdict was grounded in intuitive, inexplicable sensitivities. Judgment cannot always explain itself.

Justice Oliver Wendell Holmes knew as much. He wrote that "many honest and sensible judgments...express an intuition of experience which outruns analysis and sums up many unnamed and tangled impressions – impressions which may be beneath consciousness without losing their worth."[91] In "The Path of Law," Holmes adds that "The training of lawyers is a training in logic. The processes of analogy, discrimination, and deduction are those in which they are most at home. The language of judicial decision is mainly the language of logic. And the logical method and form flatter that longing for certainty and for repose which is in every human mind." Holmes goes on to stipulate that it is a vain flattery. "Certainty generally is illusion," he states, "and repose is

[90] Jacobellis v. Ohio, 378 U.S. 184 (1964). This case is discussed in David A. Welch, "Culture and Emotion as Obstacles to Good Judgment," in *Good Judgment in Foreign Policy: Theory and Application*, ed. Stanley A. Renshon and Deborah Welch Larson (New York: Rowman and Littlefield, 2003), p. 191.

[91] Quoted in Robert P. Burns, *A Theory of the Trial* (Princeton: Princeton University Press, 1999), pp. 209–10.

not the destiny of man. Behind the logical form lies a judgment as to the relative worth and importance of competing legislative grounds, often an inarticulate and unconscious judgment, it is true, and yet the very root and nerve of the whole proceeding."[92] The best judges, Holmes is suggesting, are not necessarily those who are best able to explain their judgments. Some skillfulness at *post festum* explanation is required. It is part of the job. But the best judges are those who ground reason upon the best intuitions, not those who can best supply reasons for their (perhaps faulty) intuitions. By way of analogy, the best dancers or athletes may not be the best choreographers or coaches. The capacity to do something well is not the same thing as the capacity to explain it well.

Post festum explanations of judgments are often beneficial, but we should not pretend that they could ever be exhaustive. "What is apparent from the literature," one study suggests, "is that explanatory models are inadequate to explain more than the most elemental kinds of judgment, those that can be structured as, and reduced to, a given preference and probability which can be quantified. Even highly sophisticated formulations of these rules have been found inadequate to describe the complex inference in natural settings such as the courtroom or the operating room."[93] The implicit capacities involved in such efforts, cognitive psychologists attest, are "always richer and more sophisticated than that which can be explicated."[94] One wonders, in turn, whether retrospective explanations of judgments, more often than not, are *rationalizations* in the pejorative sense of this term. Might *post festum* reconstructions make sense of an event without at the same time supplying the most accurate representation of the actual forces animating it?

Empirical research suggests that this is often the case. When asked how and why a particular moral judgment was made, subjects focused on attributes that seemed like plausible reasons, even though these attributes had little or no impact on their actual decision-making. Rational reckoning, in other words, did not ground the judgments. It simply infomed their explanation.[95] Studies demonstrate that exercises in moral reasoning are

---

[92] O. W. Holmes, "The Path of Law," *Harvard Law Review*, 10, (1897): 465–66; quoted in Kenneth R. Hammond, *Human Judgment and Social Policy: Irreducible Uncertainty, Inevitable Error, Unavoidable Injustice* (New York: Oxford University Press, 1996), p. 70.

[93] F. H. Low-Beer, *Questions of Judgment* (Amherst, NY: Prometheus Books, 1995), p. 68.

[94] Reber, *Implicit Learning and Tacit Knowledge*, p. 64.

[95] Haidt, "The Emotional Dog," p. 815.

"typically one-sided efforts in support of pre-ordained conclusions."[96] Judgments are often justified in rational terms. But this justification generally distorts history. The *post festum* account of a judgment is more invention than explanation.

Rodney Brooks, Director of the MIT Computer Science and Artificial Intelligence Laboratory, observes that "Just because a behavior can be described as deriving from a complex set of rules does not mean that is how it occurred.... Humans are capable of going through logical chains of reasoning, but mostly it's post hoc rationalization." To be sure, people can and do justify their judgments and actions with good reasons. But when this happens, Brooks notes and research confirms, it is usually a matter of people simply "mak[ing] stuff up."[97] In like fashion, Nietzsche argues that once a judgment finds its way into speech, it is already a misrepresentation.[98] Conscious, articulate, reasoning signals a reductive "corruption" and "falsification" of the real force behind our choices and actions.[99] The foundations for our judgments are ineffable and inherently unavailable to the conscious mind, *ad hoc* or *post hoc*.

In what might be taken as an update of Nietzsche's position, Tor Norretranders, speaks of the "user illusion." The user illusion occurs whenever we believe the conscious, rational self is driving the car when, in fact, the unconscious self is really at the wheel. The cogitating mind that thinks and explains – Norretranders calls it the *"I"* – can grapple with thirty to fifty bits of information per second, whereas the unconscious mind, the *"Me,"* processes millions more. Norretranders writes of the useful but quite limited contributions of the conscious mind:

---

[96] Greene and Haidt, "How (and where) does moral judgment work?" p. 517. This statement applies most strongly to moral reasoners who are not specifically engaged in an effort to influence other people or reach consensus.

[97] Quoted in John Horgan, *The Undiscovered Mind* (New York: The Free Press, 1999), p. 220. On empirical research confirming this phenomenon, see also R. E. Nisbet and T. D. Wilson, "Telling more than we can know: verbal reports on mental processes," *Psychological Review* 84 (1977): 231–59; Seymour Epstein and Rosemary Pacini, "Some Basic Issues Regarding Dual-Process Theories from the Perspective of Cognitive-Experiential Self-Theory," in Shelly Chaiken and Yaacov Trope, *Dual-Process Theories in Social Psychology* (New York: Guilford Press, 1999), p. 476; and Joshua and Haidt, "How (and where) does moral judgment work?" pp. 517–523.

[98] Friedrich Nietzsche, *Twilight of the Idols: or How to Philosophize with a Hammer*, trans. R. J. Hollingdale (New York: Penguin, 1968), p. 82. See also Nietzsche, *The Will to Power*, trans. Walter Kaufmann and R.J. Hollingdale (New York: Vintage, 1968), p. 243.

[99] Nietzsche, *The Gay Science*, trans. Walter Kaufmann (New York: Vintage, 1974), pp. 299, 300.

The role of the *I* in learning is precisely to force the nonconscious, the *Me*, to practice, rehearse, or just attend. The *I* is a kind of boss who tells the *Me* what it must practice. The *I* is the *Me*'s secretary. The *I* affords discipline, even though it can hold very few bits [of information] per second. . . . The bandwidth of language is far lower than the bandwidth of sensation. Most of what we know about the world we can never tell each other. . . . The *I* may say, 'I can ride a bike.' But it cannot. It is the *Me* that can. As Lao-tzu, the Chinese savant who founded Taoism, put it as he rode into the mountains to die, 'Those who know do not talk. Those who talk do not know.'[100]

Just like riding a bike, rendering a judgment inevitably relies upon the *Me*. Oftentimes, the *Me*'s secretary will be called upon after the fact to give a report. But this report speaks less to the cause of a judgment than to the correlation between prior intuitions and subsequent rationalizations. Norretranders both buttresses and amends Nietzsche's position. He puts the conscious mind in its place, but does not unduly diminish its contribution. Being a good secretary is no small task.

Athletes understand that cognitive thought can interfere with peak performance. When they are at their best, in "the zone," the *Me* is in control. At the same time, professional athletes typically work with trainers, or are adept at training themselves. Through drills and instruction, they improve their performance. Second nature, in this case, often bests first nature. And this second nature is gained, in large part, by way of disciplined training and explicit learning. Conscious thought can never replace unconscious processes on the playing field, and will never fully be able to account for the role of the unconscious after the game. But unconscious capacities are often improved through practice and pedagogy.

This is true in many situations where one would think nature leaves us well equipped (for example, running, jumping, throwing), and particularly so in sports requiring skills for which our evolutionary heritage did not directly prepare us (for example, ice hockey or surfing). What is said here of athletes applies as well to chess players, war strategists, and practical judges. Without a foundation in tacit knowledge and skills, proficiency will never be developed. But the requisite knowledge and skills can be greatly refined and improved through instruction and disciplined exercise. For the *Me* to be at its best, an exacting secretary is required.

---

[100] Tor Norretranders, *The User Illusion*. Trans. Jonathan Sydenham (New York: Viking, 1998), pp. 303, 304, 309. Jeffrey Gray arrives at the same conclusion, writing: "The conscious 'I' is not the true subject of the story: it is the unconscious brain." Gray, *Consciousness*, p. 25.

The Case for Integration: Cultivating Good Judgment

When it comes to serial processing, computers win every competition between man and machine. They are quicker and less prone to error. But for complex tasks that resist resolution through an extensive series of rule applications, the human brain still takes the prize.[101] The unconscious mind's ability to engage in parallel distributed processing, assessing multiple cues in diverse ways, allows the expert his edge over the computer. Developers of "expert systems" acknowledge that the most advanced computers fall well short of human virtuosos largely because of the machines' inability to be inventive and integrative, to go beyond tried and true decision rules.[102] The technicians who developed Deep Blue, the computer that first beat chess grandmaster Gary Kasparov in 1997, rightly understood their achievement as the construction of a sophisticated calculator, not a machine capable of artificial intelligence. All efforts by technicians to mimic the integrative judgment of a grandmaster, rather than simply relying on fast and extensive computational power, have "failed miserably."[103]

Rationality contributes to judgment in the form of analysis, calculation, logical consistency, extrapolative forecasting, and retrospective reconstruction. Tacit knowledge and skills precede and ground these rational operations while exceeding their purview. Most complex human activities, including practical judgment, bespeak the interaction of conscious and unconscious efforts.[104] Were we to expunge those facets of the mind that resist rational assessment and explanation, our judgment would be undermined rather than improved. We would be left hamstrung and disoriented in a race, as the next chapter argues, that we had no incentive to win. Good judges, therefore, integrate the intuitive capacities of the mind with its analytical and deliberative powers.

Good judgment is notoriously difficult to define. In pursuit of a definition, we do better to focus on the components that go into good judgment rather than on the results that come out of it.[105] Good judgment is best identified by the diversity and quality of its input rather than the

---

[101] Rumelhart, *Parallel Distrubuted Processing.*
[102] Dreyfus, *Mind over Machine*, p. 119.
[103] Horgan, *The Undiscovered Mind*, p. 207.
[104] Dianne Berry, "Concluding note: How implicit is implicit learning?" in *How Implicit is Implicit Learning*, ed. Dianne Berry (New York: Oxford University Press, 1997), p. 236. See also Reber, *Implicit Learning and Tacit Knowledge*, pp. 23, 133.
[105] See Welch, "Culture and Emotion," p. 191.

(*post festum*) rationality of its output. The important question to ask is whether the exercise of judgment relies on a singular, and largely unaided faculty, or whether it symphonically makes use of a wide array of explicit *and* tacit capacities.

A manager's judgment regarding the selection of the best candidate for a particular job, for example, might be the product of her intuitive insight regarding personality types (based on tacit knowledge of character traits grounded in perceptual clues and implicit memories), supplemented by a conscious effort to mitigate against known personal biases, followed by a rational, comparative analysis of the candidates' respective skills, coupled with a habit of always getting a second opinion and never jumping to conclusions. The most mysterious aspect of judgment concerns the ability to integrate such diverse and seemingly incommensurable elements.

What makes for sound judgment, in the end, are the countless micro-judgments that go into it. These micro-judgments determine when to let decision rules, habits, and intuitions play their respective parts, and when to subject these intrinsic elements of judgment to the watchful eye of reason. In turn, other micro-judgments determine how much and what kind of information to gather, how many alternative perspectives to entertain, which principles and rules to apply, how much analysis to undertake, and when and where to direct its force. The question being begged here, of course, is what makes for good micro-judgments?

Thomas Edison famously observed that "genius is one percent inspiration and ninety-nine percent perspiration." Good judgment is also a combination of what we might broadly label intuitive capacities and the hard work of gathering information, considering alternate viewpoints, and rationally analyzing options. But the optimum ratio may be quite different for judgment than Edison suggested for genius, and it assuredly varies with context. The good judge, somehow, finds the right mix given the situation at hand.

If good judgment is grounded in a well-integrated blend of wide-ranging components, it follows that relying on a single mode of perception or appraisal will generally result in poor judgment. As Isaiah Berlin argues, poor judgment consists "not in failing to apply the methods of natural science, but, on the contrary, in over-applying them. Here failure comes from resisting that which works best in each field, from ignoring or opposing it either in favor of some systematic method or principle claiming universal validity ... or else from a wish to defy all principles, all methods as such, from simply advocating trust in a lucky star or personal inspiration; that is, mere irrationalism."[106] Poor judgment is poor because it is monolithic and meager. It fails to make good use of the diverse capacities of the mind. And it fails to integrate. Good judgment, in contrast, puts a panoply of deliberative and intuitive faculties to work in the perception and appraisal of multi-faceted problems.

Like Arendt, Berlin, and Steinberger, I employ the word *mysterious* in conjunction with judgment because the mind remains a largely undiscovered continent, notwithstanding tremendous advances in cognitive neuroscience. Commenting on the dearth of knowledge of how the mind integrates its capacities to arrive at a coherent picture of the world, John Horgan aptly writes: "Like a precocious eight-year-old tinkering with a radio, mind-scientists excel at taking the brain apart, but they have no idea how to put it back together again."[107] Fortunately, the judging mind functions well enough despite our enduring ignorance of its workings.

Embodied Learning

A vast literature in decision-making investigates various means to hone the deliberative and analytical skills that feature in judgment. In contrast, there is a patent dearth of scholarship exploring the use of unconscious capacities. How does one best exploit something one does not control? Once again, cognitive neuroscience is suggestive.

The first example concerns memory. The neurological home for the names of things or actions is located near the part of the brain concerned with how these things or actions are encountered or executed in the world. Though memories could not be secured without the hippocampus, they are not stored in the hippocampus but in the cortex. The memory of a thing, in other words, is stored in the same neural networks that were activated in its perception.[108] The linguistic representation of things that we see, for instance, is located near the visual cortex, just as the linguistic representation of things that we hear is located near the auditory cortex, and the linguistic representation of things that we manipulate is located near the motor cortex. Thus in brain-injured subjects, anomia for nouns – the inability to recall or use object words – is caused when the part of the temporal lobe adjacent to the visual occipital lobe is damaged. In turn,

[106] Berlin, *The Sense of Reality*, p. 51–52.
[107] Horgan, *The Undiscovered Mind*, p. 23.
[108] Goldberg, *The Wisdom Paradox*, pp. 110–114.

anomia for verbs – the loss of action words – is caused by damage to the frontal lobe adjacent to the motor cortex.

Now it so happens that anomia for the words that represent living things occurs as a result of brain damage much more frequently than anomia for words that represent inanimate objects. There is a straightforward reason. Elkhonon Goldberg explains:

Most inanimate objects we come into contact with are man-made. Man-made objects are created for a purpose; we do things with them. In most cases, this implies that the mental representations of inanimate objects have an additional aspect: the representation of actions implicit in the objects. This aspect is for the most part absent in the mental representations of living things. As a result, the mental representations of inanimate things are more widely distributed, involve more parts of the brain, and are therefore less vulnerable to the effects of brain damage.[109]

Because the words for inanimate objects are located near the parts of the brain that attend to the way these objects are actively encountered, and because these encounters entail diverse physical abilities, the homes for these words in the brain are widely distributed and therefore less vulnerable to disruption when a single part of the brain becomes damaged. How does all this relate to the cultivation of unconscious capacities?

Conscious efforts to retrieve memories can be frustrating and, on occasion, may prove to be fruitless or even counterproductive. But one can improve the power of recollection by recalling the way the thing is encountered. For instance, one might try to remember a particular term by visualizing an encounter with it as a word on a page or in a conversation. Or one might attempt to recall the name of a new acquaintance by imagining his face, or the context of a recent meeting with him. Likewise, one might best retrieve the forgotten name of an object by imagining one's most recent use of it. In such cases, we are stimulating the brain region that is the neurological home of the sensory components activated by our encounter with the forgotten thing, and in so doing, stimulating adjacent brain regions that house its linguistic representation.

Such efforts are suggestive of a much wider range of pedagogical techniques, wherein we enhance our ability to comprehend and remember things by stimulating the part of the brain associated with their worldly encounter. In essence, this is the neuroscientific basis for the pragmatist doctrine that we learn best through action. Getting our body and

---

[109] Goldberg, *The Executive Brain*, pp. 62–67.

its unconscious capacities more involved aids conscious learning and retention.

For most of human history, learning was a product of activity that included movement and, broadly speaking, experiential performances. Most learning retains this character today. Indeed, even formal learning and thinking remain "anchored by movement." Carla Hannaford writes:

> Actions such as doodling, eye movement, speaking aloud to oneself and to others, writing things down, are familiar movements that occur during thinking. Without movement of some kind, you don't get conscious thought. . . . We tend to relegate muscles to the domain of the body, not the mind. But it is through expression that we advance and solidify our understanding. Usually this expression takes the form of speech (or sign language in the case of deaf people) or writing, which of course use a great deal of very highly coordinated muscular actions.[110]

Of course, one can cogitate while mute and motionless. But hushed immobility is not a recipe for dynamic thinking. You might attempt the experiment of trying to think while remaining completely still, without any facial tension or eye movement, and with a fully relaxed tongue (let it fall to the front of a slightly open mouth). Engaging the conscious brain without muscular motion or tension of any sort is no easy task. We simply were not wired to think and learn in motionless silence, and it should come as no surprise that two brain regions originally associated solely with muscle control – the cerebellum and the basal ganglia – are now known to be involved in the coordination of thought.[111] What is said here of learning through movement applies as well to the involvement of other faculties. Learning is best facilitated through experiences that involve not only the cognitive, rational centers of the brain but also the visual, auditory, tactile, proprioceptive, and affective faculties as well.

Good judgment develops from learning that taps into bodily awareness. This learning, gounded in implicit cognition, proves to be robust. As Oakeshott suggests of tacit knowledge: "If it is learned, it can never be forgotten, and it does not need to be recollected in order to be enjoyed. It is, indeed, often enough, the residue which remains when all else is forgotten; the shadow of lost knowledge."[112] While the name of a thing may easily be forgotten, the procedural memory of its physical

---

[110] Carla Hannaford, *Smart Moves: Why Learning Is Not All in Your Head* (Arlington: Great Ocean Publishers, 1995), p. 87.

[111] Hannaford, *Smart Moves*, p. 99. See also Steven R. Quartz and Terrence J. Sejnowski, *Liars, Lovers, and Heroes: What the New Brain Science Reveals about How We Became Who We Are* (New York: William Morrow, 2002), pp. 247–250.

[112] Oakeshott, *The Voice of Liberal Learning*, p. 60.

encounter or use forms a synaptic residue in the brain. This shadow of lost knowledge, which often takes the form of intuitive insight and tacit skills, figures prominently in practical judgment. As Alfred Tennyson observed, "Knowledge comes, but wisdom lingers."[113]

Getting the right parts of the brain involved in our experiences is key to the development of good judgment. In this vein, William Connolly asks "how . . . can the amygdala be educated?" The amygdala is a primitive brain region almost wholly impervious to conscious control. But it greatly influences decision-making, regulating fear responses, engaging emotional processes, and participating in procedural (implicit) memory. Its education is crucial for those who would cultivate practical judgment. Connolly answers his own question: "Since [the amygdala's] specific organization is shaped to an uncertain degree by previous intensities of cultural experience and performance, either it or, more likely, the network of relays in which it is set may be susceptible to modest influence by rituals and intersubjective arts."[114] Connolly's recommendation is well taken, though its target is too restrictive given the prominent role brain regions other than the amygdala play in tacit knowledge and skills. But the point remains that good judgment is grounded in the habit of exercising by way of performative and, broadly speaking, cultural engagements, facets of our minds that remain inaccessible to direct intervention or pedagogy. These experiential encounters remap the brain to make a wider assortment of its faculties more accessible. In other words, the good judge provides his *Me* with a good secretary who doubles as a personal trainer.

Consider empirical research in the area of "strategic automaticity." Strategic automaticity or "instant habits" originate from single acts of will that are designed to put unconscious capacities of the mind to work.[115] All participants involved in such studies develop general goals. In addition, some participants are also requested to articulate clear, concrete "implementation intentions." These may take the form: "If x happens, then I will (or will not) do y." Participants who articulate implementation intentions

---

[113] Alfred Tennyson, *Locksley Hall*, 1:143 (1842). The lingering of wisdom, Elkhonon Goldberg argues, is largely a left-hemisphere phenomenon. See Goldberg, *The Wisdom Paradox*.

[114] William E. Connolly, *Why I Am Not a Secularist* (Minneapolis: University of Minnesota Press, 1999), p. 29.

[115] Peter Gollwitzer, Ute Bayer, and Kathleen McCulloch, "The Control of the Unwanted," in *The New Unconscious*, ed. Ran Hassin, James Uleman, and John Bargh (Oxford: Oxford University Press, 2005), p. 485.

not only demonstrate greater follow through in achieving their goals, but also demonstrate enhanced capacities to achieve them. These enhanced capacities are grounded in the activation of automatic or unconscious skills.[116]

Participants of one study, for instance, were asked to classify geometric shapes such as circles, ellipses, triangles, and squares as either rounded or angular objects by pressing a left or a right button. All participants had the same goal – to push the correct button as quickly and accurately as possible. In turn, some participants also articulated the implementation intention: "And if I see a triangle, then I press the respective button particularly fast." Implementation intention participants showed a substantial increase in speed of response when triangles were shown compared with control subjects. Importantly, they also displayed faster reponses for angular figures when triangles were presented subliminally. Though consciously unaware of the presentation of a triangle (prime), their ability to recognize and respond to similar shapes was enhanced. In other words, people were able to improve the unconscious aptitudes implicated in their endeavors by consciously articulating tactics. The more difficult the goals, the more effective were the willful efforts to enhance the tacit skills involved in their achievement.

The articulation of clear intentions can activate parts of the brain that control unconscious capacities. As the experimental psychologists conducting one study observed, "delegating control" to our unconscious capacities by way of such efforts is an effective and efficient means to meet goals.[117] Indeed, the use of implementation intentions has been shown to enhance perceptual and motor abilities, facilitate effective operation in the midst of distractions, reduce stereotyped or prejudicial reactions, attentuate the negative effects of emotions and moods, aid the shunning of temptations that thwart goal achievement, and offset disruptive priming effects. Importantly, the use of concrete implementation strategies did not foster rigid reactions. Indeed, it increased innovative and imaginative behavior in many instances. Future studies may confirm how implementation intentions can best be employed to harness the unconscious capacities involved in practical judgment.

Consider a second example. The brain's right hemisphere copes with innovation and is considered "highly sensitive to perturbation." The left

---

[116] Gollwitzer, "The Control of the Unwanted," pp. 485–515.
[117] Gollwitzer, "The Control of the Unwanted," pp. 509, 511.

hemisphere, in contrast, is more oriented to routinized tasks and fitting new phenomena into preexisting models. It is posited as "conformist."[118] At times, the conservatism of the left hemisphere steers individuals into extreme acts of denial. Stroke victims whose right hemispheres have been damaged provide fascinating test cases. Depending on the severity of the trauma, victims may exhibit an uncanny tendency to deny the paralysis of their left sides. They may even invent – and fully embrace – elaborate stories that explain why they cannot perform requested tasks requiring the use of both arms. The damage to the right hemisphere has not only left these victims with lifeless left limbs, it has also undermined their brains' ability to grapple with the novelty of discrepant sensory inputs concerning body image. Consequently, the victims deny their paralysis rather than physically compensate for it.[119]

One woman suffering from this affliction was asked to lift a tray holding drinks. Rather than placing her functional right hand in the middle of the tray, as stroke victims who are conscious of their paralysis would do, she grabbed the tray from one end. The left arm remained lifeless at her side. Not surprisingly, the tray tipped over and the drinks spilled onto her lap. When asked what had happened, the woman stated matter of factly that she had successfully lifted the tray. She remained oblivious to the mishap and her soaked legs.

The right side of the brain that would allow the woman to cope with an altered physical reality had been too badly damaged by the stroke. Her conformist left hemisphere therefore went about the Procrustean task of fitting a novel world where partial paralysis disallowed certain actions to a preexisting body image. Consequently, she acted as if both her arms were fully functional, and subsequently rewrote her personal history to correspond with this fabrication. The left hemisphere first ignored the anomaly and subsequently distorted memory to reinforce its account. This, Ramachandran suggests, is also the neuropsychology behind the well-known "Freudian defenses" of denial, repression, and self-delusion that make regular appearances in daily life.[120]

Scholars of decision-making suggest that one of the best things one can do to offset common (intuitive) heuristics that impede good judgment is to regularize the use of a devil's advocate, or to play the role for oneself.

---

[118] Ramachandran, *Phantoms in the Brain*, p. 141.
[119] Ramachandran, *Phantoms in the Brain*, p. 141.
[120] See Ramachandran, *Phantoms in the Brain*, p. 134.

This tactic facilitates a surveying of alternative perspectives and options, thus mitigating stereotyping, excessive optimism, inaccurate self-images, and other common biases. From a neurological perspective, it is a good suggestion. We must find ways to stimulate the novelty-receptive right hemisphere of the brain, lest the left side carry through its conformist mandate of rationalizing and legitimizing expectations, habits, and prejudices.

With the aforementioned stroke victim, the physical stimulation of the damaged part of the brain did indeed produce welcome results. By irrigating the left ear of the afflicted woman with ice-cold water, doctors were able to stimulate her right hemisphere. Directly after the ear irrigation, the patient acknowledged the paralysis of her left arm and acted accordingly. However, in as little as half an hour, her former state of denial returned. The physical stimulation of the right hemisphere provided only temporary relief from its counterpart's Procrustean tendencies.

Good judgment may be cultivated by the equivalent of periodic ear washing. At times, the primary need might be arousal of the right hemisphere, perhaps by employing a devil's advocate or some other means of fostering ingenuity and the appreciation of novelty. At times, the arousal of the neural networks bearing implicit memories and tacit knowledge might be most helpful. This might be achieved through action that stimulates the motor cortex near which a form of learning found its cerebral home. And, at times, the stimulation of the seat of reason in the pre-frontal cortex will prove to be of greatest benefit. How best to target such neurological capacities is a fitting subject for experiential research.

Whole-Brain Judgment

Knowledge is a measure of what one knows. Practical wisdom is demonstrated less by *what* one knows than by *how* one knows it. The question is: does one know it affectively as well as rationally, intuitively as well as cognitively, tacitly as well as explicitly? Was the knowledge gained through formal study employing restricted neural circuitry, or through worldly experience that elicited whole-brain learning?

Logical deliberation and rational assessment are crucial skills for the proficient judge. These reflective, analytical capacities correct for flaws inherent in intuition. Indeed, it is possible that reflective consciousness evolved in human beings because it enabled the fine-tuning of implicitly acquired knowledge and skills.[121] Particularly in its deliberative and analytical modes, consciousness facilitates the *post facto* detection and correction of errors that result from the unconscious perceptions, memories, and actions that make up the lion's share of life. So an education in reason is all for the good. As Mark Twain observed, however, we should never let our education get in the way of our learning.

If formal education does not engage the whole-brain, including those areas specific to the acquisition of tacit knowledge and skills, then it may be acquired at the expense of real learning. That is Sheldon Wolin's worry. His charge is that *methodism* – the standardization of rigorous, formalized, step-by-step procedures for inquiry and research – is impeding the acquisition of an entire realm of knowledge and skills. Wolin writes that "The triumph of methodism constitutes a crisis in political education and . . . the main victim is the tacit political knowledge which is so vital to making judgments, not only judgments about the adequacy and value of theories and methods, but about the nature and perplexities of politics as well."[122] The first step to averting this crisis entails acknowledging that much learning occurs, to recall Oakeshott's phrase, "obliquely in the course of instruction" as students absorb the manner of thinking and judging of their teachers.

Oblique learning in the classroom is the product of a hermeneutic grappling with relationships and performances. It is facilitated by "field work" that takes students and scholars out of classrooms and libraries to explore the world through first-hand encounters. A combination of oblique, classroom-style learning and hands-on, experiential fieldwork is evident in apprenticeships. Here, explicit learning and "learning without awareness" are synchronous, as multiple brain regions are stimulated by diverse hands-on tasks accompanied by instruction. Because they are initially employed together in the learning process, a broad constellation of neural maps become available again when judgments are subsequently demanded.

Whole-brain judgment is based on whole-brain learning. The logic hemisphere of the brain, generally the left, deals mostly with details, acquired language processes, routines, and linear patterns. The gestalt

---

[121] See John Bargh, "Bypassing the Will: Toward Demystifying the Nonconscious Control of Social Behavior," in *The New Unconscious*, ed. Ran Hassin, James Uleman, and John Bargh (Oxford: Oxford University Press, 2005), pp. 37–58. Gray, *Consciousness*, p. 104.

[122] Wolin, "Political Theory as a Vocation," p. 1077.

hemisphere, generally the right, deals mostly with images, novelty, and intuition. The corpus callosum, a transverse band of 200 million nerve fibers, connects the two hemispheres, and allows for integrated thought.[123] Whole-brain judgment is a product of bi-hemispheric activity that is linguistic and imagistic, symbolic and concrete, habituated and inventive, calculative and intuitive, explicit and tacit.[124] In turn, whole-brain judgment taps into the contributions of sub-cortical regions, again building upon, rather than neglecting, unconscious capacities. It follows that efforts to assess practical wisdom must not deny practitioners the fully experiential encounters that elicit whole-brain responses.[125]

The task of integrating the various parts of the brain active in judging falls chiefly upon the frontal lobes. Elkhonon Goldberg maintains that "The frontal lobes do not have the specific knowledge or expertise for all the necessary challenges facing the organism. What they have, however, is the ability to 'find' the areas of the brain in possession of this knowledge and expertise for any specific challenge, and to string them together in complex configurations according to the need."[126] From a neurological point of view, good judgment occurs when the frontal lobes marshal other brain regions into service, utilizing diverse capacities and orchestrating their integrated effort. As noted earlier, the myelination of axons in the pre-frontal cortex is not completed until individuals reach their mid- to late twenties. Physiologically speaking, that is why practical wisdom is not a characteristic of the young. This does not mean that practical wisdom is the product of (late maturing) reason. Rather, it suggests that practical wisdom is the product of the (late maturing) cortical ability to integrate reason with the intuitive and affective capacities that find their origins

---

[123] Women generally have as much as 10 percent more fibers in the corpus callosum than men. This may suggest a greater ability and tendency to integrate intuitive elements into judgment.

[124] Experimental studies have confirmed the role of imagistic intelligence even in mathematical exercises. Here the processing of images (of greater or lesser), as opposed to the calculation of actual numbers, allows for a sense of approximation that is stored and retrieved figuratively rather than symbolically or linguistically. See David and Ann Premack, *Original Intelligence* (New York: McGraw Hill, 2003), pp. 218–224.

[125] The use of oral and written examinations, interviews, and surveys to determine subjects' capacity for and exercise of practical wisdom largely ignores the contribution of tacit skills, as the recent work of psychologists employing such methodologies demonstrates. See Robert Sternberg, ed., *Wisdom: Its Nature, Origins, and Development* (Cambridge: Cambridge University Press, 1990), and Robert Sternberg and Jennifer Jordan, eds. *A Handbook of Wisdom: Psychological Perspectives* (Cambridge: Cambridge University Press, 2005).

[126] Goldberg, *The Executive Brain*, p. 218.

in other brain regions. Such integration would appear to be an obvious good. But, at least in the Western tradition of thought, it has often been spurned so that reason might achieve monopolistic power.

Socrates insisted that it was worse to be at "odds" with oneself than in disagreement with a multitude of others. Moral integrity and courage are praiseworthy virtues. But Nietzsche may have been onto something when he argued that Socrates gained tranquility of the soul by establishing the tyranny of reason. While a despotic rationality may yield greater conscious control, it will not produce better judgments. Tyrannies do not foster the most productive use of diverse resources. Conscious control gained at the expense of a richer, more insightful, and more integrated whole-brain encounter with the world is a net loss.

Socrates, of course, took to heart the Delphic dictum to "Know thyself." Yet the ironic legacy of his teaching has been the extensive exploration and utilization of the tip of the self's iceberg to the exclusion of most everything that lies beneath the surface of consciousness. Antonio Gramsci wrote that knowing oneself was a matter of insight into the "historical process" that has "deposited in you an infinity of traces, without leaving an inventory."[127] Good judgment makes use of the uninventoried resources deposited over eons of ancestral experience and a lifetime of personal experience. Utilizing these deposited traces may on occasion lead one astray. Too often we intuit badly and glean the wrong lessons from our encounters with the world. So we are well advised to study reason and work to mitigate noxious biases. Learning, in most cases, is enhanced when it makes good use of explicit knowledge and rational processes.[128] At the same time, we are operating at a severe deficit if we limit ourselves to conscious, rational effort. Good judgment is an integrated, whole-brain activity. Relying solely on the small portion of the neurological capacities that we have managed to inventory – the conscious mind – can produce only impoverished judgments.

Good judgment, almost everyone since Aristotle agrees, cannot be taught. It has to be gained through experience. That is why Aristotle deemed politics a field of study and practice unfit for the young. But Aristotle never tells us what it is about experience, as opposed to formal pedagogy, that lends itself to the cultivation of judgment. Cognitive neuroscience helps us understand. Formal pedagogy well conveys explicit

[127] Antonio Gramsci, *Selections from the Prison Notebooks*, trans./ed. Quintin Hoare and Geoffrey Nowell Smith (New York: International Publishers, 1971), p. 324.

[128] Reber, *Implicit Learning and Tacit Knowledge*, p. 159.

information. Most of the knowledge that goes into our practical judgments, however, is implicitly acquired. It is absorbed obliquely. Notwithstanding the tremendous benefits of formal education, the cultivation of good judgment demands whole-brain learning. That is primarily offered in the school of life. To properly educate intuition, we must concern ourselves with the awesome task of understanding – and improving – the lessons learned in this academy.

4

The Imperative of Affect

Every faculty in one man is the measure by which he judges of the like faculty in another. I judge of your sight by my sight, of your ear by my ear, of your reason by my reason, of your resentment by my resentment, of your love by my love. I neither have, nor can have, any other way of judging about them.

Adam Smith[1]

Not everyone who understands his own mind understands his heart.

La Rochefoucauld[2]

Scooping Freud by more than a decade, Friedrich Nietzsche argued that the conscious mind is mostly a façade and that the vast majority of what really goes on in the brain remains unavailable to us. In *The Gay Science*, we read: "For the longest time, conscious thought was considered thought itself. Only now does the truth dawn on us that by far the greatest part of our spirit's activity remains unconscious and unfelt."[3] Unlike Freud, Nietzsche did not suggest that prodding the unconscious into speech would yield liberating knowledge. Rather, he insisted that making instinct articulate would result in its misrepresentation, if not corruption.

In grappling with the unconscious, Nietzsche asessed the role of innate knowledge and skills. But his primary focus was passion. Its exclusion from

[1] Adam Smith, *The Theory of Moral Sentiments* (Amherst: Prometheus Books, 2000), p. 18.
[2] La Rochefoucauld, *Maxims*, trans. Leonard Tanock (London: Penguin Books, 1959), p. 50; #103.
[3] Friedrich Nietzsche, *The Gay Science*, trans. Walter Kaufmann (New York: Vintage, 1974), pp. 261, 262.

discussion in the last chapter marks a glaring omission. No account of practical judgment is complete without an adequate understanding of the role of emotion.

Though we hold our conscious thoughts in high esteem, Nietzsche observes, they really represent "the last link of a chain."[4] The first link is passion. The retrospective task of the intellect, he maintains, is simply to justify and defend emotional predispositions.[5] Intellect is in the business of rationalization, supplying the *post hoc* paperwork that spells out the settlement of an internal struggle between competing affects. At its best, the intellect is secretarial. The deliberative mind constitutes a pale reflection of the "hidden roots" of desires and aversions. Our thoughts are always "the shadows of our feelings."[6]

Rationality never really prevails over emotion. If an obnoxious emotion is to be overcome, Nietzsche insists, this cannot be achieved by way of reason, but only by another, stronger emotion (that may well impress reason into service for its purposes).[7] The most independent thinker, therefore, is he who realizes that his thoughts are but the efflux of imperceptible affects. The man Zarathustra loves for his honesty acknowledges that "his head is only the bowels of his heart."[8] With Hume, Nietzsche held that reason is and ought to remain passion's slave.

Nietzsche does not stand alone in highly appraising the significance of emotion. However, with the partial exception of Aristotle, Machiavelli, Hume, Rousseau (who in the *Second Discourse* substitutes pity or commiseration for reason as the foundation of human justice), and certain thinkers of the Scottish Enlightenment, notably Adam Smith, emotion has gained rather bad press in the history of moral and political thought. Modern theorists generally endorse Immanuel Kant's deontological deprecation of emotion. Affects are portrayed as unwelcome intrusions to the rational judgments of moral agents. They are impediments that cloud what otherwise might be more reasonable, unbiased assessments, evaluations, and choices.

---

4 Nietzsche, *Gesammelte Werke*, vol. 16 (Munich: Musarion, 1920–29), p. 61. See also Nietzsche, *The Gay Science*, p. 261.

5 Nietzsche, *The Will to Power*, trans. Walter Kaufmann and R. J. Hollingdale (New York: Vintage, 1968), p. 208.

6 Nietzsche, *Gesammelte Werke*, p. 60. Nietzsche, *The Gay Science*, p. 203.

7 Nietzsche, *Beyond Good and Evil*, trans. R. J. Hollingdale (New York: Penguin, 1973), p. 79.

8 Nietzsche, *Thus Spoke Zarathustra: A Book for Everyone and No One*, trans. R. J. Hollingdale (New York: Penguin, 1969) p. 45.

Certainly the exclusion or disparagement of emotion has continued to be the norm in contemporary efforts to improve decision-making. Summing up a vast literature from Plato through the American Founding Fathers to contemporary theorists and behavioral political scientists, George Marcus writes: "Thus we seem to have settled on the need to secure a politics without emotion if we are to realize a politics of judgment and justice. A defensible democracy, at least at those moments of political judgment, especially in determining collective outcomes (i.e., the public good) as well as matters of justice, seemingly has to shield such judgments from the contaminating effects of passion."[9] Among current theorists of human judgment, strengthening reason remains the primary goal. To strengthen reason, emotion must be curbed. It is a zero-sum game.

In the 1980s, studies in social psychology, evolutionary psychology, and primatology began to reassess the importance of emotions to moral and political decision-making. After a quarter century of work centered on information processing models of the mind, theorists of judgment drifted away from the cognitive revolution. These scholars, along with philosophers more in touch with Aristotle than Kant, argued that affective states are indispensable components of judgment. In turn, empirical research increasingly demonstrated that emotions are inextricably involved in assessments, evaluations, and choices at a foundational level and do not simply function as impediments to rational deliberation.[10]

Denying the possibility of a wholly rational decision-maker, Irving Janis examines "hot cognitive processes." He acknowledges from the outset that "We see man not as a cold fish but as a warm-blooded mammal, not as a rational calculator always ready to work out the best solution but as a reluctant decision maker – beset by conflict, doubts, and worry, struggling with incongruous longings, antipathies, and loyalties, and seeking relief by procrastinating, rationalizing, or denying responsibility for his own choice."[11] It is salutary that contemporary scholars such as Janis recognize the fundamental influence of affect. But it would be better if they acknowledged that emotions are intrinsic components of *good* judgment rather than simply unavoidable factors in the generation of bad

9 George E. Marcus, *The Sentimental Citizen: Emotion in Democratic Politics* (University Park, PA: Pennsylvania State University Press, 2002), p. 6.

10 See, for example, Joshua Greene and Jonathan Haidt, "How (and where) does moral judgment work?" *Trends in Cognitive Sciences* 6 (2002): 517–523.

11 Irving L. Janis and Leon Mann, *Decision Making: A Psychological Analysis of Conflict, Choice, and Commitment* (New York: The Free Press, 1977), p. 15.

judgments. Particular emotions in specific situations can and often do impede sound judgment. But one should not throw out the baby with the bathwater. To put the point bluntly: rational judgment in moral and political affairs simply cannot arise in the absence of emotion. Affect gets reason off the ground and subsequently directs its operations. If we are to improve human judgment, there is no alternative but to grapple with the rich, multi-layered, typically clandestine, occasionally deleterious, generally beneficial, and always vital interaction between reason and emotion.

Affect Over Reason

The historical touchstone of psychological inquiry into the role of emotion in judgment occurred in 1884, with William James's publication of "What is an Emotion" in the philosophy journal, *Mind.* It was widely held at that time that a person's perception of the environment produced a conscious affective state. This affective state then gave rise to a bodily response. James argued that the reverse was true – namely, that one's perception of the environment produced a bodily response, and this bodily response gave rise to feelings. In short, one did not run from the bear because one was scared; rather, one became scared because one found oneself running from the bear.

James's insight is at least partially born out by contemporary neuroscience. The vast majority of emotions are generated in or induced by the limbic region, a sub-cortical area of the brain that includes the amygdala, the brain-stem, the hypothalamus, and the basal forebrain.[12] This region plays a prominent role in our first reactions to external stimuli. Our sense organs register the world by relaying information, via the thalamus, to the amygdala. The amygdala triggers an emotional response in the body that is largely executed by the basal forebrain, hypothalamus, and brain stem.[13] The physical reactions stimulated by the amygdala

[12] Early conceptions of the limbic region were overly simplistic, as the neural structures involved in emotions proved more widespread and interactivie. See Joseph LeDoux, *The Synaptic Self: How Our Brains Become Who We Are* (New York: Penguin Books, 2002), p. 212. Still, regions of the limbic system do specialize in particular emotions. A patient with severe damage to the amygdala, for instance, will not express fear, perceive danger normally, or recognize expressions of fear in others' faces. See Antonio R. Damasio, *The Feeling of What Happens: Body and Emotion in the Making of Consciousness* (New York: Harcourt, Brace and Company, 1999), pp. 60–67.

[13] Antonio Damasio, *Looking for Spinoza: Joy, Sorrow, and the Feeling Brain* (New York: Harcourt, 2003), p. 64.

often are not (immediately) available to consciousness. For example, in response to some external stimuli, the amygdala may stimulate increased heart rate and perspiration. This affective response generally takes place without conscious effort or awareness. Only subsequently might one register a *feeling* of this affective (emotional) response, or engage in a cognitive evaluation of it. Feeling scared, in the sense of being conscious of being frightened, does indeed chronologically *follow* rather than *precede* our first physical reactions (increased heart rate and perspiration, if not actual running) to a threatening situation. When we consciously feel our emotions – and it is not always the case that we do – we are perceiving an already-in-progress change in body state.[14] Indeed, we often "discover" our feelings by observing our physical reactions and behavior.[15] With this in mind, one might define emotions as affective states that (usually) have an observable physical effect. A feeling, in turn, is the conscious registry of an emotion.

To say that emotional responses literally precede our feelings of them as well as our cognitive awareness and deliberative responses to them is to say that emotions induce biases before they have the opportunity to stimulate judgment. Subjects hooked up to machines that measure galvanic skin response will give physical evidence of emotional reactions to choices they are offered even though they remain unaware of any personal preferences. In other words, they become emotionally biased in favor of certain alternatives and yet remain wholly unconscious of these biases.[16] Polygraph tests are based on this fact. Those undergoing polygraphs give physical evidence of unconscious, emotive reactions (to lying) even though their conscious thoughts and verbal responses may remain unaffected. One does not have to feel nervous or guilty or consciously register any remorse or anxiety at lying to fail a polygraph test. The changes in levels of skin conductance, like the emotional reactions that caused these changes, generally occur far below the subject's conscious awareness or control.

The phenomenon of unconscious affect's altering behavior is well demonstrated in people afflicted with various brain maladies. For instance, patients with visual agnosia (the inability to recognize faces) demonstrate measurable increases in skin conductance when shown a

---

[14] Damasio, *The Feeling of What Happens*; Damasio, *Looking for Spinoza*, pp. 101, 105.

[15] Scott Plous, *The Psychology of Judgment and Decision Making* (Philadelphia: Temple University Press, 1993), p. 25.

[16] Damasio, *The Feeling of What Happens*, p. 301.

photograph of the face of an acquaintance.[17] Yet they insist that they do not recognize the person and will act fully in accordance with their disability regardless of how this action deleteriously affects their interests. Likewise, people suffering from Korsakoff's syndrome or other forms of extensive brain damage to both temporal lobes are unable to learn any new facts or recognize people they have met a day, or an hour, before. Yet they will display an aversion to people who have treated them brusquely or otherwise negatively. Though Korsakoff victims completely fail to recognize these individuals when introduced for the second or third time, remember nothing of the rudeness shown them, and feel no emotions regarding these individuals, their behavior demonstrates an unconscious emotional bias.[18] Like the rest of us, Korsakoff victims have emotional reactions. Like us, they act upon these emotional reactions. But, because of neurological injuries that sever the link between their emotional faculties and their conscious, reflective capacities, they remain unaware that emotional reactions are affecting their actions. The rest of us become aware of this linkage, though we generally do so *post facto*. Hence we claim to act based on our feelings, when our actions are likely driven by unconscious, affective, physical reactions that, in quick order, give rise to feelings.

Studies in cognitive psychology underline the role of affective states in producing unconscious biases and behavior. Consider the effects of mood.[19] Fed bogus feedback about themselves from confederates, subjects of one study were induced to feel mildly elated, neutral, or despondent. Subsequently, subjects interviewed candidates for a middle-management position and assessed their merits. Happy subjects rated the candidates as more talented, more motivated, more attractive, and more likeable than did neutral subjects. Despondent subjects rated candidates worse on all counts. Moods spark congruent memories and thoughts: positive moods tend to produce more positive memories and more optimistic assessments and predictions, whereas negative moods elicit more critical – and self-critical – judgments. Hence, happy subjects displayed

---

[17] James H. Austin, *Zen and the Brain: Towards an Understanding of Meditation and Consciousness* (Cambridge: MIT Press, 1998), p. 597.

[18] Damasio, *The Feeling of What Happens*, pp. 43–46.

[19] A mood might be defined as an affective state more prolonged and diffuse than an emotion. Emotions are usually about something particular, while moods often do not have an identifiable, proximate object or cause. See Norbert Schwarz and Gerald Clore, "Feelings and Phenomenal Experiences," in *Social Psychology: Handbook of Basic Principles* (New York: Guilford Press, 1996), pp. 433–465.

strong mood-congruent recall, remembering mostly the positive things said by the candidates, whereas despondent subjects remembered mostly the negative things that were conveyed.[20] They judged accordingly.

In a related study, participants were asked to make judgments about topical issues (for example, evaluating political figures). Subjects who had just seen an uplifting film made more positive and lenient judgments about candidates, whereas those seeing a sad film were more negative and severe in their assessments.[21] Other research confirms that people (unconsciously) employ their affective state as a quick heuristic when generating judgments.[22] Importantly, mood states do not need to be radically altered to influence decision-making. Studies of dozens of stock exchanges in multiple countries confirm that investors are more optimistic about their returns, hence pushing the market up, on sunny days. Cloudy days have the opposite effect.[23] Even subtle alterations of mood can skew judgment.

Emotions that skew judgment do not have to constitute something as substantial, pervasive, and sustained as a mood. Experiments that involve "priming" demonstrate that more discrete emotions also have noticeable effects. Conscious processing of an external object does not begin until a stimulus has persisted for 30 milliseconds or more in the visual field.[24] In priming studies, participants view words or objects that appear for only a few milliseconds at a randomized location on a computer screen that is outside of their foveal (conscious) area of visual processing. Subsequent to their brief appearance, the prime words or objects are masked (by a string of other letters, for example), ensuring that participants are not aware of them and cannot recall their appearance. Phenomenally, participants only experience and recall brief flashes of light on the computer screen. Yet participants subliminally primed, say,

[20] Gordon Bower, "Mood Congruity of Social Judgments," in Joseph P. Forgas, ed., *Emotion and Social Judgment* (Oxford: Pergamon Press, 1991), pp. 31–53.

[21] Joseph Forgas, "The role of emotion in social judgments," *European Journal of Social Psychology* 24 (1994): 1–24.

[22] Nyla Branscombe and Brian Cohen, "Motivation and Complexity Levels as Determinants of Heuristic Use in Social Judgments," in *Emotion and Social Judgment*, pp. 145–160.

[23] Norbert Schwarz, "Feelings as Information: Moods Influence Judgments and Processing Strategies," in *Heuristics and Biases: the Psychology of Intuitive Judgment*, eds. Thomas Gilovich, Dale Griffin, and Daniel Kahneman (Cambridge: Cambridge University Press, 2002), pp. 534–35.

[24] Jeffrey Gray states that "Conscious perception requires a minimum duration of [between 30 and 200 milliseconds of] continuous firing in the pool of neurons that generates it." Jeffrey Gray, *Consciousness* (Oxford: Oxford University Press, 2004), p. 309.

with achievement oriented words (for example, strive, goal, attain) or aggression-oriented words (for example, fight, struggle, resist) will subsequently act, respectively, more instrumentally or more aggressively than non-primed subjects.

In one study, subjects subliminally exposed to a frowning or smiling face for 1/200th of a second followed by a masking image were subsequently shown a neutral image, known as a target stimulus, and asked to express their like or dislike of it. The target stimulus was evaluated in predictable ways: those targets preceded by (unconsciously processed) smiles were liked in greater proportion to those targets preceded by frowns, which were disliked in greater proportion.[25] Other subjects primed with geometric shapes subsequently expressed preference for these same shapes when exposed to them as targets.[26] Mere exposure to objects tends to create positive attitudes or preferences for them, even when this exposure is not consciously perceived.[27]

Pharmacological means of emotional priming (chemically stimulating emotional states prior to judgments) produce equally striking results.[28] And a similar sort of emotional priming can be fostered by physical movement. In one study, judgments were significantly skewed when they were made while a subject simultaneously exercised particular muscles. Judgments made by subjects moving their arms in a manner typically associated with pushing things away displayed more critical attitudes. Those subjects moving their arms in a manner typically associated with pulling things toward themselves displayed more positive attitudes.[29] Such experiments demonstrate that perceptions, assessments, evaluations, and choices can be affectively biased in a well-targeted fashion without a subject's awareness.[30] In short, emotions are relatively easy to manipulate, and these manipulations can significantly skew judgment.

[25] Joseph LeDoux, *The Emotional Brain* (New York: Simon and Schuster, 1996), p. 59.

[26] Jeffrey P. Toth, "Nonconscious Forms of Human Memory," in *The Oxford Handbook of Memory*, ed. Endel Tulving and Fergus Craik (Oxford: Oxford University Press, 2000), p. 249.

[27] Paul Slovic, Melissa Finucane, Ellen Peters, and Donald MacGregor, "The Affect Heuristic," in *Heuristics and Biases: The Psychology of Intuitive Judgment*, eds. Thomas Gilovich, Dale Griffin, and Daniel Kahneman (Cambridge: Cambridge University Press, 2002), p. 400.

[28] LeDoux, *The Emotional Brain*, p. 48.

[29] Schwarz, "Feelings as Information," pp. 545–46.

[30] John A. Bargh, "The Automaticity of Everyday Life," in *The Automaticity of Everyday Life: Advances in Social Cognition*, ed. Robert Wyer, Jr., Vol. X (Mahwah, NJ: Lawrence Erlbaum Associates, 1997), pp. 1–61.

Affective biases often induce *post hoc* rationalizations. Here, reason truly displays its slavish relation to passion. In one study, subjects were asked to judge the merits of, and subsequently choose between, two job applicants. The applicants differed in only one salient respect: one had better computing skills whereas the other was better at writing. Each paper application was accompanied by a photograph. Before the study began, participants were exposed for 4 milliseconds to a photograph of the face of one of the applicants followed by the word GOOD. Such an exposure is far too short to allow recognition: all participants consciously registered was a flicker of light. But participants were twice as likely to choose as the best person for the job the candidate whose face had been subliminally presented. This result confirms hundreds of other similar studies that demonstrate the effect of emotional priming. Of greater interest, however, is the fact that participants in this study justified their choices with reasoned arguments. They would either emphasize the importance of computer skills, or, if choosing the other candidate, argue that computer skills could always be learned on the job whereas good writing skills were of more substantial benefit.[31] The reasons subjects gave for their judgments were completely spurious. They constituted *post facto* justifications of (unconscious) emotional preferences. Just as we often employ reason to justify decisions grounded in tacit knowledge and skills, so we co-opt it to legitimate judgments grounded in unconscious emotional attachments or aversions.

Priming does not have to be artificially produced in experimental settings. In many different ways, people are biologically primed from birth. They are predisposed to react in an emotionally biased fashion to things naturally encountered in the environment. People react emotively to non-verbal cues and facial expressions, for instance, and these reactions influence judgment. Oftentimes, these reactions are not mediated by any cognitive processing.[32] For example, we generally react more positively to individuals whose pupils are dilated and more negatively to individuals with constricted pupils even though we register no conscious perception

---

[31] R. F. Bornstein, T. S. Pittman, eds., *Perception without Awareness: Cognitive, Clinical and Social Perspectives* (New York: Guilford Press, 1992).

[32] See Roger D. Masters and Denis G. Sullivan, "Nonverbal Behavior and Leadership: Emotion and Cognition in Political Information Processing," in *Explorations in Political Psychology*, ed. Shanto Iyengar and William J. McGuire (Durham: Duke University Press, 1993), pp. 150–182; Victor C. Ottati and Robert S. Wyer, Jr., "Affect and Political Judgment," in *Explorations in Political Psychology*, pp. 296–315.

of this distinction in appearance.[33] Likewise, most of us are naturally primed to demonstrate an "order effect," preferring things that appear in a particular order or placement. Generally, we express a right-sided placement preference. In one study, participants consistently selected one of four or five identical items simply because the "preferred" item appeared at the far right of a display, with the unchosen items, all identical, set to the left. Participants offered various reasons for their choice of the right-hand item, none of which were factually based.[34] Here, again, reason came into play *post facto*, spuriously justifying an emotional bias.

Much moral reasoning follows this pattern. When deliberative judgment takes place, it generally operates as a rationalization in defense of affectively determined choices.[35] "One thing only do I know for certain," Sigmund Freud once stated, "and that is that man's judgments of value follow directly his wishes for happiness – that, accordingly, they are an attempt to support his illusions with arguments."[36] Moral judgments often signal an attempt to support affective predispositions with arguments. One might say, to recall Nietzsche, that reason supplies the *post hoc* paperwork. Our moral judgments, while openly displaying a rational defense, reflect choices determined by the hidden roots of emotion.

Why did human beings evolve such that emotional responses precede and often wholly escape awareness? This feature of human nature might seem to constitute a biological design flaw. After all, would not unconscious, emotive reactions repeatedly get us into trouble? In fact, the opposite is true. From an evolutionary perspective, unreflective emotional reactions served the purpose of quickly getting us out of trouble.

Consider the physiology of the brain. As noted earlier, the major senses first send information about the environment via the thalamus to the amygdala, where an affective response is issued. In turn, a second, slower signal travels from the thalamus to the neocortex, where a

---

[33] Paula Niedenthal and Carolin Showers, "The Perception and Processing of Affective Information and its Influences on Social Judgment," in *Emotion and Social Judgment*, pp. 125–143.

[34] Timothy Wilson, *Strangers to Ourselves: Discovering the Adaptive Unconscious* (Cambridge, MA: Belknap Press, 2002), pp. 102–104.

[35] Greene and Haidt, "How (and where) does moral judgment work?" p. 517. Leanne S. Woolhouse and Rowan Bayne, "Personality and the use of intuition: Individual differences in strategy and performance on an implicit learning task," *European Journal of Personality*, 14: 2 (March/April 2000), pp. 157–169.

[36] Sigmund Freud, *Civilization and its Discontents*, trans. James Strachey (New York: W.W. Norton, 1961), p. 111.

deliberative assessment takes place. It takes a full quarter of a second (250 milliseconds) after sense organs have been exposed to an event for a person to become consciously aware of it.[37] In contrast, the affective import of all incoming sensory streams is rapidly determined by the amygdala. It occurs in less than half the time it takes for an assessment to become available to conscious awareness.[38] The more direct route, while crude, is very fast, allowing quick physical (fight, flight, or freeze) reactions.

Imagine yourself walking through the woods, when, out of the corner of your eye, you notice a snake. Immediately you freeze. At this point, a great deal is going on inside you. Your adrenal system fires up, digestion stops, your skin chills while blood is diverted to the muscles. Breathing quickens, blood pressure rises, and the heart races, infusing your body with oxygen. Meanwhile, the liver releases glucose as a quick fuel. All of this takes place without your conscious awareness or control, as a result of commands sent out from the amygdala. A moment later, perhaps even without a second glance, you realize that the "snake" was actually a harmless stick. The visual cortex has now had time to properly review the information provided by the sensory organs, and it has provided a more accurate assessment of the situation.

Though mistaken in this case, the fast, albeit crude, emotive reactions issued by the amygdala have obvious survival benefits. Slower, more accurate processes of evaluation can always follow later, once one is safely out of harm's way. If our hominid ancestors had always waited for conscious assessments before taking evasive or aggressive action, it is quite likely that our species, *homo sapiens sapiens*, would not be here today to ponder the relationship between emotions and judgment. Rather, we would constitute one of the countless casualties of natural selection.

Ever since Darwin published *The Expression of the Emotions in Man and Animals* in 1872, evolutionary biologists, if not psychologists and political scientists, have understood that emotion facilitates adaptive behavior, such as fight (anger), flight or freeze (fear), and procreation (love or lust). Emotions also give rise to intra-group communication that abets the maintenance of social hierarchies, social bonding, and other survival-enhancing traits. Emotional life proved adaptive, in part, because it made interactions among conspecifics more predictable (by way of

---

[37] Gray, *Consciousness*, p. 7.

[38] George E. Marcus, W. Russell Neuman, and Michael MacKuen, *Affective Intelligence and Political Judgment* (Chicago: University of Chicago Press, 2000), p. 37.

affective social signals) and thus supported mutually beneficial cooperation.[39] From an evolutionary perspective, emotional behavior, including
that which precedes or wholly escapes conscious awareness, increases fitness. One of the key adaptive traits that emotion facilitates is practical
judgment.[40]

Consider experiments conducted with subjects selecting cards from
stacked decks. The apparently normal decks were arranged ahead of time
such that they yielded subtly different gains and losses for card selectors.
Some decks initially yielded lower payments, but losses were also low.
Other decks produced high initial gains, but even higher subsequent
losses. To the subjects, it appeared that rewards and punishments occured
at random. After a time playing the game, however, the participants,
all hooked up to monitors, generated anticipatory skin-conductance
responses when contemplating choosing a card from a "bad" deck, which
yielded slightly larger pay-offs early on but even larger subsequent penal-
ties. Yet the participants would insist at this time that they had no clue
as to what was going on. Only much later, after many more cards were
chosen, did participants indicate a hunch that certain decks were better
than others. Though intuiting their interests and acting to serve them,
they nonetheless remained incapable of saying how or why their behavior
was actually achieving a desired end. Still later, some, but not all, of the
subjects were able to articulate how their choices best served their interests given the environment they faced. This was labeled the "conceptual
phase."[41] At this point, participants explained their emotionally stimulated behavior by providing a (correct) rationalization for their choices.

[39] Roger D. Masters, "Naturalistic Approaches to Justice in Political Philosophy and the
Life Sciences," in *The Sense of Justice: Biological Foundations of Law*, ed. Roger D. Masters
and Margaret Gruter (Newbury Park: Sage Publications, 1992), p. 85.

[40] Roger Masters writes: "Even from a strict cost-benefit perspective, one should expect that
mechanisms of emotional response could evolve both as social signals and as devices for
behavioral regulation. If so, the sense of justice might well arise from both rational
calculations and emotional processes. Indeed, the element of emotion underlying the
sense of justice would be all the more effective from a cost-benefit perspective because
the mere process of calculating costs and benefits is itself costly, whereas allowing one's
behavior to be governed by emotion might – under some circumstances – be a relatively
efficient strategy. On the other hand, allowing emotion to get out of control would
be dangerous as soon as others in the group were able to calculate and engage in
deceptive behavior based on this calculation. Hence, one would expect from a cost-
benefit perspective that mixtures of emotion and reasoned judgment would serve as the
foundation of the sense of justice." Masters, "Naturalistic Approaches," p. 85.

[41] Antoine Bechara, Hanna Damasio, Daniel Tranel, and Antonio Damasio, "Deciding
Advantageously before Knowing the Advantageous Strategy," *Science*, 28 (1997): 1293–
95.

They now understood that selecting from certain decks provided better cards in the long run.

In this experiment, emotional (physical) reactions preceded (emotionally induced) intuitive behavior, which itself preceded (for some subjects) the ability rationally to assess the situation at hand. Reason was very much a late-comer to this game. It did not help subjects serve their best interests but rather allowed them to explain beneficial behavior after the fact. Reason was less an active player than a Monday-morning quarterback. Emotion, in contrast, allowed subjects to grapple with their world to best serve their interests in a timely fashion.

By no means do affective biases always lead us astray. Neither do beneficial biases only serve us in life or death situations. They can facilitate sound judgment in mundane situations. Reason, in turn, is not restricted to *post hoc* service. It can make constructive and prescriptive contributions. But whatever its role, reason never carries the show alone.

The Reasonableness of Emotion

The crucial contributions of emotion to judgment becomes most apparent when we observe – conceptually, phenomenologically, and neuropsychologically – how hamstrung our rational capacities would be in the absence of affect. Emotions are quite reasonable, in this respect, if we understand *reasonable* to encompass those states that precede, stimulate, and sustain coherent and consistent deliberation and action.

Conceptually, one might imagine the individual as a ship at sea grappling with the winds and currents of a challenging and ever-changing environment. Reason provides a strong rudder, allowing a specific course to be consistently pursued. Affect provides the sails, without which the ship cannot reach any destination. Absent a means of propulsion, the ship's rudder becomes quite useless. It cannot govern the ship's progress. A vessel stripped of its sails will simply drift with the current. In the absence of an emotional thrust that starts the ship in motion and carries it forward, the steering power of reason – its capacity for governance or communicative control – becomes null and void.[42]

Of course, a ship equipped with sails but no rudder is hardly better off. Absent a rudder, one could never steer a straight course. Certainly

---

[42] The Latin word for rudder is *gubernaculum*, which has the same root as *gubernare*, the word for govern. The Greek word for steersman is *kybernetes*, from which we get cybernetics, the science of control and communication.

one could never tack against the wind, reaching a desired destination by strategically zigzagging toward it. A rudderless ship could only run before the wind. It would be wholly at the mercy of every gust. No consistent course could be pursued. Working together, however, rudder and sail can achieve amazing results. They allow the ship to navigate the high seas and reach far-off destinations even in the face of opposing winds and currents.

As Aristotle observed, reason can do nothing by itself; it must be combined with desire to induce action.[43] The judgments that precede and inform action find in emotion their motivating and sustaining force. Reason requires emotion to stimulate its use, to recruit and direct its abilities, and to execute its commands.[44] The most rational judgment would not get out of port without the propulsive force of emotion.

Consider patients who have bilateral damage to their amygdalas. The amygdala is a storehouse of emotional memory. It plays a large role in producing fight, flight, or freeze reactions. It is also involved in judgments that entail the retrieval of information relating to innate biases and the interpretation of social cues.[45] People with damaged amygdalas are deprived of an emotional relationship to the world. Though suffering no cognitive impairment, and fully capable of reasoning, they will often act in ways that do not serve their interests well. In turn, they will fail to enact behavior recommended by their own rational deliberations. The same deficits occur when particular areas of the pre-frontal cortex (the medial frontal gyrus or ventromedial pre-frontal areas, for instance) have been damaged. These brain regions are believed to integrate emotion into decision-making. Prior to their accidents, people with damage to their pre-frontal cortices would act quite rationally. Subsequent to sustaining brain injuries, they make personal and social decisions involving risk and conflict that are inexplicably disadvantageous. In turn, they do

---

[43] Aristotle, *The Ethics of Aristotle* (New York: Penguin Books, 1953), p. 173. See also Arash Abizadeh, "The Passions of the Wise: *Phronesis*, Rhetoric, and Aristotle's Passionate Practical Deliberation," *The Review of Metaphysics* 56 (December 2002): 267–296. In a statement that Aristotle would have embraced, Alexander Lowen writes that "Knowledge becomes understanding when it is coupled with feeling. Only a deep understanding, charged with strong feeling, is capable of modifying structured patterns of behavior." Alexander Lowen, *Bioenergetics* (New York: Coward, McCann and Geoghegan, 1975), p. 62.

[44] George E. Marcus, "The Psychology of Emotion and Politics," in *Oxford Handbook of Political Psychology*, ed. David Sears, Leonie Huddy, and Robert Jervis (New York: Oxford University Press, 2003), p. 206.

[45] Ralph Adolphs, Daniel Tranel, and Antonio Damasio, "The human amygdala in social judgment," *Nature* 393 (1998): 470–474.

not exhibit the expected emotional response when faced with their failure to navigate the social realm. All the while, they remain demonstrably capable of employing logic and other instruments of rationality and are able to retrieve and accurately assess information about their world.

Such victims of brain damage act in ways most people would consider irrational. But they do so not from any decline in their powers of reason. Rather, they act irrationally because they no longer register emotional commitments to a certain class of individual and social goods. Without these emotional biases, reason becomes powerless to direct action. In explaining this intriguing phenomenon, neuroscientist Antonio Damasio theorizes that rationality requires the use of "somatic markers" to be effective. Somatic markers, Damasio suggests, are largely unconscious emotional responses (biases) that we associate with certain images or outcomes. When we are faced with a situation that presents the possibility of a particular outcome – either advantageous or dangerous, favorable or unpleasant – an emotional reaction is triggered. In the absence of such triggers, reason is not put to work in the pursuit or avoidance of the outcome. Patients with neurological damage that prevents the linkage of emotional faculties to cognitive capacities demonstrate that the inability "to feel [one's] way through life" disables practical judgment and leads to imprudent behavior.[46]

Damasio relates the case of a patient with trauma to the ventromedial pre-frontal area. While fully capable of analytical reasoning, the patient had lost the ability affectively to determine what things were worth reasoning about. He also lost the ability to terminate the reasoning process by invoking an affective bias. Thus the patient found himself endlessly debating the minutiae of everyday life, enumerating for half an hour on one occasion the pros and cons of each of two possible dates for a return visit to the clinic (at which point the doctors chose to intervene). The patient, one might say, was subject to the (rational) interrogations of an internal child without recourse to the (affective) authority of the parent. Severed from emotive impulses, fully functional reason remained adrift at sea, leaving the unfortunate subject forever fiddling with his rudder.

In such cases, where rational capacities have been neurologically severed from emotional centers, the limits of "pure" reason become manifest. Recall the experiment with the stacked decks of cards. Some of the participants in the study had bilateral damage of the ventromedial sector of the pre-frontal cortex, which is to say, the emotive linkage to

---

[46] Greene and Haidt, "How (and where) does moral judgment work?" p. 518.

their rational capacities was severed. Unlike healthy subjects, none of these patients demonstrated galvanic skin responses (affective biases) when contemplating "good" and "bad" decks. Nonetheless, some of these patients reached the conceptual phase, indicating that they finally understood how their interests could be best served by selecting cards from particular decks. They did so by way of purely analytical means. Surprisingly, they still did not act to achieve optimal results. The brain-damaged subjects neither emotively intuited how best to serve their interests nor acted appropriately when conscious reason eventually determined how their interests could be best served. Researchers drew the following conclusion: "[I]n normal individuals, nonconscious biases guide behavior before conscious knowledge does. Without the help of such biases, overt knowledge may be insufficient to ensure advantageous behavior."[47] Unconscious emotional responses often serve our interests while providing the foundation for subsequent (deliberative) judgment. In the absence of these affective biases, the government of reason proves impotent.

Purely rational calculation – deliberation unregulated by emotional biases – well describes how patients with pre-frontal brain damage go about making disadvantageous choices. Neurologically healthy individuals, in contrast, employ affect to ground reason and more effectively pursue personal and social goals.[48] On the basis of his laboratory studies, Damasio maintains that "emotion is integral to the processes of reasoning and decision making, for worse and for better." He concludes that the "selective reduction of emotion is at least as prejudicial for rationality as excessive emotion. . . . Well-targeted and well-deployed emotion seems to be a support system without which the edifice of reason cannot operate properly."[49] A review of the current literature in the field reinforces this position: psychologically and neurologically speaking, "emotion is, inescapably, an essential component of rationality."[50] When our emotional centers are no longer adequately connected to those areas of the brain that generate thought and rational processing, a fully functional

---

[47] Bechara, "Deciding Advantageously," 1293–95.

[48] Antonio Damasio, *Descartes's Error: Emotion, Reason and the Human Brain* (New York: Putnam, 1994), p. 172. See also Jennifer Nedelsky, "Embodied Diversity and the Challenges to Law," in *Judgment, Imagination, and Politics: Themes from Kant and Arendt*, ed. Ronald Beiner and Jennifer Nedelsky (New York: Rowman and Littlefield, 2001), p. 237. Marcus, *Affective Intelligence*, p. 34. Carla Hannaford, *Smart Moves: Why Learning Is Not All in Your Head* (Arlington: Great Ocean Publishers, 1995), p. 52.

[49] Damasio, *The Feeling of What Happens*, pp. 41–42.

[50] Rose McDermott, "The Feeling of Rationality: The Meaning of Neuroscientific Advances for Political Science," *Perspectives on Politics* 2 (2004), 699.

intellect will not protect us from disadvantageous (and, in this sense, irrational) behavior. In such situations, we fail to act rationally, quite literally, because we fail to feel.

The Benefits of "Positive" and "Negative" Emotions

The contributions of "positive" emotions to good judgment are perhaps obvious: self-love prompts self-interested behavior. Yet "negative" emotions, such as fear and anxiety, also often prove vital to rational decision-making. Certainly that is the case in fight, flight, or freeze reactions. But it also applies in more nuanced cases. For instance, experiments demonstrate that depressed subjects better judge the actual extent of their influence on uncertain events. Non-depressed subjects exhibit an "illusion of control." When an outcome is associated with failure, they demonstrate an "illusion of no control." That is to say, non-depressives overestimate their ability to achieve good results and, *post hoc*, underestimate their role in producing bad results. In turn, depressed subjects better judge the causal attribution of credit and blame, whereas non-depressives are more apt to attribute positive events to their influence and negative events to the intervention of others. Non-depressed subjects are also prone to a self-serving bias; they see themselves more positively than others bearing the same characteristics. Finally, depressives more accurately assess how other people perceive them, whereas non-depressed subjects tend to exaggerate the good impressions they make on others.[51] To summarize: non-depressed people take more credit for success and accept less blame for failure than they deserve, they see themselves more positively than is appropriate, and they believe others share in this misperception.[52] Negative emotions such as sadness, fear, and anxiety (components of depression) can very much assist our rational assessments and deliberations.

Depressed people often demonstrate analytical superiority compared with their non-depressed counterparts. But that is not a recommendation for depression. Optimism is a key component of good health, and is beneficial not only to mental but also to physical well-being.[53] In turn,

---

[51] Jon Elster, *Alchemies of the Mind: Rationality and the Emotions* (Cambridge: Cambridge University Press, 1999), p. 300.

[52] Plous, *The Psychology of Judgment*, p. 185.

[53] Medical studies demonstrate that the mental outlook of heart attack survivors, which is strongly correlated to the level of optimism, is the best predictor of extended survival, greater than any medical risk factor such as amount of damage to the heart by the first attack, cholesterol levels, artery blockage, or blood pressure. Chris Peterson et al., *Learned Helplessness: A Theory for the Age of Personal Control* (New York: Oxford University

depressed people generally have a harder time bringing themselves to take action. Notwithstanding their realistic assessment of the world, or perhaps because of it, depressives shy away from engagement. Hence they may actually accomplish less. People subject to unwarranted optimism and a slightly inflated self-image ultimately may achieve more (notwithstanding an accompanying greater number of failures) simply because they are willing to take on more challenges and risks. This would help explain why the "superachievers" of life tend to be more optimistic than the average population.[54] As Winston Churchill suggested, "To attain success one should be prepared to proceed from failure to failure with undiminished enthusiasm."[55]

Still, when the failure that ensues from a poor judgment has a very high cost, optimism may not be an optimal state of mind. Nations deliberating whether or not to go to war, for example, might well want to deny key decision-makers their Prozac (as well as ideological or religious tonics that stimulate unwarranted optimism).[56] Of course, the benefit of negative emotions is not restricted to high-cost situations and high-profile decision-makers. Assuming that anxiety does not induce wholesale disengagement, it also facilitates good judgment in average citizens. Marcus, Neuman, and MacKuen write:

> The received wisdom is that people who are emotionally engaged are less likely to make rational decisions.... That axiom depends on what we mean by 'emotionally engaged.' If we mean more anxious, then ... that emotional engagement will motivate people toward making more deeply reasoned decisions about politics than those who remain dispassionate.... People use emotions, particularly anxiety, to stimulate active reconsideration of their political views.... When the political environment demands real consideration, anxiety spurs the needed reassessment; when the political environment is relatively benign, emotional calm permits the reliance on voters' effective habits, their standing decisions guided by enthusiasm.[57]

Press, 1993). Cited in Daniel Goleman, *Emotional Intelligence* (New York: Bantam Books, 1995), p. 177.

54 Seymour Epstein, *Constructive Thinking: The Key to Emotional Intelligence* (Westport: Praeger, 1998), p. 104.

55 Quoted in Epstein, *Constructive Thinking*, p. 107.

56 Jonathan Baron, *Judgment Misguided: Intuition and Error in Public Decision Making* (New York: Oxford University Press, 1998), 85. According to Bruce Bueno de Mesquita, if state leaders considering war act as utility maximizers, then unwarranted optimism explains many of their disastrous decisions. Bruce Bueno de Mesquita, *The War Trap* (New Haven: Yale University Press, 1981).

57 Marcus, *Affective Intelligence*, pp. 95, 124.

People learn more about and more accurately assess political affairs when they are anxious, not when they are calm, emotionally neutral, or generally pleased about the political environment and their place within it.[58] Positive affects (as well as certain negative affects such as intense anger or fear) recruit simple, heuristic methods of processing information. Happy (and intensely angry or frightened) people tend to simplify their cognitive efforts, relying more on intuition, giving little attention to detail, downplaying logical consistency, and deciding quickly on less information. Indeed, there is some evidence to suggest that elated subjects avoid intensive mental processing because they believe that it will dampen their felicitious mood.[59] This can lead to more biased, less thoroughly analyzed choices. Sadness and anxiety, in contrast, trigger more careful and elaborate processing of information and thus produce more circumspect judgments.[60] Negative emotion, in these instances, works in tandem with deliberative reason.

This is not to say that positive affect cannot or does not contribute to good judgment. Positive emotions stimulate creativity and flexibility in problem-solving.[61] Particularly in enjoyable or "safe" environments, positive affect promotes exploration, helps people make more associations among ideas, and fosters the examination of novel perspectives. Although rigorous step-by-step analysis may be sacrificed in these situations, its

---

58 Marcus, *The Sentimental Citizen*, p. 103.

59 Diane Mackie and Leila Worth, "Feeling Good, But Not Thinking Straight: The Impact of Positive Mood on Persuasion," in *Emotion and Social Judgment*, pp. 201–219. See also Schwarz, "Feelings as Information."

60 Forgas, "The role of emotion in social judgments." If anxiety becomes heightened to the point of producing outright fear or anger, its salutary effects may be negated. Marcus fails to recognize this dynamic when he writes: "If we want everyone to be rational, the seemingly effective solution is to make everyone anxious. No doubt there have been occasions when events have produced such a result: the Great Depression, the bombing of Pearl Harbor ('a day which [sic] will live in infamy'), the terrorist attacks on the World Trade Center and the Pentagon." Marcus, *The Sentimental Citizen*, p. 108. The reaction of those "patriots" who violently targeted innocent Japanese or Arab Americans after the attacks on Pearl Harbor and the World Trade Center suggests that their heightened emotional reactions did not stimulate well-analyzed, discrete judgments, as would low-level anxiety and uncertainty.

61 Alice M. Islen, "Positive Affect and Decision Making," in *Handbook of Emotions*, 2nd edition, ed. Michael Lewis and Jeannette M. Haviland-Jones (New York: Guilford Press, 2000), p. 417. For a helpful account of the relation between emotion, hemispheric distinctions, and the role of neurotransmitters in exploratory and routine behavior, see Elkhonon Goldberg, *The Wisdom Paradox: How Your Mind Can Grow Stronger As Your Brain Grows Older* (New York: Gotham Books, 2005), p. 228.

loss is often more than offset by original, inventive thought and creative problem-solving.[62]

Whether positive or negative, affect is most likely to influence judgment when decision-making involves the generation or review of new, unstructured, or ambivalent information and the constructive processing required to assess complex problems. In contrast, more passive decision-making based on available recollections or the retrieval and integration of "crystallized judgments" are less susceptible to emotional influence.[63] The conclusion, perhaps counterintuitive, is that "the longer and more constructively we must think to compute a judgment, the more likely that affect will influence the outcome."[64] The problem with jumping to conclusions, then, is not that it relies too heavily on emotional reactions. Emotions and moods actually play a diminished role in quick judgments that rely on pre-formed opinions. Of course, emotions and moods may have played significant roles in the original formation of the now crystallized judgments and opinions that are invoked in new situations. In this respect, the impact of emotion is simply one step removed.

Beyond prompting rigorous (re)assessments or creative problem-solving, emotions aid decision-making in a number of ways. Both positive and negative emotions may stimulate the retention of information. Perhaps the best example of this phenomenon is known as "flashbulb memory." People more vividly and accurately remember events when these events elicit emotional reactions (assuming the degree of emotional arousal is moderate; extremely stressful situations may actually impair memory).[65] Thus many people say that they can remember exactly where they were and what they were doing when they first heard that President Kennedy was shot, or, more recently, when the Twin Towers were "bombed" on September 11, 2001. Personal (that is, less public) events that stimulate charged emotions also enhance memory.

Clinical experiments confirm that people do indeed remember episodes with emotional content better than episodes without emotional content. The phenomenon occurs even when the emotional arousal is artificially stimulated. Injecting a subject with adrenaline (which

[62] Islen, "Positive Affect and Decision Making," p. 431. Norbert Schwarz and Herbert Bless, "Happy and Mindless, But Sad and Smart? The Impact of Affective States on Analytical Reasoning," in *Emotion and Social Judgment*, p. 56.

[63] Klaus Fiedler, "On the Task, the Measures and the Mood in Research on Affect and Social Cognition," in *Emotion and Social Judgment*, pp. 83–104.

[64] Forgas, "The role of emotion in social judgments," p. 19.

[65] LeDoux, *The Synaptic Self*, p. 222.

stimulates emotional arousal) directly after his exposure to an opportunity for learning enhances the subject's memory of what was learned. Obversely, enhanced memory of events (that would normally induce an emotional reaction) is thwarted if subjects are administered adrenaline-blocking agents.[66] In turn, people with damaged amygdalas, the emotional center of the brain, often demonstrate severely diminished capacity for memory. Emotional arousal registered by the amygdala plays a significant role in modulating the retention and consolidation of memories.[67] In sum, our bodies exploit positive and negative emotional reactions to enhance our ability to remember and learn. To the extent that good judgment requires access to vivid, accurate memories and the learning such memories allow, emotion proves to be useful if not indispensable.

Judgment and Empathy

The absence of affect disables reason from pursuing self-interest. When the interests of others are at stake, affect also plays a crucial role. Without emotive perception directed outward, the analytical, reflective, and deliberative components of moral judgment could not get underway. As Dewey observes, judgment is not a purely intellectual endeavor: "there must also be personal responsiveness – there must be an emotional reaction.... Unless there is a prompt and almost instinctive sensitiveness to the conditions about one, to the ends and interests of others, the intellectual side of judgment will not have its proper material to work upon."[68] Emotions allow us to see suffering as something negative that matters, just as they allow us to see happiness as something positive that should garner our allegiance. Without emotional insight, ethico-political judgment proves to be impossible.

Arne Vetlesen writes that "Judgment presupposes perception in the sense that perception 'gives' judgment its object.... To 'see' the circumstance and to see oneself as addressed by it, and thus to be susceptible to the way a situation affects the weal and woe of others, in short, to identify

---

[66] LeDoux, *The Emotional Brain*, pp. 206–07.

[67] Elizabeth Phelps, "The Interaction of Emotion and Cognition: The Relation Between the Human Amygdala and Cognitive Awareness," in *The New Unconscious*, ed. Ran Hassin, James Uleman, and John Bargh (Oxford: Oxford University Press, 2005), pp. 61–76. Ian Glynn, *An Anatomy of Thought: The Origin and Machinery of the Mind* (Oxford: Oxford University Press, 1999), p. 343.

[68] John Dewey, *The Political Writings*, ed. Debra Morris and Ian Shapiro (Indianapolis: Hackett, 1993), p. 106.

a situation as carrying *moral significance* in the first place – all of this is required in order to enter the domain of the moral, and none of it would come about without the basic emotional faculty of empathy."[69] Empathy discloses that the welfare of others is at stake in any given situation. Without an affective attachment to people and their welfare, Vetlesen suggests, we have no *reason* to act for their benefit. Hume asserts that it is not against reason to prefer the destruction of the rest of humanity to the pricking of one's little finger. Not reason, but affect induces pro-social behavior. By making the welfare of others an object of concern, empathy supplies reason with the raw material for its analysis.

With this in mind, Vetlesen criticizes Hannah Arendt's assessment of Adolf Eichmann, the Nazi officer who helped engineer the "Final Solution." Eichmann, Arendt suggests, failed to judge morally because he failed to think. Vetlesen assails Arendt for her "intellectualist" bias. He argues that Eichmann failed to judge morally because he failed to identify emotionally with his victims. Following Kant, Arendt largely dismissed the role of emotion in moral judgment. Her notion of representative thinking lacks strong affective components. Judgment, for Arendt, is by and large a cognitive endeavor. Yet, Vetlesen argues, "To be emotionally incapacitated is a sufficient condition for the failure to exercise moral judgment, because there is no access to the domain of moral phenomena, of situations involving the weal and woe of others, other than the access provided by emotions in general and the faculty of empathy in particular."[70]

The relationship Eichmann had with his victims might be informed by the experience of people with a very peculiar brain disorder called Capgras's syndrome. This disorder is caused by damage to the neurological paths that normally link the emotional centers in the limbic system, specifically the amygdala, to the areas of the brain engaged in face recognition. People with this disorder continue to recognize friends or relatives, but do not feel any emotional attachment to them. This creates cognitive dissonance, and people with Capgras's syndrome often resolve the dissonance in bizarre ways. In a typical case, a Capgras victim denied the identity of his parents whenever they were with him. Upon a reunion, he would admit that the man and woman standing before him looked, spoke, and acted just like his parents. Nonetheless, he insisted that they

---

[69] Arne Johan Vetlesen, *Perception, Empathy, and Judgment: An Inquiry into the Preconditions of Moral Performance* (University Park: The Pennsylvania State University Press, 1994), pp. 4, 6.

[70] Vetlesen, *Perception, Empathy, and Judgment*, p. 213.

were imposters. This claim allowed him to maintain the self-image of a normal person who has emotional reactions whenever friends or relations are encountered. Failing to experience an emotional reaction when encountering his mother and father, he simply assumed that they could not actually be his parents – clever disguises notwithstanding. Since the faulty wiring was only between the emotional center and the region of the brain processing face recognition, the patient had no problem acknowledging his parents in a completely normal fashion when speaking with them on the telephone.[71]

Psychopaths provide an illustrative example of the same phenomenon. Psychopaths are, or can be, fully rational. But they do not fear punishment or pain the way most people do. In turn, they have little or no empathy regarding the pain and suffering of others. Although psychopaths often demonstrate strong intelligence, superb reasoning capacities, and are generally free of delusional or irrational thought, their inability to suffer normally from fear and pain, and their consequent inability to empathize with the suffering of others, makes them moral morons. Their wholesale lack of ethical judgment stems directly from the dissociation of reason from emotional sensitivity.[72] There is, in this regard, some truth to Chesterton's remark that "The madman is not the man who has lost his reason. The madman is the man who has lost everything except his reason."[73]

Whether Eichmann was a psychopath or had a related brain disorder is unclear. We might speculate that a lack of emotive reaction to the suffering of particular individuals prompted him to develop (or accept) a rationale that legitimated his lack of empathy. Racist ideology provided such a rationale. It denied the full humanity of certain classes of people, thus legitimating his lack of an emotional bond to them. Of course, a dearth of moral concern might be explained in any number of ways: not only by the absence of empathy, for instance, but by the overabundance of an antipodal emotion, such as hate. However, as Arendt notes, in Eichmann's case (unlike Hitler's), hate did not appear to be in play.

---

[71] See V. S. Ramachandran and Sandra Blakeslee, *Phantoms in the Brain* (New York: William Morrow and Company, 1998), pp. 158–173.

[72] H. Cleckley, *The Mask of Sanity* (St. Louis: C. V. Mosby, 1955); Jonathan Haidt, "The Emotional Dog and Its Rational Tail: A Social Intuitionist Approach to Moral Judgment," *Psychological Review*. 108 (2001): 814–834.

[73] G. K. Chesterton, quoted in Robert C. Solomon, *Spirituality for the Skeptic: The Thoughtful Love of Life* (Oxford: Oxford University Press, 2002), p. 68.

Neuroscientists are exploring whether the faulty wiring in the brain that causes Capgras's syndrome and related brain disorders might contribute to the stereotyping demonstrated by racists.[74] Whatever the cause of such dysfunctions, it is clear that moral reasoning in healthy individuals is linked to affect. Certain moral judgments – namely, those involving assessments of the direct weal or woe of others – invariably implicate parts of the brain associated with social and emotional processing. Here the brain activates those regions that interpret what other people are feeling.[75] When these brain regions or their linkages are damaged, disabling affective input, moral reasoning deteriorates or ceases.

Empathy is the capacity emotionally to extend oneself, to reach across time and space so as to experience imaginatively the dispositions of others. The practical judge takes on the task of exercising her empathetic powers upon a broad community. Effectively, she extends her affective imagination to include all who might play a role in her assessments, evaluations, and choices. That is what we mean by impartiality.

Impartiality and objectivity are often falsely equated. What is required for the exercise of practical judgment, however, is not passionless objectivity but empathetic impartiality, a form of intersubjectivity. Sound judgment demands more than "just the facts." It requires a discerning exploration of the cognitive and emotional dispositions that people might bring into play in any given circumstance. Practical judgment entails an understanding of the psychology of the people with whom one interacts. This insight is based on access to non-rational orientations and activities, of which affect is a crucial component. Practical judgment, in this respect, has at least as much to do with unreason as reason.

Ralph Waldo Emerson wrote that "Prudence is false when detached."[76] The ability to understand and acknowledge other people's perspectives and predilections, and empathize with their emotional states, is a prerequisite for sound judgment. Impartiality is not idiocy. Informed by emotional intelligence, the practical judge is spared *idio*syncratic thought and action unconnected to the world of others. By extending

---

[74] See Ramachandran, *Phantoms in the Brain*, p. 171.

[75] More impersonal forms of moral judgment (those that do not involve potential direct harm to an identified person) are processed by parts of the brain associated with working memory, the same brain regions that process non-moral judgments. Greene and Haidt, "How (and where) does moral judgment work?" p. 519. Joshua Greene et al., "An fMRI Investigation of Emotional Engagement in Moral Judgment," *Science* 293 (2001): 2105–8.

[76] Ralph Waldo Emerson, "Prudence," in *Selected Writings of Emerson*, ed. Donald McQuade (New York: Modern Library, 1981), p. 222.

the emotional self imaginatively, empathy allows insight into the perceptions and propensities of others. That is what impartiality demands.

In *The Theory of Moral Sentiments*, Adam Smith argues that good judgment requires a particular act of imagination. Smith suggests we take on the persona of the "impartial spectator." Importantly, it is less the reason than the "sentiment" of this spectator that is employed to modify assessments, evaluations, and choices. Good judgment, Smith insists, implies access to a wide range of well-balanced emotions. When judging an action, one must first submit it to the "tribunal" of the "man within the breast."[77] To judge well is to imagine how an emotionally attuned and well-informed spectator would see things: "If, upon placing ourselves in his situation, we thoroughly enter into all the passions and motives which influenced it, we approve of it, by sympathy with the approbation of this supposed equitable judge. If otherwise, we enter into his disapprobation, and condemn it."[78] The crux of good judgment is the impartiality made possible when the sentiments behind actions are sorted through, understood, and properly evaluated.

Smith deems the impartial spectator, attuned to emotions, a "demigod." By exercising fairness and open-mindedness, it mimics the divine, "all-seeing Judge."[79] But the impartial spectator remains half human, with all the baggage of this fallible condition brought in tow. Occasionally given to "self-deceit" as a result of overweening "self-love" or besieged by the "implacable passions" arising in the heat of the moment, the impartial spectator displays mortal roots.[80] Notwithstanding these shortcomings and dangers, consultation with the man within the breast is mandatory. Impartiality and good judgment depend upon it.

Martha Nussbaum critcally endorses Smith's position regarding the "emotion of the judicious spectator."[81] She writes that contemporary judges

who deny themselves the influence of emotion deny themselves ways of seeing the world that seem essential to seeing it completely. . . . Sympathetic emotion that is tethered to the evidence, institutionally constrained in appropriate ways,

---

[77] Smith, *The Theory of Moral Sentiments*, p. 185.

[78] Smith, *The Theory of Moral Sentiments*, p. 162.

[79] Smith, *The Theory of Moral Sentiments*, pp. 187, 219, 221–222.

[80] Some of these limits, to be sure, are evident in Smith's imagined demigod, whose "delicacy of sentiment" betrays the cultural and economic biases of the Scot's own class status and aspirations. Smith, *The Theory of Moral Sentiments*, pp. 28, 50.

[81] Martha C. Nussbaum, *Poetic Justice: The Literary Imagination and Public Life* (Boston: Beacon Press, 1995), p. 78. See also Martha Nussbaum, *Love's Knowledge: Essays on Philosophy and Literature* (New York: Oxford University Press, 1990), pp. 338–346.

and free from reference to one's own situation appears to be not only acceptable but actually essential to public judgment . . . [I]n order to be fully rational, judges must also be capable of fancy and sympathy. They must educate not only their technical capacities but also their capacity for humanity. In the absence of that capacity, their impartiality will be obtuse and their justice blind.[82]

Nussbaum is referring to courtroom judges. But the statement applies as well to anyone who exercises practical judgment. Affect is imperative. The absence of sympathetic insight, Nussbaum concludes, would "deprive us of information we need if we are to have a fully rational response to the suffering of others."[83]

Nussbaum focuses narrowly on the fact of suffering and the experience of sympathy. Yet ethical sensibilities are cultivated by the perception and experience of a full range of human emotions. Shelley wrote in his defense of poetry: "A man, to be truly good, must imagine intensely and comprehensively; he must put himself in the place of another and of many others; the pains and pleasures of his species must become his own."[84] Our experience and understanding of the complex interactions of joy, fear, anger, and sadness, as well as the countless variations of these primary affects, attune us to the moral world. Empathy gives imaginative access to a full emotional spectrum, taking us well beyond the misfortune and melancholy that sympathy allows us to share.

I do not want to diminish the importance of sympathy. Sympathy is one manifestation of empathy, and the capacity for empathy is requisite for good judgment. But empathy does not entail becoming absorbed into another's suffering. It is not a matter of wholly identifying with another's misfortune. Indeed, the good judge can, and should, emphasize with those whose suffering she intentionally fosters. Robert S. McNamara, former Secretary of Defense, concluded that one of the chief lessons he learned from a life of statecraft was to "empathize with your enemy."[85] There is no contradiction in cultivating empathy with one's enemy and exploiting this emotional intelligence to ensure that she suffers the soundest defeat. To be empathetic entails the ability to discern another's emotional state, to understand its origins and dynamics, and to sense what attitudes, decisions, and actions such a state will likely evoke. Judgments

---

[82] Nussbaum, *Poetic Justice*, pp. 67, 78, 121.

[83] Nussbaum, *Poetic Justice*, p. 66.

[84] Percy Shelley, "A Defense of Poetry," in *The Norton Anthology of English Literature*, Vol. 2. M. H. Abrams, ed. (New York: W.W. Norton, 2001), p. 625.

[85] Robert McNamara, in *The Fog of War*, produced and directed by Errol Morris, Sony Pictures, 2003. A second rule on McNamara's list is "rationality will not save us."

made in light of this empathetic extension will boast greater insight than those shut off from the affective register. Whether such judgments issuing in actions bring weal or woe to others is another matter.

A good judge is capable of intersubjectivity, both feeling with others and thinking from their points of view. But she does not succumb to identification with them. Identification is very prone to projection – imagining that others incarnate one's own desires and demons. Herein the other is burdened with the darkness of one's own shadows. This is, I suspect, why Arendt refused to equate an expanded mentality with empathy, which, if exercised in solitude, is subject to projection.

Projection represents an actual disabling of empathy: one ceases to think and feel from another's perspective, superimposing instead one's own dispositions. The antidote is two-fold. As addressed in Chapter 2, direct, communicative experience with people – actual interaction – rather than solitary efforts of imagination goes a long way to warding off projection. Second, the empathetic judge must learn to be at home with a wide range of emotions. Sound judgment demands access to a full register of affect. The greater the access, the more informed the judgment. Premature detachment from emotions marks a kind of repression. And by repressing rather than acknowledging emotional states, one becomes their unwitting servant. Emotions denied their due are always prey to projection. But so are overwhelmingly dominant emotions. People falling in love are notoriously bad judges, at least about qualities related to the beloved. That is why (romantic) love is blind. What makes for bad judgment in this instance is the lover's inability to distinguish what she wants or feels from the reality she encounters. To be empathetic is not to be blinded by either a repressed or dominant emotion. The fuller the spectrum of affective experience the judge has at her disposal, the less likely it is that she will become enthralled to any particular emotion.[86]

Blessed with a broad and well-rounded emotional repertoire, the good judge may take a firm stand without sacrificing the expansive intersubjectivity that begets both insight and impartiality. Adam Smith observed that "The man who feels the most for the joys and sorrows of others, is best fitted for acquiring the most complete control of his own joys and sorrows."[87] The capacity for empathy suggests access to a rich repository

---

[86] See Daniel Brudney, "*Lord Jim* and Moral Judgment: Literature and Moral Philosophy," *The Journal of Aesthetics and Art Criticism*, Vol. 56, No. 3. (Summer, 1998), p. 273.

[87] Smith, *The Theory of Moral Sentiments*, p. 214.

of emotion, to a broad and deep spectrum of affect. This access is a prerequisite for emotional maturity. But the capacity for empathy is as much the cause as the effect of emotional depth. Smith's statement could easily be reversed: she who feels most fully a wide range of her own emotions will be best equipped for empathetic extension. To resonate with a broad spectrum of affects in others, a well-established relationship with one's own heart is required. Indeed, emotional depth and the capacity for empathy develop synchronously. One's relationship to others is generally built from the same emotional resources as one's relationship to oneself.

The foundation for empathy, Abraham Maslow argues, is an "inner integration" of diverse states of mind and heart. As a result of practicing this integration, one can experience another's passion without defensively reacting to it in a way that stymies learning.[88] Good judges, like the "self-actualizing" people Maslow describes, are at home with a wide range of affect. Owing to the ease with which they experience their own emotional registers, they are free to explore and learn from others, without "fear of their own insides" getting in the way.[89] If our emotions remain foreign to us, in other words, we will be unable accurately to assess and evaluate the inner life of others.

Pierre Bourdieu insists that judgments of taste are established by way of what Nietzsche called a *pathos of distance*. We acquire good taste by learning to revile what is tasteless. "Tastes are perhaps first and foremost distastes," Bourdieu writes, "disgust provoked by horror and visceral intolerance ('sick-making') of the tastes of others."[90] Likewise, when we exercise ethico-political judgment, we are often choosing *against* as much as we are choosing *for*. The visceral reaction we have in confronting the distasteful, disgusting, and reprehensible is key to the development of judgment. But we can only find another's affects distasteful or disgusting, Adam Smith observed, if we have first met them in ourselves. With this in mind, it is crucial to explore and acknowledge one's own emotional repertoire, including but not limited to the negative emotions of anger, indignation, and resentment. Otherwise, intolerance of another may signify a flight from oneself rather than an impartial assessment. She

---

[88] Abraham Maslow, *Toward a Psychology of Being*, 2nd ed. (New York: D. Van Nostrand, 1968), p. 122.

[89] Maslow, *Toward a Psychology of Being*, p. 140.

[90] Pierre Bourdieu, *Distinction: A Social Critique of the Judgment of Taste* (Cambridge: Harvard University Press, 1984), p. 56.

who never sees her own shadow will badly judge those wrestling with their darker sides.

All this is to say that empathy is a key component of representational thinking. To truly see things from another's perspective, one has to be able to feel from another's perspective. To accurately represent a different point of view, one has to have access to the emotional triggers that generate or color that point of view. To think with an enlarged mentality – say, from the standpoint of a woman or man, wife or husband, employer or employee, youth or senior, introvert or extrovert, member of the upper or lower class, professional or blue collar worker, administrator or staff member, friend or enemy, decision-maker or rule-follower – is an act of affective imagination. Reason alone cannot get you there. Only well-integrated experience of the social world coupled with emotional sensibility does the trick. To know how others will grapple with uncertainty, pursue their interests, reach out to others, or react to the exercise of power requires access to the subtle interplay of fear, hope, love, and the host of other affects that motivate actions and stimulate reactions. An enlarged mentality integrates those parts of the mind where emotions play a pivotal role.

As a moral virtue, practical judgment does not demand the experience of particular emotions in particular circumstances. It is reasonable to assume, as most moral theorists do, that one cannot have a duty to "feel" a specific emotion at any given time. Yet it is also reasonable to assert, in line with Aristotle, that we have a duty to cultivate emotional capacities such that they might become available to us in the right measure, at the right time.[91] Untutored emotions will not afford judgment the sensibility and motivation it requires in changing circumstances, nor, generally, will such emotions be utilized with intelligence and care. To have developed "correct desire," for Aristotle, is crucial to ethical lfe.

In this regard, practical judgment involves preparing the heart and mind to work in unison. The good judge, Adam Smith writes,

Has never dared to forget for one moment the judgment which the impartial spectator would pass upon his sentiments and conduct. He has never dared to suffer the man within the breast to be absent one moment from his attention. With the eyes of this great inmate he has always been accustomed to regard whatever relates to himself. This habit has become perfectly familiar to him: he has been in the constant practice, and, indeed, under the constant necessity, of modeling,

---

[91] For a helpful analysis of Aristotle's thoughts on emotions and (moral) judgment, see Nussbaum, *Love's Knowledge*, pp. 38, 55, 79.

or of endeavouring to model, not only his outward conduct and behaviour, but, as much as he can, even his inward sentiments and feelings, according to those of this awful and respectable judge. He does not merely affect the sentiments of the impartial spectator; he really adopts them. He almost identifies himself with, he almost becomes himself that impartial spectator, and scarce even feels but as that great arbiter of his conduct directs him to feel.[92]

The good judge, Smith is saying, taps into a rich and well-balanced emotional register. To judge well is to adopt the habit of seeing and feeling from the standpoint of that composite of others that the impartial spectator represents.

Lawrence Kohlberg, following Piaget's lead, argues that the primitive stages of moral judgment displayed by children are superseded as they mature by increasingly logical processing. The most sophisticated forms of moral judgment in adults, Kohlberg concludes, are those that utilize the most systematic, abstract reasoning.[93] Empirical research disconfirms Kohlberg's thesis.[94] Or, rather, it demonstrates that rational judgment and what might broadly be called "experiential systems" of judgment that include emotive elements, "function in parallel at all stages of development . . . and they interact throughout the life span [of the individual]."[95] For systematic, abstract reasoning to be fruitfully involved in moral judgment, it must be employed in tandem with a host of affective capacities.

If we are unable to feel what others are feeling, if we lack empathy, then our practical judgments will generally fail notwithstanding the rigor of their inferential calculations. They will fail, first, because a lack of empathy will disable representative thinking and the impartiality it allows. Judgments will come to echo our own hopes and fears more than reflect the actual contours of the social world being navigated. In turn, a lack of empathy will stymie the development of the motivational force behind

---

[92] Smith, *The Theory of Moral Sentiments*, p. 206.

[93] Jean Piaget, *The Moral Judgment of the Child* (New York: Free Press, 1965); Lawrence Kohlberg, "The Development of Children's Orientations toward a Moral Order," *Vita Humana*, 6 (1963) 11–33; 11 (1963): 1–32; Anne Colby and Lawrence Kohlberg, *The Measurement of Moral Judgment, Volume 1: Theoretical Foundations and Research Validation* (Cambridge: Cambridge University Press, 1987).

[94] For a summary account of the empirical literature, see Gisela Labouvie-Vief, "Wisdom as integrated thought: historical and developmental perspectives," in *Wisdom: Its Nature, Origins, and Development* (Cambridge: Cambridge University Press, 1990), pp. 67–68.

[95] Seymour Epstein and Rosemary Pacini, "Some Basic Issues Regarding Dual-Process Theories from the Perspective of Cognitive-Experiential Self-Theory," in Shelly Chaiken and Yaacov Trope, *Dual-Process Theories in Social Psychology* (New York: Guilford Press, 1999), p. 476.

moral and political assessments, evaluations, and choices. One has to be affectively predisposed to make the right decisions; one must, all things being equal, experience one's own and others' suffering as an evil to be avoided, and one's own and others' happiness as a good to be promoted. To the extent we consider practical judgment a moral virtue, the cultivation of correct desire is crucial.

Self-Knowledge, Good Judgment, and the Role of Emotion

A good way to improve judgment is through the "debiasing" that occurs when one considers alternative points of view. Empathy is a key feature of this effort.[96] It is a matter of acknowledging, and in some sense experiencing, the emotional states and the concomitant perspectives to which others are subject. That is a feat relatively easy to accomplish when the others in question are near and dear to us. Their pains, pleasures, and perspectives may effortlessly become our own. The task is considerably more difficult when those with whom we seek to empathize are more distant in time or space.

Reason on its own, Hume rightly observed, does not care a whit more for the fate of humanity than the state of one's little finger. But emotion unaided by imagination is often little better at extending its concern. As Hume himself acknowledged, our emotional attachments diminish markedly with increased spatial or temporal distance. Those living on the other side of the globe, or in the distant future, matter to us less than family, friends, associates, and compatriots.

Emotions are largely captive to the here and now, painting the world, including its past and future, with the colors most vividly available in the present. Thus, people in particular moods or in the thrall of particular emotions will typically project these moods or emotions backward and forward when assessing and evaluating other people, distant events, or future prospects. Affect does not have a good sense of time or space. Of course, one's current emotions may relate to future expectations. Anxiety, dread, and foreboding are cases in point, as is hopefulness. But even such emotional states do not distinguish between what is now being experienced and how one might experience things from another vantage point at another time.

---

96 Plous, *The Psychology of Judgment*, p. 256. Peter Suedfeld and Philip Tetlock, "Psychological Advice about Political Decision Making: Heuristics, Biases and Cognitive Defects," in *Psychology and Social Policy*, ed. Peter Suedfeld and Philip Tetlock (New York: Hemisphere Publishing, 1992), pp. 51–70.

The problem is not simply egoism at work. To be sure, people often find it difficult to empathize with others because they remain tightly wedded to personal concerns. But people are also notoriously bad empathizers with themselves. That is to say, we have great difficulty accurately imagining (or remembering) our own future (or past) states of mind. Current affect shouts, whereas remembered past or projected future dispositions whisper. That is why able-bodied people project their own fears onto an imagined life of disability, as we observed in Chapter 2. And that is why people do not well predict how they will think, feel, and act were they to find themselves in a different emotional state.[97] Current moods or dominant affects generally prove to be overwhelming. As crucial as emotions are to good judgment, therefore, it is well to remember that they are unruly guests seldom given to systematic endeavor.

Rationality, when masterless and left wholly to its own devices, fails miserably to secure our interests or the interests of others. To serve us well, reason must be ruled by passion. As the often pernicious effects of emotional biases and the fickle nature of affect demonstrates, however, Hume's statement about reason requires some revision. With Aristotle in mind, we might say that reason is and ought to be a slave of the right passions, at the right time, on the right occasions, to the right degree.[98]

According to Aristotle, one cannot choose a prudent course of action unless one's emotional relationship to the world is properly developed and exercised. A courageous person, for example, experiences an appropriate (level of) fear such that he acts bravely but without abandon.[99] Both the dearth and the excess of fear produce vicious results. If fear wholly dominates, one will not exhibit the virtue of courage but rather will display the vice of cowardice. A person wholly without fear, in turn, embodies the vice of foolhardiness. Only the expression of the right emotions

---

[97] Iris Marion Young, "Asymmetrical Reciprocity: On Moral Respect, Wonder, and Enlarged Thought," in *Judgment, Imagination, and Politics: Themes from Kant and Arendt*, ed. Ronald Beiner and Jennifer Nedelsky (New York: Rowman and Littlefield, 2001), p. 209. McDermott, "The Feeling of Rationality," p. 698. George Loewenstein and Jennifer Lerner, "Out of control: Visceral influences on behavior," *Organizational Behavior and Human Decision Making Processes* 65 (1996): 272–92.

[98] Aristotle argued that virtue was a habitual orientation toward the good which entailed acting "at the right times on the right occasions towards the right people for the right motive and in the right way." Aristotle, *Ethics*, p. 65.

[99] As Mark Twain observed, "Courage is resistance to fear, mastery of fear – not absence of fear. Except a creature be part coward it is not a compliment to say it is brave." Twain, Mark, *Pudd'nhead Wilson's Calendar*, 1894. Quoted in Robert A. Fitton, *Leadership*. (Boulder: Westview Press, 1997), p. 114.

in the right degree in the right circumstances allows the development and exercise of virtue.[100] Since *phronesis* is a combination and integration of (all the) other virtues, according to Aristotle, it also relies on emotional foundations. Without appropriate levels of well-directed emotions, without being able to rely upon the right emotion, on the right occasions, to the right degree, one is precluded from making prudent judgments.

D. H. Lawrence wrote that "The only justice is to follow the sincere intuition of the soul, angry or gentle. Anger is just, and pity is just, but judgment is never just."[101] Judgment, which reflects a balance of reason and emotion, is indeed never just in Lawrence's sense of the term. It is never the product of pure will unencumbered by thought. Indeed, as Lawrence describes it, justice is simply the expression of an emotional bias. Such biases may be unadulterated, which is to say, unreflective. But that does not mean they are just. Justice is not that simple because the world is not that simple. Practical judgment grapples with dense and convoluted environments, and the justice it promotes reflects the contours of a multi-faceted world. Anger, though often justified, is seldom just. Hence to act in anger is often to regret, for anger, like every emotion, fails to see beyond itself. Practical judgment, in contrast, exploits emotional resources without unreflectively succumbing to any particular desire or aversion. It achieves this feat by imaginatively extending itself to better encompass a diversity of perspectives, dispositions, and propensities. Practical judgment is, for that reason, often more just and more often just than the spontaneous outpouring of untutored emotion.

Advocates for "emotional intelligence" stipulate that success in life depends on one's ability to make good use of affective resources.[102] As is always the case with important truths, the devil is in the details. Affect is a necessary but not a sufficient condition for the exercise of good judgment. Whether the influence of affect will generate a sound judgment in any particular situation allows no generalizable answer. The threat of emotional skewing is ever present. Through oratory (rhetoric), visual stimulation (priming), or pharmaceutical means, it is relatively easy to

---

[100] See Martha C. Nussbaum, *The Therapy of Desire: Theory and Practice in Hellenistic Ethics* (Princeton: Princeton University Press, 1994), p. 94.

[101] D. H. Lawrence, *Studies in Classic American Literature* (New York: Viking Press, 1922), pp. 17–18.

[102] Peter Salovey, Brian Bedell, Jerusha Detweiler, and John Mayer, "Current Directions in Emotional Intelligence Research" in *Handbook of Emotions*, 2nd ed., ed. Michael Lewis and Jeannette M. Haviland-Jones (New York: Guilford Press, 2000), p. 506.

manipulate people's emotions and deleteriously affect their judgment.[103] The fact that emotions are not easily accessible to reflection, and may remain wholly unconscious, makes them doubly dangerous. The conclusion reached by Damasio is apt:

Knowing about the relevance of feelings in the processes of reason does *not* suggest that reason is less important than feelings, that it should take a backseat to them or that it should be less cultivated. On the contrary, taking stock of the pervasive role of feelings may give us a chance of enhancing their positive effects and reducing their potential harm. Specifically, without diminishing the orienting value of normal feelings, one would want to protect reason from the weakness that abnormal feelings or the manipulation of normal feelings can introduce in the process of planning and deciding.[104]

To enhance our judgment, and our reason, we must work with and through our emotional capacities. Self-knowledge – understanding one's heart, as La Rochefoucauld would say – is key.

Empirical research has discovered an important exception to the widespread tendency of employing current mood states as heuristic devices in decision-making. If individuals are given the opportunity to attribute their current moods to some specific cause, the skewing of their judgments diminishes, and may be fully averted. In one experiment, subjects were asked to make judgments of various sorts. The nature of their assessments and evaluations – that is, their level of generosity, tendencies of approval or disapproval, and optimistic or pessimistic conclusions – proved to be significantly influenced by the weather – namely, if it was a sunny or rainy day when they were asked to submit their judgments. However, when an offhand mention of the weather was made during the interview, the effect of mood states on their judgments was largely negated.[105] When subjects were given an opportunity to attribute their moods to a particular (external) cause, such as the weather, their judgments were no longer skewed by these moods.

---

[103] Anthony Greenwald and Mahzarin Banaji, "Implicit Social Cognition: Attitudes, Self-Esteem, and Stereotypes," *Psychological Review* 102, 1: 4–27 (1995), p. 5.

[104] Damasio, *Descartes' Error*, p. 246. Martha Nussbaum comes to a similar conclusion following a different route. She writes: "To say that emotions should form a prominent part of the subject matter of moral philosophy is not to say that moral philosophy should give emotions a privileged place of trust, or regard them as immune from rational criticism: for they may be no more reliable than any other set of entrenched beliefs.... It does mean, however, that we cannot ignore them, as so often moral philosophy has done." Nussbaum, *Upheavals of Thought*, p. 2.

[105] Gerald Clore and W. Gerrod Parrott, "Moods and their Vicissitudes: Thoughts and Feelings as Information," in *Emotion and Social Judgment*, pp. 107–123.

Other studies indicate that evaluative judgments are generally not skewed by affective arousal if the judgment in question is called for directly after the arousing stimulation. In contrast, judgments are skewed by heightened arousal if they are solicited after some delay from the time of stimulation, though while the subject is still in a state of arousal. In the latter case, subjects presumably no longer link their heightened arousal to the now-distant cause. Consequently, their judgments are skewed by affective states that they no longer attribute to an external event.[106] To generalize, we might say that being under the influence of a particular mood or emotion is not in itself an impediment to good judgment. Being unaware of our moods and emotions, their causes and effects, is the real problem.

The first task at hand, then, is to acknowledge the full impact of emotion on decision-making. In an extension of the Humean position, Herbert Simon argues that "Reason is wholly instrumental. It cannot tell us where to go; at best it can tell us how to get there. It is a gun for hire that can be employed in the service of whatever goals we have, good or bad." Simon concludes that we should not "underestimate the powerful effects of emotion in setting the agenda for human problem solving."[107] Simon is right – as far as he goes. Emotions are important for judgment, but not only because they set agendas, answering the question, "What problem should be addressed"? Emotions also help define problems *as* problems, as aspects of the world in need of assessment and evaluation. They facilitate identification of the important features of a problem, determine the sort of information that is retained in memory and gathered for processing, stimulate the creative exploration of options, influence the analysis of these options, figure prominently in the selection of alternatives, and provide the motivation for the activity of judging itself as well as the execution of its choices.[108]

In turn, emotions prove to be crucial to the acquisition and retention of mental habits that facilitate sound judgment. Cognitive neuroscience confirms that the acquisition of habits is grounded in the brain's emotional systems that provide the feedback (enthusiasm and

---

[106] Schwarz, "Feelings as Information," p. 541. See also LeDoux, *The Emotional Brain*, p. 48.

[107] Herbert A. Simon, "Alternative visions of rationality," in *Judgment and decision making*, ed. H. R. Arkes and K. R. Hammond (Cambridge: Cambridge University Press, 1986), pp. 97, 110, 113.

[108] See Amitai Etzioni, *The Moral Dimension* (New York: The Free Press, 1988), p. 94. See also Marcus, *Affective Intelligence*, p. 9.

encouragement) for the learning and retaining of new skills.[109] Without emotion, one would never find or sustain the motivation to acquire the mental habits that figure prominently in judging.

Emotions color our world. But emotions are not simply attributes of judgment that might be subtracted without affecting its substance, in the way that a car remains a car, whether it is painted red or green. As core elements of our relationship to the world, emotions might best be viewed not simply as contributing to judgment, but as kinds of judgments. Robert Solomon claims that

> Every emotion is a judgment that presupposes the entire body of previous emotional judgments to supply its context and its history as well as 'paradigm cases' for it to consider if not follow. But every emotion is also an individual bit of legislation, whether striking out on its own and shifting the weight of precedent, attempting to establish itself as a new paradigm case, or merely reinforcing the biases of our already established emotional constitution. . . . and so, *every* emotion must be viewed as constitutional, as an essential decision concerning the way one is to view his world.[110]

Likewise, Martha Nussbaum defines emotions as "geological upheavals of thought." They are types of judgment that testify to an inner and outer world that often remains, for better or worse, beyond our conscious, rational control.[111] Though emotions may be unreliable and treacherous, Nussbaum notes, one cannot effectually engage the topic of moral and political life without accounting for the significant role they play.[112] By situating us in our world, framing our experiences, and motivating us to act or react, emotions are constitutive of any and all moral and political judgments.

Recall Nietzsche's critique of Socrates: there are devastating costs associated with a unified self under the tyranny of reason. Critics of the tradition of Western thinking have taken a similar position. Marimba Ani writes:

> What Plato recognizes as 'harmony' is achieved when the 'positive' term of the dichotomy controls (or destroys) the 'negative' term/phenomenon/entity: when reason controls emotion, both in the person and in the state. (In African and Eastern conceptions, harmony is achieved through the balance of complementary

---

[109] Marcus, *The Sentimental Citizen*, p. 82.

[110] Robert C. Solomon, *The Passions* (Garden City, NY: Anchor Press, 1976), pp. 186, 187, 188, 195, 196, 198, 200.

[111] Martha C. Nussbaum, *Upheavals of Thought: The Intelligence of Emotions* (Cambridge: Cambridge University Press, 2001), p. 90.

[112] Nussbaum, *Upheavals of Thought*, p. 2.

forces, and it is indeed impossible to have a functioning whole *without* harmonious interaction and the existence of balancing pairs.) ... But our notions of what constitutes intelligence have been molded by the minority Western European world-view, and so we have difficulty thinking holistically in this regard, since the European world is predicated on first separation, dichotomization, and then "dominance" of one of the opposites.[113]

The hegemonic role of reason in the (Western) approach to judgment is now being challenged both theoretically and empirically. In the absence of well-integrated emotions, studies demonstrate, reason proves to be incapable of delivering the goods.

Much contemporary work on judgment carries on the Socratic legacy, asking how we might improve judgment by strengthening reason. There is much to be gained from this endeavor, for affective biases are many, and their influence in decision-making is often insidious. Emotions leave us vulnerable to prejudice and projection. Under the influence of negative emotions, in particular, the exercise of judgment may deteriorate into a habit of hasty censure. Eagerness to blame is not practical wisdom. The good judge is not judgmental. Still, the remedy for an overly judgmental disposition is not the squelching of emotion, negative or otherwise. Quite the opposite. The cultivation of empathy is required.

What was said in the last chapter (3) regarding intuition and tacit cognition applies equally to emotion. While an education in reason is all for the good, this education should not be structured as an attempt to *replace* emotions with reason. Any such effort will prove futile and counterproductive. Good judgment depends on acknowledging, exploring, cultivating, and integrating affect. Denying or deprecating its force gets us nowhere. We stand to benefit most from investigations that chart the conditions under which emotions work synergistically with reason to produce sound, impartial, empathetic judgments.[114]

La Rochefoucauld famously observed that "The head is always fooled by the heart."[115] The truth behind this aphorism has prompted generations of scholars to denounce and denigrate emotions such that reason might be valorized. A more balanced reaction is warranted. The task

---

[113] Marimba Ani, *Yurugu: An African-Centered Critique of European Cultural Thought and Behavior* (Trenton: African World Press, 1994), pp. 35, 77.

[114] For an empirically informed, theoretically sustained, and tactically engaged effort in this direction, see William E. Connolly, *Neuropolitics: Thinking, Culture, Speed* (Minneapolis: University of Minnesota Press, 2002). See also Connolly's *Why I Am Not a Secularist* (Minneapolis: University of Minnesota Press, 1999).

[115] La Rochefoucauld, *Maxims*, p. 50; #102.

before us is to explore the potential of whole-brain judgment. William Connolly has championed the cause (without employing this term). Connolly writes:

An ethical sensibility, you might say, is composed through the cultural layering of affect into the materiality of thought. It is a constellation of thought-imbued intensities and feelings. To work on an established sensibility by tactical means, then, is to nudge the composition of some layers in relation to others. You work experimentally on the relays between thought-imbued *intensities* below the level of feeling and linguistic complexity, thought-imbued *feelings* below the level of linguistic sophistication, *images* that trigger responses at both levels.[116]

Connolly observes the importance of integrating these pre-linguistic and pre-conscious affective orientations with our rational and deliberative capacities. We cannot afford to exclude any of our neural networks. By way of worldly encounters and tactical explorations in self-development, we "nudge" ourselves into cultivating the habits of thought and feeling that allow the exercise of sound judgment.

If the head is not to be fooled by the heart, the head will have to integrate the heart. Some of the most powerful parts of the human brain allow and govern affective life. Improving practical judgment entails cultivating and exploiting this emotional intelligence. We cannot much enlarge our mentality without enlarging our access to affect. The "wise and judicious conduct" that is the mark of "superior prudence," Adam Smith observes, arises when we find "the best head joined to the best heart."[117]

The core of practical judgment is keen insight into the nature of the human psyche, a psyche inherently and fundamentally imbued with affect. To learn to judge well is to develop the sensibilities that allow us to understand the complex and often subtle role played by passion in human affairs. If the judging mind is to improve its efforts, it is the heart, increasingly, that must become the object of study, and its sympathies the object of schooling.

---

[116] Connolly, *Neuropolitics*, p. 107.
[117] Smith, *The Theory of Moral Sentiments*, p. 316.

5

The Riches of Narrative

To raise the question of the nature of narrative is to invite reflection on the very nature of culture and, possibly, even on the nature of humanity itself.
Hayden White[1]

I am always at a loss to know how much to believe of my own stories.
Washington Irving[2]

There is nothing we are more certain about than our sense of self. However confounding the world around us, however confused we may be about particular judgments, we rest assured – at the least – that there is a self being perplexed. *Cogito, ergo sum*, Descartes announced in an effort to disabuse himself and fellow philosophers of uncertainty: I think, therefore I am. While one may doubt a great deal in life, Descartes discovered, one cannot doubt that there is, minimally, a self engaged in doubting.

For most of us, the self is a stable and enduring entity. To be sure, the notion of the self has an abstract quality about it. We cannot locate the self precisely, and we do not well understand its origins, constitution, or development. But to deny the reality of the self is to court psychological and social disintegration. From well before the time we were able to think in abstract terms, the self asserted itself in our lives as an omnipresent force. It served as a fulcrum for our explorations and a foundation for our experiences.

[1] Hayden White, *The Content of the Form: Narrative Discourse and Historical Representation* (Baltimore: The Johns Hopkins University Press, 1987), p. 1.
[2] Washington Irving, "To the Reader," in *Tales of a Traveler* (1824).

Notwithstanding its ubiquitous presence in our lives, the self has no transcendental nature, no essence. It is best understood as a fabrication. I am not saying that the self has no reality. In this regard, it is misleading to speak of "the illusion of self."[3] The self is not an illusion: it exists, it serves critical functions, and it produces significant effects. Indeed, the self plays the most important role for the individual, or rather, the self constitutes each individual's most important role. Nonetheless, it is a fiction.

Fiction, in its original sense, denotes a forming or fashioning. To assert the self as a fiction is to say that the self is an artifact. More precisely, the self is a narrative artifact, a tale we tell ourselves so convincingly that, by psychological necessity, it assumes the character of a primordial, stable entity. The self is a time-bound deed that gains the status of an enduring doer. So the self is no illusion, but rather a very powerful creation. What is illusory is its essence.

Seyla Benhabib puts the point rather well when she writes, "The self is not a thing, a substrate, but the protagonist of a life's tale."[4] Yet the self is not monolithic. The individual – at least the psychologically healthy individual – does not live life's tale as a single character. Rather, the self plays multiple roles. Its characters, manifold as they are, stand intertwined. They populate diverse plots within an overarching narrative scheme. Each of these plots bears its distinct themes, relationships, problems, and resolutions (or lack thereof). Yet each overlaps sufficiently with others or, better said, is sufficiently nested within others, to forge and retain narrative coherence. When this narrative structure proves insufficient, the individual lapses into psychosis. The absence of narrative coherence indicates the pathology of personality disorders, the diseases of the self.

Notwithstanding its tremendous importance to the life and health of the individual, the self is not a substrate. It does not pre-exist (or survive) its narrative construction. The so-called unity of the self is the narratively forged identity of a protagonist. The story is primary and generative, while the self is subsidiary and responsive. Philosopher Alasdair MacIntyre writes: "Just as a history is not a sequence of actions, but the concept of an action is that of a moment in an actual or possible history abstracted for some purpose from that history, so the characters in a history are not

[margin note: very similar to C.T.]

---

3 Michael S. Gazzaniga, *The Mind's Past* (Berkeley: University of California Press, 1998), p. 1.
4 Seyla Benhabib, *Situating the Self* (New York: Routledge, 1992), 162.

a collection of persons, but the concept of a person is that of a character abstracted from a history."[5] An individual becomes a self, in other words, by abstracting a persona from its narrative passage through space-time. The self is the character-in-development distilled from the multiple, variegated, spatio-temporal sequences of events that are formatted into the story of an individual life.

We tend to think of the characters of a novel as its sub-stratum and imagine the plot to develop around them. We are wont to believe that the story forms in the wake of enduring personalities that push themselves through the world, acting into their environment as stable, autopoetic entities. The common perception is that character drives plot. But a novel's character does not predate or survive its plot. Rather, it signifies the crystallization of plot, a vector arising from temporally and spatially generated patterns of relationships. Likewise, we assume the primordial and foundational nature of the self. Yet the self does not predate or survive its narrative. The concept of a self is abstracted from its history. And if we tell stories to make sense of our lives, effectively defining sub-plots by their protagonists, these anecdotes are but reflections of deeper narratives that constitute the selves in question.[6]

All of this may seem highly abstract, perhaps even a bit of post-modern posturing. It is not. The fictioned self is not meant to be figurative or metaphorical. There is good empirical evidence for it. Exploring the neuroscience behind the self takes us through the first leg of a journey that will illuminate the nature of practical judgment and suggest opportunities for its cultivation.

The Neurological Construction of the Self

In the late nineteenth and early twentieth centuries, social scientists such as William James, Charles Horton Cooley, and George Herbert Mead proposed a quasi-Darwinian model of the self. They understood it as a product of evolution, rooted in the body and developed over the life of the individual through social interaction.[7] But it is not our instinctive,

---

[5] Alasdair MacIntyre, *After Virtue: A Study in Moral Theory* (Notre Dame: University of Notre Dame Press, 1981), pp. 201–202.

[6] See Thomas Heilke, "Realism, Narrative, and Happenstance: Thucydides' Tale of Brasidas," *American Political Science Review* 98 (2004): 128.

[7] William James, *Psychology: The Briefer Course* (New York: Harper, 1961. Charles Horton Cooley, *Human Nature and the Social Order* (New York: Scribner, 1964). George Herbert Mead, *Mind, Self and Society* (Chicago: University of Chicago Press, 1934). For a good

hard-wired neural relays that establish in us a sense of self – at least, not by themselves. Instinctive capacities are too rudimentary. That should be obvious from the fact that insects and reptiles boast great repertoires of innate skills. Yet we are loath to attribute to them a sense of self or self-consciousness. The feat of creating a self is not achieved by instinct alone. Rather, it arises from neural development undergone primarily during an individual's youth but persisting throughout life.

This neural development, as discussed in Chapter 2, is known as "brain mapping." Brain mapping (Hebbian plasticity) occurs when specific neural connections assert their dominance with repeated use. Neurons that fire together, wire together. The synaptic circuits formed by this process produce a neural inventory of life. The worldly experiences that constitute an individual's existence, coupled with the internal reactions of the individual to these experiences, are laid down as tracks in the mind. This interactive scheme of brain maps – built upon genetically acquired neural foundations – produces a sense of self. Joseph LeDoux writes: "People don't come preassembled, but are glued together by life . . . regarding questions of mind and behavior, nature and nurture are really two ways of doing the same thing – wiring up synapses – and both are needed to get the job done."[8] The job in question is the creation of a self. "You are your synapses," LeDoux concludes. "[Y]our 'self,' the essence of who you are, reflects patterns of interconnectivity between neurons in your brain."[9] The self is a complex brain map whose features, though drafted at an early age, are always under revision.

The neural inventory of life created by brain maps may be portrayed as a kind of narrative, the scripting of an existential tale. Antonio Damasio writes:

The entire construction of knowledge, from simple to complex, from nonverbal imagetic to verbal literary, depends on the ability to map what happens over time, *inside* our organism, *around* our organism, *to* and *with* our organism, one thing followed by another thing, causing another thing, endlessly. Telling stories, in the sense of registering what happens in the form of brain maps, is probably a brain obsession and probably begins relatively early both in terms of evolution and in terms of the complexity of the neural structures required to create

review of these thinkers' contributions, see James Holstein and Jaber Gubrium, *The Self We Life By: Narrative Identity in a Postmodern World* (New York: Oxford University Press, 2000).

[8] Joseph LeDoux, *The Synaptic Self: How Our Brains Become Who We Are* (New York: Penguin Books, 2002), pp. 3, 66.

[9] LeDoux, *The Synaptic Self*, pp. ix, 2.

narratives.... The brain inherently represents the structures and states of the organism, and in the course of regulating the organism as it is mandated to do, the brain naturally weaves wordless stories about what happens to an organism immersed in an environment.[10]

Neural mapping is best understood as a narrative accounting of lived experience. It constitutes a silent, synaptic story. This narrative accounting is an "obsession" for humans in the sense that, phylogenetically and ontogenetically, it constitutes our being. From the evolutionary perspective of the species and the developmental perspective of the individual organism, brain mapping makes us who we are. Synaptic storylines inventory the individual's life, serve as its engine of development, and foster a sense of self.

Neuroscientist Jeffrey Gray concurs that the "narrative of consciousness" is synaptically formed.[11] But might we not posit an enduring teller behind the neurological tale – an essential, primordial cartographer? Of course, there is brain tissue in the fetus before there is any significant amount of neural mapping. Still, the brain mass only becomes an effectively functioning brain through the development of its neural relays. And the development of these relays, beyond the most rudimentary instincts, only occurs as the organism grapples with its environment. There is no discernible (sense of) self prior to this activity. Rather, the self is generated as neural maps create increasingly complex and interactive circuits that capture the organism's march through space and time. We want to think of ourselves as transcendent authors, and, by and large, it is healthy to do so. At a neurological level, however, we are fabricated characters. Just as the brain constructs a model of the external world through its synaptic maps, so, too, it "constructs a model of the self as actor in that world."[12] We are the persona retrospectively abstracted from synaptic stories.

The brain is replete with neural maps, most of which are unavailable to introspection and beyond conscious control. These unspoken synaptic tales are nonetheless being actively interpreted. Neuroscientist Michael Gazzaniga argues that our sense of self derives largely from an unconscious hermeneutics that is the product of a "built-in" neurological mechanism found in the left hemisphere of the brain. Gazzaniga calls this neurological mechanism, appropriately enough, "the interpreter."

[10] Antonio R. Damasio, *The Feeling of What Happens: Body and Emotion in the Making of Consciousness* (New York: Harcourt, Brace and Company, 1999), p. 189.

[11] Jeffrey Gray, *Consciousness* (Oxford: Oxford University Press, 2004), p. 5.

[12] Gray, *Consciousness*, p. 293.

Gazzaniga's label might be misleading. It suggests an isolated homunculus, or, in neurological terms, a self-enclosed, hard-wired module that does all the interpreting. More likely, our self-interpretive capacities are the products of a broad synthesis of related brain activities. Undoubtedly, however, many of these activities are located in the left hemisphere. In turn, the left hemisphere serves as the primary coordinator for neural inventorying, even when the operation occurs elsewhere in the brain. Notwithstanding the question of modularity, then, Gazzaniga informatively explores how this neurological mechanism develops and how its activities, which mostly operate below the threshold of perception, eventuate in self-consciousness.

The interpeter, Gazzaniga writes, "ties the vast output of our thousands upon thousands of automatic systems into our subjectivity to render a personal story for each of us."[13] It oversees the transformation of the raw perception of temporally and spatially contiguous (internal and external) events into descriptive or explanatory narratives. The interpreter gives these events (interrelated) meanings. For the most part, this complex activity takes place well under the radar of awareness. We do not consciously interpret our brain maps nor do we consciously integrate these interpretations over time. But this hermeneutics goes on continuously, and the effort of integration eventually produces a coherent narrative we call the self.

Gazzaniga writes: "The interpreter constantly establishes a running narrative of our actions, emotions, thoughts, and dreams. It is the glue that unifies our story and creates our sense of being a whole, rational agent. It brings to our bag of individual instincts the illusion that we are something other than what we are. It builds our theories about our own life, and these narratives of our past behavior pervade our awareness."[14] The human brain (and particularly its left hemisphere) is hard-wired, given a minimally conducive social environment, to fiction a self. This self is interpreted as standing in charge, as ruling over itself and, to the extent possible, as controlling its environment. In Norretrander's terminology, the left-hemispheric secretary actively interprets its internal and external world so as to generate a coherent, enduring self. The interpreter allows the impression that an *I* is in control.

13 Michael S. Gazzaniga, *The Mind's Past* (Berkeley: University of California Press, 1998), p. 24.
14 Gazzaniga, *The Mind's Past*, p. 174. See also Gazzaniga, "Brain and Conscious Experience," in *Foundations in social neuroscience*. ed. John T. Cacioppo et al. (Cambridge, Mass.: MIT Press, 2002), pp. 203–214.

The activity of the interpreter is easily observed, as we saw in Chapters 3 and 4, whenever conscious judgment exhibits itself as the *post hoc* rationalization of an unconscious impulse. Its functioning is more graphically illustrated by individuals who have sustained brain damage. Recall the story of the unfortunate woman who had a stroke in her right hemisphere and consequently suffered the paralysis of her left arm.[15] A healthy right hemisphere takes on the charge of grappling with novelty. Damage to the woman's right hemisphere rendered it largely incapable of this task. Consequently, her "conformist" left hemisphere gained hegemony. Unchecked by the right hemisphere's prerogative to innovate and adapt, the left-hemispheric secretary morphed into Procrustes. It became a revisionist historian intent on making the recent past conform to an earlier past. When the world of experience contradicted the woman's longstanding self-image, she simply rewrote her personal history to validate an out-dated sense of self. Hence she denied the paralysis of her left arm, and subsequently concocted outrageous stories to explain away mishaps brought on by her physical limitations. Here the interpreter kept spinning stories of a fully functional self notwithstanding direct evidence to the contrary. Only a good earwashing stimulated her right hemisphere (temporarily) to update the dysfunctional narrative.

Gazzaniga provides equally striking examples of the fictioning, and malfunctioning, of selves. He discusses cases of "split-brain" patients who either have a defective corpus callosum, or, for medical reasons, have had their corpus callosum surgically severed such that the two hemispheres of the brain are no longer connected. Now the conformist, self-interpreting left side can no longer work in tandem with the innovation-attending but speechless right side. With obstructive screens separating their visual fields, split-brain patients were presented with two pictures. One picture was seen only by the right eye (and therefore registered only by the left hemisphere), while another picture was seen only by the left eye (and registered only by the right hemisphere). After the obstructive screens were removed, the patients were presented with an assortment of other pictures and asked to choose those that most suitably corresponded to the earlier viewed images.

In one case, an image of a chicken claw was exposed to the right eye/left hemisphere of a patient while his left eye/right hemisphere was exposed to a snow scene. The split screen was subsequently removed

---

[15] V. S. Ramachandran and Sandra Blakeslee, *Phantoms in the Brain* (New York: William Morrow and Company, 1998), p. 141.

and the patient was presented with assortment of other pictures. He was asked to choose those that were closely associated with the previously viewed images. The "correct" choices from among the newly presented pictures were those of a chicken (which corresponded to the chicken claw) and a shovel (which corresponded to the snow scene). The patient, as one might expect, chose the shovel with his left hand and the chicken with his right hand. However, when asked why these items were chosen, the response was intriguing. "Oh, that's simple," he said. "The chicken claw goes with the chicken, and you need a shovel to clean out the chicken shed." The left hemisphere, observing the left hand's choice of a shovel but unaware that the left eye had been previously exposed to the snow scene, set itself the task of producing a coherent story to make sense of the situation. Gazzaniga interprets the results of the experiment:

What is amazing here is that the left hemisphere is perfectly capable of saying something like, "Look, I have no idea why I picked the shovel – I had my brain split, don't you remember? You probably presented something to the half of my brain that can't talk; this happens to me all the time. You know I can't tell you why I picked the shovel. Quit asking me this stupid question." But it doesn't say this. The left brain weaves its story in order to convince itself and you that it is in full control.[16]

In split-brain patients, the secretarial left-brain finds itself at a distinct disadvantage. It must interpret the world as if a single self were interacting with its environment. Yet the inability of the corpus callosum to transmit data leaves the person with two truncated tales to coordinate. Backed into this corner, the left-brain carries on with the task of weaving an overarching narrative to make sense of its world. It makes up through poetic license what it lacks in raw information.

For split-brain or stroke patients, the stories told by the secretarial self can be quite fanciful. But narrative self-fictioning occurs no less frequently, though perhaps less spectacularly, in healthy individuals. Gazzaniga argues that our left hemisphere serves the function of a spin doctor who tries, at all costs, "to keep our personal story together."[17] This task is achieved by the construction of coherent and often quite

---

[16] Gazzaniga, *The Mind's Past*, pp. 24–25.

[17] Gazzaniga, *The Mind's Past*, pp. 25–27. Steven Pinker writes: "Each of us *feels* that there is a single 'I' in control. But that is an illusion that the brain works hard to produce.... The conscious mind – the self or soul – is a spin doctor, not the commander in chief." Steven Pinker, *The Blank Slate* (New York: Viking, 2002), pp. 42–43.

imaginative tales that demonstrate an *I* in control. Each of these short stories reflects the deeper narrative of a constructed self.

The lion's share of these tales are told silently. Relatively few rise to consciousness. Occasionally, when employed in an effort to explain our actions, these tales gain the form of *post hoc* rationalizations. Here, as Gazzaniga writes, a concocted story "liberates us from the sense of being tied to the demands of the environment and produces the wonderful sensation that our self is in charge of our destiny."[18] Consider, in this light, the *order effect* (discussed in Chapter 3). Confronted with a line of five identical items, people typically choose the item placed to the far right. This appears to be a hard-wired bias. But people also offer reasons for their choices. As all of the items are perfectly identical, none of the proffered reasons has any merit.[19] The spurious rationalizations are mini-fictions crafted to buttress the meta-fiction of a coherent, autonomous self (that bases its choices on sound reasons).

In fact, there are two biases at play here. There is the right-side bias and there is the essential-self bias. The subject of the experiment is unaware of both. Hence he lives out a story – as do all psychologically healthy individuals – of a unified self that makes assessments and evaluations on the basis of good reasons (or at least conscious ones). Having made a choice for the right-side item, the chooser needs an explanation to make sense of this turn of events. Consequently, he fabricates one. The voiceless dialogue that takes place after choosing the right-side item might go something like this: "Hmm. I chose the item to the far right. That's interesting. I must have had a good reason for doing that. Certainly I wouldn't have chosen it randomly. What might my reason have been? Ah, here's one! That item looks brighter than the others. Perhaps it's a little newer. I like newness. That's a good reason to choose it. Newness is good." Articulating the conclusion to such a conversation is not lying in the sense of uttering a falsehood with the intent of misleading. It is simply a matter of the interpretive, secretarial *I* doing its job. Indeed, the rationalization serves a crucial function. It allows the author a sense of self-directedness – a core component of psychological well-being.

The left hemisphere is always cooking up stories to lend coherence to the whirl of environmental stimuli, responses, and reflections that constitute our lives. It provides "the string that ties events together and

---

[18] Gazzaniga, *The Mind's Past*, p. 175.
[19] Timothy Wilson, *Strangers to Ourselves: Discovering the Adaptive Unconscious* (Cambridge: Belknap Press, 2002), pp. 102–104.

makes actions or moods appear to be directed, meaningful, and purposeful." As such, Gazzaniga observes, it generates the "personal narrative for
why we feel and do the things we feel and do."[20] While this sort of self-
fictioning appears grotesquely counterfeit in brain-damaged individuals,
it is the *sine qua non* of effective coping in healthy individuals. While it is
often necessary "to lie to ourselves" to keep our personal stories together,
Gazzaniga states, these lies, in most cases, facilitate our functioning
in complex social environments. He writes: "We need something that
expands the actual facts of our experience into an ongoing narrative, the
self-image we have been building in our mind for years. . . . It is probably
the most amazing mechanism the human being possesses."[21] The most
amazing aspect of this mechanism is that it provides not merely adaptive
skills for coping with life, but an adaptive self for living it.

Key to the left hemisphere's success in fabricating a narrative self is
the relative tardiness of consciousness. Compared with the speed of the
brain's automatic responses, its conscious efforts are downright sluggish.
Benjamin Libet's tenacious work in this area is informative. A *conscious*
decision to do something, Libet has demonstrated, lags behind the onset
of the initial brain activity that produces the intended behavior by up to a
half-second. Brain activity that stimulates voluntary motion, for instance,
occurs well before one becomes aware of an intention to move.[22] When
consciously choosing to act, we are not initiating a process. Rather, we are
acknowledging an already-in-progress neurological activity that puts our
body into motion. Consciousness of an intention to act in a particular
way occurs not as a stimulant to, but in the wake of, brain activity directed
toward that end.[23]

---

[20] Gazzaniga, *The Mind's Past*, p. 133.

[21] Gazzaniga, *The Mind's Past*, pp. 25–27.

[22] Benjamin Libet, "Unconscious cerebral initiative and the role of conscious will in volun-
tary action," *Behavioral and Brain Science* 8(1985): 529–566. See also Libet, "The neural
time factor in conscious and unconscious events." Cited in Guy Claxton, *Hare Brain
Tortoise Mind: Why Intelligence Increases When You Think Less* (Hopewell, NJ: The Ecco
Press, 1997), p. 161. Libet's work has been confirmed by other experiments. See Gray,
Consciousness, p. 22.

[23] Whereas the "readiness potential" indicating initial cerebral activity occurrs 550 milliseconds before muscle movement, subjects become conscious of their decision to move
100–200 milliseconds before muscle movement. Libet and others have suggested that
this delay allows enough time, roughly 350 milliseconds, for the "free will" of a conscious
subject either to allow or naysay the brain's readiness to carry out the movement. In this
vein, one might understand free will, and consciousness in general, as an evolutionary adaptation that allows humans to second-guess – that is, veto or affirm – automatic
or instinctual urges that are already in progress. See Jeffrey M. Schwartz and Sharon

The notion of consciousness acting as a tardy umpire rather than a "first mover" is most evident in non-voluntary movement. Here, consciousness truly serves as a rubber stamp, retrospectively legitimating action taken unconsciously. When a person accidentally touches a hot stove, for instance, he immediately removes his hand. In fact, he retracts his hand before feeling any pain. The sense of pain from the heat rises to consciousness well after the hand is put into motion. That is a good thing, given the sluggishness of consciousness and the potential swiftness of physical injury. From the point of view of self-consciousness, however, there is a problem. It would be disconcerting for a self-conscious being to act first and only discover the reasons for his actions later. So the mind tricks itself, retroactively assessing conscious sensations (for example, of pain) as the *cause* of actions taken.[24] It engages in a temporal sleight-of-hand. We mislead ourselves into believing that we are acting as a result of our becoming aware of a feeling when in fact the feeling only arises after our physical response is underway.

Citing Libet's studies, Gazzaniga writes that "The brain finishes the work [of initiating a behavior] half a second before the information it processes reaches our consciousness.... The brain begins to cover for this 'done deal' aspect of its functioning by creating in us the illusion that the events we are experiencing are happening in real time – not before our conscious experience of deciding to do something."[25] It would be detrimental to one's sense of (an autonomous) self to perceive actions as products of impulses that one could only retroactively endorse. Hence we are structured to remain oblivious to the tardiness of conscious responses. We can react to an event (for example, ducking the head as a reaction to a shouted warning) in one-tenth of a second or less; yet we only become conscious of our reaction half a second after the initial event. Our neurological structure, which allows the perception of behavior as if it followed from rather than preceded conscious intention, helps us fabricate a self. The phenomenon of tardy consciousness is not restricted to reactions to physical threat or pain. It applies to many of our "choices." As Jeffrey Gray observes, "There is good experimental evidence that *decisions are taken a long time before the subject becomes consciously aware of having made the decision....* Consciousness occurs after the event."[26] The fact of the

---

Begley, *The Mind and the Brain: Neuroplasticity and the Power of Mental Force* (New York: HarperCollins, 2002), pp. 304–308.

[24] Gray, *Consciousness*, p. 9.

[25] Gazzaniga, *The Mind's Past*, pp. 63–64.

[26] Gray, *Consciousness*, p. 21.

matter is that our conscious judgments are mostly afterthoughts. They bespeak the efforts of a left hemisphere, with help of the time lag of consciousness, feigning cognitive control through the narrative fabrication of a self.

The crafting of the narrative self, from a neurological point of view, arises before the first use of words. Language (acquisition) follows rather than precedes the synaptic stories that structure our early lives. The sense of self that develops as the brain imagistically maps its interactions with the world is not reliant on language. Rather, these maps constitute "a nonverbal narrative document of what is happening to the main protagonists in the process, accomplished with the elementary representation tools of the sensory and motor systems."[27] In time, the cerebral cortex facilitates conscious interpretation of some of these synaptic stories, and subsequently may give them linguistic expression. But most narration occurs well before such reflexivity. Damasio writes that "Telling stories precedes language, since it is, in fact, a condition for language, and it is based not just in the cerebral cortex but elsewhere in the brain and in the right hemisphere as well as the left."[28] The "second-order" narratives that we weave with words and the "refined" subjectivity that arises from them are both nourished by the basic, non-verbal narration that grounds brain development.[29] The conclusion reached by Damasio is that "Language enriches the human self even if it does not serve as its source."[30]

It may seem a stretch to posit storytelling as preceding linguistic expression. We get a sense of what Damasio has in mind, however, by examining the various ways we create and employ wordless neural storylines. Optical illusions illustrate the point. Recall the Titchener circles employed in Chapter 3 to demonstrate the power of tacit, non-cognitive skills. Although the two central medium-sized disks are physically identical in size, the one surrounded by the large objects looks smaller than the one surrounded by the small objects. Neural maps in the brain cause us to evaluate the sizes of the disks comparatively, in reference to contiguous objects. Contiguous evaluation is a good habit for humans operating in a natural environment to develop. The ability speedily to pick the largest fruit from a limb, for example, is much facilitated by a quick comparative

---

[27] A. R. Damasio and H. Damasio, "Making Images and Creating Subjectivity," in *The Mind-Brain Continuum: Sensory Processes*, ed. Rodolfo Llinas and Patricia Churchland (Cambridge: MIT Press, 1996), p. 25.

[28] Damasio, *The Feeling of What Happens*, p. 189.

[29] Damasio, "Making Images and Creating Subjectivity," p. 26.

[30] Damasio, "Making Images and Creating Subjectivity," p. 22.

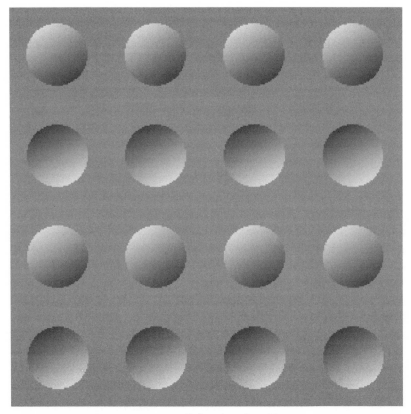

FIGURE 5.1. Spheres and cavities.

assessment of the size of nearby fruit. Although it can produce perverse results on occasion, for the most part it is an adaptive trait. Our penchant for contiguous evaluation is the product of brain maps that render a wordless story about the accurate assessment of the sizes of nearby objects. We follow that well-established plot even when particular circumstances demonstrate its shortcomings.

Consider another optical illusion. Here, a series of circular disks appear scattered on a uniform background, as in Figure 5.1. The disks are all identical except that half of them are light near the top, shading into grey in the middle, and dark near the bottom. The remaining disks are lighter on their bottom hemispheres, shading into grey in a middle band, and darker at the top. People viewing disks that are lighter on top see them as spheres bulging out of the page. The disks that are darker on the top are perceived as cavities. Why this difference in perception?

Why don't people simply see numerous shaded disks, half of which are inverted?

The answer is that we live in an environment where light sources typically shine from above. Our brains have developed neural maps that interpret the optical world as if it were being illuminated by a heavenly sun or moon (or ceiling-mounted light bulbs). In such a world, objects with lighted top hemispheres and darkened (shaded) bottom hemispheres are correctly seen as spheres, whereas objects with darkened (shaded) top hemispheres and lightened bottom hemispheres are correctly perceived as concavities.[31] The neural mapping that invests us in this optical storyline works well enough in the natural environment. The exception posed by an optical illusion simply proves the rule.

Finally, and perhaps most persuasively, consider the phenomenon known as "filling-in." Every eye has its "blind spot," a small area in the normal range of peripheral vision where one cannot see. The blind spot occurs because the part of the retina that is physically connected to the optic nerve is insensitive to light. You can become aware of your blind spot by closing one eye and focusing on a particular point, say a black dot on a page held a few inches away. Some distance to the left and right of the dot is your blind spot. A small figure placed in this blind spot will not be perceived.

Filling-in occurs when a small figure falling in one's blind spot disrupts a larger figure that surrounds or is contiguous to it. The small figure is not seen. Yet one perceives the larger figure situated in one's peripheral vision as if it were continuous, with no disrupting blind spot. For instance, when the white box that bisects the thick, vertical black line in Figure 5.2 falls into one's blindspot, one does not perceive a thick black line with a white box bisecting it. Nor does one perceive a thick black line with an empty space in its middle section. Rather, one perceives a continuous thick black line. The brain simply invents a segment of thick black line and fills in the blind spot with it, allowing the perception of continuity.

Even more intriguing, consider what happens when two misaligned vertical black lines are drawn with a white box occupying the blind spot, as in Figure 5.3. Now the brain not only fills in the blind spot with a concocted segment, but actually realigns the black lines. One perceives a single, continuous, vertical, *straight* black line.[32] The brain unabashedly invents the continuity of its visual world.

[31] See Ramachandran, *Phantoms in the Brain*, p. 69.
[32] Ramachandran, *Phantoms in the Brain*, pp. 92–97.

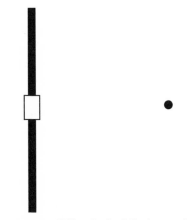

FIGURE 5.2. Filling-in for blind spots (1).

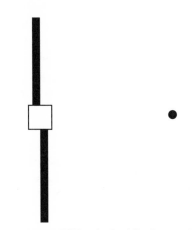

FIGURE 5.3. Filling-in for blind spots (2).

Why does the brain fill-in? Ramachandran explains: "The answer lies in a Darwinian explanation of how the visual system evolved. One of the most important principles in vision is that it tries to get away with as little processing as it can to get the job done. To economize on visual processing, the brain takes advantage of statistical regularities in the world – such as the fact that contours are generally continuous or that table surfaces are uniform – and these regularities are captured and wired into the machinery of the visual pathways early in visual processing."[33] In other

---

[33] Ramachandran, *Phantoms in the Brain*, pp. 103–104.

words, neural mapping is responsible. Brains maps are constructed early in life to facilitate the individual's efficient interactions with its environment. Optical illusions notwithstanding, filling-in serves environmentally adaptive purposes well enough in a world where most surfaces are continuous. Our retinas receive visual information and transmit this accurately to our brains. And in those instances where our retinas fall short – that is, where the optic nerve interferes with the reception of light – the brain fabricates information to fill in that which it cannot receive from the environment. Brain maps fiction an optical scene to mesh with a larger visual narrative.

The optical centers of the brain are not the only ones that fill-in. Brain regions involved in memory are often engaged in an analogous activity. Try this experiment. Think back to something you did yesterday, perhaps a moment spent reading, or writing, or jogging, or dining, or tending to children. Take a moment to remember everything that you can of the activity, in great detail. Now recall the images that were formed in your mind's eye while remembering yesterday's event. Did you see yourself in the picture? Did you visualize your body in something close to its entirety, perhaps from a "God's eye" view? Most people do. They remember events from a perspective that allows them to see the whole scene, with themselves playing the role of a (visible) protagonist. Of course, this is a patent fabrication (unless the activity recalled was gazing into a mirror). If the event being remembered was the reading of a book, for instance, then an exact, unreconstructed memory would produce an image of hands holding a book on a lap and occasionally turning pages. It would not produce an image of a person seated in a chair in an office. Yet this is the sort of image we typically "remember."

Memory is actively reconstructive. It does not retrieve exact copies of past experiences but reconstructs these experiences from selected perceptions, filling in gaps and ensuring (that is to say, fabricating) consistency.[34] One of the most persistent acts of recollective filling-in we engage in generates the sense of self – that is to say, the memory of an individual identity. Just as the brain tells optic tales to ensure the perception of a continuous, coherent visual world, so it forges and recalls more sophisticated narratives to allow the perception of a continuous, coherent self.

[34] Scott Plous, *The Psychology of Judgment and Decision Making* (Philadelphia: Temple University Press, 1993), p. 31.

The Importance of Words

The neural capacity for narrative allows us to develop and maintain an abiding, reflexive identity. Language is necessary for these narrative accountings to achieve the richness and depth required for full self-consciousness. We discover who we are, and come to know ourselves, through the stories we and others tell.[35] The enigma of a self – that peculiar mix of conscious effort operating atop a large iceberg of unconscious perceptions, drives, habits, and skills – receives its illumination in the stories that verbally chart its travels through space and time.

Many of the narratives that make up our sense of self are of the silent, synaptic kind. But, as Daniel Dennett points out, there is a special role for stories constructed with words:

We, in contrast [to spiders, beavers and most other animals], are almost constantly engaged in presenting ourselves to others, and to ourselves, and hence *representing* ourselves – in language and gesture, external and internal.... Our human environment contains not just food and shelter, enemies to fight or flee, and conspecifices with whom to mate, but words, words, words. These words are potent elements of our environment that we readily incorporate, ingesting and extruding them, weaving them like spiderwebs into self-protective strings of *narrative*.... Our fundamental tactic of self-protection, self-control, and self-definition is not spinning webs or building dams, but telling stories, and more particularly concocting and controlling the story we tell others – and ourselves about who we are.[36]

Dennett suggests that storytelling is *the* human artifice. It defines us as a species.

As importantly, storytelling defines us as individuals. The sense of personal self, no less than the sense of species-being, is generated through storytelling. The point is not simply that human self-consciousness and stories go together. That is true, but trite. The point is that the former is derived from the latter. Narrative is cause, selfhood (self-consciousness) is effect. Narratives construct us before we ever get a chance to construct them. Dennett writes: "Our tales are spun, but for the most part we don't spin them; they spin us. Our human consciousness, and our narrative selfhood, is their product, not their source. These strings or streams of

---

[35] See Hannah Arendt, *The Human Condition* (Chicago: Chicago University Press, 1958), pp. 181–82. See also Seyla Benhabib, *The Reluctant Modernism of Hannah Arendt* (Thousand Oaks, CA: Sage, 1996), p. 125.

[36] Daniel C. Dennett, *Consciousness Explained* (Boston: Little, Brown and Company, 1991), pp. 417–18.

narrative issue forth *as if* from a single source. . . . Their effect on any audience is to encourage them to (try to) posit a unified agent whose words
they are, about whom they are: in short, to posit a center of *narrative gravity.*"37 Narratives are not simply powerful tools employed by *homo faber* to
facilitate its worldly navigations. Rather, the human self is the product of
a narrative way of being. Ontologically speaking, we are told by stories.
And if we self-consciously assume the role of storytellers, we do so only
insofar as this assumed identity reflects the deeper reality of a narratively
constructed existence.

The self, one might say, is fictioned to ensure the viability of the human
organism's narrations. To call the self a fiction, however, is not to deny
that it is fabricated for the best of reasons. Dennett writes:

A self . . . is . . . an abstraction defined by the myriads of attributions and interpretations (including self-attributions and self-interpretations) that have composed
the biography of the living body whose Center of Narrative Gravity it is. As such, it
plays a singularly important role in the ongoing cognitive economy of that living
body, because, of all the things in the environment an active body must make
mental models of, none is more crucial than the model the agent has of itself.38

The self forms an indispensable mental grid by way of which the individual
interacts with its world. It constitutes a crucial centripetal force ensuring
that the web of stories that develop from worldly life do not spin out of
control.

Neuroimaging studies of "inner speech" validate the importance of
words in the narrative construction of the self.39 Research suggests that
"The self, in the normative 'self-representation' sense that has interested
philosophers, is created and expressed by the narratives generated by
constant activity in the brain's language production and comprehension
regions."40 We speak to ourselves about ourselves in a running dialogue.
Out of this ever-expanding tale, a sophisticated sense of self emerges.

37 Dennett, *Consciousness Explained*, p. 418.
38 Dennett, *Consciousness Explained*, pp. 426–27.
39 There are various neuroimaging techniques. Positron emission tomography, also known
   as a PET scan, produces images of the brain by detecting the radiation from tiny particles called positrons emitted from a radioactive substance administered to the patient.
   Functional magnetic resonance imaging, also known as fMRI, determines which parts of
   the brain are involved in activity by non-invasively monitoring the increased blood flow
   that accompanies heightened neural activity in the activated areas. Other techniques
   include magnetoencephalography (MEG) and computerized axial tomography (CAT).
40 John Bickle, "Empirical Evidence for a Narrative Concept of Self," in Gary Fireman, Ted
   McVay, Jr., and Owen Flanagan, *Narrative and Consciousness: Literature, Psychology and the
   Brain* (New York: Oxford University Press, 2003), pp. 198–99.

In the absence of words to populate its narratives, full self-consciousness would likely not develop and individual identity would not meet the threshold of human selfhood.

Evolutionary psychologists have argued that language developed as a means of grappling with the increasing complexity of social interaction. Mental representation of others became a mechanism for establishing and maintaining social cohesion and enabling individuals to evaluate the likelihood of cooperation or cheating among fellow group members. In all likelihood, these mental representations were originally produced by way of wordless pantomime. In this crude narrative format, tribal members might have relived the major events of the day by acting them out in a manner that established the characteristics, status, and social functions of the actors involved. Such wordless stories undoubtedly were accompanied by primitive vocalizations. In time, oft-repeated sounds congealed into sequences of phonemes and formed the beginning of a basic vocabulary. Eventually, fully linguistic narratives came to serve as an efficient means of social bonding within large, complex groups, perhaps taking up the prominent role played by mutual grooming among primates. With this prehistory in mind, the central importance of oral tradition to all primitive peoples is understandable. Narrativity was the original and chief means of knowledge acquisition and retention for human society, and supplied a crucial tool for social bonding. It continues to serves these purposes today. [41]

There is a great deal about our world that we are patently ill equipped to understand. As products of evolution, we should not be surprised by this. Our minds have evolved by way of natural selection. Mental capacities were selected for their ability to help solve life-or-death matters in the rough-and-tumble world of our forebears. Non-essential capacities might have developed over time, but they would not have had natural selection to increase the probability of their long-term survival. Hence we lack the cognitive equipment to do many things, such as hold more than a handful of unrelated items in memory at one time, do complex algebraic calculations in our heads, and rotate objects in the fourth dimension. Such limitations attest to our evolutionary heritage.[42] Notwithstanding the mind's many limitations, an abiding strength displays itself. We are

---

[41] See Stephen John Read and Lynn Carol Miller, "Stories are Fundamental to Meaning and Memory: For Social Creatures, Could It Be Otherwise," in *Knowledge and Memory: The Real Story – Advances in Social Cognition*, ed. Robert Wyer, Jr., Vol. VIII (Mahwah, NJ: Lawrence Erlbaum Associates, 1995), p. 148.

[42] See Steven Pinker, *How the Mind Works* (New York: W. W. Norton, 1997), p. 561.

talented storytellers. The narration of experience is a highly complex endeavor. But it comes easily to most of us. Indeed, we cannot help but engage in the activity, whether awake or asleep. Computers effortlessly learn and retrieve thirty-digit numbers. Yet they fail miserably at relaying the import of a child's fairy tale. For humans, the situation is reversed. Compacting the blooming, buzzing world around us into meaningful stories is almost effortless for *homo sapiens*. We are hardwired to think in and through narratives, and our cerebral software develops on the basis of this foundation.

Narrative texts are recalled approximately twice as well as expository texts. Compared with topic familiarity and level of interest, which has little effect on recall, narrativity proves very robust in its relationship to the accurate retention of information. Likewise, recall is much enhanced when individuals form a narrative impression rather than attempt to memorize discrete data. The conclusion drawn by social scientists and psychologists is that narrative has a "privileged status in the cognitive system."[43] The unconscious mind sifts through a plethora of stimuli every moment of the day. It excludes most of this information, and by way of streamlining, contextualization, and filling-in, produces a coherent narrative. The same holds true for our consciously produced, linguistic stories.[44] Narratives give form to the flux. They weave the hurly-burly of the phenomenal world into recognizable and recollectible patterns.[45] Narratives are bite-size slices of space-time. Human beings cut up and digest reality in stories.

Hayden White maintains that historical happenings lack the resolution needed to constitute identifiable events. The eye of the historian provides the focus. In telling his story, the historian ensures that events "display the coherence, integrity, fullness, and closure of an image of life that is and can only be imaginary."[46] In this sense, White insists, "every historical narrative has as its latent or manifest purpose the desire to *moralize* the events of which it treats."[47] Moralization is evident, minimally, in the

---

[43] Arthur Graesser and Victor Ottati, "Why Stories? Some Evidence, Questions, and Challenges," in *Knowledge and Memory*, p. 124.

[44] See Robert C. Mathews and Lewis Roussel, "Abstractness of implicit knowledge: A cognitive evolutionary perspective," in *How Implicit is Implicit Learning*, ed. Dianne Berry (New York: Oxford University Press, 1997), p. 42.

[45] Mathews and Roussel, "Abstractness of implicit knowledge," p. 42.

[46] White, *The Content of the Form*, p. 24.

[47] Quoted in Lewis P. Hinchman and Sandra K. Hinchman, eds. *Memory, Identity, Community: The Idea of Narrative in the Human Sciences* (Albany: State University of New York Press, 1997), p. xxvi.

imparting of coherence and purposiveness to (sequences of) happenings. Narrative develops when thick descriptions are linked temporally by way of a plot. This thick sequencing of events displays inherent moralizing in the form of attributed causality.

What can be said of history in general applies as well to individual sagas, the personal stories that generate self-understanding. Philosopher Charles Taylor writes that a "basic condition of making sense of ourselves [is] that we grasp our lives in a *narrative*. . . . [W]e cannot but strive to give our lives meaning or substance, and . . . this means that we understand ourselves inescapably in narrative'"[48] What Joan Didion says of the novelist, in this regard, applies equally to the rest of us: "We tell ourselves stories in order to live." By way of selective exclusions and filling in, stories "freeze the shifting phantasmagoria which is our actual experience of life to produce stable images." Thus, Didion writes, "we live entirely . . . by the imposition of a narrative line upon disparate images."[49] Likewise, David Carr observes that narrative provides a "synthesis of the heterogenous."[50] In so doing, it gives the bounded human mind access to an unbounded and deeply complex world.

Though multiple and variegated in its forms, narrative is the human universal. We think, learn, heal, and feel in and through narrative. Our attitudes and actions are initiated and recalled, forecast and recollected, in stories. As Roland Barthes observes, narrative is "simply there like life itself . . . international, transhistorical, transcultural."[51] Barbara Hardy concurs: "We dream in narrative, day-dream in narrative, remember, anticipate, hope, despair, believe, doubt, plan, revise, criticize, construct, gossip, learn, hate and love by narrative."[52] In everyday life, people operate much like jurors trying to interpret fragmentary evidence given in testimony. Achieving narrative coherence is crucial. To the extent that a story can be told about the world around us, sense can be made of its complex relationships, and judgments can be levied upon them. The mental acts of understanding and judging, cognitive psychologists suggest, is achieved through the organization of perceptions into narrative

---

[48] Charles Taylor, *The Sources of the Self* (Cambridge: Cambridge University Press, 1989), pp. 47, 51.

[49] Joan Didion, *The White Album*, 1979. Quoted in Wilson, *Strangers to Ourselves*, p. 67.

[50] David Carr, "Narrative and the Real World: An Argument for Continuity," in *Memory, Identity, Community*, p. 10.

[51] Quoted in White, *The Content of the Form*, p. 1.

[52] Barbara Hardy, "Towards a Poetics of Fiction: An Approach Through Narrative," *Novel*, 2, 1968: 5–14. Quoted in MacIntyre, *After Virtue*, p. 197.

format, and, subsequently, the integration of newly acquired narratives into available, already internalized tales.[53]

This capacity arises because narrative, and narrative alone, allows us to forge a coherent temporal/historical context for existence while making sense, and justifying, actions in terms of plans and goals. "There is no other cognitive-experiential structure that blends these two basic dimensions of human existence," Mark Johnson writes, "Consequently, while we can capture certain aspects of our experience via concepts, models, propositions, metaphors, and paradigms, only narrative encompasses both the temporality and the purposive organization at the general level at which we pursue overarching unity and meaning in our lives."[54] By slicing up space-time into bite-size chunks, and ensuring that these slices are linked by causation and purpose, narrative allows us to digest a diverse, dynamic world and evaluate its components.

The instinctive drive to tell and hear stories is evident to every parent. As my two sons were being readied for bed one evening, the younger one asked about options for reading. There was a large selection of books available, recently garnered from the local library. The subject matter included dinosaurs, sea otters (my son's favorite animal at the time), and the pilgrims, as Thanksgiving was approaching. He chose dinosaurs, and I selected a volume from the many available on the topic. But the boy was wary, knowing my penchant for pedagogy. With suspicious eyes cast to the tome I was opening, he asked: "Is that a real book that tells stories, or one that just teaches?" At five years of age, my son was keenly aware that narratives provide the most fecund source for learning, one more in line with his innate capacities than books that merely supply information. By fostering vivid impressions, stimulating imagination, and securing memories, narrative teaches in a way that the transmission of facts and concepts cannot.

Montaigne, with keen psychological insight, insisted that he was not a pedagogue but rather a storyteller.[55] Montaigne well knew, however,

---

53 Roger C. Schank and Robert P. Abelson, "Knowledge and Memory: The Real Story," in *Knowledge and Memory: The Real Story – Advances in Social Cognition*, ed. Robert Wyer, Jr., Vol. VIII (Mahwah, NJ: Lawrence Erlbaum Associates, 1995), pp. 81–82. See also Mathews and Roussel, "Abstractness of Implicit Knowledge," p. 42. John A. Bargh, "The Automaticity of Everyday Life," in *The Automaticity of Everyday Life: Advances in Social Cognition*, ed. Robert Wyer, Jr., Vol. X (Mahwah, NJ: Lawrence Erlbaum Associates, 1997), p. 33.

54 Mark Johnson, *Moral Imagination: Implications of Cognitive Science for Ethics* (Chicago: University of Chicago Press, 1993), pp. 170–71.

55 Montaigne, *The Complete Works of Montaigne*, trans. Donald Frame (Stanford: Stanford University Press, 1957/1965), p. 612.

that the best education is often delivered through narratives. Certainly that is the type of education to which humans find themselves naturally predisposed. As Martha Nussbaum observes, "one of the child's most pervasive and powerful ways of learning its society's values and structures is through the stories it hears and learns to tell."[56] Social and cognitive psychologists demonstrate that things are not much different for adults.

David Carr explains that we live so much of our lives via narrative format because we assume the role not only of the lead character of our tales but that of the chief reporter as well as the primary audience. Carr writes:

> We are constantly striving, with more or less success, to occupy the story-teller's position with respect to our own actions. . . . The fact that we often need to tell such a story even to ourselves, in order to become clear on what we are about, brings to light two important things: the first is that such narrative activity, even apart from its social role, has a practical function in life, that is, it is often a constitutive part of action, and not just an embellishment, commentary or other incidental accompaniment. The second is that we sometimes assume, in a sense, the point of view of audience to whom the story is told, with regard to our own action, as well as . . . those of agent or character and of story-teller.[57]

We act in particular ways, in other words, because it corresponds well to our role in an unfolding tale. Indeed, an act may be defined as a meaningful, intentional, purposeful effort rather than, say, a behavioral tick, only if it can be embedded within a story. Psychologically speaking, we are, first and foremost, inhabitants of narrative.

Self-consciousness – what neuroscientist Gerald Edelman calls "higher-order consciousness" – is not based on the experience of the here and now. Rather, it is grounded in "the ability to model the past and future."[58] To be human is to be self-conscious, and to be self-conscious is to perceive, comparatively reflect upon, express, and attempt to (re)direct the story of one's life. Narrative frameworks do not simply supply reasons for taking action, something ostensibly available in rudimentary fashion to other animals and even to computers. Narratives furnish the opportunity comparatively to assess, evaluate, and choose these reasons. This is possible because we can tell stories about our

---

56 Martha Nussbaum, *Love's Knowledge: Essays on Philosophy and Literature* (New York: Oxford University Press, 1990), pp. 293–94.

57 David Carr, *Time, Narrative, and History* (Bloomington: Indiana University Press, 1986), p. 61.

58 Gerald Edelman, *Bright Air, Brilliant Fire: On the Matter of the Mind* (New York: Basic Books, 1992), pp. 167–68.

present state of affairs, relate it to our history, and narratively imagine our future.[59] Scientists will know they have created true self-consciousness in a machine, it is said, when the computer's response to a particularly demanding question is: "That reminds me of a good story!" Constructing, entertaining, and comparatively evaluating stories of past, present, and future is the distinguishing mark of human beings, the central feature of moral development, and the chief activity of the practical judge.[60]

Narrative and Moral Life

"Man is always a storyteller!" Jean-Paul Sartre wrote. "He lives surrounded by his and others' myths. With them he sees everything in his life, no matter what befalls him."[61] Sartre is onto something. But the events that compose our lives do not await a retrospective embedding in stories. Actions are taken because they are perceived to contribute to a plot. Reflecting on man the storyteller, Sartre goes on to say that "he seeks to live his life as though he were telling it."[62] We act in the world by inserting ourselves into existing narratives, half-told stories that await our words and deeds for their consummation. To be sure, retrospective storytelling brings into awareness the full narrative context of our efforts. But we are called into action by yet-to-be completed scripts. Our actions arise as the sorts of things the protagonists of our lives' tales would initiate.

To say that one lives life as though one were telling its story is not to say that actions are never authentic or original or that they are rigidly prescribed. Authenticity and originality may well constitute key virtues of the characters we play, and the capacity for spontaneity may feature as a prominent trait. One can live life "in character" and fully retain

---

[59] See Alasdair MacIntyre, *Dependent Rational Animals* (Chicago: Open Court, 1999), pp. 56–57, 96.

[60] See Johnson, *Moral Imagination*, p. 164. See also Leslie Paul Thiele, "Evolutionary Narratives and Ecological Ethics," *Political Theory* 27 (1999): 6–38. Empirical research suggests that a significant portion of this comparative storytelling may occur at an unconscious level. See Neal Roese, Lawrence Sanna, and Adam Galinsky, "The Mechanics of Imagination: Automaticity and Control in Counterfactual Thinking," in *The New Unconscious*, ed. Ran Hassin, James Uleman, and John Bargh (Oxford: Oxford University Press, 2005), pp. 138–170.

[61] From *La Nausée*, quoted in Kenneth J. Gergen and Mary M. Gergen, "Narrative of the Self," in *Memory, Identity, Community*, p. 161.

[62] Quoted in Gergen, "Narrative of the Self," p. 161.

opportunities for autonomy and initiative. In turn, our thoughts and actions always bear the potential of starting new tales. MacIntyre's assertion that the "unity" of a self issues from the "unity of a character" that develops out of the "unity of a narrative" is problematic in this regard.[63] Narratives can be open-ended. Henry James characterized modern novels as "loose, baggy monsters." The narrative of the self, likewise, often depicts plurality and flux more than unity and stability. In other words, a narrative context enables at least as much as it restricts. In literature, as in life, story lines are always open to realignment. Unexpected actions and events are to be expected. Even in the midst of the most radical realignment, however, the narrative thread is never completely severed. The autonomous, inventive individual continues to act in response to or in anticipation of stories in the making.[64]

To live a life as though one were telling its story does not suggest a narrow, egoistic perspective. It does not indicate a static, inwardly focused, self-interested point of view. A rich narrative exceeds the exploits of a single protagonist, and it avoids flat, one-dimensional, supporting characters. Readers or listeners of a good story should be able to identify, at least partially, with everyone in the cast. Odysseus first feels the pathos of his heroics in Troy, and, more importantly, comes to understand the suffering of the Trojans, not during his pillaging of the city but only later, as he listens to the bard Demodocus sing of the war. Overcome by the minstrel's tale, Odysseus weeps. The mighty warrior's tears, Homer writes, fell like those of a woman throwing her arms around a fallen husband. It is the story of the war, not his particpation in it, that allows Odysseus to show empathetic impartiality and a moral perspective.

Morally mature individuals live in light of such narrative understanding. If a life's tale can only be imagined from the author's standpoint, narcissism will preclude moral concern. If it can only be told from the perspective of others, a lack of autonomy will inhibit moral courage. When the narrative web that generates an individual's identity is characterized by the right mix of authorial presence and empathetic extension, the development of an autonomous self capable of moral relationships is in progress.[65] As Iris Murdoch observed, we tell stories about ourselves, and in time come to resemble the

---

[63] MacIntyre, *After Virtue*, pp. 202–203. For a good critique of MacIntyre's position, see Samantha Vice, "Literature and the Narrative Self," *Philosophy* 78 (2003): 93–108. See also Galen Strawson, "Against Narrativity," *Ratio* 17 (2004): 428–452.

[64] See Carr, "Narrative and the Real World," p. 17.

[65] Benhabib, *Situating the Self*, 198.

protagonists of which we speak. Moral philosophy describes and analyzes this process.[66]

The ethical ability to detach ourselves from immediate desires and preoccupations so as to judge the lived past and plan possible futures is a function of our capacity to inhabit narratives. Moral life is best described as the scripting of a story of human flourishing, with particular attention paid to the obligations and responsibilities that devolve to the protagonist and other characters given their respective roles. Alasdair MacIntyre makes this point succinctly when he writes: "I can only answer the question 'What am I to do?' if I can answer the prior question 'Of what story or stories do I find myself a part?'"[67] Of course, the individual's effort to determine what he is to do is not a matter of passively locating himself in a settled narrative. Neither is he adopting a monolithic role. Inevitably, competing story lines arise. An individual's moral judgments are grounded in stories that capture his multiple roles in diverse scripts, defining him, for instance, as an able parent, caring spouse, skilled professional, mild hypochondriac, active environmentalist, and middle-of-the-road Episcopalian. As diverse as these narrative roles may be, many will overlap. Indeed, the narrative that is the self is the composite of such intertwining tales.

The moral judge sets himself the task of discovering and interpreting the stories that structure his life while recasting his parts within them. His reliance on narrative is both retrospective and prospective. He finds meaning in his past by situating it within a broader narrative framework. In turn, he envisions alternate narratives as possible models for his future.[68] Of course, embracing new, empowering narratives entails the hard work of rescripting deeply etched identities grounded in oft-told tales. Psychotherapists are well aware of the difficulties encountered by clients who engage in such rescriptings, as are moral reformers.

Narrative underlines the relative contingency of events. Other futures are always possible, as are various interpretations of the past. The moral judge traces out the implications of alternative scripts, playing through various scenes in his mind. In the end, he attempts to settle upon a script that offers the best guide to future action by extrapolating key themes of earlier narratives. Mark Johnson describes how a person involved in a

---

[66] Iris Murdoch, "Metaphysics and Ethics," in *Existentialists and Mystics: Writings on Philosophy and Literature*, ed. Peter Conradi (Harmondsworth: Penguin, 1999), p. 75.

[67] MacIntyre, *After Virtue*, p. 201.

[68] See Bent Flyvbjerg, *Rationality and Power: Democracy in Practice* (Chicago: University of Chicago Press, 1998), p. 8.

moral conundrum finds a story line that is suitable: "The agonizing process of narrative exploration drags on as she runs over in her imagination, again and again, how she feels as she projects herself into each type of situation. There will be 'moral principles,' of course, brought into play in all of this. But they will be only one part of the relevant considerations which she must try to blend into a narrative whole."[69] Moral principles often play a role in the effort to mesh scripts coherently and negotiate moral conundrums. But they can effectively do so only within an overarching narrative framework. "The great instrument of moral good," Shelley wrote, "is the imagination."[70] The tool of imagination uncovers the moral good by exploring diverse plots.

Some moral systems boast principles that purportedly stand prior to and supersede narrative. Neo-Kantian morality, for instance, claims to be divorced from (or at least asserts its priority over) any story of human flourishing. Consider John Rawls's theory of justice. Right action, for Rawls, is to be pursued independently of the good it produces, however this good is conceived. The concept of right, Rawls insists, is prior to that of the good. It follows that narratives of human flourishing cannot, and should not, structure ethical life or provide the engine of moral development. At best, they stand in service to deontological principles. Their subordination to principle arises because the self, understood as an essential being, is prior to any ends it might affirm, and hence prior to any stories (of human flourishing) that might illustrate these ends.[71]

Defending this Kantian understanding of justice in the tradition of social contract thinkers, Rawls maintains that justice, like truth, is a "first virtue." Its principles should never be compromised, not by the pursuit of any particular good, not by any particular story of human flourishing, not even by "the welfare of society as a whole."[72] For Rawls, justice is a

---

[69] Johnson, *Moral Imagination*, p. 183.

[70] Percy Shelley, "A Defense of Poetry," in *The Norton Anthology of English Literature*, Vol. 2. ed. M. H. Abrams (New York: W.W. Norton, 2001), p. 625.

[71] John Rawls writes: "We should not attempt to give form to our life by first looking to the good independently defined. It is not our aims that primarily reveal our nature but rather the principles that we would acknowledge to govern the background conditions under which these aims are to be formed and the manner in which they are to be pursued. For the self is prior to the ends which are affirmed by it; even a dominant end must be chosen from among numerous possibilities. There is no way to get beyond deliberative rationality. We should therefore reverse the relation between the right and the good proposed by teleological doctrines and view the right as prior." John Rawls, *A Theory of Justice* (Cambridge: Harvard University Press, 1971), p. 560.

[72] Rawls, *A Theory of Justice*, pp. 3–4.

first virtue because it allows us to realize our nature as human beings. "The desire to express our nature as a free and equal rational being," Rawls stipulates, "can be fulfilled only by acting on the principles of right and justice as having first priority.... Therefore in order to realize our nature we have no alternative but to plan to preserve our sense of justice as governing our other aims. This sentiment cannot be fulfilled if it is compromised and balanced against other ends as but one desire among the rest."[73] Rawls's theory of justice makes all stories of the human good subservient to principles that reflect human nature.

That, at least, is how the early Rawls has been interpreted, and, perhaps, how the early Rawls understood himself. Upon closer inspection of *A Theory of Justice*, however, and quite explicitly in Rawls's later works, it becomes clear that deontological principles derive from a vision of the flourishing of a particular people. They gain traction by being embedded in a narrative – namely, the story of how a specific (political) culture came to understand itself as composed, fundamentally, of free and equal rational beings. The concept of the primacy of right is the historical product of the "considered judgments" of a people whose socially cultivated sensibilities have been fine-tuned and rationalized.[74] The considered judgments that Rawls depends upon are those of individuals socialized to understand themselves, first and foremost, as free and equal beings who perceive the good to entail a "rational plan of life" and who understand the systematic pursuit of this plan to be subject to principles that are universalizable.[75] This attachment to justice is meant to align with our moral predispositions, buttress our latent if not actual socio-political commitments, and slide frictionlessly into our conceptual world. For many modern liberals, it does just that – but only as a result of the (understated) narrative depicting the rise of liberal culture and its psycho-social effects.

The status of truth and justice as first virtues is a historical achievement. Only within the narrative context of this development does allegiance to the priority of right, and deontological morality more generally, arise. Alasdair MacIntyre makes this point succinctly, observing that "Man is in his actions and practice, as well as in his fictions, essentially a story-telling animal. He is not essentially, but becomes through his history, a teller of stories that aspire to truth."[76] We might say, in like fashion, that man is not

---

[73] Rawls, *A Theory of Justice*, p. 574.
[74] Rawls, *A Theory of Justice*, pp . 48–51.
[75] Rawls, *A Theory of Justice*, p. 561.
[76] MacIntyre, *After Virtue*, p. 201.

essentially, but becomes through his history, a teller of stories that assert the rule of reason and the priority of the right over the good.[77] Absent narrative foundations, (deontological) principles lose their punch.

Provincial Stories

Hegel claimed that Kantian moral concepts only become functional once ethical substance is (clandestinely) incorporated into them. Likewise, Richard Rorty suggests that the "universality" of a moral claim only ever gains motivational force when it finds a home in the "provinciality" of narrative.[78] Minimally, this provincial tale must illustrate how a particular morality came to claim universal, non-contingent status. Rorty asserts the primacy of narrative over deontology. As usual, he makes his case in deceivingly straightforward terms: it is simply a matter of audience appeal.

To make a moral claim, Rorty argues, is to suggest that one's position is or should be persuasive in (re)forging the values and behavior of a particular audience. Jürgen Habermas and other neo-Kantians argue that their moral claims ought to be persuasive to all rational, sincere audiences. For Rorty this makes little sense. Sincere, rational Nazis – embedded as they are in particular narratives of Aryan supremacy – would remain unconvinced by Habermas's (or Rorty's) liberal arguments. The same is true for any number of other imaginable audiences. There are no trans-historical, culturally universal, non-contingent principles of right. There are only more or less persuasive stories (that may or may not address the singular importance of principles of right).

Nietzsche casts this problem in broad, epistemological terms. Even the "most industrious and most scrupulously conscientious analysis and self-examination of the intellect," Nietzsche insists, cannot determine how other intellects, or audiences, might view things. In short, "we cannot look around our own corner." Beings who are "able to experience time backward, or alternatively forward and backward (which would involve another direction of life and another concept of cause and effect)" are beyond the scope of our imaginative powers. These potential audiences exist out of moral sight, around the corner. But, Nietzsche concludes,

---

[77] For a similar interpretation of how Rawlsian theory secretively relies on narrative power, see Eldon J. Eisenach, *Narrative Power and Liberal Truth* (Lanham: Rowman and Littlefield, 2002), pp. 11–14.

[78] Richard Rorty, "Universality and Truth," in Robert B. Brandom, ed. *Rorty and his Critics* (Oxford: Blackwell Publishers, 2000), p. 23.

"I should think that today we are at least far from the ridiculous immodesty that would be involved in decreeing from our corner that perspectives are permitted only from this corner."[79] Habermas may not have imagined, and perhaps cannot imagine, an audience for which his moral claims, if sincerely entertained, would remain unconvincing. But that does not suggest his moral claims are universally valid. It simply means that his imagination is quite limited. We all ply these waters.

Notwithstanding the inherent provincialism of our moralities, Rorty states, we can successfully and unabashedly propagate democratic, liberal politics grounded in the aspiration of moral growth. And we can do so without a theory of the "universal validity" of reason or reliance upon "context-independent truth." Only one thing is crucial. We need persuasive stories. Moral claims make little sense, or, at least, have little appeal or persuasive ability beyond those audiences sharing allegiance to crucial components of cultural narratives. These narratives foster certain forms of self-consciousness and certain patterns of self-development. This is not to say that conversing with those who disagree with us is pointless. Common ground can always be discovered. In any case, everyone likes a good story. So it is simply a matter of providing a narrative that offers readers and listeners something of appeal – namely, a better (that is, more persuasive) way to understand themselves and their opportunities for flourishing.

Rorty opts for what he calls "a narrative of maturation." Essentially, this is a Deweyan tale embellished with neo-Darwinian claims. Its moral purpose is to foster solidarity and diminish cruelty. Rorty quickly admits that he "cannot offer anything remotely approaching a knock-down argument, based on commonly accepted premises, for this narrative." The best he can do is tell a "fuller story, encompassing more topics" that convincingly fleshes out the pragmatic narrative of ethico-political maturation.[80] The absence of philosophically compelling arguments does not signal defeat. It simply reinforces the inescapable need for persuasive stories, and the rhetoric that facilitates their delivery. The simple fact, for Rorty, is that all philosophically informed moral arguments, at least those that are

---

79 Friedrich Nietzsche, *The Gay Science*, trans. Walter Kaufmann (New York: Vintage, 1974), p. 336.
80 Rorty, "Universality and Truth," p. 24. Richard Rorty, *Contingency, Irony, and Solidarity*, (Cambridge: Cambridge University Press, 1989) p. xv. For the empirical validation of a maturation narrative, see Gisela Labouvie-Vief, "Wisdom as integrated thought: historical and developmental perspectives," in *Wisdom: Its Nature, Origins, and Development* (Cambridge: Cambridge University Press, 1990), pp. 52–83.

not straightforwardly circular or tautological, ultimately have narrative foundations.

I focus briefly on Rorty not to belabor his debate with Habermas or highlight his Nietzschean roots, but to underscore the narrative dimension of moral claims.[81] As a result of the character of human experience, moral reasoning always finds itself embedded in, and nourished by, narrative understanding. If, as Seyla Benhabib claims, the self is not a sub-strate but the protagonist of life's tale, then it follows that selves cannot be individuated prior to the narratives that foster them.[82] Morality is not so much produced by (pre-existing, autonomous) selves as selves are generated from morally saturated narratives.

Once formed, selves are not easily reconstructed. Neither are they infinitely plastic. With the exception of the sort of brainwashing that occurs in cults or concentration camps, mature adults generally do not adopt wholly new narratives to realign their lives. Notwithstanding certain post-modern readings of Rorty (and Foucault), we are not free to swap out narrative identities at will. When reconstructions do occur, they typically arise from the painstaking work of editing the narratives that already nourish the self.

In this vein, Rorty speaks of "redescription." He holds that people do not change their "central projects" as a consequence of rational argument. If they undergo a significant change, it is because they come to embrace a revised narrative that offers a retooled plot, set of characters, and themes.[83] Ethico-political moorings, in other words, do not get settled or even much realigned with the lever of logic. Theories and first principles are supportive, not generative, of these moorings and their adjustments. Metaphor and mythology have always played, and will continue to play, a greater role than axioms and argument in the generation and transformation of moral selves.[84]

Moral development, it follows for Rorty, is not "a matter of getting closer to the True or the Good or the Right." Rather, it arises as a product

---

[81] For a concise account of the implicit narrative basis of all political and moral theorizing, and the explicit narrative foundations of pragmatist theory, see Eisenach, *Narrative Power and Liberal Truth*, pp. 1–19.

[82] Benhabib, *Situating the Self*, p. 162.

[83] Richard Rorty, *Philosophy and Social Hope* (London: Penguin Books, 1999), pp. 64–65.

[84] See George Lakoff *Moral Politics: How Liberals and Conservatives Think*, 2nd ed. (Chicago: University of Chicago Press, 2002). See also George Lakoff and Mark Johnson, *Metaphors We Live By* (Chicago: University of Chicago Press, 1980) and George Lakoff and Mark Johnson, *Philosophy in the Flesh* (New York: Basic Books, 1999).

of "imagination." What gets imagined, and redescribed, are notions of "possible communities" and the moral relationships that feature promi- nently in these communities. Iconic historical figures exhibiting such imagination, and consequently inciting moral (political, religious, or sci- entific) revolutions, manage to "redescribe the familiar in unfamiliar terms."[85] These individuals are more responsible than others for the (co)authorship of narratives that largely define a culture. But even the most original and radically revolutionary figures do not begin with virgin parchment. No one starts a story from scratch. Authorship is always a rewriting.

The art of narrative redescription is what all revolutionary thinkers (in the Kuhnian sense) master, regardless of their field of inquiry or action. Insofar as their redescriptions produced rescriptings of life, Rorty equates the efforts of Newton, Freud, and Christ. What makes for a *moral* redescription (as opposed, say, to a Newtonian/scientific or Freudian/psychological redescription) is its concern with expanding or otherwise altering relations of solidarity. Throughout history, narrative has always been the chief vehicle for this effort. In the world Rorty wishes to inaugurate, the power of narrative to effect such change, and its pri- macy over other means of moral suasion, would become widely acknowl- edged. Rorty writes:

This process of coming to see other human beings as 'one of us' rather than as 'them' is a matter of detailed description of what unfamiliar people are like and of redescription of what we ourselves are like. This is a task not for theory but for genres such as ethnography, the journalist's report, the comic book, the docud- rama, and, especially, the novel. Fiction . . . gives us details about kinds of suffer- ing being endured by people to whom we had previously not attended . . . [and] details about what sorts of cruelty we ourselves are capable of, and thereby lets us redescribe ourselves. That is why the novel, the movie, and the TV program have, gradually but steadily, replaced the sermon and the treatise as the principal vehicles of moral change and progress. In my liberal utopia, this replacement would receive a kind of recognition which it still lacks. That recognition would be part of a general turn against theory and toward narrative.[86]

As a result of the relative hegemony of a particular set of stories told and retold across the Western tradition, many of us aspire to a direct

---

[85] Rorty, *Philosophy and Social Hope*, p. 87.

[86] Richard Rorty, *Contingency, Irony, and Solidarity* (Cambridge: Cambridge University Press, 1989), p. xvi. On the turn toward narrative and away from theory among political the- orists, see Sanford Shram and Philip Neisser, *Tales of the State* (Lanham, MD: Rowman and Littlefield, 1997), pp. 1–14; Maureen Whitebrook, *Real Toads in Imaginary Gardens: Narrative Accounts of Liberalism* (Lanham: Rowman and Littlefield, 1995), p. 22; John Schaar, *Legitimacy in the Modern State* (New Brunswick: Transaction Books, 1981), p. 79.

(intellectual) relationship to truth. This direct relationship begets ethical principles that are equally universal and non-contingent. The motivational force to pursue and embrace truth and its ethico-political correlates, however, arises only within the context of a narrative that describes how these truths gained and deserve a foothold in the mind of the universe's star, rational actor. Without such a story, deontology fails, for even if one admits (the very dubious claim) that reason dictates particular sorts of action, the Humean question "Why ought I be rational?" remains unanswered. It remains unanswered until a particular narrative (for example, of human dignity discovered in the unimpeded rational mind apprehending moral law) is constructed and embraced.

Perhaps Plato provides the best example of the surreptitious use of narrative to buttress the universal claims of the True, the Good, and the Right. The battle of philosophy versus poetry begins with this ancient thinker, who pits the metaphysical and moral truths discovered through dialectical reason against the opinions and biases generated from mythology. "No man," Coleridge wrote, "was ever yet a great poet without being at the same time a profound philosopher."[87] Plato certainly would have disagreed. And clearly the reverse of Coleridge's claim is false, as the turgid prose of many philosophers, such as Kant or Habermas, give painful testimony. Yet Plato proved to be a very poetic philosopher, notwithstanding his explicit denunciation of bards.

Plato's Socrates employs dialectic as his chief weapon. But oftentimes, markedly in the *Protagorus* but evident in many dialogues, dialectic does not emerge victorious over sophistry and the telling of tales.[88] Myths and other misleading stories, Plato feared, would continue to win the hearts and minds of his fellow citizens notwithstanding Socratic methods of persuasion. *Theoria* would fight the good fight, but, in the end, could not hold its ground against the poetic arts. Somehow the playing field had to be leveled, lest the doomed exercise of pursuing sufficient reason – the essence of dialectic – forever suffer under the rule of rhetoric. Reason would have to enlist its own rhetorical device – namely, the narrative in dialogue format – to defend philosophy against rhetoric.

Content as well as form must pay homage to narrative. Plato only gets a third of the way through his most renowned dialogue, *The Republic*, before

---

[87] Penned in reference to Shakespeare, Coleridge made this claim in his *Biographia Literaria*. Quoted in H. P. Rickman, *Philosophy in Literature* (Madison: Associated University Presses, 1996), p. 23.

[88] For an excellent discussion of this point, see Peter Levine, *Living Without Philosophy: On Narrative, Rhetoric, and Morality* (Albany: State University of New York Press, 1998), pp. 83–121.

Socrates is forced to fall back on the authoritative myth of the metals. And the dialogue resorts to the Myth of Er in the concluding chapter to defend the judgment that justice is intrinsically good for the city and the soul. When Socrates's own efforts to supply exhaustive rationales for his assessments and evaluations fall short, as they always do, poetry and myth step into the breach.

When Plato inscribed upon the portals of his Academy, "Let no one enter who has not studied geometry," he was setting in place the mandate of his teaching. It would pursue truths that require no stories; for there is no better example of a storyless (timeless, context-independent) truth than a mathematical axiom.[89] Ethico-political life, like a geometrical relationship, was to be viewed not as a product of historical circumstance, but *sub specie aeternitatis*. The irony is that Plato saw fit to convey his love of wisdom primarily in narrative form (the dialogue), and often by way of narrative content (myths). Faced with losing the battle between philosophy and poetry, Plato took up the tools of his opponents. Unable to secure the high ground by dialectic alone, he countered the pernicious tales told by sophists and poets with his own narratives. It was the power of vivid stories to shape minds and direct actions that Plato explicitly feared and implicitly venerated. By his actions he acknowledged the truth penned by Shelley (who deemed Plato one of his "gods"), that "Poets are the . . . founders of civil society . . . [and] the unacknowledged legislators of the world."[90]

What MacIntyre says of children, Plato grudgingly acknowledges for all citizens: deprive them of stories and you "leave them unscripted, anxious stutterers in their actions as in their words." MacIntyre goes on to state: "Hence there is no way to give us an understanding of any society, including our own, except through the stock of stories which constitute its initial dramatic resources. Mythology, in its original sense, is at the heart of things."[91] Moral dispositions are not secured by rational analysis. They are generated by reflective mythologizing. We learn what is right and good by discovering our roles in a story that concretely situates us in the world. In the absence of such stories, we would stagger through life.

[89] Like quantum physicists, high-caliber mathematicians often understand their theoretical explorations within a narrative framework that is better described in terms of symphony and beauty than logical consistency and truth. Plato's love for mathematics is perhaps best interpreted in this light.

[90] Shelley, "A Defense of Poetry," pp. 622, 632.

[91] MacIntyre, *After Virtue*, p. 201.

Philosophy that aspires to universal validity must conceal its mythological roots. Whether the appeal is to dialectic, communicative reason, the priority of first virtues, the golden rule, the word of God, or the categorical imperative, all such efforts ultimately gain authoritative status by situating themselves within narratives that generate and sustain the motivation for moral action. Of course, only some philosophers acknowledge the fundamentally narrative nature of their enterprise, and even then only at certain junctures in their careers.[92]

Consider Heidegger. He originally developed a fundamental ontology as a replacement for metaphysics. Then, in a transitional period of his life known as the "turning" or *Kehre*, he shifted story lines. After completing *Being and Time*, Heidegger revises his own redescription of the human condition. Realizing that he, too, had been charmed by metaphysical subjectivism, Heidegger no longer assigns human being the status of lead actor on the world stage. He re-scripts *Dasein* to take on the role of a humble participant in the historical saga of Being's disclosure. No longer the sole, heroic protagonist, *Dasein* becomes part of the supporting cast.

The later Heidegger portrays human being as a witness uniquely gifted with, and uniquely made responsible for, the disclosure of Being. To disclose is not to control. Most fundamentally, to be the voice of Being is to be a caretaker of its mystery. Beginning with the ancient Greeks, Heidegger suggests, we observe humanity's increasing abandonment of the role of witness and caretaker in favor of the role of master and possessor.[93] This new project originally manifests itself in the pursuit of conceptual control

---

[92] See Jonathan Ree, *Philosophical Tales: An Essay on Philosophy and Literature* (London: Methuen, 1987); Joshua Foa Dienstag, *Dancing in Chains: Narrative and Memory in Political Theory* (Stanford: Stanford University Press, 1997); Leslie Paul Thiele, "The Ethics and Politics of Narrative: Heidegger + Foucault," in *Foucault and Heidegger: Critical Encounters*, ed. Alan Milchman and Alan Rosenberg, Minneapolis: University of Minnesota Press, 2003, pp. 206–234.

[93] Heidegger eventually admits that his story of a pristine and transparent relation to Being at the Greek origins of Western thought is more myth than history. By 1954, he would acknowledge that "that which really gives us food for thought did not turn away from man at some time or other which can be fixed in history – no, what really must be thought keeps itself turned away from man since the beginning." Martin Heidegger, *What is Called Thinking*, trans. J. Gray (New York: Harper and Row, 1968), p. 7. In his lecture on "Time and Being," given in 1962, Heidegger would be more specific: neither Homer, other Greek poets, nor everyday Greek speakers used *aletheia* in the sense of unconcealment but also largely understood it as correctness of representation, as *orthotes*. Heidegger admits that his earlier assertion about the "essential transformation" of the historical understanding of truth from unconcealment to correctness is "untenable." Martin Heidegger, *On Time and Being*, trans. J. Stambaugh (New York: Harper and Row, 1972), p. 70.

by Plato and his like. Over time, however, the metaphysical pursuit finds a concrete counterpart in technological exploits.

At the climax of Heidegger's story, humanity's historical effort to achieve conceptual and technological mastery produce a sort of amnesia. We increasingly forget how to let Being be. Concomitantly, we forget how to let human being be. We instrumentalize ourselves no less than our world, becoming our own tools and each other's resources. In the endless pursuit of mastery and possession, we forget our role and responsibility as witnesses and caretakers and assume the mandate of master technicians. Heidegger's portrayal of the rise of technology is a reworked tale of the fall from grace. Rather than proffering a set of deontological principles, analytical statements, or axiomatic truths to define our ethico-political obligations, Heidegger's historical/mythological saga provides us with new, or rather revised, scripts.

If Heidegger provides a grand narrative to contest the conceptual terrain of metaphysics, Foucault produces multiple genealogical tales to destablize the topography of power. In the contemporary world, Foucault insists, the most fecund form of power circulates through the capillaries of the body politic largely unnoticed. Foucault's uncanny knack was to make the invisible visible. He redescribes modern societies as "demonic."[94] The individuals composing them are disciplined to think, feel, and act in certain ways, within certain limits. Yet this soulcraft is clandestine. Indeed, the subjection to particular forms of thought and life proves most efficacious when it is internalized as an identity. Power triumphs not when it collides with victims but when it flows through participants. We are not flies caught in a despotic spider's web of power. We are the spider-flies, and the webs that we unwittingly spin become our disciplinary homes.

The capacity of rationality to mask the mechanisms of power, cloaking it in the garb of principle, makes it an efficient vehicle of domination. Ethical codes and the rationalities that support them are portrayed by Foucault as Trojan horses. They surreptitiously gain entry to the soul, and subsequently open its doors to the enemy lying in wait. Foucault takes on the role of Cassandra. He tells a cautionary tale of the rational guise of disciplinary power. In the face of such power, Foucault counsels resistance. We are urged to reconstitute ethico-political relations such that they become governed less by codes or rules and more by an aesthetically

94 Michel Foucault, *Politics, Philosophy, Culture: Interviews and Other Writings, 1977–1984*, ed. Lawrence Kritzman (New York: Routledge, 1988), p. 52.

oriented care of self and other. This ethical and aesthetic reconstitution promises a reduction in disciplinary domination.

Genealogy is not meta-narrative. Meta-narration provides closure to the storytelling process. It is the grand saga that encapsulates, and subordinates, all other tales. Foucault's genealogies do not universalize, nor display teleological movement toward a final denouement. Rather, they are descriptive accounts of unique, diverse, contingent struggles. Far more than Heidegger, Foucault remains conscious of his role as a time- and space-bound storyteller. Indeed, he is eager to admit the fabricated nature of his narratives. Foucault writes: "I am well aware that I have never written anything but fictions. I do not mean to say, however, that truth is therefore absent. It seems to me that the possibility exists for fiction to function in truth, for a fictional discourse to induce effects of truth, and for bringing it about that a true discourse engenders or 'manufactures' something that does not as yet exist, that is, 'fictions' it."[95] Foucault explodes the meta-narrative of universally valid reason into countless micro-narratives of contingent, power-infested rationalities. These micro-narratives illustrate how historical efforts in the service of particular concentrations of power take on the color of ahistorical objectivity. Foucault's fictions, in this sense, battle against other temporally and spatially bound fabrications that wear the cloak of metaphysical transcendence.

Foucault's narratives are not designed to facilitate the discovery of a "true" self that lies hidden beneath webs of power. Indeed, such a pursuit, typically motivated by meta-narrative, only further envelopes the subject in a disciplinary matrix. Rather, Foucault's stories stimulate conscious acts of self-fictioning. Such artistry turned inward is both a positive goal and a prophylactic. By constantly transforming the self, one presents normalizing power with a target more difficult to hit. Self-transformation, in this context, is another name for resistance. "The target nowadays," Foucault explains, "is not to discover what we are, but to refuse what we are." We are urged to move beyond "the subject as a pseudosovereign" to a self whose most prominent virtue is the courage to rescript its life.[96] In turn, Foucault's storytelling is meant to cultivate practical judgment in the face of omnipresent yet ever-changing threats. "The 'best' theories do not constitute a very effective protection against disastrous political

[95] Foucault, *Power/Knowledge: Selected Interviews and Other Writings 1972–1977*, ed. Colin Gordon (New York: Pantheon Books, 1980), p. 193.
[96] Foucault, "The Subject and Power," in Hubert Dreyfus and Paul Rabinow, *Beyond Structuralism and Hermeneutics*, (Chicago: University of Chicago Press, 1982), p. 216.

choices," Foucault insists. [97] Hence he opts for genealogies that elicit the hermeneutic, phronetic skills required for concrete struggles.

Heidegger's and Foucault's rejections of metaphysical foundations and transcendental standards are often assailed for undermining morality and principled politics. Despite the brilliance and originality of their thought, critics charge, Heidegger and Foucault remain ethically ungrounded and divorced from political responsibility. I would argue, in contrast, that Heidegger and Foucault highlight the importance of moral and political judgment by providing compelling narratives to foster its cultivation. Heidegger pens an ontological tale of the plight of *Dasein* in the maw of technology. Foucault crafts genealogical stories of the creation of subjects through disciplinary power. Both narratives develop a hermeneutics of engagement. These stories are meant to help us navigate late modern life, providing fertile soil from which practical wisdom might grow.

Novel Judgments

Moral and political theory relies on narrative, openly or surreptitiously, to achieve its ends. But narratives need not be steeped in philosophical erudition to contribute to moral and political life. Indeed, literary fiction often offers greater benefits. Our ethico-political judgments are much enhanced by the sort of lessons literature provides.[98] Citing Milan Kundera, Rorty argues that the novel – an "imaginative realm where no one owns the truth and everyone has the right to be understood" – provides for moral education in ways that philosophy cannot.[99] Novels portray life in rich detail, and present experiences in concrete forms that attract and cultivate the moral imaginations of readers. Hence the "wisdom of the novel," Rorty states, invoking Kundera.[100] Practical judgment finds in literature a workshop where its skills and sensibilities may be finely honed. Like Vico, Rorty maintains that rhetoric, in the form

---

[97] Foucault, "Politics and Ethics: An Interview," in *The Foucault Reader*, ed. Paul Rabinow (New York: Pantheon, 1984), p. 374.

[98] Jon Elster, *Alchemies of the Mind: Rationality and the Emotions* (Cambridge: Cambridge University Press, 1999), p. 33.

[99] Rorty, *Philosophy and Social Hope*, p. 20.

[100] Rorty, *Philosophy and Social Hope*, p. 20. See also John S. Nelson, "Prudence as Republican Politics in American Popular Culture," in *Prudence: Classical Virtue, Postmodern Practice*, ed. Robert Harriman (University Park, PA: Pennsylvania State University Press, 2003), pp. 244–45.

of narrative, supplies the images that abet the cultivation of practical judgment.

Reflecting the age-old Platonic tension between theory and mythology, Colin McGinn, an ethics teacher, writes:

I often notice how much more engaged and perceptive my students are when I teach ethics from literature rather than from a philosophical text. Nor do I detect much of the usual (depressing) sophomoric relativism in their moral comments when their minds are focused on the deeds of particular characters. I take this as evidence that the literary works are recruiting their real moral faculties: they are down in the moral trenches, outraged or compassionate, fully immersed in moral concepts, not distracted by philosophical irrelevancies . . . Scepticism about morality seems hollow when the moral faculties are practically engaged – just as skepticism about the external world is the furthest thing from one's mind in the heat of battle.[101]

The statement is reminiscent of the experience of the biographer-boss of Alexis Zorba in Kazantzakis's novel, *Zorba the Greek*. Zorba, an earthy man with a lust for life and an appetite for dance, does not read much. Certainly he reads no philosophy. His foreign employer, in contrast, is erudite. For all his book learning, however, Zorba's boss proves deficient in the art of moral suasion, as the futile efforts to reform the employee make patent. Scratching his head in confusion after one such effort, Zorba responds:

I've got a thick skull, boss, I don't grasp these things easily. . . . Ah, if only you could dance all that you've just said, then I'd understand. . . . Or if you could tell me all that in a story, boss. Like Hussein Aga did. He was an old turk, a neighbor of ours. Very old, very poor, no wife, no children, completely alone. His clothes were worn, but shining with cleanliness. He washed them himself, did his own cooking, scrubbed and polished the floor, and at night used to come in to see us. . . . One day he took me on his knee and placed his hand on my head as though he were giving me his blessing. 'Alexis,' he said, 'I'm going to tell you a secret. You're too small to understand now, but you'll understand when you are bigger. Listen, little one: neither the seven stories of heaven nor the seven stories of the earth are enough to contain God; but a man's heart can contain him. So be very careful, Alexis – and may my blessing go with you – never to wound a man's heart!'

The erudite man is rueful. "If only I could never open my mouth," he muses, "until the abstract idea had reached its highest point – and had become a story! But only the great poets reach a point like that, or a people, after centuries of silent effort."[102] Reversing a common prejudice,

---

[101] Colin McGinn, *Ethics, Evil, and Fiction* (Oxford: Clarendon Press, 1997), p. 176.
[102] Nikos Kazantzakis, *Zorba the Greek* (New York: Simon and Schuster, 1952), pp. 278–79.

Kazantzakis suggests that storytelling marks the maturity rather than the youth of moral education. Narrative is not a weak, thin form of ethical teaching that requires beefing up to achieve the vigor and vitality of abstract principle. In this regard, Kazantzakis would endorse Michael Walzer's assertion that morality starts off "thick" and robust, fully integrated in the concrete details of social life. Only on special occasions, for particular purposes, is it thinned out in argumentative form to gain the status of abstract principle.[103] Essence is thin. Existence is thick. We learn and grow, morally and politically, primarily by way of the thick.

Charles Larmore observes that "Theory can carry us only so far in our attempt to grasp the nature of moral judgment. To go further, we must turn above all to the great works of imaginative literature."[104] Moral judgment is not the product of general theories. It arises in the context of lived experience and grapples with its contingencies. Theory and contingency are, in a manner of speaking, oil and water. Narrative, in contrast, is incident-friendly. It is not forged from thinly articulated generalities, but from the thick description of specific circumstances that house distinct opportunities and obstacles. Parsimony is a virtue for theorists, but a vice for storytellers. The rich detail of narrative provides moral judgment its key resource.

"It is easier to know man in general than to understand one man in particular,"[105] La Rochefoucauld wrote. Moral judgment requires this more difficult knowledge. It is not that theory has no role to play in ethics. But only practical judgment can determine when, where, and to whom abstract rules apply and how they should be adjusted to context. "Ethics admits of no exactitude," Aristotle insists, "Those who are following some line of conduct are forced in every collocation of circumstances to think out for themselves what is suited to these circumstances."[106] Aristotle's "allegiance" to narrative follows therefrom, and pits him against the conceptual abstractions of Plato no less than the generalizations of Kant.[107]

In the *Poetics*, Aristotle states that dramatic narratives allow an appreciation of the "universals" of the human condition. Such knowledge provides

[103] Michael Walzer, *Thick and Thin: Moral Argument at Home and Abroad* (Notre Dame: University of Notre Dame Press, 1994), pp. 16–17.

[104] Charles E. Larmore, *Patterns of Moral Complexity* (Cambridge: Cambridge University Press, 1987), p. 21.

[105] La Rochefoucauld, *Maxims*, trans. Leonard Tanock (London: Penguin Books, 1959), p. 92; #436.

[106] Aristotle, *The Ethics of Aristotle* (New York: Penguin Books, 1953), p. 57.

[107] Levine, *Living Without Philosophy*, p. 128.

a significant resource for moral judges. The universals of the human condition – the lust for power or the fear of death, for example – form the thematic backdrops of narrative accounts. Every universal, however, has its antipode. Altruistic caring (or timid complacency) stands opposed to the lust for power just as heroic self-sacrifice (not to mention suicidal depression) contests the fear of death. Like great truths, whose opposites are also true, universal themes always exist with their shadows. In this respect, universals do not dictate practical solutions to concrete problems. They simply provide recognizable ways of structuring questions. They are raw materials awaiting the scriptwriter's touch. Only the narrative itself, filled with particular characters fighting their way through particular plots, provides a "collocation of circumstances" ripe for assessment, evaluation, and choice. Universals and their antipodes display themselves as thematic backdrops setting the boundaries of a moral landscape. Only practical judgment, immersed in the fray of the stage production, can provide adequate direction to the characters involved.[108]

Narratives, unlike principles and maxims, do not issue imperatives. They facilitate understanding. The listener or reader, as Louis Mink states, must render meaningful "a complex event by seeing things together in a total and synoptic judgment which cannot be replaced by an analytical technique."[109] In this respect, narratives cultivate the development of hermeneutic skills. These skills, Heidegger and Gadamer observe, are essentially phronetic in nature. The interpretation of narrative relies on the same sort of skill as the exercise of practical judgment.

To interpret a story is to discern a plot, to transform a chronicle of discontinuous events into a sequence of meaningful relationships. It demands a synoptic vision that lays out the contribution of each of the parts to the whole.[110] Interpretation is not a straightforward activity. The "moral" of a story is not its most literal accounting. Every good tale has twists and turns. These reversals, ironies, *aporia*, and contradictions challenge the reader to make sense of a hurly burly of activities and characters. What Martha Nussbaum says of tragedy applies equally

---

[108] See Marilyn Friedman, "Care and Context in Moral Reasoning," in *Women and Moral Theory*, ed. Eva Kittay and Diana Meyers (Lanham: Rowman and Littlefield, 1987), p. 200.

[109] Louis O. Mink, "The Autonomy of Historical Understanding," in *Philosophical Analysis and History*, ed. William Dray (New York: Harper and Row, 1966), p. 184. Quoted in Donald E. Polkinghorne, *Narrative Knowing and the Human Sciences* (Albany: State University of New York Press, 1988), p. 52.

[110] See Polkinghorne, *Narrative Knowing and the Human Sciences*, pp. 18–19.

to most literary fiction: it "does not display the dilemmas of its characters as pre-articulated; it shows them searching for the morally salient; and it forces us, as interpreters, to be similarly active." Interpreting narrative, Nussbaum concludes, is "a messier, less determinate, more mysterious matter" than the parsing of a philosophic argument.[111] Zdravko Planinc's messy interpretation of *The Republic* is illuminating in this regard.

Planinc argues that the most significant contribution of Plato's dialogue is not its development of conceptual arguments or the provision of philosophic truths. Rather, its chief contribution is the fostering of *phronetic* skills. Readers must rely on their own practical judgment to determine how content and form conflict and converge, how themes stand in tension, what each character represents, above, beyond, and below its specific articulations, which of the characters, if any, speak for truth at any particular juncture, and what their developmental paths suggest. "In short," Planinc writes, "the reader must exercise his judgment prudently in order to understand how 'every word counts.'"[112]

Every word counts, but each word can be counted in multiple ways. The same phrase may mean quite different things in different contexts, depending on who is speaking, who is listening, how it is spoken, and what events it is voiced in anticipation of or in response to. Moral and political conundrums abound in Platonic dialogues, and it is up to the reader to determine their practical resolution. Digging beneath the surface, the reader realizes that a rhetorical victory may actually constitute an ethical failure, an encomium may mask disparagement, a proposed ideal may underline the need for common sense, just as a pragmatic compromise may drive home the importance of principled vision.

The *Republic's* just regime, the ideal city or *kallipolis*, is anything but pragmatic. Dictatorial rule, eugenics, communism, and the full equality of the sexes (in the context of a severely patriarchal society) are its radical components. By proposing the most imprudent of political schemes, Plato effectively goads the reader into exercising prudence. The *Republic* provides a schooling in practical wisdom by way of its impractical idealizations. A literal accounting of the dialogue quite misses this point. Like its interlocutors, the *Republic's* readers are encouraged to engage

---

[111] Martha Nussbaum, *The Fragility of Goodness: Luck and Ethics in Greek Tragedy and Philosophy* (Cambridge: Cambridge University Press, 1986), p. 14.

[112] Zdravko Planinc, *Plato's Political Philosophy: Prudence in the Republic and the Laws* (Columbia: University of Missouri Press, 1991), p. 15.

their own phronetic skills.[113] It is fitting that the dialogue concludes with its interlocutors admonished to practice "justice with prudence in every way."[114]

In "The Death of the Author," Roland Barthes asserts that a text is not stamped by an authorial presence with a singular meaning. Authorial intent does not determine the significance of a text. Meaning arises through a text's interactions with readers and other texts.[115] To be sure, an author may aim to convey a specific lesson. A good author, however, will be guided by a deep reservoir of tacit knowledge in forging his tale. Thus what he conveys to the attentive reader may be much more (or less) than he intends to convey. An author's explicit intent is often but a pale ghost of a text's meaning. Indeed, writers may explicitly deny that which they implicitly convey, just as people often act on the basis of implicit beliefs that contradict their explicitly stated convictions.[116] A text, most fundamentally, is not what an author says it is. A text is what it does in the world.

Barthes writes that "Literature is the question minus the answer." No singular message or principle can encapsulate a tale and exhaust its meaning. That is because narratives, as Barthes maintains, are not concerned with imitation (of the forms of truth) or representation (of an ultimate, or even mundane reality). The function of narrative, primarily, is to "constitute a spectacle."[117] The spectacle presents itself as ripe for engagement. It solicits the exercise of *phronetic* skills that will discern its themes, lessons, and moral bearing. Authorial intent takes a back seat. Ernest Hemingway once observed that if he knew the answer, he would not have to tell the story.[118] Narrative presents us with the spectacle of life, and demands the exercise of practical judgment to uncover its riches.

Joseph Conrad's classic, *Lord Jim,* is illustrative. Young Jim is smart, strong, ambitious, and brimming with integrity. His life is in front of

---

[113] Planinc, *Plato's Political Philosophy*, p. 36.

[114] Plato, *The Republic of Plato*, translated by Allan Bloom (New York: Basic Books, 1968), p. 303 (621c).

[115] Roland Barthes, *Image, Music, Text* (New York: Hill and Wang, 1977).

[116] Pawel Lewicki, Thomas Hill and Maria Czyzewska, "Nonconscious acquisition of information," *American Psychologist* 47 (1992):796–801. See also Guy Claxton, *Hare Brain Tortoise Mind: Why Intelligence Increases When You Think Less* (Hopewell, NJ: The Ecco Press, 1997).

[117] Quoted in White, *The Content of the Form*, p. 43.

[118] Quoted in Michael Roemer, *Telling Stories: Postmodernism and the Invalidation of Tra͏ͅ Narrative* (Lanham, MD: Rowman and Littlefield, 1995), p. 100.

him – until one day when, serving as first mate aboard a doomed ship, judgment fails him. The decrepit *Patna*, ferrying Muslims to Mecca, begins to break up in open seas. Jim is initially set on gallant efforts to save the pilgrims. But he pauses, yielding to the example of the cowardly German skipper who quickly abandons ship. Jim ignores his noble impulse and gives reign to a growing panic. He deserts the sinking ship and its forlorn passengers. Later, Jim recounts that he simply was not "ready" for the moral challenge that confronted him that fateful day at sea. His hard and fast principles, his strong sense of "moral identity," proved insufficient when the chips were down.[119]

Jim desperately wants to redeem himself, to prove once and for all his courage and trustworthiness, to regain his honor. In his adopted tropical home of Patusan, he gets the chance. Here he takes on the responsibility of governing. Again Jim is in a position of authority and obligation. But now he puts himself on the line for each and every decision he makes. He vouches for his judgments and actions with his life. As the story unwinds, Jim gives a newly arrived buccaneer the second chance that he feels all men deserve. The buccaneer betrays Jim's trust, dastardly attacking the innocent natives of Patusan. Though a victim of his own naiveté, Jim refuses to wash his hands of the bloodshed. His sense of integrity costs him his life, a price he seems almost eager to pay.

Before his death, Jim has the opportunity to relay a message that summarizes his moral development and the dilemmas of his life to those he leaves behind in Britain. Marlow, the teller of the tale, recalls:

> When I was leaving him for the last time he had asked whether I would be going home soon, and suddenly cried after me, 'Tell them ...' I had waited – curious, I'll own, and hopeful too – only to hear him shout, 'No – nothing.' That was all then – and there will be nothing more; there will be no message, unless such as each of us can interpret for himself from the language of facts, that are so often more enigmatic than the craftiest arrangement of words.[120]

Conrad supplies a moral spectacle, but refuses to provide the axioms and principles that would make otiose the reader's hermeneutic efforts. Phronetic skills are obligatory if the "language of facts" is to surrender its meaning. In the end, like Lord Jim, the reader must make his own judgments, and is asked to vouch for them.

---

[119] Joseph Conrad, *Lord Jim* (London: Penguin, 1986), p. 103.
[120] Conrad, *Lord Jim*, p. 293.

Narrative as Ersatz Experience

Moral imagination is the capacity to situate oneself in competing and complementary narratives, to play these narratives out into possible futures, and comparatively to assess their dangers and merits. This faculty is undeveloped in the young. Mark Johnson writes of the youthful judge: "What she really needs here is something that the young are least likely to have, namely, mature moral imagination. As young artists of their lives, they typically do not have an experience that is broad enough, rich enough, and subtle enough to allow them to understand who they are, to imagine who they might become, to explore possibilities for meaningful action, and to harmonize their lives with those of others."[121] Lacking experience, youth typically lack the ability to imagine what twists and turns a plot in progress might take to complement and extend the narratives that have largely defined their existence to date. Practical judgment suffers as a result.

While steering well clear of the language of morality, Niccolo Machiavelli joins Aristotle in identifying the same shortcoming in youth. The young may rightfully lay claim to strength, courage, and passion. But only age, Machiavelli states in *The Discourses*, begets prudential judgment.[122] The reason is not simply that people acquire knowledge with age. Rather, extensive experience fosters psycho-social insight, an appreciation of how people act and react in context. This insight helps one figure out what sort of knowledge is apposite to the problem at hand, what principles apply, and when and how rules should be bent or broken.

Whether counseling the prince, or his fellow citizens, Machiavelli's prime mission is the cultivation of practical judgment. If prudence is the gift of experience, however, what could Machiavelli be offering in his essays? The answer is second-hand experience. Machiavelli's interpretations of Roman history and contemporary events offer a substitute for those lacking extensive worldly encounters. Princes and citizens might gain through the mediated experience of historical narrative what a dearth of direct experience denies them. In this manner, prudential judgment, a trait of the aged, might be combined with the physical and emotional wherewithal possessed by the young. In the hands of a young hermeneut, historical narrative proves a reliable proxy for wordly

---

[121] Johnson, *Moral Imagination*, p. 183.
[122] Niccolò Machiavelli, *The Prince and The Discourses* (New York: Modern Library, 1950), p. 274.

experience.[123] Machiavelli might well have adopted Terence's counsel, appropriately mouthed by a character named *Phronimus*: "'Tis every young man's first concern, From other's faults experience to learn."[124] Machiavelli's writings provide those who boast the strength, courage, and passion of youth a means for premature aging.

Like Machiavelli, Thomas Hobbes found historical narrative the best substitute for direct experience. Accordingly, Hobbes thought it a good use of his time to translate the *History of the Peloponnesian War*. In his preface to the reader, Hobbes writes of Thucydides:

> He filleth his narrations with that choice of mater, and ordereth them with that judgment, and with such perspicuity and efficacy expresseth himself, that, as Plutarch saith, he maketh his auditor a spectator. For he setteth his reader in the assemblies of the people and in the senate, at their debating; in the streets, at their seditions; and in the field, at their battles. So that look how much a man of understanding might have added to his experience, if he had then lived a beholder of their proceedings, and familiar with the men and business of the time: so much almost may he profit now, by attentive reading of the same here written. He may from the narrations draw out lessons to himself, and of himself to be able to trace the drifts and counsels of the actors to their seat.[125]

History, Hobbes concludes, finds its "principal and proper work" in the enabling of men "by knowledge of actions past, to bear themselves prudently in the present and providently towards the future."[126] Regarding such instruction, Hobbes insists, Thucydides never met his match.

History is a fine teacher. However, by his own efforts, Hobbes implies that fables prove better pedagogues. Hobbes presents his political theory as a branch of science, a kind of geometry. But, like Plato, he casts this scientific erudition within a fictive framework. He tells the tale of the rise of the Leviathan out of the anarchy of nature, an epic saga that helps the reader understand and accept the wisdom of unified leadership. With Machiavelli, Hobbes underlines the practical limitations of formal

---

[123] Arguably Machiavelli's comedies, *Mandragola* and *Clizia*, offered a similar exposure through fiction.

[124] Terence, *The prologue, interludes, and epilogue to the* Heautontimoroumenos *of Terence* (Hull: G. and J. Ferraby, 1757), p. 12.

[125] Thomas Hobbes, "To the Readers," in *Hobbes's Thucydides*, ed. Richard Schlatter (New Brunswick, NJ: Rutgers University Press, 1975), p. 7.

[126] Thomas Hobbes, *Hobbes's Thucydides*, p. 6. For Hobbes, judgment is simply the "last Opinion" one has before one's deliberation, the "chayn of a mans Discourse," is broken off. In this respect, judgment mimics will, which Hobbes identifies as the last appetite one is subjected to before one's deliberation, for whatever reason, is broken off. Thomas Hobbes, *Leviathan*, ed. C. B. Macpherson (New York: Penguin Books, 1968), pp. 130–31.

knowledge and principle, notwithstanding his deep bow to mathematics. Following the footsteps of ancient mentors, Hobbes writes that "narration itself doth secretly instruct the reader, and more effectually than can possibly be done by precept."[127] Formulae and precepts are easy to learn. But they are difficult to apply in an ever-changing world. The most effective route to prudential judgment is well-digested experience. Unable to supply this to his readers, Hobbes provides an ersatz remedy.

The narratives that serve as a training ground for practical judgment are both directly available through personal experience and indirectly available through fiction and history. Henry James observed that "Character is plot." The idea is that a writer first creates strong characters, and the events that naturally follow as these characters interact drive the plot. To forecast how the plot of life will unfold given the characters at hand (and how characters, in turn, will be rescripted by the plot) is the task of the practical judge. Indeed, practical judgment might be defined as the faculty that allows one to apprehend stories in progress – to predict with some assurance what events will occur based on the characters involved and the circumstances at hand, and to state with some authority what events should occur to achieve the best practicable results.

Kant observed that the "sharpening of judgment is indeed the one great benefit of examples."[128] Examples are narrative accounts that illustrate, though never straightforwardly, a principle in its concrete form. When Aristotle suggests that being just entails acting as the *phronimos* would act, he is asking us to follow the right example. Aristotle suggests we adopt the counsel of the (imagined) *phronimos*, just as Adam Smith suggests we act upon the counsel of the (imagined) impartial spectator. Effectively, we are asked to construct a narrative setting for our deliberations. Martha Nussbaum writes that "good legal judgment is increasingly being seen as Aristotle sees it – as the wise supplementing of the generalities of written law by a judge who imagines what a person of practical wisdom *would* say in the situation, bringing to the business of judging the resources of a rich and responsive personality. It is not surprising that such reflections have recently led lawyers to take a keen interest in literature and to claim that works of literature offer insight into norms of legal

---

[127] Thomas Hobbes, "Of the Life and History of Thucydides," in *Hobbes's Thucydides*, ed. Richard Schlatter (New Brunswick, NJ: Rutgers University Press, 1975), p. 18.

[128] Immanuel Kant, *Critique of Pure Reason*, trans. N. Kemp Smith (London: Macmillan, 1985), p. 178.

judgment."[129] What is said here of legal judgment applies, *a fortiori*, to practical judgment in daily life. Its inculcation comes less from principles than from examples, including those that inhabit personal experience, history, literature, and popular culture.[130] Good judgment, as Arendt held, is grounded upon good examples.

Examples offer an escape from the endless spiral of reasoned argument. Every step in a logical argument begs the support of justificatory reasons; and these reasons cry out for their own support. Examples provide a means of stanching the infinite regress that ensues from the pursuit of sufficient reason. They "fill-in" when deduction, logic, and conceptual argument reach the end of their tethers. Charles Larmore writes that "Reasons must come to an end somewhere; otherwise, on pain of infinite regress, there could be no reasons – although this does not imply that where reasons come to an end we have reached the bedrock of self-evidence and certainty – far from it in the case of moral judgment. I would suggest that the important role of moral examples lies in their suitability as just such reasons, and that they are useful precisely to the extent to which they are examples of the exercise of moral judgment.[131] A good example, Larmore is suggesting, *is* a good reason. Indeed, it is the only reason that stands fully on its own, without requiring a chain of other reasons to support it.[132]

Phronetic skills are developed through interpretive encounters with narratives populated with illustrative models. The task is to determine what particular examples are examples of, and whether they are worthy of emulation, emendation, or condemnation.[133] The literary narratives that best cultivate practical judgment, it follows, are not whitewashed tales of Pollyannas triumphing over black-hatted villains. Like historical narratives, good fiction is rife with unruly ambiguities. Amidst scenes of justice triumphant, it showcases unrequited love, well-rewarded treachery, and disastrous good intentions. Were this not the case, hermeneutic skills would be unnecessary.

---

[129] Nussbaum, *Love's Knowledge*, pp. 100, 101.
[130] Levine, *Living Without Philosophy*, p. 43.
[131] Charles Larmore, "Moral Judgment," in *Judgment, Imagination, and Politics: Themes from Kant and Arendt*, ed. Ronald Beiner and Jennifer Nedelsky (New York: Rowman and Littlefield, 2001), p. 52.
[132] Larmore, "Moral Judgment," p. 63. Charles E. Larmore, *Patterns of Moral Complexity* (Cambridge: Cambridge University Press, 1987), p. 21.
[133] See Bent Flyvbjerg, *Making Social Science Matter: Why Social Inquiry Fails and How It Can Succeed Again* (Cambridge, U.K.: Cambridge University Press, 2001), pp. 85–86.

The novelist's particular forte, according to D. H. Lawrence, is his access to the full spectrum of the human condition. With patent bravado, Lawrence writes: "I, who am a man alive, am greater than my soul, or spirit, or body, or mind, or consciousness, or anything else that is merely a part of me.... For this reason I am a novelist. And being a novelist, I consider myself superior to the saint, the scientist, the philosopher, and the poet, who are all great masters of different bits of man alive, but never get the whole hog."[134] The statement is reminiscent of Coleridge's claim that every great bard is also a profound philosopher – and presumably more than that. Strictly speaking, the statement is false. And yet there is a kernel of truth in Lawrence's boast. To study science or philosophy may aid the development of skills conducive to practical judgment. Even staunch rationalists acknowledge that science may never match literature's capacity to plumb the human psyche.[135] But to write or read a good novel is to be exposed to the broad, variegated spectrum of human experience. It throws one into a multi-dimensional world, and thus solicits the broad cultivation of practical judgment with an urgency just short of life.

Authors take on the task of providing their readers with ersatz experience. The novel's richness of detail – its provision of a "spectacle" that is conveyed imaginatively to multiple senses – is its genius. It provides thickly textured opportunities and obstacles for the reader to navigate. This surfeit is fecund. Novels provide a cornucopia of simulated encounters. "In great fiction," John Gardner writes, "we not only respond to imaginary things – sights, sounds, smells – as though they were real, we respond to fictional problems as though they were real: We sympathize, think, and judge. We act out, vicariously, the trials of the characters and learn from the failures and successes of particular modes of action, particular attitudes, opinions, assertions, and beliefs exactly as we learn from life.[136] Novels present the reader with the challenge of discovery and discrimination amidst a deeply complex reality.[137]

---

[134] D. H. Lawrence, quoted in Philip Stevick, ed. *The Theory of the Novel* (New York: The Free Press, 1967), p. 405.

[135] Noam Chomsky, for example, acknowledges that "It is quite possible ... that we will always learn more about human life and personality from novels than from scientific psychology." Quoted in John Horgan, *The Undiscovered Mind* (New York: The Free Press, 1999), p. 47. Likewise, Jon Elster writes: "With respect to an important subset of the emotions we can learn more from moralists, novelists, and playwrights than from the cumulative findings of scientific psychology." Jon Elster, *Alchemies of the Mind: Rationality and the Emotions* (Cambridge: Cambridge University Press, 1999), p. 48.

[136] John Gardner, *The Art of Fiction* (New York: Vintage Books, 1983), p. 31.

[137] See White, *The Content of the Form*, p. 48.

The novel's evocative wealth, philosopher Iris Murdoch argues, raises it above philosophy.[138] In this respect, the novel constitutes a fertile middle ground between the conceptually rich but perceptually impoverished prose of philosophy and the conceptually impoverished but perceptually overwhelming nature of direct experience. Anthony Cunningham writes: "Real life can be traumatic, disorienting, distracting, and confused, and sometimes it is all we can do to live through it and construct any coherent account of what happened, much less one that gets to the heart of what matters. Again, the right kind of novel can function as a moral filter, centering our attention on what is morally salient with words that can do greater justice to experience than the words we can sometimes muster after an actual experience."[139] The *ersatz* experience provided by narrative is not inherently inferior to direct experience. Indeed, vicarious, indirect experience may be more fecund, and more conducive to the cultivation and exercise of practical wisdom. Novels filter reality by way of thick sequencing, and this unity of phenomenal richness and restricted scope stimulates and directs our perceptions and sensibilities.

The English romantic poets (for example, Coleridge and Shelly) and the German romantic theorists (for example, Schelling and Schiller) suggest that literature cultivates sensibilities that allow one better to perceive the complex and subtle textures of life. They argue that literature heightens and refines moral awareness. In keeping with the English and German romantics, but taking her lead from Aristotle and Henry James, Martha Nussbaum extols the literary enhancement of perception. Literature enriches our insight, she insists, and refines our appreciation of the "concrete features" of moral life. Greater moral awareness and a greater sense of responsibility follow therefrom.[140] Literature sharpens the perceptive skills that underpin practical judgment in ways that philosophical treatises cannot.

Describing his own novels, Joseph Conrad writes: "My task, which I am trying to achieve, is by the power of the written word to make you hear, to make you feel – it is before all, to make you *see*."[141] Before any systemic judgments can be made, one must first hear and see the subtle and intricate features of moral life. But, as Conrad notes,

[138] Iris Murdoch, "Against Dryness: A Polemical Sketch," *Encounter*, 16:(1961): 16–20.
[139] Anthony Cunningham, *The Heart of What Matters: The Role for Literature in Moral Philosophy* (Berkeley: University of California Press, 2001), p. 92.
[140] Nussbaum, *Love's Knowledge*, p. 7.
[141] Joseph Conrad, 1914 Preface to *The Nigger of the Narcissus* (1897), quoted in David Lodge, *Consciousness and the Novel* (Cambridge: Harvard University Press, 2002), p. 13.

heightened perception is not restricted to our visual and auditory senses. It is also affective. Narrative makes you *feel*. In a similar vein, but with a nod to Aristotle, Cunningham writes: "Good character involves seeing the world in particular ways. Novels can help us see by helping us feel the right things at the right times, to the right degree, toward the right objects, and the depiction can make all the difference."[142] To see the world well is to feel the world well. Acute perception requires attuned sensibilities.

The problem with myth and poetry, Plato states in Book X of the *Republic*, is that they appeal to emotion rather than to reason alone. Emotions are easy to manipulate, hard to control, and frequently skew judgment. Plato is right to worry about them. But even Plato could not bring himself to throw out the baby with the bathwater. By writing narrative dialogues with mythological components, Plato implicitly acknowledged the imperative of appealing to affect, however fraught with danger such appeals remain. His most famous student explicitly endorsed the effort.[143]

A prominent means of developing the emotional resources requisite for good judgment, Nussbaum insists, is literature in general, and novels in particular. Borrowing from Adam Smith, Nussbaum argues that literary works cultivate the "emotion of the judicious spectator."[144] What Aristotle said of tragic drama can equally be said of the novel. As Nussbaum writes: "the very form constructs compassion in readers, positioning them as people who care intensely about the sufferings and bad luck of others, and who identify with them in ways that show possibilities for themselves."[145] Any appeal to emotion threatens to skew judgment. The likelihood of such distortion, however, is decreased if we are in the habit of exercising our affective capacities imaginatively. Untutored emotion tends to moral blindness. It is shortsighted and largely incapable of spatial extension. By regular exposure to the rich descriptions of narrative, we encourage our emotions to travel in space and time, creating opportunities for empathetic extension. In this regard, novels cultivate practical judgment in

---

[142] Cunningham, *The Heart of What Matters*, p. 5.

[143] Aristotle, *Ethics*, p. 173.

[144] Martha C. Nussbaum, *Poetic Justice: The Literary Imagination and Public Life* (Boston: Beacon Press, 1995), p. 78.

[145] Nussbaum, *Poetic Justice*, p. 66. Nussbaum focuses on sympathy and pity, neglecting how literature sensitizes us to a full range of the delights, aspirations, worries, irritations and rages that occupy its characters. Like Rorty, she dwells primarily on solidarity as our foremost ethical responsibility and achievement. And, like Rorty, she understands solidarity as "the imaginative ability to see strange people as fellow sufferers." Rorty, *Contingency, Irony, and Solidarity*, p. xvi.

the same manner as direct experience: by sensitizing us to the hearts and minds of others.

Nussbaum argues that affective sensibilities cannot be developed via formal pedagogy. Following Marcel Proust, she writes that "the most important truths about human psychology cannot be communicated or grasped by intellectual activity alone: powerful emotions have an irreducibly important cognitive role to play. If one states this view in a written form that expresses only intellectual activity and addresses itself only to the intellect of the reader (as is the custom in most philosophical and psychological treatises), a question arises. Does the writer really believe what his or her words seem to state? If so, why has this form been selected above others, a form that itself implies a rather different view of what is important and what dispensible?"[146] Relying on a purely conceptual, abstract format to foster ethico-political judgment courts contradiction if the capacity for good judgment is reliant on emotional sensibilities that arise only in relation to particular individuals and events. The novel, with all its messiness, not the internally consistent moral treatise, avoids this contradiction.

Nussbaum has done more than any other contemporary philosopher to champion the development of ethical sensibilities by way of literature. She rightfully emphasizes the importance of emotions and the limitations of rationality in the cultivation of practical judgment. Unfortunately, Nussbaum is largely blind to the tacit register. She assumes that the development and subsequent exercise of nuanced perception and affective sensibilities, primarily if not completely, is a conscious activity. Yet the reader or listener of stories is not always aware of the ways and means by which his own perceptive capacities and emotions are sharpened, refined, and exercised. As with direct experience, literary experience taps into and cultivates implicit knowledge and skills.

The Tacit Register

Scholars who celebrate the cultivation of practical judgment through literature generally accept Thomas Hobbes's pronouncement that narrative "secretly" instructs the reader. Stories illuminate us indirectly. The precise nature of this indirect instruction is seldom addressed, except to say that it arises as a result of "incalculability in the complexity of human

---

[146] Nussbaum, *Love's Knowledge*, p. 7.

affairs."[147] The idea is that life is too variegated and unpredictable to be successfully navigated through precepts. The nuances of narrative better capture this complexity. Scholars generally leave it at that.

The power of narrative *is* secretive, but only in the sense that it involves unconscious aptitudes. Isaiah Berlin states that the "gifted novelist" makes use of "that vast number of small, constantly altering, evanescent colours, scents, sounds, and the psychical equivalents of these, the half noticed, half inferred, half gazed-at, half unconsciously absorbed minutiae of behaviour and thought and feeling which are at once too numerous, too complex, too fine and too indiscriminable from each other to be identified, named, ordered, recorded, set forth in neutral scientific language."[148] The gifted novelist, Berlin holds, is educated by the unconscious. This education is central to the development of practical judgment.

It follows, for Berlin, that practical wisdom is displayed most frequently not in the "learned," but in "historians and novelists and dramatists and ordinary persons endowed with understanding of life."[149] Berlin places the geniuses of politics – Bismarck, Talleyrand, Mirabeau, Lincoln, Franklin Roosevelt, Cavour, Disraeli, Gladstone, and Ataturk – alongside "the great psychological novelists." What marks the political genius and great novelist are their highly sensitive psychological antennae. They receive and process much more information from the social world than can be consciously perceived or catalogued. Though Berlin did not employ the language of cognitive psychology, he understood that much of what we gain from literature, as from life, is implicitly appropriated and utilized.

Rich in detail, literature abounds in "peripheral cues" that inform our tacit capacities.[150] In his study of the means of educating intuition, Robin Hogarth observes that "The tacit system is particularly sensitive to the narrative mode, which persuades in ways that differ from the more direct, deliberative approaches.... We understand by *seeing*. And what we see [in stories] is often a connection that would not otherwise have been made. The implication for educating intuition is that we should

---

[147] Heilke, "Realism, Narrative, and Happenstance," pp. 129, 136.

[148] Isaiah Berlin, *The Sense of Reality: Studies in Ideas and their History*, ed. Henry Hardy (London: Chatto and Windus, 1996), p. 23.

[149] Berlin, *The Sense of Reality*, p. 25.

[150] Deborah Prentice and Richard Gerrig, "Exploring the Boundary between Fiction and Reality," in Shelly Chaiken and Yaacov Trope, *Dual-Process Theories in Social Psychology* (New York: Guilford Press, 1999), p. 535.

consciously use narrative."[151] Much of what we absorb from a novel, as from life, is stored in procedural rather than declarative memory. It secures a more fertile, deeper, and longer-lasting impression in our neural networks than do facts or conceptual knowledge, and hence becomes manifest in unconscious habits of thought and emotion, in the *Me* rather than the *I*. Literature invites rational apprehension. But it also stimulates whole-brain learning.[152] It solicits the use of tacit capacities, which may prove more effective than conscious efforts at discovering patterns and investing meaning.[153]

"Ultimately, nobody can get more out of things, including books, than he already knows," Nietzsche wrote. "For what one lacks access to from experience one will have no ear."[154] Heidegger concurred, adding that "The most difficult learning is to come to know actually and to the very foundations what we already know"[155] Nietzsche and Heidegger suggest that we first learn implicitly, with our unconscious minds. Subsequently, with considerable effort, we acquire a conceptual understanding of this embodied knowledge. Likewise, one intuits the meaning of a narrative long before one cognitively registers it. The explicit interpretation of stories brings to the reader (arguably no less than to the author) a conscious awareness of a tacit apprehension. Michael Roemer writes that "The truth we seek in story is a truth we already know. We want to evade it even as we are drawn to it. If we did not already know it, we would not be looking for it."[156] Roemer, like Nietzsche and Heidegger, underlines the subtle ways in which cognition interacts with the tacit register. In our encounters with literature no less than with life, conscious, analytical learning is mostly a *re*education.

Karl Polanyi argued that the sense we have of our bodies constitutes the "paradigm" case of tacit knowing.[157] When we experience the world

---

[151] Robin Hogarth, *Educating Intuition* (Chicago: University of Chicago Press, 2001), p. 210.

[152] Jane Adamson, "Against tidiness: Literature and/versus moral philosophy," in *Renegotiating Ethics in Literature, Philosophy, and Theory*, ed. Jane Adamson, Richard Freadman, and David Parker (Cambridge: Cambridge University Press, 1998), p. 89.

[153] Jeffrey Gray, *Consciousness* (Oxford: Oxford University Press, 2004), pp. 9, 50, 115.

[154] Friedrich Nietzsche, *Ecco Homo*, trans. Walter Kaufmann. New York: Vintage, 1967), p. 261.

[155] Martin Heidegger, "Modern Science, Metaphysics, and Mathematics," in *Basic Writings*, ed. David Farrell Krell (New York: Harper and Row, 1977), p. 252.

[156] Roemer, *Telling Stories*, p. 147.

[157] Karl Polanyi, *Knowing and Being*, ed. Majorie Greene (Chicago: University of Chicago Press, 1969), p. 183.

subsidiarily, Polanyi writes, "we feel it in a way similar to that in which we feel our body." Effectively, we "interiorize" aspects of the world and, in so doing, "make them mean something."[158] Narrative is a catalyst for interiorization. To read novels imaginatively, with the whole body, is to experience its scenes and characters internally. Transforming this meaning into explicit knowledge via cognition is always a challenge. Just as we tacitly apprehend how to ride a bicycle without knowing how we know it, so we learn from a novel. When we do attempt an explanation, it typically lacks both the depth and breadth of our embodied knowledge. Explaining a good joke is not the same thing as enjoying one, and interpreting a novel is not the same as dwelling in it subsidiarily.

The writer, no less than the reader, finds himself in the position of not understanding everything he knows. The effort to make his implicit knowledge explicit can prove counterproductive. Award-winning novelist Ursula Le Guin advises authors to "trust the story," observing that "during the actual composition it seems to be best if conscious intellectual control is relaxed." For Le Guin, novels are not a "rational presentation of ideas by means of an essentially ornamental narrative." Rather, they are creatures of evolution that resist rational assimilation and require the "unconscious mind" for their development.[159] Likewise, novelist Anne Lamott observes that a good writer puts his skills in the service of tacit perceptions and intuitive insights. He pursues a subsidiary awareness of his characters, learning to dwell in them. The characters thus appear to exhibit lives of their own, speaking and acting in ways that may surprise the author. Lamott states: "For us, for writers . . . we need to align ourselves with the river of the story, the river of the unconscious, of memory and sensibility, of our characters' lives, which can then pour through us."[160] Elie Wiesel maintains that characters "force the writer to tell their stories."[161] The writer in touch with his tacit register becomes a mouthpiece for his characters. A subsidiary awareness allows him to cohabitate their minds and bodies. It is not always clear, in such cases, who is speaking and who is listening.

---

[158] Polanyi, *Knowing and Being*, p. 183.

[159] Ursula K. Le Guin, "A Response, by Ansible, from Tau Ceti," in Laurence Davis and Peter Stillman, eds. *The New Utopian Politics of Ursula K. Le Guin's* The Dispossessed (Lanham: Rowman and Littlefield, 2005), pp. xxiv, 305.

[160] Anne Lamott, *Bird by Bird: Some Instructions on Writing and Life* (New York: Random House, 1994), p. 121.

[161] Elie Wiesel, "A Sacred Magic Can Elevate the Secular Storyteller," in *Writers on Writing: Collected Essays from* The New York Times (New York: Henry Holt, 2001), p. 262.

Characters are seldom if ever wholly preconceived. Like the plot that carries them along, characters are discovered as much as created. That is just to say that intuition, for the novelist, precedes and directs explicit effort. Lamott explains: "You create these characters and figure out little by little what they say and do, but this all happens in a part of you to which you have no access – the unconscious. This is where the creating is done. We start out with stock characters, and our unconscious provides us with real, flesh-and-blood, believable people." She adds, as advice to aspiring novelists: "Just don't pretend you know more about your characters than they do, because you don't. Stay open to them. It's teatime and all the dolls are at the table. Listen. It's that simple."[162] In fact, learning to listen to one's tacit capacities is not that simple. It's one of the most difficult challenges for the novelist. But when the conduits to the unconscious are opened, writing seems effortless, a product of inspiration.

There are tricks of the trade. Prescriptive books for young novelists generally underline the importance of routine: writing at the same time each day, with set procedures that seldom vary. The point is not simply to avoid procrastination and ensure the allocation of sufficient time to one's craft. Rather, the intention is to habituate the engagement of tacit capacities. Popular fiction writer Stephen King observes:

When you're writing, you're creating your own worlds. I think we're actually talking about creative sleep. . . . Your schedule – in at about the same time every day, out when your thousand words are on paper or disk – exists in order to habituate yourself, to make yourself ready to dream just as you make yourself ready to sleep by going to bed at roughly the same time each night and following the same ritual as you go. . . . Your job [as a writer] is to make sure the muse knows where you're going to be every day from nine 'til noon or seven 'til three. If he does know, I assure you that sooner or later he'll start showing up.[163]

Lamott offers a similar counsel, observing that rituals signal the unconscious that it is time to become active.[164] Like King, she suggests that "You try to sit down [to write] at approximately the same time every day. This is how you train your unconscious to kick in for you creatively."[165] Routines prepare one to tap into implicit memories and skills and otherwise unavailable emotional resources. Novelists, like athletes, need to

---

[162] Lamott, *Bird by Bird*, pp. 71–72, 53.
[163] Stephen King, *On Writing: A Memoir of the Craft* (New York: Pocket Books, 2000), pp. 152–53.
[164] Lamott, *Bird by Bird*, p. 117.
[165] Lamott, *Bird by Bird*, p. 6.

warm up to find their rhythm. It is a matter of utilizing embodied habits to prime the pump of tacit capacities. For novelists, the routine of sitting down at the same time each day, hands hovering over a keyboard, effectively instructs the heart and mind to open themselves to subsidiary awareness. It summons the muse.

According to Freud, the motto of civilization reads "Where id was there shall ego be." The id – what we have termed the *Me* – stands in uneasy alliance with the *I*, or ego. The Viennese psychologist focused his attention and hope on the suppression of the (instinctual) id and the rise of the ego and superego (conscience). But the dominance of the ego and superego in civilized man is not an unmitigated victory. The suppression of instinct, Freud argued, brings with it the neuroses and psychoses of the caged animal. The writer of fiction, and its reader, need not be invested in this Freudian trade-off. It is not a matter of *replacing* the *Me* with the *I*. Their cooperation is invoked. Narrative reunites id with ego by stimulating intuition to take disciplined action. In this light, the creation and interpretation of narrative might be seen as the foundation for civilization. By paying homage to the unconscious and, at the same time, demanding the diligence of the secretarial ego and the oversight of the superego, narrative allows for a balanced expression of our most basic humanity. It brings together, in Nietzschean terms, Dionysian flux and Apollinian form.

Finding a Balance

Like the good novelist, the good judge relying on tacit skills may not know what he thinks until after he speaks.[166] Still, it would be a terrible waste – and a considerable danger – were the secretarial ego underemployed. Wholesale reliance on the tacit registers evoked by narrative without the benefit of reason and explicit knowledge leaves one prey to a host of biases. Consider, for instance, the representativeness heuristic (discussed in Chapter 1).

Narratives are rich in detail. That is why stories "come alive" for us. But the abundance of detail often leads the reader or listener to assume that the (historical or fictional) events described are representative of larger trends. The probability of an event's (re)occurrence, however, actually

---

[166] Robert Harriman, "Prudence in the Twenty-First Century," in *Prudence: Classical Virtue, Postmodern Practice*, ed. Robert Harriman (University Park, PA: Pennsylvania State University Press, 2003), p. 303.

decreases in direct proportion to its specificity. The more detailed the
description, the less likely the event.

Logic dictates that the concurrence of A *and* B is always less likely than
the occurrence of A *or* B. Yet when A and B are richly described, people
frequently assume their concurrence to be more likely. Subjects of one
study, for instance, deemed it unlikely that they would come across a doctor and a lawyer conversing on the street corner. But they thought it more
likely to encounter a doctor and a lawyer bantering on the curb about
a round of golf that they had recently played at the local country club.
Here the more detailed image of professionals playing golf and forming
friendships prompts the falacious heightening of the statistical probability of a concurrent event. Likewise, when subjects were asked what the
chances were of a nuclear exchange occurring in the next decade, most
thought it very unlikely. However, when they were asked the probability
of nuclear war breaking out as a result of a terrorist act committed on
American soil by foreign agents, they considered it much more likely.
Here, again, the conjuction of A – a nuclear war – and B – a terrorist act
carried out by foreign agents on American soil – is thought to be more
likely to occur together than A occurring alone. Reviewing the evidence,
Tversky and Kahneman observe that "As the amount of detail in a scenario
increases, its probability can only decrease steadily, but its representativeness and hence its apparent likelihood may increase. The reliance on
representativeness, we believe, is a primary reason for the unwarranted
appeal of detailed scenarios and the illusory sense of insight that such
constructions often provide."[167] When presented with an abstract version of a problem, subjects generally observe correctly that two independent events are less likely to occur than one. However, when these events
are placed in a narrative context, the conjunction fallacy grounded in
the representativeness heuristic reappears.[168] Narrative wealth can be
treacherous.

In a related phenomenon, people tend to assume the probability of
an event increases with the ease with which instances of it can be brought
to mind. As we saw in Chapter 1, this is known as the availability heuristic. The chance of being injured by a shark attack while on holiday at

[167] A. Tversky and K. Kahneman, "Judgments of and by representativeness," in *Judgment
    under Uncertainty: Heuristics and Biases*, ed. D. Kahneman, P. Slovic, and A. Tversky (Cam-
    bridge: Cambridge University Press, 1982), p. 98.
[168] Seymour Epstein and Rosemary Pacini, "Some Basic Issues Regarding Dual-Process
    Theories from the Perspective of Cognitive-Experiential Self-Theory," in *Dual-Process
    Theories in Social Psychology*, p. 473.

the beach in Florida is 200 times less than the chance of getting hit by lightening during the same holiday, and 30 times less than the probability of being killed by a falling airplane. Yet most people would rate their chances of getting mauled by a shark much higher. Because shark attacks make headlines, and inspire films and books, it is much easier for people to recall instances of (real or fictional) shark attacks. The availability of detail (either supplied, recalled, or imagined) promotes a false belief in the likelihood of its (re)occurring. If they can imagine an event easily, people think it more likely to occur.[169]

In sum, reliance on narrative knowledge uninformed by logic, the laws of probability, demographics, and social statistics will produce an over-emphasis on salient events and individuals. "Great man" theories of history that celebrate the heroic, transformative deeds of particular statesmen while ignoring larger socio-economic trends are cases in point. Fernand Braudel of the French *Annales* group writes: "To the narrative historians, the life of men is dominated by dramatic accidents, by the actions of those exceptional beings who occasionally emerge, and who often are the masters of their own fate and even more of ours. And when they speak of 'general history,' what they are really speaking of is the intercrossing of such exceptional destinies, for obviously each hero must be matched against another."[170] Wholly fictional tales, like narrative history, may mislead in similar ways.[171] While we inform our judgment with embellished memories of graphic scenes, we ignore, unfairly, important background conditions, trends, and diffuse but significant forces operating off-stage.

Our proclivity for coherent narratives may falsely inform perceptions and memories in other ways. When we give narrative accounts of our lives, we introduce intentionality and causality to connect disparate events. Subsequently, we tend to remember these events with the fabricated attributions intact.[172] William James observed this tendency. "The most frequent source of false memory is the accounts we give to others of our experiences," James wrote. "Such accounts we almost always make both more simple and more interesting than the truth. We quote what we should have said or done, rather than what we really said or did; and in the first telling we may be fully aware of the distinction. But ere long the

---

[169] See Scott Plous, *The Psychology of Judgment and Decision Making* (Philadelphia: Temple University Press, 1993), pp. 121–130.

[170] Quoted in White, *The Content of the Form*, p. 32.

[171] Prentice and Gerrig, "Exploring the Boundary," pp. 529–46.

[172] Schank and Abelson, "Knowledge and Memory," p. 34.

fiction expels the reality from memory and reigns in its stead alone."[173]
Contrived stories, though originally apprehended and acknowledged as
fiction, may subsequently be recalled as fact. During his presidency, for
example, Ronald Reagan was known to attribute historical truth to events
that he witnessed or partook of on stage as a Hollywood actor. When
internalized narratives take precedence over reference to historical data
and comparative analysis, the *"illusion* of understanding" often takes the
place of comprehension.[174]

Baunch Spinoza originally hypothesized, and contemporary research
confirms, that people generally *assume* the truth of data (or memories)
unless their falsity is explicitly demonstrated. Belief in the veracity of
data is simultaneous with its apprehension. Disbelief, in contrast, entails
a conscious effort. Given this psychological reality, fictional information
may often "gain acceptance [as fact] by default."[175] To the extent that a
fictional account explores new terrain – characters, settings, or themes
that are unfamiliar – readers or listeners are even less likely to challenge
the veracity of unsupported assertions.[176] This occurs, in part, because
readers of fiction are employing implicit cognition to assimilate information, and these tacit capacities are less accessible to systematic, critical
processing.[177]

Fiction is also prone to biased assimilation. It is often employed to
buttress pre-existing beliefs. When viewers of the television comedy *All in
the Family* were asked about their experience, those demonstrating high
racial prejudice saw Archie Bunker as the hero of the show and Mike, his
liberal son-in-law, as the butt of most jokes. Viewers demonstrating low
racial prejudices interpreted the program as a satire of Archie Bunker's
racist beliefs, and saw Mike as winning most arguments with his father-
in-law.[178] The danger here is not restricted to fiction, of course. History
and science are also prone to biased assimilation. However, consumers
of fiction are more likely to give "free reign to their prior attitudes" than
readers of factual accounts.[179] As a result of the richness of its detail and

---

[173] William James, *The Principles of Psychology*, Vol. I (New York: Henry Holt, 1890),
pp. 373–74.
[174] Robyn M. Dawes, *Everyday Irrationality* (Boulder: Westview, 2001), p. 141.
[175] Prentice and Gerrig, "Exploring the Boundary," p. 182.
[176] Prentice and Gerrig, "Exploring the Boundary," p. 539.
[177] Prentice and Gerrig, "Exploring the Boundary," p. 542.
[178] N. Vidmar and M. Rokeach, "Archie Bunker's bigotry: A study in selective perception
and exposure," *Journal of Communication* 24 (1974): 36–47.
[179] Prentice and Gerrig, "Exploring the Boundary," p. 541.

its inherent ambiguity, fiction offers more latitude for interpretation, including that which buttresses pre-existing dispositions and biases.

In our worldly encounters, we often fail to learn the right lessons despite repeated opportunities. And all too often, we learn the wrong lessons. The same lapses occur in our encounters with fiction. Extended exposure to thickly described characters and plots does not ensure the development of practical wisdom. The question of *how* one encounters texts (and life) is key. We should not expect avid students of history or literature to be better judges based solely on the length of their reading list. Old dullards abound. Likewise, bookish fools. Ersatz experience must be well-interpreted and well-integrated to become of use. The pertinent question is not how many fictional or historical narratives one has under one's belt, but are they well digested. And, of course, the quality of the literature at hand is germane. Not all experiences, direct or literary, are created equal. What Oakeshott says of life also pertains to literature. One's reading may be replete with "a ceaseless flow of seductive trivialities which invoke neither reflection nor choice but instant participation."[180] The consumption of pulp fiction, and much film and television viewing, offers more of an escape from moral and political judgment than a stimulant for its exercise.

What is said here of readers and watchers of fiction applies equally to authors. Saddam Hussein, the former Iraqi dictator, became an avid writer of romantic fantasies. Indeed, he was feverishly completing his fourth novel in as many years when the invasion of Iraq that led to his capture began. Rather than planning for the defense of his regime, Saddam spent many of his remaining days as a free man describing in florid prose the heroic resistance of a mythical people to an imperial army. Most of the forty thousand copies of *Be Gone Demons!* rolling off the presses when the bombs started dropping on Baghdad were destroyed. It has been suggested that the Iraqi dictator sought in fiction the absolute control over people and events that increasingly slipped from his hands in life. This motivation may explain the literary aspirations of other tyrants, including Nero, Napoleon, Hitler, Mao Zedong, and Ghaddafi.[181]

---

[180] Michael Oakeshott, *The Voice of Liberal Learning* (Indianapolis: Liberty Fund, 2001), p. 33.

[181] "Saddam, the great dictator of fairy tales," *The Daily Telegraph,* accessed at http://www.telegraph.co.uk/news/main.jhtml?xml = /news/2003/12/17/wbook17.xml&s Sheet = /news/2003/12/17/ixnewstop.html "Contemplating Saddam, the Romance Novelist," by Jo Tatchel, National Public Radio, *All Things Considered,* November 15, 2004.

The pitfalls of narrative are very real, and advocates of the educative power of literature are not unaware of them.[182] Any unmitigated endorsement of fiction as a tonic for the development of practical judgment is mistaken. In many cases, the strengths and weaknesses of narrative arise from the very same source – namely, its ability to stimulate emotion and imagination. Oftentimes, the discipline of deliberative reason is the best counterweight. But narrative also provides its own remedy. After an engaging discussion of the psychological biases, flawed logic, and statistical errors that hinder decision-makers, Scott Plous maintains that a fertile imagination is often the best recourse. Imagination in general, and empathetic imagination in particular, allows decision-makers to gain insight into alternative perspectives and outcomes, thus avoiding many of the biases that waylay judgment.[183] Envisioning alternative points of view really amounts to constructing alternative narratives. Good judges both construct these competing narratives and consult others who can provide them.[184]

Mark Twain observed that "You can't depend on your judgment when your imagination is out of focus."[185] Most people prove to be quite competent at making good choices when presented with the available options. Ignorance of alternatives is fatal to judgment, and the failure to compare various perspectives and possibilities is generally a failure of the mind's eye.[186] Judgment lacking in imagination is moribund. The good judge, it follows, is someone adept at calling to mind any number of competing narrative accounts of the world he wishes to assess and evaluate without, at the same time, falling prey to the seductive power of his own stories.

Practical judgment cannot be distilled into algorithms. It is both reliant upon (alternative) narratives in its formation and, retrospectively, is best explained by way of narratives that describe its exercise.[187] As problematic as stories can be for the practical judge, they provide the invaluable service of fostering psychological insight into ethical literacy. Narratives

[182] Nussbaum, *Love's Knowledge*, pp. 296–97.
[183] Plous, *The Psychology of Judgment*, p. 256.
[184] Hubert Dreyfus and Stuart Dreyfus, "What is morality: A phenomenological account of the development of ethical expertise," in *Universalism vs. Communitarianism: Contemporary Debates in Ethics*, ed. David Rasmussen (Cambridge: MIT Press, 1990), p. 249.
[185] Mark Twain, *Mark Twain's Notebook*, ed. A.B. Paine (New York: Cooper Square Publishers, 1972), p. 344.
[186] Dawes, *Everyday Irrationality*, p. 3.
[187] Gary Klein, *Sources of Power: How People Make Decisions* (Cambridge: MIT Press, 1998), p. 189.

surround and permeate us. To steer clear of their wealth because of inherent risks is to leave oneself intuitionally hamstrung and emotionally impoverished, and hence more, not less, prey to the influence of fragmented perception and impulse.

Nested Narratives and the Pursuit of Meaning

Ruminating about negative experiences does not relieve, and may exacerbate, their psychologically deleterious effects. In contrast, writing or talking about these experiences – something that generally takes a narrative form – alleviates symptoms, allowing greater recuperation from trauma, more insightful responses, and more emotionally balanced moods.[188] On their own, negative experiences can prove to be debilitating. When they are contextualized, placed in terms of a coherent (perhaps even causal) series of events, their negativity is offset by the self-empowerment that arises from the activity of sense-making. The emotional "lift" we receive by translating misery into meaning derives from the creation of a narrative context. What is intolerable, Nietzsche observes, is not pain and suffering, but meaningless pain and suffering.[189] Narrative does not obviate the former, but it helps us avoid the latter. Narrative therapy proceeds on this premise, as do various forms of cognitive therapy.[190]

In *The Human Condition*, Hannah Arendt refers to Isak Dinesen's remark that "All sorrows can be borne if you put them into a story or tell a story about them."[191] The statement underlines the significance of narrative to psychological health. Indeed, Arendt seems to suggest that

---

[188] Wilson, *Strangers to Ourselves*, pp. 175–181.

[189] Friedrich Nietzsche, *The Will to Power*, trans. Walter Kaufmann and R. J. Hollingdale (New York: Vintage, 1968), p. 35.

[190] See Jeffrey M. Schwartz and Sharon Begley, *The Mind and the Brain: Neuroplasticity and the Power of Mental Force* (New York: HarperCollins, 2002), pp. 246–50; Lynne Angus and John McLeod, eds. *The Handbook of Narrative and Psychotherapy: Practice, Theory, and Research* (Thousand Oaks, CA: Sage Publications, 2004); Peter Salovey, Brian Bedell, Jerusha Detweiler, and John Mayer, "Current Directions in Emotional Intelligence Research" in *Handbook of Emotions*, 2nd ed., ed. Michael Lewis and Jeannette M. Haviland-Jones (New York: Guilford Press, 2000), p. 512; J. W. Pennebaker, "Writing about emotional experiences as a therapeutic process," *Psychological Science*, 8(1997): 162–166; and Wilson, *Strangers to Ourselves*, pp. 175–181. For a selected bibliography of articles and books on narrative therapy, see http://www.iona.edu/academic/arts_sci/orgs/narrative/Sawchuk.htm

[191] Hannah Arendt, *The Human Condition* (Chicago: University of Chicago Press, 1958), p. 175.

the only possible way to redeem the human condition is through stories and the retrospective judgments they allow. For Arendt, our narrative evaluations make the ultimately tragic world of phenomenal existence meaningful, and thus bearable.

To consider something meaningful is to understand it as part of a greater whole, and, often, as an element in a series of cause and effect relationships.[192] Meaning is the perception of pattern. We pursue meaning by way of stories that lend coherence, salience, and significance to the world we encounter and our place within it. John Dewey asserts that truth is a subset of meaning. He writes that "Meaning is wider in scope as well as more precious in value than is truth, and philosophy is occupied with meaning rather than with truth.... Truths are but a class of meanings, namely, those in which a claim to verifiability by their consequences is an intrinsic part of their meaning."[193] Any truth can become meaningful for us. But it does so not by virtue of its internal consistency, but rather by its being fit into a larger scheme of relationships. The contextualization of a truth, its placement within an overarching pattern, generates an affective charge. Without this charge, meaning is absent. That is why we can always gain greater appreciation of truthful statements, come to know them on deeper levels, and be reawakened to their power. It is not the internal attributes of the factual statement that change, but its meaningfulness – that is, its placement within a larger pattern of relationships. In the absence of a narrative setting to which we are emotionally disposed, the truths that animate our lives would remain stale and flat.

The word narrative derives from the Latin *narrare*, which means to relate. It is, in turn, rooted in the Greek *gno*, which refers to knowing and knowledge. To know is to relate or connect. Narrative knowledge is a knowing of relationships. Narratives bring to light connections that generate patterns. Gifted with the intellectual ability and burdened with the emotional need to make connections between the diverse relationships that structure our lives, we are, first and foremost, makers of meaning. Storytelling is the primary means by which human experience gains meaning.[194] As Hayden White observes, "The absence of narrative capacity or a refusal of narrative indicates an absence or refusal of meaning

---

[192] Polkinghorne, *Narrative Knowing and the Human Sciences*, p. 6.
[193] John Dewey, *The Political Writings*, ed. Debra Morris and Ian Shapiro (Indianapolis: Hackett, 1993), p. 33.
[194] Polkinghorne, *Narrative Knowing and the Human Sciences*, p. 1.

itself."[195] Humans are in the meaning business. And the coin of the realm is narrative.

In a borderless flow of time and excess of space, amidst a surplus of life's details, narrative configures a pattern. Practical judgment exploits this capacity.[196] To judge the particular is to bring it within the purview of an overarching design, to insert it in a narrative that gives it durability and resilience. In this respect, human action, as Arendt suggested, is redeemed by judgment, understood as the retrospective imposition of narrativity.[197] By thinking the particular in context of the universal, judgment redresses the potential meaninglessness of a contingent world.

Anti-essentialists such as Rorty are often understood to say that core narratives are incommensurable. The stories that justify the judgments of scientists and those employed by theists, for instance, set parallel trajectories that never cross. The language of science stands diametrically opposed and without relation to the language of religion. This, I believe, is a misreading of Rorty. Certainly it mischaracterizes the narrative structure of life.

Narratives that distinguish us from others, or distinguish parts of ourselves from other parts, are not wholly incommensurable. Strict incommensurability would leave no room for communication or interaction of any sort. Even the most diverse practical judgments and worldviews, however, bring to their defense narrative resources to which the fiercest opponents have some access. Distinct narratives might be thought of as two prime numbers, incapable of division by common multiples (other than 1). Prime numbers are not wholly incommensurable, however, in that they can easily be compared (for example, in size) and may display many shared characteristics (for example number of digits).[198] Nonetheless, they cannot be reduced to a single set of common elements. They are unique, but not incommensurable.

To reduce something to a single set of common elements would be to discover its essence. Narratives cannot be so distilled. They have no

---

[195] White, *The Content of the Form*, p. 2.

[196] See Martin Heidegger, *History of the Concept of Time: Prolegomena*, trans. T. Kisiel (Bloomington: Indiana University Press, 1985), pp. 203, 210.

[197] Hannah Arendt, *Lectures on Kant's Political Philosophy*, ed. with an interpretive essay by Ronald Beiner (Chicago: University of Chicago Press, 1982), p. 118.

[198] For example, 13 and 19 are both numbers between 10 and 20; both are formed by two digits, with 1 being the first digit. Like countless other pairs of numbers, both are separated by an interval of six. And they both share the unique status of forming the endpoints of the "teens." Notwitstanding these comparisons and commonalities, as prime numbers 13 and 19 are uniquely irreducible.

essence. Their analysis will never reach bedrock. To take a narrative approach to knowledge, then, is to be an anti-essentialist but not an incommensurablist. Rorty writes:

We antiessentialists would like to convince you that it does not pay to be essentialist about tables, stars, electrons, human beings, academic disciplines, social institutions, or anything else. . . . There is nothing to be known about them except an initially large, and forever expandable, web of relations to other objects. Everything that can serve as the term of a relation can be dissolved into another set of relations, and so on forever. There are, so to speak, relations all the way down, all the way up, and all the way out in every direction: you never reach something which is not just one more nexus of relations.[199]

Temporalizing Rorty's assertion yields the statement that there is nothing but stories all the way down, all the way up, and all the way out in every direction. Anything we may wish to hold onto as original, indivisible, and elementary can always be narratively re-described. Terminal truth, conceived either as epistemological bedrock or teleological finale, is never reached. Still, the stories that spread out in every direction share many common traits and their trajectories frequently cross. Strict incommensurability is not their burden.

Each and every narrative can be *nested* within another narrative. Narrative nests, like bird nests, are open-ended. They do not fully encompass what they enclose. Rather, they encircle what lies inside and, at the same time, leave it available to a further nesting by other stories. When a narrative is nested within a larger narrative structure, its basic meaning may be retained or fundamentally altered. The story of a boy's youthful exploits might be nested within the larger narrative of his family's role in its community, or his country's cultural development, without changing its basic meaning, just as physiology can be nested within biology, which, in turn, can be nested within chemistry and physics without subverting its scientific import. Alternately, re-nestings may significantly alter the gist of a story. Foucault's nesting of Bentham's utilitarian design for the Panopticon within the overarching narrative of the pernicious rise of bio-power, or Nietzsche's nesting of Christian ethics within a genealogy of morality are cases in point.

A narrative is a temporally and spatially defined pattern of relationships that, like any pattern of stars, can always be viewed as part of a larger constellation. From a geocentric point of view, we might see a particular constellation as a Big Dipper. From a perspective beyond our galaxy, the perception of a ladle might endure, though now it will be seen within

---

[199] Rorty, *Philosophy and Social Hope*, pp. 53–54.

the hands of a tired man at a drinking well. From a still more expansive viewpoint, the stars making up the Big Dipper may not appear as a ladle at all, but rather form a small portion of a completely different pattern, say the stitching on a horse's bridle. There is, theoretically, no end to the nesting process. Isolated components of a narrative, or entire narratives, may always be made part of larger constellations. This is not a strictly linear process, but can proceed along multiple axes. And there is no Archimedian point from which one might nest all other narratives while remaining unavailable to being nested oneself.

Because there are only stories up, down, and in every direction, with no Archimedian center, the question of which narrative is the nester and which the nestee is always open to debate. Marxists, for example, nest theistic narratives by placing them within an overarching history of inegalitarian economic development and the alienated consciousness that class structures produce. Religious narratives are the efflux of dysfunctional relations of production. Meanwhile, theists (of, say, an Augustinian persuasion) might situate Marxist narratives within the ongoing story of an arrogant humanism that elevates the city of man above the city of God. From this perspective, Marx's atheism is just another historical example of the pride that comes before a fall. Such competing stories are not wholly incommensurable. As Gadamer suggests, a fusion of horizons is always possible. In any case, rival narratives can and do engage in battle, and they are susceptible to multiple points of comparison. But they are irreducible to common sets of fundamental facts or principles. They do not share an essence. Rather, they are involved in a potentially interminable nesting game.

Likewise, Freudians might describe Sophocles's tale of Oedipus as a primitive narrative that unknowingly reflects but fails systematically to grapple with the fundamental sexual psychology of the human animal. Devotees of Sophocles, for their part, might cast the Freudian narrative as yet another display of the hubristic claim to knowledge that doomed Oedipus to his tragic fate.[200] On this reading, Freudians, like Oedipus, are blinded to larger truths by their cleverness. Whether Freud best nests Sophocles, or Sophocles Freud, is an open question.

Practical judgment is grounded in narrative knowledge. The practical judge assesses which stories provide the optimal narrative nests in any

---

[200] Alternatively, as Arendt suggested, the Freudian tale might be seen as a symptom of the "curious neurotic concern with the self" that characterizes modernity. Hannah Arendt, "Letter to Mary McCarthy, May 28–31, 1971," from *Between Friends* (New York: Harcourt and Brace, 1995), p. 295. Quoted in Adriana Cavarero, *Relating Narratives: Storytelling and Selfhood*, trans. Paul Kottman (London: Routledge, 2000), pp. 14–15.

particular context. The question one asks of fiction – what is the example of a particular character's action an example of – is the same question the moral and political judge asks of life's experiences. He seeks to discover the narrative nest that captures the most important lessons to be learned from any particular situation. He then assesses how the plot might (best) unfold.

That narratives always nest other narratives has long been understood. C. S. Lewis observed in 1936 that parable, the expression of one story within another, was not simply a literary device. It was a fundamental component of understanding and a basic structure of the human mind.[201] As meaning makers, human beings pursue linkages. They try to relate parts to greater wholes; they seek overarching patterns. As such, they are naturally disposed to the interminable nesting of narratives. Human beings are also disposed, it seems, to yearn for the mother of all narrative nests.

Jean-François Lyotard famously observed that post-modernism constituted an "incredulity toward metanarratives." A meta-narrative is a narrative nest that explicitly or implicitly claims an unnestable status for itself. It denies reliance on an inexhaustible web of relations. Lyotard counsels us to reject such narrative monopolies. In their stead, we are to (re)deploy micro-narrative, the *petit récit*, as a means of legitimating socio-political life and grounding judgment.[202] Even those sympathetic to the post-modern cause have worried about Lyotard's deprecation of meta-narrative. Stephen White writes: "Lyotard is right in his critique of generalizing narratives fixed upon an unshakable philosophical foundation. But the simple image of proliferating small narratives neglects the unavoidable pressures toward generalization in a world where my or our narrative sooner or later runs up against yours."[203] White's point is

---

[201] See Mark Turner, *The Literary Mind* (New York: Oxford University Press, 1996), pp. 7, 147.

[202] Jean-François Lyotard, *The Postmodern Condition* (Minneapolis: University of Minnesota Press, 1984), p. 60.

[203] Stephen K. White, *Sustaining Affirmation: The Strengths of Weak Ontology in Political Theory* (Princeton: Princeton University Press, 2000), p. 12. White proposes "weak ontology" as a substitute for meta-narrative (strong ontology). Weak ontologies articulate "our most fundamental intimations of human being" but not in the form of "crystalline truth." Rather, they develop the underdetermined meaning of "various existential universals" under the "gravitational pull of ethico-political judgments and historical-cultural interpretations." In line with this underdetermination of meaning, a weak ontology does not simply declare its contestability but rather "enacts it in some way." White, *Sustaining Affirmation*, pp. 10–11, 89, 108.

well-taken. There is no escape from the need for more encompassing narratives that focus our cognitive attention and secure our emotional allegiance.[204] Micro-narratives inevitably beg nesting. And such nesting efforts will always be tempted by the possibility of closure.

Stories are manifold, but truth is one. Stories demonstrate a diversity of actors and outcomes, while truth is unitary. Stories display, in Paul Ricoeur's words, a *plurivocité*, soliciting multiple interpretations from multiple perspectives.[205] Truth is singular and unambiguous. The practical judge embraces the inexhaustibility of narrative. But he also appreciates the human aspiration to truth, the universal longing to nest the stories that inform contextual judgment in ever more comprehensive, inclusive tales. In themselves, such aspirations are not pathological. They are intrinsic to the human condition. The problem arises when metanarrative becomes the substitute for – rather than the stimulant of – ongoing discovery and learning.

Narrative, Multi-Dimensionality, and Moral Principle

Stories limn temporal and spatial development. They supply historically and geographically specific descriptions rather than timeless, universal definitions. We find it useful to define many things, of course, notwithstanding their temporal and spatial contingencies. Indeed, most definitions bandied about are really descriptions of things seen from the viewpoint of a two-legged mammal that happens to occupy a small, blue-green planet – a planet swirling in a galaxy of 200 billion stars that is itself one of 125 billion other galaxies in a universe dotted with black holes and "singularities" where all the known laws of physics cease to exist. Thus the peculiar ring of "universalist" claims. We humanoids should be wary of definitions, and all the other trappings of essentialism.

What, then, is the status of the rules and principles that inform moral narrative wary of definitions? Citing Dewey, Mark Johnson explains that principles "have an important bearing on our moral deliberations. However, they must be seen, not as recipes for action, but as reminders of what one's tradition has found, through its ongoing experience and reflection, to be important considerations in reflecting on past actions, courses of action open to us, and the choices of people we regard as possessing

[204] White, *Sustaining Affirmation*, p. 69.
[205] Paul Ricoeur, *From Text to Action: Essays in Hermeneutics, II* (Evanston, Illinois: Northwestern University Press 1991), p. 16.

practical wisdom."[206] Rules and principles are important components of moral life. But they gain significance only within a narrative that tells the story of how they came to be developed and legitimated, and how they reflect, and aid, good judgment. Their virtue arises not from their foundational status, but from their role within a narrative that outlines a history of moral development.

Seyla Benhabib rightly holds that the "interpretive and narrative skills that are essential to good judgment" require "guidance" by rules and principles. These rules and principles support the narratively grounded efforts of the practical judge. Still, Benhabib displays a Habermasian tendency. She veers toward the claim of unnestability for particular rules and principles – namely, those of "universal moral respect and reciprocity."[207] Such a claim for the foundational status of the principle of reciprocity may be justified within the context of contemporary Western culture. But that is simply to say that it is can be nested within a particular historical tale.

Rorty asserts, with Dewey, that practical judgment is the whole of morality. It trumps any and all rules or principles. Better said, it rejects their foundational status. Rorty insists, in contrast to Habermas and Benhabib, that the distinction between morality and prudence, the universal and the contingent, simply marks a "transitional stage" on the way to a fuller moral development that dissolves the distinction.[208] He nests (Habermasian) narratives of universalism within a temporally more expansive narrative of moral maturation.

Narratives that endorse incontestable rules and principles assume a preponderant role in the moral development of youth. With adulthood come increasing opportunities to nest purported truths within larger webs of relations. The years of college, Rorty writes, are often when this transition occurs. By the time young people are in college, they "should have finished absorbing the best that has been thought and said and should have started becoming suspicious of it."[209] Becoming suspicious of the inviolability of rules and principles ought not occur too early in life. Rorty explains that "There is only the shaping of an animal into a human being by a process of socialization, followed (with luck) by the self-individuation and self-creation of that human being through his or her

---

[206] Johnson, *Moral Imagination*, p. 105.
[207] Benhabib, *Situating the Self*, 54.
[208] Rorty, "Universality and Truth," p. 24. See also Rorty, *Philosophy and Social Hope*, pp. xvi, xxix.
[209] Rorty, *Philosophy and Social Hope*, p. 124.

own later revolt against that very process.... Socialization has to come before individuation, and education for freedom cannot begin before some constraints have been imposed."[210] Pre-college education, Rorty argues, has the task of producing "literate citizens."[211] It bears the obligation of teaching intellectual skills (literacy) as well as the attitudes and values that inform (democratic) citizenship. These attitudes and values are inculcated by way of (national) myths. What Nietzsche said of early religious beliefs, Rorty holds for ethico-political myths: like our baby teeth, they should not extend beyond childhood. Still, they prove to be quite useful prior to maturity, enabling proper nourishment and a good bite.[212]

Rorty believes in the necessity of grand, socializing narratives. But these stories need not claim the status of unnestable meta-narratives. Rather, their power may simply derive from the (largely) unchallenged authority of the individuals (for example, parents) and institutions (for example, schools) that propagate them. The socializing power of micro-narratives can be well illustrated by children modeling themselves on superheroes or other inspiring characters from storybooks or television. This modeling occurs notwithstanding the fact that the children may be fully aware of the fictional status of their exemplars. Narratives making no claim to foundational status are quite sufficient for the socialization of youth.

Since the time of Homer, if not earlier, narratives have served the forces of traditionalism. For cultural conservatives, stories link us to the past and prompt us to reinscribe customary values. Critics suggest that philosophers who celebrate storytelling view our narrative nature as "a limit, rather than an opportunity." As traditionalists, they deny "authorship to individuals," and maintain that narratives cannot be "radically rewritten."[213] It is well to remember, however, that revolutionary thinkers also rely on narratives to achieve their purposes. Like conservatives, they employ stories as a means of integrating individuals into existent or idealized ethico-political communities. In this sense, narrative knowledge, while harboring political relevance, "has no unambiguous partisan or ideological allegiances."[214] Some narrative accounts, such as Karl Marx's,

---

[210] Rorty, *Philosophy and Social Hope*, p. 118.
[211] Rorty, *Philosophy and Social Hope*, p. 118.
[212] Friedrich Nietzsche, *Gesammelte Werke, Musarionausgabe*, vol. 9 (Munich: Musarion Verlag, 1920–1929), p. 405.
[213] Joshua Foa Dienstag, *Dancing in Chains: Narrative and Memory in Political Theory* (Stanford: Stanford University Press, 1997), p. 13.
[214] Hinchman, *Memory, Identity, Community*, p. xxvii.

promote revolutionary efforts. Others serve as "the tools of self-satisfied moralism or raw power."[215] There are canonic narratives and counter-hegemonic narratives. In the end, revolutionary, liberatory, and progressive tales will compete against reactionary, traditionalist, and conservative ones for the hearts and minds of citizens, motivating individual and collective action by communicating and transforming the roles people assume and the plots they inhabit.

Unlike axiomatic theories, stories invite multiple, and occasionally diametrically opposed, interpretations. Even those narratives that gain hegemonic status are not monolithic tales. The narrative of Christ's life, for instance, has been employed to buttress both revolutionary socialism (via liberation theology) and reactionary capitalism (via Christian fundamentalism). This inherent *plurivocité* of narrative has prompted many contemporary literary critics to deny the ethical functions of narrative altogether.[216] Narrative, they suggest, is simply too malleable to be helpful in establishing moral standards.

The practical judge is aware that there is always more than one side to a story, and usually more than two. But he is also actively involved in appraising competing stories. Martha Minow argues that a judge is perspectivist in a crucial sense, but he does not, for that reason, abandon the responsibilities of normative evaluation. Minow writes: "Once we see that any point of view, including one's own, *is* a point of view, we will realize that every difference we see is seen in relation to something already assumed as the starting point. Then we can expose for debate what the starting points should be. The task for judges is to identify vantage points, to learn how to adopt contrasting vantage points, and to decide which vantage points to embrace in given circumstances."[217] The assimilation of multiple perspectives is a prerequisite for sound judgment. Indeed, in the absence of diverse points of view, the normative task of the judge would evaporate.

---

[215] Robert P. Burns, *A Theory of the Trial* (Princeton: Princeton University Press, 1999), p. 226.

[216] Jane Adamson observes that "It is doubly ironic that during the last twenty years the ethical functions of literature – for centuries of prime concern to imaginative writers and literary critics – have been repudiated by a majority of literary theorists (all driven in various ways, as Mark Edmundson has recently argued, by the centuries-old platonic will to disenfranchise art), while at the same time so many philosophers have sought to re-enfranchise literature by arguing for its special value as a mode of moral inquiry." Adamson, "Against tidiness," p. 84.

[217] Martha Minow, "Justice Engendered," in Robert E. Goodin and Philip Pettit, eds, *Contemporary Political Philosophy* (Oxford: Blackwell Publishers, 1997), p. 506.

To say that the judge is a perspectivist is perhaps misleading. The term *perspectivism* suggests a visual subject. It posits a single, optical axis of differentiation between competing claims. Narratives operate on multiple dimensions. They speak in different voices, appeal to different senses, and access different cognitive and affective capacities. They can be analyzed upon historical, social, cultural, economic, political, ethical, and aesthetic planes.

All of us participate in the dimensions of space and time. All share in (self) consciousness and employ tacit knowledge and skills.[218] We all partake, to greater or lesser extent, in the dimension of rationality as a result of our highly developed cortices. We all inhabit an affective dimension, owing to our well-developed limbic systems. Each of these dimensions enables us to experience the world in particular ways. No single plane of existence can encompass all the others, notwithstanding significant overlaps and interdependencies.

Good judgment reflects the capacity simultaneously to inhabit various stories, to experience an issue from multiple vantage points, and, as importantly, in multiple frames of mind, emotional states, or moods. It reflects the *multi-dimensionality* of life. The "inability to think and judge a thing apart from its function or utility," writes Arendt, indicates a "utilitarian mentality," a kind of "philistinism." She continues: "And the Greeks rightly suspected that this philistinism threatens...the political realm, as it obviously does because it will judge action by the same standards of utility which are valid for fabrication, demand that action obtain a predetermined end and that it be permitted to seize on all means likely to further this end."[219] Narrative judgment refuses philistinism. What differentiates politics from fabrication is what differentiates a story from a technical manual. The former is multi-dimensional and transformative, the latter not. The former teaches various lessons and bears many messages. The latter has a single lesson to teach, and wholly exhausts itself therein. Once its purpose has been achieved, re-reading a technical manual is pointless. It might as well be thrown out. Being a multi-dimensional entity, however, a narrative can never be exhausted. It resists evaluation along a single axis, inviting numerous re-readings, new interpretations, and fresh judgments.

---

[218] Friedrich Nietzsche, *The Gay Science*, trans. Walter Kaufmann (New York: Vintage, 1974), pp. 299–300.

[219] Hannah Arendt, *Between Past and Future: Eight Exercises in Political Thought* (New York: Penguin, 1954), p. 216.

Rorty argues that there is no difference between finding a text useful and interpreting it correctly. Texts and narratives, for pragmatists like Rorty, are kinds of tools. To wield a tool (most) usefully is to use it correctly. We can argue about which interpretations are better or worse, in the sense of more or less useful given the tasks at hand, but the categories of "right" and "wrong" simply do not apply. This approach veers toward the philistinism that Arendt disparaged. At the same time, Rorty recognizes that the fullest appreciation of a narrative requires moving beyond crass instrumentalism. A narrative is of greatest value when approached openly, without static, preconceived ideas about how it will be put to use.

Kant made the distinction between things, which may be valued, and people, who must be respected for their intrinsic worth (and who, in addition, may be valued for sundry reasons). Rorty designates texts as "honorary persons."[220] He writes that there is a "useful distinction ... between knowing what you want to get out of a person or thing or text in advance and hoping that the person or thing or text will help you want something different – that he or she or it will help you to change your purposes, and thus to change your life."[221] Narratives offer us the opportunity to navigate between dimensions, and hence to experience life, and ourselves, anew.

To remain open to transformation when confronting a text constitutes what Rorty calls an "inspired" reading. This receptivity to the riches of narrative allows the reader not only to inform his judgment, but fundamentally to change what, how, and why he judges. An inspired reading, Rorty writes, constitutes "an encounter with an author, character, plot, stanza, line or archaic torso which has made a difference to the critic's conception of who she is, what she is good for, what she wants to do with herself: an encounter which has rearranged her priorities and purposes."[222] In effect, the inspired reader acknowledges, as MacIntyre observed, that the question "What is to be done?" can only be answered after first figuring out one's place in a story. To approach a narrative in an inspired way is to remain receptive to the fundamental rescripting of roles.[223] This

---

[220] Rorty, *Philosophy and Social Hope*, p. 144.
[221] Rorty, *Philosophy and Social Hope*, p. 145.
[222] Rorty, *Philosophy and Social Hope*, p. 145.
[223] Ironically, Rorty has made the redescription of great philosophical works in his own image into something of an art form. That is to say, he openly utilizes texts to serve his pragmatist purposes, seemingly without being much changed by them. In this repect, Rorty, like most of us, has difficulty practicing what he preaches.

receptivity allows one not only to inform judgment, but fundamentally to change what, how, and why one judges.

In like fashion, Gadamer writes that the fusion of horizons that occurs in an interpretive encounter with a text is always "dangerous" because all *bona fide* interpretation threatens fundamentally to alter the self whose horizons are being fused.[224] An inspired encounter with narrative transforms the self, then, in the same way that the democratic exercise of power implies not only acting and effecting change, but being acted upon and undergoing change.[225] In both cases, transformation arises out of an openness to the "reemplotment" of one's own life story, the renesting of narratives that structure one's life within other, more encompassing narratives.[226]

A narrative, most fundamentally, is not what an author says it is but what it does in the world. It is the product of hermeneutic effort. That is because meaning, as Gadamer observes, is often discovered where it was not intentionally put.[227] Although thick, narratives are not rigid. Narratives teach, but do not speak for themselves. They await interpretation. But just as every aphorism has its antipode, so every narrative may beget opposing interpretations, and, for some, teach the wrong lessons. Though we might well acknowledge the indispensability of narratives to human understanding and the crucial role of narratives in constructing psychological and moral selves, therefore, a troubling question remains. What prevents us from being led astray by Thrasymachean tales, fascist history, or fundamentalist fables?

That is an age-old question, and it resists facile answers. But the problem at hand is less the proliferation of dangerous stories than the closed, restrictive manner in which narratives of all sorts are approached and interpreted. Undoubtedly, closed readings are often products not only or even primarily of personal attributes, but of the particular position of an interpreter within structures of power. This presents a vast and complex problem to which genealogical investigation, the sociology of knowledge,

---

[224] Hans-Georg Gadamer, *Reason in the Age of Science*, trans. Frederick Lawrence (Cambridge: MIT Press, 1981), pp. 109–110.

[225] Sheldon Wolin, "What Revolutionary Action Means Today," in *Dimensions of Radical Democracy: Pluralism, Citizenship, Community*, ed. Chantal Mouffe (London: Verso, 1992), pp. 251–52.

[226] Alison Brysk, " 'Hearts and Minds': Bringing Symbolic Politics Back In," *Polity* 27 (1995): 580.

[227] Hans-Georg Gadamer, *Philosophical Hermeneutics*, translated and edited by David Linge (Berkeley: University of California Press, 1976), p. 9.

and the critique of ideology are partial answers. What is evident, however, is that moral development hinges on open, inspired readings. It occurs through the hermeneutic engagement with narratives that, at times, are radically different from those that have shaped one's own being. The solution to the problems of democracy, it is often said, is more democracy. In the same vein, the solution to the problems posed by dangerous narratives is a deeper, richer, fuller, and more self-conscious assimilation of the riches that narratives provide.

A predilection for stories is often understood as the vestige of youth, something to be given up with age as one embraces reason and science. But things are not that simple. In J. M. Barrie's classic tale, *Peter Pan*, the protagonist recruits Wendy Darling to join him in Neverland because she can tell stories, something wholly absent in his homeland of endless adventure. One suspects that it is the dearth of stories in Neverland, the lack of narrative knowledge, that prevents Peter Pan and the Lost Boys from ever growing up. For all their escapades, Peter and his youthful pirate-fighters will never become practically wise. They prefer to live without the burden of prudence. Hence Wendy the storyteller must return to her home in London.

It is not that practical wisdom is adverse to adventure. It is simply incompatible with eternal youth. To remain forever young, Peter Pan foregoes the riches of narrative. There will be no learning from experience. Those of us who live this side of Neverland ought to make a wiser choice.

Conclusion

I have the same title to write on prudence that I have to write on poetry or holiness. We write from aspiration and antagonism, as well as from experience. We paint those qualities which we do not possess.

Ralph Waldo Emerson[1]

Throughout history, practical judgment has been addressed by a broad spectrum of philosophers and theorists. But it holds particular significance for thinkers who do not avail themselves of what might be called hard foundations for their ontologies, epistemologies, or ethics. In this respect, practical judgment has been of interest to Aristotelians more than Platonists, to Humeans more than Kantians, to hermeneuticists more than analytical philosophers, and to pragmatists and post-modernists more than (neo)structuralists and strict behavioralists. Of course, Plato, Kant, and many modernist thinkers have made important contributions to our understanding of practical judgment. Still, those who temper the pursuit of essences with the narrative investigation of experience generally find practical judgment of utmost significance. So much depends upon good judgment, anti-essentialists agree, because so little is available to greater certainty. Judgment is a crucial faculty as a result of the multiple (cognitive) paradoxes and (normative) dilemmas that infuse contemporary life, notwithstanding the impact of scientific methodologies, metaphysical principles, or religious doctrine.

---

[1] Ralph Waldo Emerson, "Prudence," in *Selected Writings of Emerson*, ed. Donald McQuade (New York: Modern Library, 1981), p. 221.

To valorize judgment is not to condone relativism. Quite the contrary. To the extent that relativism connotes an "anything goes" attitude, it wholly negates the importance of judgment. Good judgment is what is most needed in a world burdened by claims that subjective preferences are the final word. Relativism gets its punch from positing epistemologically and ethically isolated subjects. In contrast, the practical judge lives in a multi-dimensional, shared world.

Democritus first observed the skeptic's problem over two millennia ago: "Poor mind, "he mused," from the senses you take your arguments, and then want to defeat them? Your victory is your defeat."[2] Likewise, contemporary relativists assert the wholly subjective nature of reality and then suggest the impossibility of welding together subjective perception with an objective world. Rather than getting caught on the horns of this dilemma, we might follow Heidegger in positing a corporeal human being that is always already in the world with others. That is to say, the relativist's notion of purely subjective preferences proves vacant if we challenge the premise of a "merely 'inner' " self that subsequently comes to doubt its ability to discern and partake of a common reality.[3]

What Heidegger said of radical skepticism applies equally to relativism – namely, that it "makes sense only on the basis of a being whose constitution is Being-in-the-world.... World in its most proper sense is just that which is already on hand for any questioning."[4] Heidegger insists that we do not *have* bodies. Rather, "we 'are' bodily."[5] In the same respect, we do not *have* a world and social relations. Rather, we *are* worldly and socially. And we do not have skills; rather, we are skillfully. Or, as Heidegger puts it more pointedly, skills have us. To question, to doubt, or to assert the pure subjectivity of the individual is already to give witness to the shared world and the common (cognitive and linguisitic) skills that allow such questions, doubts, and assertions to be formulated, understood, and articulated. Being-in-the-world-with-others is the presupposition for all apprehension and all doubt.

---

[2] Diels, *Fragmente der Vorsokratiker* (4th ed., 1922), frag B125. Quoted in Hannah Arendt, *The Human Condition* (Chicago: University of Chicago Press, 1958), p. 275 n.31.

[3] Martin Heidegger, *Being and Time* (New York: Harper and Row, 1962), p. 250.

[4] Martin Heidegger, *History of the Concept of Time: Prolegomena*, trans. T. Kisiel (Bloomington: Indiana University Press, 1985), p. 215 (and see p. 161). See also Heidegger, *The Basic Problems of Phenomenology* (Bloomington: Indiana University Press, 1982), p. 164.

[5] Heidegger, *Nietzsche, Vol. 1: The Will to Power as Art*, trans. D. Krell (New York: Harper and Row, 1979), p. 99.

The practical judge exercises her craft neither burdened by the relativist's radical doubt nor inflated by the self-assurance of the positivist who makes claim to non-perspectival knowledge. Indeed, the positivist quest for a God's eye view is simply the epistemological flip side of the relativist's coin. In moving beyond subjectivism and objectivism, the practical judge skillfully reasserts her being-in-the-world-with-others. It is with this in mind, one suspects, that Hannah Arendt, Heidegger's student, wrote: "Judging is one, if not the most, important activity in which this sharing-the-world-with-others comes to pass."[6] Far from leaving us isolated in a relativist hell or an objectivist heaven, practical judgment embeds us in a common world.

Grappling with Multi-Dimensionality

In 1967, physicist Nobel laureate P. W. Anderson observed that "More is different." The whole is not simply the aggregate of its parts. When enough parts are added to a physical system, more is not simply more (of the same). It becomes different. As the quantity of components grows, so do interactions between them, and by means of these interactions, quantitative differences translate into qualitative differences. Reducing a system to the laws that govern the interactions of its parts does not mean those laws can be employed to reconstruct the whole.[7] More eventually becomes more complex, not simply more abundant. With more components, more time, more interactions, even more laws and rules, one witnesses the emergence of new properties.[8]

Practical judgment is grounded in the understanding that more is different. The practical judge affirms that we cannot attain a firm grasp of a multi-dimensional, dynamic world through a reductive, analytical application of epistemological or ethical rules. In today's high-tech, data-driven societies, many judgments are best informed by statistical knowledge. And a good dose of rationality will cut through much confusion. But the assessment and evaluation of ethico-political life remains grounded in the intuitive capacities, tacit skills, and affective imagination that allow insight into a deeply complex realm of interaction and emergence.

[6] Hannah Arendt, *Between Past and Future* (New York: Penguin Books, 1954), p. 221.
[7] See Tor Norretranders, *The User Illusion*. Trans. Jonathan Sydenham (New York: Viking, 1998), p. 356.
[8] On emergence, see Roger Penrose, *Shadows of the Mind* (Oxford: Oxford University Press, 1994).

That is not to demean rules and principles, particularly in the moral realm. The good judge knows their worth. For one, the observance of rules often shields us from the biases that inevitably infiltrate decision-making. Moreover, bending or breaking rules, even when warranted, may set a dangerous precedent. Others may follow suit for the wrong reasons. In turn, like all novel action, the flouting of rules bears the potential of rewiring the brain. While one may bend or break rules for good reasons, such action will make it easier and more likely for these rules to be ignored in the future, even without the reflection that prompted their initial rejection. The Law of Karma, of willed effort, announced two and a half millennia ago by Gautama Buddha still resonates with Aristotelian wisdom: we become heirs to our own acts of will. At a minimum, neuroscientists observe, the retribution of karma arises in the form of remapped brains.[9] Taking exception to good rules is always a dangerous business. It easily becomes a bad habit.

William James observed that "There is no more miserable human being than one in whom nothing is habitual but indecision."[10] Indeed, to be without good habits is not only to be miserable but to lack practical wisdom. The practical judge actively cultivates good habits of thought and behavior – repertoires of tacit skills and knowledge – that make her more perceptive, adaptive, and mentally resilient in environments of deep complexity. Most importantly, she is in the habit of learning from experience. In this respect, Aristotle and cognitive neuroscientists concur that the practical judge is the architect of her own mind.

Our brains sport a good many hard-wired synaptic pathways. But, as Schwartz and Begby observe, "Neuronal circuits also change when something as gossamer as our thoughts changes, when something as inchoate as mental effort becomes engaged – when, in short, we choose to attend with mindfulness. The power of attention not only allows us to choose what mental direction we will take. It also allows us, by actively focusing attention on one rivulet in the stream of consciousness, to change – in

---

9   Gautama's statement reads: "All Beings are owners of their Karma. Whatever volitional actions they do, good or evil, of those they shall become the heir." Quoted in Jeffrey M. Schwartz and Sharon Begley, *The Mind and the Brain: Neuroplasticity and the Power of Mental Force* (New York: HarperCollins, 2002), p. 375.

10 William James, *The Principles of Psychology* (Cambridge: Harvard University Press, 1981), p. 126. Cited in Russell Hardin, *Morality with the Limits of Reason* (Chicago: University of Chicago Press, 1988), p. 17.

scientifically demonstrable ways – the systematic functioning of our own neural circuitry."[11] The effort to rewire our brains through mindfulness, Schwartz and Begby argue, is "the true moral act."[12] We bear the responsibility of choosing our habits before they choose us.

Gadamer wrote that "It is not so much our judgments as it is our prejudices that constitute our being."[13] Our lives, and our identities, largely develop from cognitive and affective activities that are only marginally within conscious control. At the same time, we can reprogram our neural circuits to transform constitutional prejudices, and improve practical judgment as a result. Whole-brain learning cultivates such resourcefulness of mind.[14]

Immanuel Kant, a man convinced of the importance of rules, declared that science was the organization of knowledge, and wisdom was the organization of life. Kant was much given to organization: so much so that the people of his hometown Koenigsberg, it is said, set their watches by the philosopher's daily walks with his dog. A more apt definition of wisdom might acknowledge the disorganization of life, its inherent uncertainties and insuperable complexity, the emergence of novelty, and the role of fortune, which, as Isaiah Berlin observes, "mysteriously enough, men of good judgment seem to enjoy rather more often than others."[15] The good judge does not let rule breaking become a bad habit, but neither does she allow rule-following to become so routinized as to prevent skillful adaptation. She develops and continually renovates brain maps to facilitate navigation of a complex, ever-changing terrain.

Practical wisdom allows us to make the best of life's murky depths, to surf its chaotic waves, grapple with its time- and space-bound contingencies, and ably wrestle with fortune. Reason has an important contribution to make to this effort. But its domain is limited. The pursuit of analytical rigor should supplement rather than supplant the exercise of intuition and emotional intelligence. To judge well is to reject both sterile logic and reactive impulse. Only whole-brain judgment allows for

[11] Schwartz, *The Mind and the Brain*, p. 367.
[12] Schwartz, *The Mind and the Brain*, p. 325.
[13] Hans-Georg Gadamer, *Philosophical Hermeneutics*, trans./ed. David Linge (Berkeley: University of California Press, 1976), p. 9.
[14] Joseph Dunne, *Back to the Rough Ground: 'Phronesis' and 'Techne' in Modern Philosophy and in Aristotle* (Notre Dame: University of Notre Dame Press, 1993), pp. 272, 292.
[15] Isaiah Berlin, *The Sense of Reality: Studies in Ideas and their History*, ed. Henry Hardy (London: Chatto and Windus, 1996), p. 53.

robustness in our assessments and responsiveness in our evaluations and choices.

Reading Embodied Minds

A key feature distinguishing human beings from even the smartest of the apes, evolutionary psychologists assert, is our capacity for "mind reading." This is not a reference to parapsychology, but to the fact that humans effectively operate with a "theory of mind," which is to say, people understand that other people act in reference to particular mental states. We interpret others' actions within the context of their beliefs, intentions, and goals.[16]

Young children, autistic adults, and many other mammals prove to be quite adept at interpreting and predicting behavior so long as an interpretion of the mental state behind the behavior is not required. They do not evidence a sophisticated ability to read minds. This is well demonstrated in experiments where four-year-old children consistently fail to predict the behavioral reactions of individuals holding false beliefs. Though aware that a false belief is held, the child will nonetheless expect the individual to act on the basis of available, accurate knowledge. In such experiments, six-year-old humans perform at about the same level as adult chimpanzees. They remain, in many respects, mind-blind.[17] In older children, mind-reading abilities quickly develop.

Mind reading is a crucial component of practical judgment.[18] What the practical judge reads, however, are not simply minds filled with true or false beliefs and sundry intentions and goals, but minds subject to unconscious biases, intuitive insights, variable moods, affective reactions, emotional understanding, and rational (mis)calculations. To exercise good judgment is to be a fluent reader of the hearts and minds of fellow

---

[16] See David Premack and Ann Premack, *Original Intelligence* (New York: McGraw Hill, 2003), pp. 139–157.

[17] See Angeline Lillard and Lori Skibbe, "Theory of Mind: Conscious Attribution and Spontaneious Trait Inference," in *The New Unconscious*, ed. Ran Hassin, James Uleman, and John Bargh (Oxford: Oxford University Press, 2005), pp. 277–305. Recent studies suggest that chimpanzees are capable of rudimentary mind reading, but do not have a "full-blown, human-like theory of mind." Michael Tomasello, Josep Call, and Brian Hare, "Chimpanzees understand psychological states – the question is which ones and to what extent," *Trends in Cognitive Sciences* 7 (2003): 153–156.

[18] See Robin Dunbar, "On the origin of the human mind," in *Evolution and the human mind: Modularity, language and meta-cognition*, ed. Peter Carruthers and Andrew Chamberlain (Cambridge: Cambridge University Press, 2000), pp. 238–253.

men and women. Such reading skills are the prerogative of an enlarged mentality.[19]

Edward de Bono has suggested that the generation of new ideas is best achieved by "lateral" thinking.[20] Vertical thinking pursues a solution to a puzzle along a singular axis. It is like looking for gold by digging the same hole ever deeper. Lateral thinking is more like digging multiple, erratically spaced holes. While vertical thinking is an exercise in logical, step-wise progression, lateral thinking is less ordered. It might be prompted by random stimuli, by intentionally zigzagging, or reversing directions.[21] Practical judgment integrates vertical and lateral thinking. If creative ideas are the products of two-dimensional (lateral) thinking, then practical judgment may rightly be described as thinking in three (or more) dimensions. Three-dimensional thought is grounded in mind reading.

Consider King Solomon's quandary. Two women deliver babies, only one of which survives birth. Each woman claims the living infant as her own. After some consideration, Solomon decides that the living child should be cut in two, with each of the claimants receiving half of the corpse. This is an example of reversing direction. Rather than straightforwardly rendering justice between the two women and seeking the good of the child, Solomon proposes a murderous injustice. But the ancient king was a keen student of human psychology. Understanding that emotions generally get the better of us, he foresaw that an overpowering love would force the real mother to deny her rightful claim rather than see her offspring killed. And so it came to pass. Solomon returned the child to the woman who (falsely) admitted to being an imposter.

In a multi-dimensional world, strict adherence to step-wise logic is dysfunctional, for there are no logical means by which to cross over from one dimension to another. Logic only allows one to pursue better solutions along a single axis, by digging deeper holes. Solomon achieves the best of all possible outcomes by moving beyond systematic reason, offering

---

[19] Mind-reading abilities appear to require the integration of various brain activities, including executive control (employing the pre-frontal cortex) and introspection. Bertram Malle, "Folk Theory of Mind: Conceptual Foundations of Human Social Cognition," in *The New Unconscious*, ed. Ran Hassin, James Uleman, and John Bargh (Oxford: Oxford University Press, 2005), p. 229.

[20] Edward de Bono, *New Think: The Use of Lateral thinking in the Generation of New Ideas* (New York: Basic Books, 1968).

[21] Bono, "The Virtues of Zigzag Thinking," *Chemtech* 20 (1990): 80–85.

each of the plaintiff mothers the worst of all possible outcomes (half of a dead child). He was privy to an enlarged mentality because he was able to think, and feel, from the point of view of both mothers. Likewise, Aesop's wily fox gets the juicy grapes from the wary crow neither through force, nor threat, nor bribery, nor reasoned argument, but through an unlikely appeal to vanity. And, as we saw, the much-derided lad choosing dimes over dollars retires a rich man, and has the last laugh. In each case, the practical judge escapes the confines of logic to benefit from empathetic understanding. She is capable of exploring a problem, and its potential solutions, from multiple perspectives. The practical judge understands that people are not essentially rational animals, but rather creatures capable of rationality.[22] And she understands that her own reason, almost always a helpful resource, contributes most when it operates in conjunction with, not as a replacement for, the exercise of intuitive and emotional capacities.

A good reasoner might well be able to predict what a wholly rational person would do in any particular situation, but she will not be able to predict, since more is different, what wholly rational people will do in the aggregate. In turn, she will fail miserably at predicting what an *actual* (quasi-rational) person will do. Yet this is the domain of ethico-political life. What is needed in this realm, as Cicero observes, is the ability to incisively assess and evaluate peoples' convoluted "thoughts and feelings and beliefs and hopes."[23] A good judge starts with the premise "that people have . . . divided minds with different aspirations, that decision making, even for the individual, is an act of compromise among the different selves."[24] Common experience reinforces this conviction. Most of the tough decisions we have to make – the ones that leave us bewildered and hungry for good counsel – are just those that pit us against ourselves. As Nietzsche understood, our decisions and actions are largely products of unconscious struggles, as instinct, embodied knowledge, and emotions wage an internal battle to assert themselves. The eventual victor often marshals reason, *post facto*, to justify its rule. But we should not mistake

---

[22] Reuven Bar-Levav, *Thinking in the Shadow of Feelings* (New York: Simon and Schuster, 1988), pp. 19–20.

[23] Cicero, "On the Orator (I)," in *On the Good Life*, trans. Michael Grant (New York: Penguin, 1971), p. 316.

[24] David E. Bell, Howard Raiffa, and Amos Tversky, "Descriptive, Normative, and Prescriptive Interactions in Decision Making," in *Decision Making: Descriptive, Normative, and Prescriptive Interactions*, ed. David Bell, Howard Raiffa, and Amos Tversky (Cambridge: Cambridge University Press, 1988), p. 9.

the calm announcement of victory for the melee of battle.[25] To be proficient in reason without knowing the soul of the reasoner does not get one very far in understanding or predicting human behavior. The experienced judge reads the hearts and minds of those with whom she interacts. Oftentimes, it is necessary to read between the lines.

In a letter to Mersennes, René Descartes famously asserted that "Nothing can be in me, that is, in my mind, of which I am not conscious: I have proved it in the *Meditations*."[26] John Locke concurred, observing that it was unintelligible to think that any thought could occur without consciousness of itself. In his *Essay Concerning Human Understanding*, Locke insisted that consciousness was intrinsic to intelligent thought and definitive of the self. Nietzsche exploded this myth, and Freud fashioned a psychology out of the pieces. It is contemporary neuroscience, however, that has provided the firmest foundation for inquiry into the nature of affect and the unconscious, and their fundamental contributions to practical judgment.[27]

There is no "direct route" by which we can access the unconscious mind. But the body provides the surest indirect route. Just as we can measure unconscious reactions by way of changes in galvanic skin conductance and heart rate, so we can access other unconscious states by attention to affect, gesture, posture, voice, and facial expression. In the field of psychotherapy, it is widely recognized that the body bears the brunt of unconscious fears and their repression. For those who can read its signs, the body serves as a palimpsest of the mind. A renowned psychotherapist writes: "Our aim is not to make the unconscious conscious [as was Freud's self-assigned task], but to make it more familiar and less frightening. When we descend to that border area where body consciousness touches the unconscious, we become aware that the unconscious is our

[25] Friedrich Nietzsche, *Gesammelte Werke, Musarionausgabe,* vol. 1 (Munich: Musarion Verlag, 1880–82), p. 414, vol. 7, p. 395; Nietzsche, *The Will to Power,* trans. Walter Kaufmann and R.J. Hollingdale (New York: Vintage, 1968), p. 270; and see Leslie Paul Thiele, *Friedrich Nietzsche and the Politics of the Soul* (Princeton: Princeton University Press, 1990).

[26] Quoted in Guy Claxton, *Hare Brain Tortoise Mind: Why Intelligence Increases When You Think Less* (Hopewell, NJ: The Ecco Press, 1997), p. 205.

[27] A research team of cognitive neuroscientists writes: "First of all, strictly speaking, conscious thought does not exist. Thought, when defined as producing meaningful associative constructions, happens unconsciously. One may be aware of some of the elements of a thought process or one may be aware of a product of a thought process, but one is not aware of thought itself." Ap Dijksterhuis, Henk Aarts, and Pamela Smith, "The Power of the Subliminal: On Subliminal Persuasion and other Potential Applications, in *The New Unconscious,* ed. Ran Hassin, James Uleman, and John Bargh (Oxford: Oxford University Press, 2005), p. 81.

strength, while consciousness is our glory."[28] We are only now recuperating from Descartes's egregious error of hermetically separating mind from body. Emerson wrote that prudence is "but a name for wisdom and virtue conversing with the body and its wants."[29] If practical judgment is to be cultivated in contemporary times, our attention must be redirected to the corporeal nature of thought and the hidden strengths of embodied mindfulness.

Practical Wisdom, Neuroscience and Narrative

Cognitive neuroscience takes on the challenge of investigating the corporeal nature of practical wisdom. Empirical studies have discovered specific, concrete recipes for developing whole-brain learning and judgment. But the knowledge we have gained thus far only further underlines the importance of remaining questions. In many respects, we have not got much beyond Aristotle in determining how best to blend reason with emotion, conscious efforts with unconscious habits and tacit skills, holistic appraisal with deductive calculations, and, perhaps most importantly, narrative knowledge with abstract principle.

This last dyad, in many respects, subsumes all the former. Until the mid-seventeenth century, the distinction between narrative and non-narrative forms of knowledge was ill-defined. Notwithstanding Plato's early battle with myth and poetry, it was only modern science that categorically proclaimed the inferiority of narrative knowledge. What Plato essayed for philosophy – to ground it on non-narrative certainties – modern empiricists consummated for science. Lord Kelvin stated: "When you can measure what you are speaking of and express it in numbers, you know that on which you are discoursing, but when you cannot measure it and express it in numbers, your knowledge is of very meagre and unsatisfactory kind."[30] In modern times, narrative ceased to be a serious form of inquiry. Consequently, its prerogative to sit at the table of knowledge was revoked.[31]

Science often has cause to be suspicious of narrative, for many of the reasons originally voiced by Plato. Stories can undermine logic, heighten

---

[28] Alexander Lowen, *Bioenergetics* (New York: Coward, McCann and Geoghegan, 1975), p. 320.

[29] Emerson, *Selected Writings of Emerson*, p. 222.

[30] Quoted in James Robertson, "Shaping the Post-Modern Economy," in *Business and the Environment*, eds. Richard Welford and Richard Starkey (Washington, DC: Taylor and Francis, 1996), p. 22.

[31] Stephen Toulmin, *Return to Reason* (Cambridge: Harvard University Press, 2001), p. 15.

bias, and manipulate emotion. Stories often mislead, in no small part because of their unique capacity to heighten sensibilities, stimulate imagination and emotion, and invoke tacit capacities. There is, Henry James observed, a common fear of literature's "insidious" nature: the "danger of its hurting you before you know it."[32] Narrative's clandestine effects are not to be dismissed. Let there be no doubt: the uninformed reliance on narrative to the exclusion of rational inquiry may keep people from exercising the best judgment.

While narrative bears its own dangers and shortcomings, its contributions to ethico-political life are undeniable. It is informative and transformative in a manner and to a degree that has no contender. Narrative enlarges mentality by fostering mind-reading skills, heightening perceptive abilities, and enhancing moral sensitivity. It serves as a key source of mediated experience. Unlike conceptual arguments, narratives do not wield deductive power. They exhibit and clarify rather than decisively demonstrate. But they are not, for that reason, any less effective.[33] Their strength, as C. S. Peirce said of good philosophy, comes from "the multitude and variety" of their ingredients, rather than the "conclusiveness" of any single component. Their capacity to persuade does not form a chain of reasons, which is only ever as strong as its weakest link, but, as Peirce suggested, "a cable whose fibers may be ever so slender, provided that they are sufficiently numerous and intimately connected."[34] Indeed, it is the thick, complexly interdependent, multi-dimensional character of narrative that primarily fosters the development of phronetic skills.

Aristotle insisted that practical wisdom concerns matters given to change, things that are temporally and spatially variable. As such, practical wisdom pertains to matters that cannot be defined by a singular truth but may, nonetheless, be illuminated by diverse narratives. Like the metaphors that populate them, narratives can carry us from one dimension to another.[35] They help us negotiate connections between diverse jursidictions. To the extent that we remain open to the power of narrative, we remain open to the experience of multi-dimensionality. That openness is the hallmark of worldly wisdom.

[32] Henry James, "The Art of Fiction" in *Partial Portraits* (Ann Arbor: University of Michigan Press, 1970), p. 381.
[33] Donald E. Polkinghorne, *Narrative Knowing and the Human Sciences* (Albany: State University of New York Press, 1988), p. 21
[34] Quoted in Martha Minow, "Justice Engendered," in Robert E. Goodin and Philip Pettit, eds, *Contemporary Political Philosophy* (Oxford: Blackwell Publishers, 1997), p. 517.
[35] The Greek word *metaphorein* means to transfer or carry over.

Oral tradition, mythology, religious scripture, history, biography, fairy tales, classic literature, and, as Sheldon Wolin suggests, "epic" political philosophy, provided the narrative foundations for the cultivation of judgment in the pre-modern world. With the rise of the novel in the nineteenth century, prose fiction came to augment these traditional forms of narrative learning. In the twentieth century, film and television took center stage. During the twenty-first century, the role of narrative in cultural life may be usurped by other forms of entertainment and information. To the extent that popular culture becomes defined by cyber-interactions, the ersatz experience delivered by immersion in narratives may evaporate. In turn, direct experience may also decline owing to a preoccupation with the "virtual reality" available on motion picture, television, video, and computer screens. As such, a post-modern, televisual, and web-based culture may undermine opportunities for both the direct and mediated experiences that serve to cultivate judgment.

In the contemporary world, an accelerated age where leisure steadily morphs into work or entertainment, the time for reflective storytelling may be ebbing away. Yet one wonders if stories are really disappearing, or simply changing form. As the epic waned while the novel waxed, so too television, motion pictures, and weblogs may simply be taking the place of the literary novel. Of course, the changing form of narrative presents its own problems. Story lines in motion pictures are increasingly overshadowed by the technology of film making. Plot and character development take a back seat to the "special effects" that determine both the pace of the film and its subject matter. Parallel developments are observable in other media. The fascination with pastiche, sound bites, and clips has eroded narrative design. Plot, always a product of temporal and spatial continuity, gives way to an episodic blur of juxtaposing images. "The electronic culture," Jeffrey Scheuer writes, "fragments information into isolated, dramatic particles and resists longer and more complex messages."[36] In such a culture, a sense of history is lost, and connective geographical tissue atrophies. The result, to employ Pierre Bourdieu's description of the effect of watching television, is "structural amnesia."[37] We are endlessly bombarded with fragmented images. These images, unlike narratives, do not solicit the synthetic powers of interpretation. They merely induce

[36] Jeffrey Scheuer, *The Sound Bite Society: Television and the American Mind* (New York: Four Walls Eight Windows, 1999), p. 9.

[37] Pierre Bourdieu, *On Television* (New York: The New Press, 1998), p. 7. See also Roderick Hart, *Seducing America: How Television Charms the Modern Voter* (New York: Oxford University Press, 1994), p. 86.

consumption. At least in its traditional form, narrative arguably has been displaced in post-modernity.[38]

To the extent that our lives are increasingly divorced from narratives, exemplary tales that demand hermeneutic effort, the faculty of judgment is threatened. But storytelling is not about to disappear from our lives. The genre of narrative is co-extensive with the human condition. If it is depressed in one venue, it will likely emerge in another. Perhaps that is how we should interpret the rise of narrative to philosophical prominence in the midst of its decline (or transformation) in popular culture. Defining post-modernity as an "incredulity toward metanarratives," Jean-François Lyotard opts for the redeployment of micro-narratives to legitimate socio-political life and its institutions. Richard Rorty contends that there is no other recourse: we have only our (culturally and historically specific) narratives to serve as banisters for ethical and political life. The post-modern rejection of religious, metaphysical, and scientific foundations leaves narrative shouldering much of the burden of structuring social mores. Philosophically, narrative has regained its place at the table of knowledge, and found surprising allies within the scientific community. Indeed, there is perhaps no better advocate for a narrative understanding of the human condition than cognitive neuroscience, the protagonist of the tale told here. Brandishing the most advanced weapons of science, it courageously affirms narrative as the source of the self and a chief resource for the cultivation of practical judgment.

To speak of the death of narrative is decidedly premature. Even the demise of *meta*-narrative has been greatly exaggerated. To be sure, meta-narratives are out of fashion today among the highly educated. But meta-narratives have not disappeared from post-modernity. As Fredric Jameson observes, most have simply gone underground.[39] And many that operate in open air are flourishing. The rise of Islamic and Christian fundamentalism are cases in point. In the face of such totalizing and ferociously competitive meta-narratives, the cultivation of practical judgment takes on a new urgency, as does the deployment of salutary micro-narratives.

This book celebrates practical judgment. But I do not mean to romanticize it. If practical judgment is good at anything, it is good at knowing

---

[38] Michael Roemer, *Telling Stories: Postmodernism and the Invalidation of Traditional Narrative* (Lanham, MD: Rowman and Littlefield, 1995), p. 179.

[39] Fredric Jameson, Foreword to Jean-François Lyotard, *The Postmodern Condition* (Minneapolis: University of Minnesota Press, 1984), p. xii.

its own limits. Just as the practical judge recognizes the respective short-comings of reason, intuition, and affect operating in isolation, so she recognizes the restricted domain of judgment itself. Practical judgment is no panacea. Ever open to improvement, it can never be perfected. Increasing its precision and consistency will, in most cases, decrease its flexibility and robustness. The converse also holds. The problem here has as much to do with the indeterminacies of the world as the weaknesses of the human mind. Practical judgment is a faculty relatively well adapted to its environment. But life is complex, even paradoxical. One simply should not expect to too much of our synaptic hardware given the tasks at hand. In any case, human beings are not only the judges of life, but also, as Heidegger and Nietzsche respectively suggested, its enchanted witnesses and celebratory yea-sayers. It would be "strange" indeed, Aristotle held, to assert the sovereignty of *phronesis* given its limited domain. Though a crucial part of life, judgment is not the whole of life. That is a truth obvious to most. It is a lesson best remembered by an embodied mind.

The wise judge understands that the depths of life cannot fully be plumbed. But ignorance provides no excuse for inaction. We cannot escape the responsibilities that define our place in a web of relations, nor wash our hands of its stickiness. Not to act is still to be acted upon, and sins of omission may overtake those of commission in a complex, interdependent society. To act is to introduce a new vector in the world. It is always, in part, an endeavor of hope. This hope need not be unfounded. The practical judge may be sanguine that action will yield expected results when grounded upon well-integrated experience. At the same time, she must expect the unexpected. Wrestling with fortune is always an adventure.

The best hedge against fortune is experience. Of course, experience is, or at least can be, an adventure in itself. In his essay, "The Art of Fiction," Henry James counsels the aspiring novelist to 'Write from experience and experience only." But he is quick to add, lest the triteness of his counsel veil an intended gravity: "Try to be one of the people on whom nothing is lost!"[40] James's admonition to writers applies equally to readers, especially those readers of men and women who would interpret the grand text of life. The mindful judge makes every experience her teacher, and every teaching an adventure.

It is fitting to conclude with a story. In a *Thousand and One Nights*, a mighty king is betrayed by his wife and, after summarily executing her,

---

[40] James, *Partial Portraits*, pp. 389–90.

swears never to be so humiliated again. In order to avoid future cuck-oldings, the king initiates a brutal custom: he always weds a virgin, con-summates the marriage that evening, and beheads the unfortunate girl the next morning. His viceroy, the Wezir, a man of good judgment, is well-schooled in the art of government. But his practical wisdom fails him after some months when he has to provide yet another victim for the insatiable king in a land wholly depleted of virgins.

The Wezir's daughter, Shahrazad, offers to wed the king in order to save her father from the potentate's wrath. Reluctantly, the Wezir agrees, sensing that his daughter has some smarts of her own. Indeed, the wily Shahrazad saves her life by keeping her new groom awake and amused, telling story after story for a thousand and one nights. The consumma-tion of the marriage is indefinitely postponed as each evening the mighty king hangs upon his bride's every word until the light of morning arrives. Shahrazad keeps her head about her, and undermines tyrannical ambi-tion. Her practical wisdom finds its ultimate resource in narrative.

That is a good lesson for democrats to learn, at least for those who share the ideal of a meditative culture. In such a culture, one neither mes-merized by technology nor disparaging of science, judgment grounded in experience would serve as a prophylactic against dogma and despot. Here the spoils of widely cultivated practical wisdom would be the fine balance between liberty and law, autonomy and obligation, innovation and order, creativity and custom that defines the best of democratic life. For those who share the ideal of a meditative culture, wise judgments follow from inspired readings of a deeply complex world. And what is an ideal but a tale that wants to be told.

Bibliography

Abizadeh, Arash. "The Passions of the Wise: *Phronesis*, Rhetoric, and Aristotle's Passionate Practical Deliberation," *The Review of Metaphysics* 56 (December 2002): 267–296.

Abram, David. *The Spell of the Sensuous: Perception and Language in a More-Than-Human World*. New York: Pantheon Books, 1996.

Adamson, Jane. "Against tidiness: Literature and/versus moral philosophy." In *Renegotiating Ethics in Literature, Philosophy, and Theory*, pp. 84–110. Ed. Jane Adamson, Richard Freadman, and David Parker. Cambridge: Cambridge University Press, 1998.

Adolphs, Ralph, Daniel Tranel, and Antonio Damasio. "The human amygdala in social judgment." *Nature* 393 (1998): 470–474.

Allison, Graham. *The Essence of Decision*. Boston: Little, Brown and Company, 1971.

Angus, Lynne and John McLeod, eds. *The Handbook of Narrative and Psychotherapy: Practice, Theory, and Research*. Thousand Oaks, CA: Sage Publications, 2004.

Ani, Marimba. *Yurugu: An African-Centered Critique of European Cultural Thought and Behavior*. Trenton, NJ: African World Press, 1994.

Arendt, Hannah. *Between Past and Future: Eight Exercises in Political Thought*. New York: Penguin Books, 1954.

Arendt, Hannah. *The Human Condition*. Chicago: University of Chicago Press, 1958.

Arendt, Hannah. "Thinking and Moral Considerations: A Lecture," *Social Research* 38: 3 (1971): 417–446.

Arendt, Hannah. *The Life of the Mind — Thinking*. New York: Harcourt Brace Jovanovich, 1978.

Arendt, Hannah. "On Hannah Arendt." In Melvyn A. Hill *Hannah Arendt: The Recovery of the Public World*, pp. 301–339. New York: St. Martin's Press, 1979.

Arendt, Hannah. *Lectures on Kant's Political Philosophy*. Ed. Ronald Beiner. Chicago: University of Chicago Press, 1982.

Arendt, Hannah. "Understanding and Politics." In Hannah Arendt, *Essays in Understanding, 1930–1954*, pp. 307–327. Ed. Jerome Kohn. New York: Harcourt Brace & Company, 1994.

Aristotle. *The Ethics of Aristotle: The Nichomachean Ethics*. Trans. J. A. K. Thomson. New York: Penguin Books, 1953.

Aristotle. *The Politics*. Trans. T. A. Sinclair. New York: Penguin Books, 1962.

Austin, James H. *Zen and the Brain: Towards an Understanding of Meditation and Consciousness*. Cambridge: MIT Press, 1998.

Barber, Benjamin. *The Conquest of Politics: Liberal Philosophy in Democratic Times*. Princeton: Princeton University Press, 1988.

Barber, Benjamin. "Foundationalism and Democracy." In *Democracy and Difference: Contesting the Boundaries of the Political*, pp. 348–359. Ed. Seyla Benhabib. Princeton: Princeton University Press, 1996.

Bargh, John A. "The Automaticity of Everyday Life." In *The Automaticity of Everyday Life: Advances in Social Cognition*, Vol. X, pp. 1–61. Ed. Robert Wyer, Jr. Mahwah, NJ: Lawrence Erlbaum Associates, 1997.

Bargh, John. "Bypassing the Will: Toward Demystifying the Nonconscious Control of Social Behavior." in *The New Unconscious*, pp. 37–58. Ed. Ran Hassin, James Uleman, and John Bargh. Oxford: Oxford University Press, 2005.

Bar-Levav, Reuven. *Thinking in the Shadow of Feelings*. New York: Simon and Schuster, 1988.

Baron, Jonathan. *Judgment Misguided: Intuition and Error in Public Decision Making*. New York: Oxford University Press, 1998.

Barry, Brian. *Political Argument*. New York: Humanities Press, 1965.

Barthes, Roland. *Image, Music, Text*. New York: Hill and Wang, 1977.

Bechara, Antoine, Hanna Damasio, Daniel Tranel, and Antonio Damasio. "Deciding Advantageously before Knowing the Advantageous Strategy." *Science*, 28(1997): 1293–95.

Beiner, Ronald. "Interpretive Essay." In Hannah Arendt, *Lectures on Kant's Political Philosophy*, pp. 89–156. Ed. Ronald Beiner. Chicago: University of Chicago Press, 1982.

Beiner, Ronald. *Political Judgment*. Chicago: University of Chicago Press, 1983.

Beiner, Ronald. *Philosophy in a Time of Lost Spirit: Essays on Contemporary Theory*. Toronto: University of Toronto Press, 1997.

Beiner, Ronald and Jennifer Nedelsky, eds. *Judgment, Imagination, and Politics: Themes from Kant and Arendt*. New York: Rowman and Littlefield, 2001.

Bell, David E., Howard Raiffa, and Amos Tversky, "Descriptive, Normative, and Prescriptive Interactions in Decision Making." In *Decision Making: Descriptive, Normative, and Prescriptive Interactions*, pp. 9–30. Ed. David Bell, Howard Raiffa, and Amos Tversky. Cambridge: Cambridge University Press, 1988.

Benhabib, Seyla. *Situating the Self: Gender, Community and Postmodernism in Contemporary Ethics*. New York: Routledge, 1992.

Benhabib, Seyla. *The Reluctant Modernism of Hannah Arendt*. Thousand Oaks, CA: Sage, 1996.

Benhabib, Seyla. "Judgment and the Moral Foundations of Politics in Hannah Arendt's Thought." In *Judgment, Imagination, and Politics: Themes from Kant and Arendt*, pp. 183–204. Ed. Ronald Beiner and Jennifer Nedelsky. New York: Rowman and Littlefield, 2001.

Berlin, Isaiah. *Four Essays on Liberty.* Oxford: Oxford University Press, 1969.

Berlin, Isaiah. *Concepts and Categories.* Ed. Henry Hardy. New York: Viking Press, 1979.

Berlin, Isaiah. *The Sense of Reality: Studies in Ideas and Their History.* Ed. Henry Hardy. London: Chatto and Windus, 1996.

Berlin, Isaiah. *The Power of Ideas.* Ed. Henry Hardy. Princeton: Princeton University Press, 2000.

Bernstein, Richard. *Beyond Objectivism and Relativism: Science, Hermeneutics, and Praxis.* Philadelphia: University of Pennsylvania Press, 1985.

Bernstein, Richard. *The New Constellation: The Ethical-Political Horizons of Modernity/ Postmodernity.* Cambridge: MIT Press, 1991.

Berry, Dianne. "Concluding note: How implicit is implicit learning." in *How Implicit is Implicit Learning,* pp. 235–40. Ed. Dianne Berry. New York: Oxford University Press, 1997.

Bickle, John. "Empirical Evidence for a Narrative Concept of Self." In *Narrative and Consciousness: Literature, Psychology and the Brain,* pp. 195–208. Ed. Gary Fireman, Ted McVay, Jr., and Owen Flanagan. New York: Oxford University Press, 2003.

Booth, Wayne C. *The Company We Keep: An Ethics of Fiction.* Berkeley: University of California Press, 1988.

Bornstein, R. F. and T. S. Pittman, eds. *Perception without Awareness: Cognitive, Clinical and Social Perspectives.* New York: Guilford Press, 1992.

Bourdieu, Pierre. *Distinction: A Social Critique of the Judgment of Taste.* Cambridge: Harvard University Press, 1984.

Bourdieu, Pierre. *On Television.* New York: The New Press, 1998.

Bower, Gordon. "Mood Congruity of Social Judgments." In *Emotion and Social Judgment,* pp. 31–53. Ed. Joseph P. Forgas. Oxford: Pergamon Press, 1991.

Branscombe, Nyla and Brian Cohen. "Motivation and Complexity Levels as Determinants of Heuristic Use in Social Judgments." In *Emotion and Social Judgment,* pp. 145–160. Ed. Joseph P. Forgas. Oxford: Pergamon Press, 1991.

Brehmer, Berndt. "In a word: Not from experience." In *Judgment and decision making,* pp. 705–719. Ed. Hal Arkes and Kenneth Hammond. Cambridge: Cambridge University Press, 1986.

Browne, Stephen. "Edmund Burke's *Letter to the Sheriffs of Bristol* and the Texture of Prudence." In *Prudence: Classical Virtue, Postmodern Practice,* pp. 127–144. Ed. Robert Harriman. University Park, PA: Pennsylvania State University Press, 2003.

Brudney, Daniel. "*Lord Jim* and Moral Judgment: Literature and Moral Philosophy." *The Journal of Aesthetics and Art Criticism,* 56 (1998): 265–81.

Bruner, Jerome. "The Narrative Creation of Self." In *The Handbook of Narrative and Psychotherapy: Practice, Theory, and Research,* pp. 3–14. Ed. Lynne Angus and John McLeod. Thousand Oaks, CA: Sage Publications, 2004.

Brysk, Alison. "'Hearts and Minds': Bringing Symbolic Politics Back In." *Polity* 27(1995): 559–585.

Bueno de Mesquita, Bruce. *The War Trap.* New Haven: Yale University Press, 1981.

Burke, Edmund. *Reflections on the Revolution in France.* Garden City, NJ: Doubleday and Co., 1961.

Burns, Robert P. *A Theory of the Trial.* Princeton: Princeton University Press, 1999.

Cacioppo, John T. et al., eds. *Foundations in social neuroscience.* Cambridge, MA: MIT Press, 2002.

Campbell, John. *Lives of the Chief Justices of England,* vol. 4. Ed. James Cockcroft. Northport, NY: E. Thompson 1894–99.

Camus, Albert. *The Rebel.* New York: Vintage Books, 1956.

Cape, Robert, Jr. "Cicero and the Development of Prudential Practice at Rome." In *Prudence: Classical Virtue, Postmodern Practice,* pp. 35–65. Ed. Robert Harriman. University Park, PA: Pennsylvania State University Press, 2003.

Carr, David. "Narrative and the Real World: An Argument for Continuity," In *Memory, Identity, Community: The Idea of Narrative in the Human Sciences,* pp. 7–25. Ed. Lewis P. Hinchman and Sandra K. Hinchman. Albany: State University of New York Press, 1997.

Carr, David. *Time, Narrative, and History.* Bloomington: Indiana University Press, 1986.

Carroll, John and Eric Johnson. *Decision Research: A Field Guide.* Newbury Park CA: Sage Publications, 1990.

Carruthers, Peter and Andrew Chamberlain, eds. *Evolution and the human mind: Modularity, language and meta-cognition.* Cambridge: Cambridge University Press, 2000.

Cavarero, Adriana. *Relating Narratives: Storytelling and Selfhood.* Trans. Paul Kottman. London: Routledge, 2000.

Ceci, S. and U. Bronfenbrenner. "Don't forget to take the cupcakes out of the oven: Strategic time-monitoring, prospective memory and context," *Child Development* 56 (1985): 175–90.

Choi, Y. Susan, Heather Gray, and Nalini Ambady. "The Glimpsed World: Unintended Communication and Unintended Perception." In *The New Unconscious,* pp. 309–333. Ed. Ran Hassin, James Uleman, and John Bargh. Oxford: Oxford University Press, 2005.

Chomsky, Noam. "*Review of* Verbal Behavior," *Language* 35 (1959): 26–58.

Cicero. *De Inventione.* Cambridge: Harvard University Press, 1949.

Cicero. *On the Good Life.* Trans. Michael Grant. New York: Penguin, 1971.

Cicero. *The Republic and The Laws.* Trans. Niall Rudd. Oxford: Oxford University Press, 1998.

Claparede, Edouard. "Recognition and 'me-ness.'" In *Organization and Pathology of Thought,* pp. 58–75. Ed. D. Rapaport. New York: Columbia University Press, 1951.

Claxton, Guy. *Hare Brain Tortoise Mind: Why Intelligence Increases When You Think Less.* Hopewell, NJ: The Ecco Press, 1997.

Cleckley, H. *The Mask of Sanity.* St. Louis: C. V. Mosby 1955.

Clore, Gerald and W. Gerrod Parrott. "Moods and their Vicissitudes: Thoughts and Feelings as Information." In *Emotion and Social Judgment,* pp. 107–123. Ed. Joseph P. Forgas. Oxford: Pergamon Press, 1991.

Coates, John. *The Claims of Common Sense: Moore, Wittgenstein, Keynes and the Social Sciences.* Cambridge: Cambridge University Press, 1996.

Cohen, L. J. "Can Human Irrationality Be Experimentally Demonstrated?" *The Behavioral and Brain Sciences* 4 (1981): 317–331.

Colby, Anne and Lawrence Kohlberg. *The Measurement of Moral Judgment, Volume 1: Theoretical Foundations and Research Validation.* Cambridge: Cambridge University Press, 1987.

Connolly, William E. *Why I Am Not a Secularist.* Minneapolis: University of Minnesota Press, 1999.

Connolly, William E. *Neuropolitics: Thinking, Culture, Speed.* Minneapolis: University of Minnesota Press, 2002.

Cooksey, Ray W. *Judgment Analysis: Theory, Methods, and Applications.* San Diego: Academic Press, 1996.

Cooley, Charles Horton. *Human Nature and the Social Order.* New York: Scribner, 1964.

Conrad, Joseph. *Lord Jim.* London: Penguin, 1986.

Csikszentmihalyi, Mihaly and Jeanne Nakamura. "The Role of Emotions in the Development of Wisdom." In *A Handbook of Wisdom: Psychological Perspectives*, pp. 220–242. Ed. Robert Sternberg and Jennifer Jordan. Cambridge: Cambridge University Press, 2005.

Cummins, Denise Dellarosa and Conlin Allen. *The Evolution of Mind.* New York: Oxford University Press, 1998.

Damasio, Antonio. *Descartes' Error: Emotion, Reason and the Human Brain.* New York: Putnam, 1994.

Damasio, A. and H. Damasio. "Making Images and Creating Subjectivity." In *The Mind-Brain Continuum: Sensory Processes*, pp. 19–27. Ed. Rodolfo Llinas and Patricia Churchland. Cambridge: MIT Press, 1996.

Damasio, Antonio. *The Feeling of What Happens: Body and Emotion in the Making of Consciousness.* New York: Harcourt, Brace and Company, 1999.

Damasio, Antonio. *Looking for Spinoza: Joy, Sorrow, and the Feeling Brain.* New York: Harcourt, 2003.

Davis, Laurence and Peter Stillman, eds. *The New Utopian Politics of Ursula K. LeGuin's* The Dispossessed (Lanham: Rowman and Littlefield, 2005), pp. xxiv, 305.

Dawes, Robyn M. *Everyday Irrationality.* Boulder: Westview, 2001.

Dawes, R., D. Faust, and P. Meehl, "Clinical versus actuarial judgment." *Science* 243 (1989): 1688–74.

de Bono, Edward. *New Think: The Use of Lateral Thinking in the Generation of New Ideas.* New York: Basic Books, 1968.

de Bono, Edward. "The Virtues of Zigzag Thinking." *Chemtech* 20 (1990): 80–85.

Dennett, Daniel C. *Consciousness Explained.* Boston: Little, Brown and Company, 1991.

Dennett, Daniel C. *Darwin's Dangerous Idea: Evolution and the Meanings of Life.* New York: Simon and Schuster, 1995.

Den Uyl, Douglas J. *The Virtue of Prudence.* New York: Peter Lang, 1991.

Derrida, Jacques. "Force of Law: The 'Mystical Foundation of Authority.'" Trans. Mary Quaintance. In *Deconstruction and the Possibility of Justice*, pp. 3–67. Ed. Drucilla Cornell, Michel Rosenfeld, and David Gray Carlson. New York: Routledge, 1992.

Derrida, Jacques. "The Villanova Roundtable: A Conversation with Jacques Derrida," In *Deconstruction in a Nutshell*, pp. 3–28. Ed. John D. Caputo. New York: Fordham University Press, 1997.

Dienstag, Joshua Foa. *Dancing in Chains: Narrative and Memory in Political Theory.* Stanford: Stanford University Press, 1997.

Dewey, John. *The Political Writings.* Ed. Debra Morris and Ian Shapiro. Indianapolis: Hackett, 1993.

Diamond, Peter J. "The 'Englightement Project' Revisited." In *Prudence: Classical Virtue, Postmodern Practice*, pp. 99–123. Ed. Robert Harriman. University Park, PA: Pennsylvania State University Press, 2003.

Dijksterhuis, Ap, Henk Aarts, and Pamela Smith. "The Power of the Subliminal: On Subliminal Persuasion and other Potential Applications." In *The New Unconscious*, pp. 77–106. Ed. Ran Hassin, James Uleman, and John Bargh. Oxford: Oxford University Press, 2005.

Dostal, Robert. "Judging Human Action: Arendt's Appropriation of Kant." In *Judgment, Imagination, and Politics: Themes from Kant and Arendt*, pp. 139–164. Ed. Ronald Beiner and Jennifer Nedelsky. New York: Rowman and Littlefield, 2001.

Dreyfus, Hubert and Stuart Dreyfus, with Tom Athanasiou. *Mind over Machine: The Power of Human Intuition and Expertise in the Era of the Computer.* New York: The Free Press, 1988.

Dreyfus, Hubert and Stuart Dreyfus. "What is morality: A phenomenological account of the development of ethical expertise." In *Universalism vs. Communitarianism: Contemporary Debates in Ethics*, pp. 237–264. Ed. David Rasmussen. Cambridge: MIT Press, 1990.

Dreyfus, Hubert L. *Being-in-the-World: A Commentary on Heidegger's* Being and Time, *Division I.* Cambridge MA: MIT Press, 1991.

Dreyfus, Hubert and Stuart Dreyfus. "What is Moral Maturity: Towards a Phenomenology of Ethical Expertise." In *Revisioning Philosophy*, pp. 111–131. Ed. James Ogilvy. Albany: State University of New York Press, 1992.

Dunbar, Robin. "On the origin of the human mind." In *Evolution and the human mind: Modularity, language and meta-cognition*, pp. 238–253. Ed. Peter Carruthers and Andrew Chamberlain. Cambridge: Cambridge University Press, 2000.

Dunne, Joseph. *Back to the Rough Ground: 'Phronesis' and 'Techne' in Modern Philosophy and in Aristotle.* Notre Dame: University of Notre Dame Press, 1993.

Edelman, Gerald. *Neural Darwinism.* New York: Basic Books, 1987.

Edelman, Gerald. *Bright Air, Brilliant Fire: On the Matter of the Mind.* New York: Basic Books, 1992.

Edwards, Ward. "The Theory of Decision Making." *Psychological Bulletin*, 41: 380–417.

Eisenach, Eldon J. *Narrative Power and Liberal Truth.* Lanham: Rowman and Littlefield, 2002.

Ellis, Henry and R. Hunt. *Fundamentals of Cognitive Psychology*, 5th ed. Madison: Brown and Benchmark, 1993.

Elster, Jon. *Alchemies of the Mind: Rationality and the Emotions.* Cambridge: Cambridge University Press, 1999.

Emerson, Ralph Waldo. *Selected Writings of Emerson.* Ed. Donald McQuade. New York: Modern Library, 1981.

Epstein, Seymour. *Constructive Thinking: The Key to Emotional Intelligence.* Westport: Praeger, 1998.

Epstein, Seymour and Rosemary Pacini. "Some Basic Issues Regarding Dual-Process Theories from the Perspective of Cognitive-Experiential Self-Theory." In *Dual-Process Theories in Social Psychology*, pp. 462–482. Ed Shelly Chaiken and Yaacov Trope. New York: Guilford Press, 1999.

Ericsson, K. A. and J. Smith, eds. *Toward a General Theory of Expertise: Prospects and Limits*. Cambridge: Cambridge University Press, 1991.

Etzioni, Amitai. *The Moral Dimension*. New York: The Free Press, 1988.

Everitt, Anthony. *Cicero: The Life and Times of Rome's Greatest Politician*. New York: Random House, 2003.

Ferguson, Kennan. *The Politics of Judgment: Aesthetics, Identity, and Political Theory*. Lanham, MD: Lexington Books, 1999.

Ferrara, Alessandro. *Justice and Judgment*. London: Sage, 1999.

Fiedler, Klaus. "On the Task: The Measures and the Mood in Research on Affect and Social Cognition." In *Emotion and Social Judgment*, pp. 83–104. Ed. Joseph P. Forgas. Oxford: Pergamon Press, 1991.

Fishburn, Peter. "The Making of Decision Theory." In *Decision Science and Technology*, pp. 369–388. Ed. James Shanteau, Barbara Mellers, and David Schum. Boston: Kluwer Academic Publishers, 1999.

Fitton, Robert A., ed. *Leadership*. Boulder: Westview Press, 1997.

Fleishacker, Samuel. *A Third Concept of Liberty: Judgment and Freedom in Kant and Adam Smith*. Princeton: Princeton University Press, 1999.

Flyvbjerg, Bent. *Rationality and Power: Democracy in Practice*. Chicago: University of Chicago Press, 1998.

Flyvbjerg, Bent. *Making Social Science Matter: Why Social Inquiry Fails and How It Can Succeed Again*. Cambridge, U.K.: Cambridge University Press, 2001.

Forgas, Joseph. "The role of emotion in social judgments." *European Journal of Social Psychology* 24 (1994): 1–24.

Foucault, Michel. *Power/Knowledge: Selected Interviews and Other Writings 1972–1977*. Ed. Colin Gordon. New York: Pantheon Books, 1980.

Foucault, Michel. "The Subject and Power." In *Beyond Structuralism and Hermeneutics*, pp. 208–226. Ed. Hubert Dreyfus and Paul Rabinow. Chicago: University of Chicago Press, 1982.

Foucault, Michel. *The Foucault Reader*. Ed. Paul Rabinow. New York: Pantheon, 1984.

Foucault, Michel. *Politics, Philosophy, Culture: Interviews and Other Writings, 1977–1984*. Ed. Lawrence Kritzman. New York: Routledge, 1988.

Friedman, Marilyn. "Care and Context in Moral Reasoning." In *Women and Moral Theory*, pp. 190–204. Ed. Eva Kittay and Diana Meyers. Lanham: Rowman and Littlefield, 1987.

Freud, Sigmund. *Civilization and its Discontents*. Trans. James Strachey. New York: W. W. Norton, 1961.

Gadamer, Hans-Georg. *Truth and Method*. New York: Crossroad, 1975.

Gadamer, Hans-Georg. *Philosophical Hermeneutics*. Trans. David Linge. Berkeley: University of California Press, 1976.

Gadamer, Hans-Georg. *Reason in the Age of Science,*. Trans./Ed. Frederick Lawrence. Cambridge: MIT Press, 1981.

Gadamer, Hans-Georg. *Heidegger's Ways*. Trans. John Stanley. Albany: State University of New York Press, 1994.

Gadamer, Hans-Georg. *The Enigma of Health*. Trans. Jason Gaiger and Nicholas Walker. Stanford: Stanford University Press, 1996.

Gardner, John. *The Art of Fiction*. New York: Vintage Books, 1983.

Garver, Eugene. "After Virtū: Rhetoric, Prudence, and Moral Pluralism in Machiavelli." In *Prudence: Classical Virtue, Postmodern Practice*, pp. 67–97. Ed. Robert Harriman. University Park, PA: Pennsylvania State University Press, 2003.

Gazzaniga, Michael S. *The Mind's Past*. Berkeley: University of California Press, 1998.

Gazzaniga, Michael S. "Brain and Conscious Experience." In *Foundations in social neuroscience*, pp. 203–214. Ed. John T. Cacioppo et al. Cambridge, Mass.: MIT Press, 2002.

Geertz, Clifford. *The Interpretation of Cultures*. New York, Basic Books, 1973.

Gergen, Kenneth J. and Mary M. Gergen. "Narrative of the Self." In *Memory, Identity, Community: The Idea of Narrative in the Human Sciences*, pp. 161–184. Ed. Lewis P. Hinchman and Sandra K. Hinchman. Albany: State University of New York Press, 1997.

Gigerenzer, Gerd, Peter M. Todd, and the ABC Research Group. *Simple Heuristics That Make Us Smart*. New York: Oxford University Press, 1999.

Gigerenzer, Gerd. *Adaptive Thinking: Rationality in the Real World*. Oxford: Oxford University Press, 2000.

Gigerenzer, Gerd. "Ecological Intelligence: An Adaptation for Frequencies." In *The Evolution of Mind*, pp. 9–29. Ed. Denise Dellarosa Cummins and Conlin Allen. New York: Oxford University Press, 1998.

Gilbert, Daniel T. "Inferential Correction," In *Heuristics and Biases: the Psychology of Intuitive Judgment*, pp. 167–184. Ed. Thomas Gilovich, Dale Griffin, and Daniel Kahneman. Cambridge: Cambridge University Press, 2002.

Gillespie, Michael. "Martin Heidegger's Aristotelian National Socialism," *Political Theory* 28:2 (April 2000), 140–166.

Gilovich, Thomas, Dale Griffin, and Daniel Kahneman, eds. *Heuristics and Biases: the Psychology of Intuitive Judgment*. Cambridge: Cambridge University Press, 2002.

Gladwell, Malcolm. *Blink: The Power of Thinking without Thinking*. New York: Little, Brown, 2005.

Glaser, Jack and John Kihlstrom. "Compensatory Automaticity: Unconscious Volition is not an Oxymoron." In *The New Unconscious*, pp. 171–195. Ed. Ran Hassin, James Uleman, and John Bargh. Oxford: Oxford University Press, 2005.

Glynn, Ian. *An Anatomy of Thought: The Origin and Machinery of the Mind*. Oxford: Oxford University Press, 1999.

Goldberg, Elkhonon. *The Executive Brain: Frontal Lobes and the Civilized Mind*. New York: Oxford University Press, 2001.

Goldberg, Elkhonon. *The Wisdom Paradox: How Your Mind Can Grow Stronger As Your Brain Grows Older*. New York: Gotham Books, 2005.

Goleman, Daniel. *Emotional Intelligence*. New York: Bantam Books, 1995.

Gollwitzer, Peter, Ute Bayer, and Kathleen McCulloch. "The Control of the Unwanted." in *The New Unconscious*, pp. 485–515. Ed. Ran Hassin, James Uleman, and John Bargh. Oxford: Oxford University Press, 2005.

Gould, Stephen Jay. *Bully for Brontosaurus: Reflections in Natural History.* New York: W.W. Norton, 1991.

Graesser, Arthur and Victor Ottati. "Why Stories? Some Evidence, Questions, and Challenges," In *Knowledge and Memory: The Real Story – Advances in Social Cognition*, Vol. VIII. Ed. Robert Wyer, Jr. Mahwah, NJ: Lawrence Erlbaum Associates, 1995.

Gramsci, Antonio. *Selections from the Prison Notebooks.* Trans. /ed. Quintin Hoare and Geoffrey Nowell Smith. New York: International Publishers, 1971.

Gray, Jeffrey. *Consciousness.* Oxford: Oxford University Press, 2004.

Greene, Joshua et al. An fMRI Investigation of Emotional Engagement in Moral Judgment," *Science* 293 (2001): 2105–8.

Greene, Joshua and Jonathan Haidt. "How (and where) does moral judgment work?" *Trends in Cognitive Sciences* 6 (2002): 517–523.

Greenwald, Anthony and Mahzarin Banaji. "Implicit Social Cognition: Attitudes, Self-Esteem, and Stereotypes," *Psychological Review* 102 (1995): 4–27.

Grenberg, Jeanine. "Feeling, Desire and Interest In Kant's Theory of Action," *Kant-Studien* 92 (2001): 153–179.

Griffin, Dale and Amos Tversky. "The Weighing of Evidence and the Determinants of Confidence." In *Heuristics and Biases: the Psychology of Intuitive Judgment*, pp. 230–249. Ed. Thomas Gilovich, Dale Griffin, and Daniel Kahneman. Cambridge: Cambridge University Press, 2002.

Hacking, Ian. *The Emergence of Probability.* Cambridge: Cambridge University Press, 1975.

Hacking, Ian. *The Taming of Chance.* Cambridge: Cambridge University Press, 1990.

Haidt, Jonathan. "The Emotional Dog and Its Rational Tail: A Social Intuitionist Approach to Moral Judgment." *Psychological Review.* 108 (October 2001): 814–834.

Hammond, Kenneth R. *Human Judgment and Social Policy: Irreducible Uncertainty, Inevitable Error, Unavoidable Injustice.* New York: Oxford University Press, 1996.

Hanley, Ryan Patrick. "Political Science and Political Understanding: Isaiah Berlin on the Nature of Political Inquiry," *American Political Science Review* 98 (May 2004): 327–339.

Hannaford, Carla. *Smart Moves: Why Learning Is Not All in Your Head.* Arlington, VA: Great Ocean Publishers, 1995.

Hardin, Russell. *Morality with the Limits of Reason.* Chicago: University of Chicago Press, 1988.

Harriman, Robert. "Theory without Modernity." In *Prudence: Classical Virtue, Postmodern Practice*, pp. 1–32. Ed. Robert Harriman. University Park, PA: Pennsylvania State University Press, 2003.

Harriman, Robert. "Prudence in the Twenty-First Century." In *Prudence: Classical Virtue, Postmodern Practice*, pp. 287–321. Ed. Robert Harriman. University Park, PA: Pennsylvania State University Press, 2003.

Hart, Roderick. *Seducing America: How Television Charms the Modern Voter.* New York: Oxford University Press, 1994.

Heidegger, Martin. *Being and Time.* Trans. John Macquarrie and Edward Robinson. New York: Harper and Row, 1962.

Heidegger, Martin. *What is Called Thinking,* Trans. J. Gray. New York: Harper and Row, 1968.

Heidegger, Martin. *On Time and Being.* Trans. J. Stambaugh. New York: Harper and Row, 1972.

Heidegger, Martin. *Basic Writings.* Ed. David Farrell Krell. New York: Harper and Row, 1977.

Heidegger, Martin. *Nietzsche, Vol. 1: The Will to Power as Art.* Trans. D. Krell. New York: Harper and Row, 1979.

Heidegger, Martin. *The Basic Problems of Phenomenology.* Trans. Albert Hofstadter. Bloomington: Indiana University Press, 1982.

Heidegger, Martin. *History of the Concept of Time: Prolegomena.* Trans. T. Kisiel. Bloomington: Indiana University Press, 1985.

Heidegger, Martin. *The Fundamental Concepts of Metaphysics: World, Finitude, Solitude.* Trans. William McNeill and Nicholas Walker. Bloomington: Indiana University Press, 1995.

Heidegger, Martin. *Plato's Sophist.* Trans. Richard Rojcewicz and Andre Schuwer. Bloomington: Indiana University Press, 1997.

Heilke, Thomas. "Realism, Narrative, and Happenstance: Thucydides' Tale of Brasidas." *American Political Science Review* 98 (2004): 121–138.

Hinchman, Lewis P. and Sandra K. Hinchman eds. *Memory, Identity, Community: The Idea of Narrative in the Human Sciences.* Albany: State University of New York Press, 1997.

Hobbes, Thomas. *Leviathan.* Ed. C. B. Macpherson. New York: Penguin Books, 1968.

Hobbes, Thomas. *Hobbes's Thucydides.* Ed. Richard Schlatter. New Brunswick, NJ: Rutgers University Press, 1975.

Hoffman, James E. "The Psychology of Perception." In *Mind and Brain: Dialogues in Cognitive Neuroscience,* pp. 7–32. Ed. Joseph Ledoux and William Hirst. Cambridge: Cambridge University Press, 1986.

Hogarth, Robin. "Beyond discrete biases: Functional and dysfunctiional aspects of judgmental heuristics." In *Judgment and decision making,* pp. 680–704. Ed. Hal Arkes and Kenneth Hammond. Cambridge: Cambridge University Press, 1986.

Hogarth, Robin. *Educating Intuition.* Chicago: University of Chicago Press, 2001.

Holstein, James and Jaber Gubrium. *The Self We Live By: Narrative Identity in a Postmodern World.* New York: Oxford University Press, 2000.

Horgan, John. *The Undiscovered Mind.* New York: The Free Press, 1999.

Howard, Dick. *Political Judgments.* Lanham, MD: Rowman & Littlefield, 1996.

Hume, David. *An Inquiry Concerning Human Understanding.* Indianapolis: Bobbs-Merrill, 1955.

Islen, Alice M. "Positive Affect and Decision Making." In *Handbook of Emotions,* 2nd edition, pp. 417–435. Ed. Michael Lewis and Jeannette M. Haviland-Jones. New York: Guilford Press, 2000.

Jaeger, Werner. *Paideia: The Ideals of Greek Culture,* 2nd ed., 3 Vols. New York: Oxford University Press, 1973.

James, Henry. *Partial Portraits.* Ann Arbor: University of Michigan Press, 1970.

James, William. *The Principles of Psychology.* Vol. I (New York: Henry Holt, 1890), pp. 373–74. Cambridge: Harvard University Press, 1981.

James, William. *Psychology: The Briefer Course.* New York: Harper, 1961.

Janis, Irving. *Victims of Groupthink.* Boston: Houghton Mifflin, 1972.

Janis, Irving and Leon Mann. *Decision Making: A Psychological Analysis of Conflict, Choice, and Commitment.* New York: The Free Press, 1977.

Janis, Irving L. *Crucial Decisions: Leadership in Policymaking and Crisis Management.* London: The Free Press, 1989.

Johnson, Mark. *Moral Imagination: Implications of Cognitive Science for Ethics.* Chicago: University of Chicago Press, 1993.

Kahneman, Daniel, Paul Slovic, and Amos Tversky, eds. *Judgment under Uncertainty: Heuristics and Biases.* Cambridge: Cambridge University Press, 1982.

Kant, Immanuel. *The Philosophy of Kant.* Ed. Carl J. Friedrich. New York: Modern Library, 1949.

Kant, Immanuel. *Religion Within the Limits of Reason Alone.* Trans. Theodore Greene and Hoyt Hudson. New York: Harper and Row, 1960.

Kant, Immanuel. *Groundwork of the Metaphysics of Morals.* Trans. H. J. Paton. New York: Harper and Row, 1964.

Kant, Immanuel. *The Doctrine of Virtue.* Trans. Mary Gregor. Philadelphia: University of Pennsylvania Press, 1964.

Kant, Immanuel. *The Metaphysical Elements of Justice: Part I of the Metaphysics of Morals.* Trans. John Ladd. Indianapolis: Bobbs-Merrill, 1965.

Kant, Immanuel. *Critique of Pure Reason.* Trans. N. Kemp Smith. London: Macmillan, 1985.

Kateb, George. "The Judgment of Arendt." In *Judgment, Imagination, and Politics: Themes from Kant and Arendt,* pp. 121–137. Ed. Ronald Beiner and Jennifer Nedelsky. New York: Rowman and Littlefield, 2001.

Kazantzakis, Nikos. *Zorba the Greek.* New York: Simon and Schuster, 1952.

King, Stephen. *On Writing: A Memoir of the Craft.* New York: Pocket Books, 2000.

Klein, Gary. *Sources of Power: How People Make Decisions.* Cambridge: MIT Press, 1998.

Koh, K. and D. E. Meyer. "Function learning: Induction of continuous stimulus-response relations." *Journal of Experimental Psychology: Learning, Memory, and Cognition,* 17 (1991): 811–836.

Kohlberg, Lawrence. "The Development of Children's Orientations toward a Moral Order." *Vita Humana,* 6 (1963): 11–33; 11(1963): 1–32.

Konner, Melvin. *The Tangled Wing: Biological Constraints on the Human Spirit.* New York: Holt, Rinehart and Winston, 1982.

Kuhn, Thomas. *The Structure of Scientific Revolutions,* 2nd ed. Chicago: University of Chicago Press, 1970.

Labouvie-Vief, Gisela. "Wisdom as integrated thought: historical and developmental perspectives." In *Wisdom: Its Nature, Origins, and Development,* pp. 52–83. Cambridge: Cambridge University Press, 1990.

Lakoff, George and Mark Johnson, *Metaphors We Live By*. Chicago: University of Chicago Press, 1980.

Lakoff, George and Mark Johnson. *Philosophy in the Flesh*. New York: Basic Books, 1999.

Lakoff, George. *Moral Politics: How Liberals and Conservatives Think*, 2nd edition. Chicago: University of Chicago Press, 2002.

Lamott, Anne. *Bird by Bird: Some Instructions on Writing and Life*. New York: Random House, 1994.

Larmore, Charles E. *Patterns of Moral Complexity*. Cambridge: Cambridge University Press, 1987.

Larmore, Charles E. "Moral Judgment." In *Judgment, Imagination, and Politics: Themes from Kant and Arendt*, pp. 47–64. Ed. Ronald Beiner and Jennifer Nedelsky. New York: Rowman and Littlefield, 2001.

La Rochefoucauld. *Maxims*. Trans. Leonard Tanock. London: Penguin Books, 1959.

Lawrence, D. H. *Studies in Classic American Literature*. New York: Viking Press, 1922.

LeDoux, Joseph. *The Emotional Brain*. New York: Simon and Schuster, 1996.

LeDoux, Joseph. *The Synaptic Self: How Our Brains Become Who We Are*. New York: Penguin Books, 2002.

Levinas, Emmanuel. *Basic Philosophical Writings*. Ed. Adriaan T. Peperzak, Simon Critchley, and Robert Bernasconi. Bloomington: Indiana University Press, 1996.

Levine, Peter. *Living Without Philosophy: On Narrative, Rhetoric, and Morality*. Albany: State University of New York Press, 1998.

Lewicki, P., M. Czyzewska, and H. Hoffman. "Unconscious acquisition of complex procedural knowledge." *Journal of Experimental Psychology: Learning, Memory, and Cognition*, 13 (1987): 523–530.

Lewicki, Pawel, Thomas Hill, and Maria Czyzewska. "Nonconscious acquisition of information." *American Psychologist* 47 (1992): 796–801.

Lewicki, Pawel, Maria Czyzewska, and Thomas Hill. "Nonconscious information processing and personality." In *How Implicit is Implicit Learning*, pp. 48–72. Ed. Dianne Berry. New York: Oxford University Press, 1997.

Libet, Benjamin. "Unconscious cerebral initiative and the role of conscious will in voluntary action." *Behavioral and Brain Science* 8(1985): 529–566.

Lieberman, Matthew D. "Intuition: A Social Cognitive Neuroscience Approach." *Psychological Bulletin*, 126 (2000): 109–137.

Lillard, Angeline and Lori Skibbe. "Theory of Mind: Conscious Attribution and Spontaneious Trait Inference." In *The New Unconscious*, pp. 277–305. Ed. Ran Hassin, James Uleman, and John Bargh. Oxford: Oxford University Press, 2005.

Lodge, David. *Consciousness and the Novel*. Cambridge: Harvard University Press, 2002.

Lodge, Milton and Kathleen M. McGraw eds. *Political Judgment: Structure and Process*. Ann Arbor: The University of Michigan Press, 1995.

Loewenstein, George and Jennifer Lerner. "Out of control: Visceral influences on behavior." *Organizational Behavior and Human Decision Making Processes* 65(1996): 272–92.

Lopes, Lola L. "The Rhetoric of Irrationality," *Theory and Psychology* 1 (1991): 65–82.

Low-Beer, F. H. *Questions of Judgment*. Amherst, NY: Prometheus Books, 1995.

Lowen, Alexander. *Bioenergetics*. New York: Coward, McCann and Geoghegan, 1975.

Lyotard, Jean-François. *The Postmodern Condition*. Trans. Geoff Bennington and Brian Massumi. Minneapolis: University of Minnesota Press, 1984.

Lyotard, Jean-François. *Just Gaming*. Trans. Wlad Godzich. Minneapolis: University of Minnesota Press, 1985.

Lyotard, Jean-François. *The Differend: Phrases in Dispute*. Trans. Georges Van Den Abbeele. Minneapolis: University of Minnesota Press, 1988.

Machiavelli, Niccolò. *The Prince and The Discourses*. New York: Modern Library, 1950.

Machiavelli, Niccolò. *The Prince*. Trans. Robert Adams. New York: Norton, 1977.

MacIntyre, Alasdair. *After Virtue: A Study in Moral Theory*. Notre Dame: University of Notre Dame Press, 1981.

MacIntyre, Alasdair. *Whose Justice? Which Rationality*. Notre Dame: University of Notre Dame Press, 1988.

MacIntyre, Alasdair. *Dependent Rational Animals*. Chicago: Open Court, 1999.

Mackie, Diane and Leila Worth. "Feeling Good, But Not Thinking Straight: The Impact of Positive Mood on Persuasion." In *Emotion and Social Judgment*, pp. 201–219. Ed. Joseph P. Forgas. Oxford: Pergamon Press, 1991.

Malle, Bertram. "Folk Theory of Mind: Conceptual Foundations of Human Social Cognition." in *The New Unconscious*, pp. 225–255. Ed. Ran Hassin, James Uleman, and John Bargh. Oxford: Oxford University Press, 2005.

Marcus, George E., W. Russell Neuman, and Michael MacKuen, *Affective Intelligence and Political Judgment*. Chicago: University of Chicago Press, 2000.

Marcus, George E. *The Sentimental Citizen: Emotion in Democratic Politics*. University Park, PA: Pennsylvania State University Press, 2002.

Marcus, George E. "The Psychology of Emotion and Politics" in *Oxford Handbook of Political Psychology*, pp. 182–221. Ed. David Sears, Leonie Huddy, and Robert Jervis. New York: Oxford University Press, 2003.

Martin, R. D. *The Specialist Chick Sexer: A History, A World View, Future Prospects*. Melbourne: Bernal Publishing, 1994.

Marton, F., P. Fensham, and S. Chaiklin. "A Nobel's Eye View of Scientific Intuition." *International Journal of Science Education* 16 (1994): 457–73.

Maslow, Abraham. *Toward a Psychology of Being*, 2nd ed. New York: D. Van Nostrand, 1968.

Masters, Roger D. "Naturalistic Approaches to Justice in Political Philosophy and the Life Sciences." In *The Sense of Justice: Biological Foundations of Law*, pp. 67–92. Ed. Roger D. Masters and Margaret Gruter. Newbury Park: Sage Publications, 1992.

Masters, Roger D. and Denis G. Sullivan. "Nonverbal Behavior and Leadership: Emotion and Cognition in Political Information Processing." In *Explorations in Political Psychology*, pp. 150–182. Ed. Shanto Iyengar and William J. McGuire. Durham: Duke University Press, 1993.

Masters, R. S. W. "Knowledge, knerves and know-how: The role of explicit vs. implicit knowledge in the breakdown of a complex skill under pressure." *British Journal of Psychology* 83(1992): 343–58.

Mathews, Patricia M. "Kant's Sublime: A Form of Pure Aesthetic Reflective Judgment," *The Journal of Aesthetics and Art Criticism*, 54 (1996): 165–180.

Mathews, Robert C. and Lewis Roussel. "Abstractness of Implicit Knowledge: A cognitive evolutionary perspective." In *How Implicit is Implicit Learning*, pp. 13–47. Ed Dianne Berry. New York: Oxford University Press, 1997.

McCarty, Richard. "Motivation and Moral Choice in Kant's Theory of Rational Agency," *Kant-Studien* 85 (1994): 15–31.

McDaniel, James P. and John Sloop, "Hope's Finitude." In *Judgment Calls: Rhetoric, Politics, and Indeterminacy*, pp. 1–10. Ed. John Sloop and James McDaniel. Boulder: Westview Press, 1998.

McDermott, Rose. "The Feeling of Rationality: The Meaning of Neuroscientific Advances for Political Science." *Perspectives on Politics* 2(2004): 691–706.

McGinn, Colin. *Ethics, Evil, and Fiction*. Oxford: Clarendon Press, 1997.

McMackin, J. and P. Slovic "When does explicit justification impair decision-making?" *Journal of Applied Cognitive Psychology*, 14 (2000): 527–541.

Mead, George Herbert. *Mind, Self and Society*. Chicago: University of Chicago Press, 1934.

Merleau-Ponty, Maurice. *Phenomenology of Perception*, trans. Colin Smith. London: Routledge and Kegan Paul, 1962.

Merleau-Ponty, Maurice. "The Primacy of Perception and its Philosophical Consequences," In *The Essential Writings of Merleau-Ponty*, pp. 47–63. Ed. Alden Fisher. New York: Harcourt, Brace and World, Inc., 1969.

Merzenich, M. M. and R. C. deCharms, "Neural Representations, Experience, and Change." In *The Mind-Brain Continuum: Sensory Processes*, pp. 61–81. Ed. Rodolfo Llinas and Patricia Churchland. Cambridge: MIT Press, 1996.

Milner, A. and M. Goodale. *The visual brain in action*. Oxford: Oxford University Press, 1995.

Minow, Martha. "Justice Engendered," In *Contemporary Political Philosophy*, pp. 504–24. Ed. Robert E. Goodin and Philip Pettit. Oxford: Blackwell Publishers, 1997.

Montaigne. *The Complete Works of Montaigne*. Trans. Donald Frame. Stanford: Stanford University Press, 1957/1965.

Mullen, John and Byron Roth. *Decision-Making: Its Logic and Practice*. Savage, MD: Rowman and Littlefield, 1991.

Murdoch, Iris. "Against Dryness: A Polemical Sketch." *Encounter*, 16 (1961): 16–20.

Murdoch, Iris. "Metaphysics and Ethics." In *Existentialists and Mystics: Writings on Philosophy and Literature*, pp. 59–75. Ed. Peter Conradi. Harmondswort Penguin, 1999.

Myers, David G. *Intuition: Its Powers and Perils*. New Haven: Yale University Press, 2002.

Natali, Carlo. *The Wisdom of Aristotle*. Trans. Gerald Parks. Albany: State University of New York Press, 2001.

Nedelsky, Jennifer. "Embodied Diversity and the Challenges to Law." In *Judgment, Imagination, and Politics: Themes from Kant and Arendt*, pp. 229–256. Ed. Ronald Beiner and Jennifer Nedelsky. New York: Rowman and Littlefield, 2001.

Nelson, John S. "Prudence as Republican Politics in American Popular Culture." In *Prudence: Classical Virtue, Postmodern Practice*, pp. 229–257. Ed. Robert Harriman. University Park, PA: Pennsylvania State University Press, 2003.

Niedenthal, Paula and Carolin Showers. "The Perception and Processing of Affective Information and Its Influences on Social Judgment." *Emotion and Social Judgment*, pp. 125–143. Ed. Joseph P. Forgas. Oxford: Pergamon Press, 1991.

Nietzsche, Friedrich. *Gesammelte Werke, Musarionausgabe*. Munich: Musarion Verlag, 1920–29.

Nietzsche, Friedrich. *Ecce Homo*. Trans. Walter Kaufmann. New York: Vintage, 1967.

Nietzsche, Friedrich. *The Will to Power*. Trans. Walter Kaufmann and R. J. Hollingdale. New York: Vintage, 1968.

Nietzsche, Friedrich. *The Anti-Christ*. Trans. R. J. Hollingdale. New York: Penguin, 1968.

Nietzsche, Friedrich. *Twilight of the Idols: or How to Philosophize with a Hammer.* Trans. R. J. Hollingdale. New York: Penguin, 1968.

Nietzsche, Friedrich. *Thus Spoke Zarathustra: A Book for Everyone and No One*. Trans. R. J. Hollingdale. New York: Penguin, 1969.

Nietzsche, Friedrich. *Beyond Good and Evil: Prelude to a Philosophy of the Future*. Trans. R. J. Hollingdale. New York: Penguin, 1972.

Nietzsche, Friedrich. *The Gay Science*. Trans. Walter Kaufmann. New York: Vintage, 1974.

Nietzsche, Friedrich. *Daybreak: Thoughts on the Prejudices of Morality*. Trans. R. J. Hollingdale. Cambridge: Cambridge University Press, 1982.

Nietzsche, Friedrich. *Untimely Meditations*. Trans. R. J. Hollingdale. Cambridge: Cambridge University Press, 1983.

Nietzsche, Friedrich. *Human, All Too Human: A Book for Free Spirits*. Trans. R. J. Hollingdale. Cambridge: Cambridge University Press, 1986.

Nisbet, R. E. and T. D. Wilson. "Telling more than we can know: Verbal reports on mental processes," *Psychological Review* 84 (1977): 231–59.

Norretranders, Tor. *The User Illusion*. Trans. Jonathan Sydenham. New York: Viking, 1998.

Nussbaum, Martha. *The Fragility of Goodness: Luck and Ethics in Greek Tragedy and Philosophy*. Cambridge: Cambridge University Press, 1986.

Nussbaum, Martha. *Love's Knowledge: Essays on Philosophy and Literature*. New York: Oxford University Press, 1990.

Nussbaum, Martha. *The Therapy of Desire: Theory and Practice in Hellenistic Ethics*. Princeton: Princeton University Press, 1994.

Nussbaum, Martha. *Poetic Justice: The Literary Imagination and Public Life*. Boston: Beacon Press, 1995.

Nussbaum, Martha. *Upheavals of Thought: The Intelligence of Emotions*. Cambridge: Cambridge University Press, 2001.

Oakeshott, Michael. *The Voice of Liberal Learning*. Indianapolis: Liberty Fund, 2001.

O'Neill, Daniel I. *The Burke-Wollstonecraft Debate: Savagery, Civilization, and Democracy.* University Park, PA: Penn State University Press, forthcoming 2007.

Ottati, Victor C. and Robert S. Wyer, Jr. "Affect and Political Judgment." In *Explorations in Political Psychology,* pp. 296–315. Ed. Shanto Iyengar and William J. McGuire. Durham: Duke University Press, 1993.

Pateman, Carole. *Participation and Democratic Theory.* Cambridge: Cambridge University Press, 1970.

Pennebaker, J. W. "Writing about emotional experiences as a therapeutic process," *Psychological Science,* 8(1997): 162–166.

Penrose, Roger. *Shadows of the Mind.* Oxford: Oxford University Press, 1994.

Phelps, Elizabeth. "The Interaction of Emotion and Cognition: The Relation Between the Human Amygdala and Cognitive Awareness." in *The New Unconscious,* pp. 61–76. Ed. Ran Hassin, James Uleman, and John Bargh (Oxford: Oxford University Press, 2005).

Piaget, Jean. *The Moral Judgment of the Child.* New York: Free Press, 1965.

Pinker, Steven. *How the Mind Works.* New York: W. W. Norton 1997.

Pinker, Steven. *The Blank Slate.* New York: Viking, 2002.

Pitken, Hannah Fenichel. *Fortune is a Woman: Gender and Politics in the Thought of Niccolò Machiavelli.* Berkeley: University of California Press, 1984.

Pizarro, David and Paul Bloom. "The intelligence of the moral intuitions: A reply to Haidt." *Psychological Review,* 110 (2001): 193–196.

Planinc, Zdravko. *Plato's Political Philosophy: Prudence in the Republic and the Laws.* Columbia: University of Missouri Press, 1991.

Plato. *Collected Dialogues.* Princeton: Princeton University Press, 1989.

Plato. *The Republic of Plato.* Trans. Allan Bloom. New York: Basic Books, 1968.

Plous, Scott. *The Psychology of Judgment and Decision Making.* Philadelphia: Temple University Press, 1993.

Polanyi, Michael. *Knowing and Being.* Ed. Majorie Greene. Chicago: University of Chicago Press, 1969.

Polkinghorne, Donald E. *Narrative Knowing and the Human Sciences.* Albany: State University of New York Press, 1988.

Pope, Alexander. *An Essay on Man,* Vol. 2 of *The Works of Alexander Pope.* London: John Murray, 1871.

Premack, David and Ann Premack. *Original Intelligence.* New York: McGraw Hill, 2003.

Prentice, Deborah and Richard Gerrig. "Exploring the Boundary between Fiction and Reality." In *Dual-Process Theories in Social Psychology,* pp. 529–46. Ed. Shelly Chaiken and Yaacov Trope. New York: Guilford Press, 1999.

Quartz, Steven R. and Terrence J. Sejnowski. *Liars, Lovers, and Heroes: What the New Brain Science Reveals about How We Became Who We Are.* New York: William Morrow, 2002.

Ramachandran, V. S. and Sandra Blakeslee. *Phantoms in the Brain.* New York: William Morrow and Company, 1998.

Rawls, John. *A Theory of Justice.* Cambridge: Harvard University Press, 1971.

Read, Stephen John and Lynn Carol Miller. "Stories are Fundamental to Meaning and Memory: For Social Creatures, Could It Be Otherwise." In *Knowledge and*

Memory: The Real Story – Advances in Social Cognition, Vol. VIII, pp. 139–152. Ed. Robert Wyer, Jr. Mahwah, NJ: Lawrence Erlbaum Associates, 1995.

Reber, Arthur. "Implicit learning of artificial grammars." *Journal of Verbal Learning and Verbal Behavior* 6(1967): 317–327.

Reber, Arthur. *Implicit Learning and Tacit Knowledge: An Essay on the Cognitive Unconscious.* New York: Oxford University Press, 1993.

Reeve, C. D. C. *Practices of Reason: Aristotle's Nicomachean Ethics.* Oxford: Clarendon Press, 1992.

Renshon, Stanley A. "Appraising Good Judgment Before It Matters." In *Good Judgment in Foreign Policy: Theory and Application*, pp. 61–101. Ed. Stanley A. Renshon and Deborah Welch Larson. New York: Rowman and Littlefield, 2003.

Ree, Jonathan. *Philosophical Tales: An Essay on Philosophy and Literature.* London: Methuen, 1987.

Rickey, Christopher. *Revolutionary Saints: Heidegger, National Socialism and Antinomian Politics.* University Park, PA: Pennsylvania State University Press, 2002.

Rickman, H. P. *Philosophy in Literature.* Madison: Associated University Presses, 1996.

Ricoeur, Paul. *From Text to Action: Essays in Hermeneutics, II.* Evanston, IL: Northwestern University Press, 1991.

Roemer, Michael. *Telling Stories: Postmodernism and the Invalidation of Traditional Narrative.* Lanham, MD: Rowman and Littlefield, 1995.

Roese, Neal, Lawrence Sanna, and Adam Galinsky. "The Mechanics of Imagination: Automaticity and Control in Counterfactual Thinking." In *The New Unconscious*, pp. 138–170. Ed. Ran Hassin, James Uleman, and John Bargh. Oxford: Oxford University Press, 2005.

Rorty, Richard. *Contingency, Irony, and Solidarity.* Cambridge: Cambridge University Press, 1989.

Rorty, Richard. "Justice as a Larger Loyalty." In *Justice and Democracy: Cross-Cultural Perspectives*, pp. 9–22. Ed. Ron Bontekoe and Marietta Stepaniants. Honolulu: University of Hawai'i Press, 1997.

Rorty, Richard. *Philosophy and Social Hope.* New York: Penguin, 1999.

Rorty, Richard. "Universality and Truth." In *Rorty and his Critics*, pp. 1–30. Ed. Robert B. Brandom. Oxford: Blackwell Publishers, 2000.

Rousseau, Jean-Jacques. *Emile.* Trans. Allan Bloom. New York: Basic Books, 1979.

Ruderman, Richard S. "Aristotle and the Recovery of Political Judgment." *American Political Science Review* 91(1997): 409–420.

Rumelhart, David E., James L. McClelland, and the PDP Research Group. *Parallel Distributed Processing: Explorations in the Microstructure of Cognition*, Volume 1. Cambridge: MIT Press, 1986.

Rushton, J. Philippe. "Social Learning Theory and the Development of Prosocial Behavior." In Nancy Eisenberg, ed. *The Development of Prosocial Behavior*, pp 77–105. New York: Academic Press, 1982.

Sadato, N., A. Pascula-Leone, J. Grafman, V. Ibanez, M. P. Deiber, G. Dold, and M. Hallett. "Activation of the primary visual cortex by Braille reading in blind subjects," *Nature* 380(1996): 526–28.

Salovey, Peter, Brian Bedell, Jerusha Detweiler, and John Mayer. "Current Directions in Emotional Intelligence Research." in *Handbook of Emotions*, 2nd edition, pp. 504–520. Ed. Michael Lewis and Jeannette M. Haviland-Jones. New York: Guilford Press, 2000.

Schaar, John. *Legitimacy in the Modern State.* New Brunswick: Transaction Books, 1981.

Schank, Roger C. and Robert P. Abelson. "Knowledge and Memory: The Real Story." In *Knowledge and Memory: The Real Story – Advances in Social Cognition*, Vol. VIII, pp. 1–85. Ed. Robert Wyer, Jr. Mahwah, NJ: Lawrence Erlbaum Associates, 1995.

Shelley, Percy. "A Defense of Poetry." In *The Norton Anthology of English Literature*, Vol. 2., pp. 620–32. Ed. M. H. Abrams. New York: W. W. Norton, 2001.

Scheuer, Jeffrey. *The Sound Bite Society: Television and the American Mind.* New York: Four Walls Eight Windows, 1999.

Schooler, J. and T. Engstler-Schooler. "Verbal Overshadowing of Visual Memories: Some Things Are Better Left Unsaid." *Cognitive Psychology* 22 (1990): 36–71.

Schwartz, Jeffrey M. and Sharon Begley. *The Mind and the Brain: Neuroplasticity and the Power of Mental Force.* New York: HarperCollins, 2002.

Schwarz, Norbert and Herbert Bless. "Happy and Mindless, But Sad and Smart? The Impact of Affective States on Analytical Reasoning." In *Emotion and Social Judgment*, pp. 55–71. Ed. Joseph P. Forgas. Oxford: Pergamon Press, 1991.

Schwarz, Norbert and Gerald Clore. "Feelings and Phenomenal Experiences." In *Social Psychology: Handbook of Basic Principles*, pp. 433–465. New York: Guilford Press, 1996.

Schwarz, Norbert. "Feelings as Information: Moods Influence Judgments and Processing Strategies." In *Heuristics and Biases: the Psychology of Intuitive Judgment*, pp. 534–547. Ed. Thomas Gilovich, Dale Griffin, and Daniel Kahneman. Cambridge: Cambridge University Press, 2002.

Scott, James C. *Seeing Like a State: How Certain Schemes to Improve the Human Condition Have Failed.* New Haven: Yale University Press, 1998.

Shram, Sanford and Philip Neisser. *Tales of the State.* Lanham, MD: Rowman and Littlefield, 1997.

Simon, Herbert. *The Sciences of the Artificial.* 2nd ed. Cambridge: M.I.T. Press, 1981.

Simon, Herbert. "Alternative visions of rationality." In *Judgment and decision making: An interdisciplinary reader*, pp. 97–113. Ed. H. R. Arkes and K. R. Hammond. Cambridge: Cambridge University Press, 1986.

Simonton, Dean Keith. *Origins of Genius: Darwinian Perspectives on Creativity.* New York: Oxford University Press, 1999.

Slovic, Paul, Melissa Finucane, Ellen Peters, and Donald MacGregor. "The Affect Heuristic." In *Heuristics and Biases: the Psychology of Intuitive Judgment*, pp. 397–420. Ed. Thomas Gilovich, Dale Griffin, and Daniel Kahneman. Cambridge: Cambridge University Press, 2002.

Smith, Adam. *The Theory of Moral Sentiments.* Amherst, MA: Prometheus Books, 2000.

Solomon, Robert C. *The Passions.* Garden City, NY: Anchor Press, 1976.

Solomon, Robert C. *Spirituality for the Skeptic: The Thoughtful Love of Life.* Oxford: Oxford University Press, 2002.

Somech, Anit and Ronit Bogler. "Tacit Knowledge in Academia: Its Effects on Student Learning and Achievement." *The Journal of Psychology*, 133 (1999): 605–616.

Sophocles. *Antigone*, in *The Norton Book of Classical Literature*, ed. Bernard Knox. New York: W. W. Norton 1993; also in *Sophocles I* (Chicago: University of Chicago Press, 1954.

Stadler, Michael and Peter Frensch, eds. *Handbook of Implicit Learning*. Thousand Oaks: Sage Publications, 1998.

Staudinger, Ursula. "Older and wiser? Integrating results on the relationship between age and wisdom-related performance." *International Journal of Behavioral Development*, 23 (1999): 641–664.

Steinberger, Peter J. *The Concept of Political Judgment*. Chicago: University of Chicago Press, 1993.

Sternberg, Robert, ed. *Wisdom: Its Nature, Origins, and Development*. Cambridge: Cambridge University Press, 1990.

Sternberg, Robert and Jennifer Jordan, eds. *A Handbook of Wisdom: Psychological Perspectives*. Cambridge: Cambridge University Press, 2005.

Stevick, Philip, ed. *The Theory of the Novel*. New York: The Free Press, 1967.

Strawson, Galen. "Against Narrativity." *Ratio* 17 (2004): 428–452.

Suedfeld, Peter and Philip Tetlock. "Psychological Advice about Political Decision Making: Heuristics, Biases and Cognitive Defects. In *Psychology and Social Policy*, pp. 51–70. Ed. Peter Suedfeld and Philip Tetlock. New York: Hemisphere Publishing, 1992.

Taylor, Charles. *The Sources of the Self*. Cambridge: Cambridge University Press, 1989.

Terence. *Heautontimorumenos*. Oxford: Dodsley, Payne and Jackson, 1777.

Tetlock, Philip. "Is it a Bad Idea to Study Good Judgment." *Political Psychology* 13 (3): 429–434, 1992.

Tetlock, Philip. "Theory-Driven Reasoning about Plausible Pasts and Probable Futures in World Politics." In *Heuristics and Biases: the Psychology of Intuitive Judgment*, pp. 749–762. Ed. Thomas Gilovich, Dale Griffin, and Daniel Kahneman. Cambridge: Cambridge University Press, 2002.

Tetlock, Philip. *Expert Political Judgment: How Good Is It? How Can We Know?* Princeton: Princeton University Press, 2005.

Thiele, Leslie Paul. *Friedrich Nietzsche and the Politics of the Soul*. Princeton: Princeton University Press, 1990.

Thiele, Leslie Paul. "Love and Judgment: Nietzsche's Dilemma," *Nietzsche-Studien*, 20 (1991): 88–108.

Thiele, Leslie Paul. "Evolutionary Narratives and Ecological Ethics," *Political Theory* 27 (February 1999): 6–38.

Thiele, Leslie Paul. "Common Sense, Judgment and the Limits of Political Theory." *Political Theory*, 28 (August 2000): 565–588.

Thiele, Leslie Paul. "The Ethics and Politics of Narrative: Heidegger + Foucault." In *Foucault and Heidegger: Critical Encounters*, pp. 206–234. Ed. Alan Milchman and Alan Rosenberg. Minneapolis: University of Minnesota Press, 2003.

Thiele, Leslie Paul. "A (Political) Philosopher by Any Other Name: The Roots of Heidegger's Thought," *Political Theory* 32 (August 2004): 570–579.

Thiele, Leslie Paul. "Ontology and Narrative," *The Hedgehog Review*, Vol. 7, No 2: 77–85, Summer 2005.

Thiele, Leslie Paul. "Judging Hannah Arendt: A Reply to Zerilli," *Political Theory* 33 (October 2005): 706–714.

Thiele, Leslie Paul. "Making Intuition Matter," in *Making Political Science Matter: The Flyvbjerg Debate and Beyond*, eds. Sanford E. Schram and Brian Caterino (New York: New York University Press), 2006.

Thompson, Leigh. *The Mind and Heart of the Negotiator*, 2nd edition. Upper Saddle River, NJ: Prentice Hall, 2001.

Tomasello, Michael, Josep Call, and Brian Hare. "Chimpanzees understand psychological states – the question is which ones and to what extent," *Trends in Cognitive Sciences* 7(2003): 153–156.

Toth, Jeffrey P. "Nonconscious Forms of Human Memory." In *The Oxford Handbook of Memory*, pp. 245–261. Ed. Endel Tulving and Fergus Craik. Oxford: Oxford University Press, 2000.

Toulmin, Stephen. *Return to Reason*. Cambridge: Harvard University Press, 2001.

Turner, Mark. *The Literary Mind*. New York: Oxford University Press, 1996.

Tversky, A. and D. Kahneman. "Judgments of and by representativeness." In *Judgment under Uncertainty: Heuristics and Biases*, Ed, D. Kahneman, P. Slovic, and A. Tversky. Cambridge: Cambridge University Press, 1982.

Tversky, Amos and Daniel Kahneman. "Extensional Versus Intuitive Reasoning: The Conjunction Fallacy in Probability Judgment." In *Heuristics and Biases: the Psychology of Intuitive Judgment*, pp. 19–48. Ed. Thomas Gilovich, Dale Griffin, and Daniel Kahneman. Cambridge: Cambridge University Press, 2002.

Twain, Mark. *Mark Twain's Notebook*. Ed. A. B. Paine. New York: Cooper Square Publishers, 1972.

Uleman, James. "Introduction: Becoming Aware of the New Unconscious." In *The New Unconscious*, pp. 3–15. Ed. Ran Hassin, James Uleman, and John Bargh. Oxford: Oxford University Press, 2005.

Underwood, Geoffrey, ed. *Implicit Cognition*. Oxford: Oxford University Press, 1996.

Urmson, J. O. "Aristotle's Doctrine of the Mean." In *Essays on Aristotle's Ethics* pp. 157–170. Ed. Amelie Oksenberg Rorty. Berkeley: University of California Press, 1980.

Vetlesen, Arne Johan. *Perception, Empathy, and Judgment: An Inquiry into the Preconditions of Moral Performance*. University Park: The Pennsylvania State University Press, 1994.

Vice, Samantha. "Literature and the Narrative Self." *Philosophy* 78 (2003): 93–108.

Vidmar, N. and M. Rokeach. "Archie Bunker's bigotry: A study in selective perception and exposure." *Journal of Communication* 24 (1974): 36–47.

Walzer, Michael. *Thick and Thin: Moral Argument at Home and Abroad*. Notre Dame: University of Notre Dame Press, 1994.

Weintraub, Sandra. *The Hidden Intelligence: Innovation through Intuition*. Boston: Butterworth Heinemann, 1998.

Welch, David A. "Culture and Emotion as Obstacles to Good Judgment." In *Good Judgment in Foreign Policy: Theory and Application*, pp. 191–215. Ed. Stanley A. Renshon and Deborah Welch Larson. New York: Rowman and Littlefield, 2003.

Welford, Richard and Richard Starkey, eds. Business and the Environment (Washington DC: Taylor and Francis, 1996), p. 22.

White, Hayden. *The Content of the Form: Narrative Discourse and Historical Representation.* Baltimore: The Johns Hopkins University Press, 1987.

White, Stephen K. *Sustaining Affirmation: The Strengths of Weak Ontology in Political Theory.* Princeton: Princeton University Press, 2000.

Whitebrook, Maureen. *Real Toads in Imaginary Gardens: Narrative Accounts of Liberalism.* Lanham: Rowman and Littlefield, 1995.

Whitehead, A. N. *Introduction to Mathematics.* London: Williams and Norgate, 1911.

Whyte, Lancelot Law. *The Unconscious before Freud.* New York: St. Martins, 1978.

Wiesel, Elie. "A Sacred Magic Can Elevate the Secular Storyteller." In *Writers on Writing: Collected Essays from* The New York Times, pp. 258–262. New York: Henry Holt, 2001.

Wiggins, David. "Deliberation and Practical Reason." In *Essays on Aristotle's Ethics*, pp. 221–240. Ed. Amelie Oksenberg Rorty. Berkeley: University of California Press, 1980.

Willingham, Daniel B. and Laura Preuss. "The Death of Implicit Memory." Psyche, 2 (October 1995):15; http://psyche.cs.monash.edu.au/v2/psyche-2-15-willingham.html

Wilson, Timothy. *Strangers to Ourselves: Discovering the Adaptive Unconscious.* Cambridge: Belknap Press, 2002.

Wilson, T. D. and J. W. Schooler. "Thinking too much: Introspection can reduce the quality of preferences and decisions." *Journal of Personality and Social Psychology*, 60 (1991): 181–192.

Wolin, Sheldon. "Political Theory as a Vocation." *American Political Science Review* 63 (1969): 1062–82.

Wolin, Sheldon. "What Revolutionary Action Means Today." In *Dimensions of Radical Democracy: Pluralism, Citizenship, Community*, pp. 240–53. Ed. Chantal Mouffe. London: Verso, 1992.

Wolin, Sheldon. *Tocqueville Between Two Worlds: The Making of a Political and Theoretical Life.* Princeton: Princeton University Press, 2001.

Woolhouse, Leanne S. and Rowan Bayne. "Personality and the use of intuition: Individual differences in strategy and performance on an implicit learning task." *European Journal of Personality*, 14 (March/April 2000): 157–169.

Young, Iris Marion. "Asymmetrical Reciprocity: On Moral Respect, Wonder, and Enlarged Thought." In *Judgment, Imagination, and Politics: Themes from Kant and Arendt*, pp. 205–228. Ed. Ronald Beiner and Jennifer Nedelsky. New York: Rowman and Littlefield, 2001.

Zimmerman, Manfred. "The Nervous System in the Context of Information Theory." In *Human Physiology*, 2nd ed., pp. 166–73. Ed. R. F. Schmidt and G. Thews. Berlin: Springler-Verlag, 1989.

Index